Thoughts and Thinkers

THOUGHTS
AND
THINKERS

Anthony Quinton
President of Trinity College, Oxford

Holmes & Meier Publishers, Inc.
New York

First published in the United States of America 1982 by
Holmes & Meier Publishers, Inc.
30 Irving Place, New York, N.Y. 10003

Library of Congress Cataloging in Publication Data

Quinton, Anthony.
    Thoughts and thinkers.

    Bibliography: p.
    Includes index
    1. Philosophy – Addresses, essays, lectures. I. Title.
B29.Q56   190   81-13372
ISBN 0-8419-0772-2   AACR2
ISBN 0-8419-0773-0 (pbk.)

Printed in Great Britain

Contents

ACKNOWLEDGMENTS

The chapters in this book first appeared as follows, and thanks are due to the editors and publishers involved for permission to include them. 1: *Nature and Conduct* (Royal Institute of Philosophy lectures, vol. 8, 1973/4), ed. R. S. Peters (1975). 2, 3 & 7: *Times Literary Supplement*, July 27, 1973; Jan. 24, 1975; May 17, 1974. 4: *Purnell's History of the World*, ed. J. M. Roberts. 5: *New Review*, Jan. 1976. 8: *Proceedings of the Philosophy of Education Society of Great Britain*, July 1971. 9 & 10: *Proceedings of the Aristotelian Society*, 1975/6; Supplementary Volume, 1960. 11 & 26: *Philosophy*, 1962; 1960. 12: *The American Scholar*, Jan. 1976. 14: *Conference*, Oct. 1974. 15, 16, 21, 25, 30, 31, 32 & 33: *New York Review of Books*, May 18, 1967; June 12, 1975; Feb. 13, 1969; Nov. 23, 1967; July 23, 1970; Jan. 12, 1966; Nov. 21, 1968; April 25, 1968. 17: *Victorian Studies*, March 1958. 18: *Proceedings of the British Academy*, 1971. 19: *Biology and Personality*, ed. I. T. Ramsey (1965). 20: *Mind*, Jan. 1976. 22: *Freud*, ed. Jonathan Miller (1972). 24 & 27: *Encounter*, Oct. 1974; Dec. 1973. 28: *Contemporary Political Philosophers*, ed. Anthony de Crespigny & Kenneth Minogue (1975).

Preface

The various chapters of this book, collected here for the first time, reflect some persistent and related interests of mine, two of which have been particularly influential: an interest in the connections between philosophy and the other activities of the mind and an interest in the history of philosophy. These two interests are aspects of a single concern for the openness of philosophy, to the rest of intellectual life and to its own past. It should not be a confined debate between a handful of specialists about a few topics of current and strictly professional concern.

I do not think there are any eternal truths about either the actual or the ideal relation between philosophy and other forms of intellectual life or its own history that are substantial enough to be worth trying to formulate very precisely. At any time philosophy will receive some influence from the general intellectual style and preoccupations of its age, since no one is born a philosopher pure and simple and most who become philosophers do not abandon all other intellectual interests. On the other hand, philosophy will usually exercise some reciprocal influence on the general life of the mind in the world around it, even if it has no apparent intention of doing so, such as would be revealed by the choice of generally interesting problems and the provision of solutions to them in readily intelligible terms.

I imagine most philosophers would agree that philosophy ought to have some influence on the non-philosophical thinking of those who are not philosophers themselves. But there would be many different ideas about the form this influence should take and the manner in which it should be pursued. At one extreme the ideal might be seen as a matter of purely exemplary influence, as the provision of a model of serious and rationally self-conscious thinking. At the other philosophy would be seen as failing in its task if it did not chiefly address itself to the 'problems of men', as they most insistently present themselves to ordinary reflection.

Something a little less bland and amorphous can be said if the special character of recent philosophy, and here I mean academic philosophy in the English-speaking world, is made a subject for consideration. For most of the twentieth century it has been conducted in an unusually enclosed, deliberately autonomous way and, in contrast to the anglicised Hegelian idealism that preceded it, in a resolutely unhistorical fashion.

Wittgenstein, notoriously, had no use for the philosophy of the past. He did, of course, quote St Augustine to start a discussion of his own, but found Hume unbearable to read. Moore and Russell, who stand, in a way, as Lenin and

Trotsky respectively to Wittgenstein's Stalin, were not hostile to it, but either did not practise it or practised it in a deliberately naive way. Moore went no further than a few historical allusions. The most quaintly unhistorical of these was the assumption, implicit in his 'Refutation of Idealism' of 1903, that Berkeley's problem about the nature of the immediate objects of perception was of central importance to the kind of watered-down Hegelian philosophy in which he himself had been brought up.

Russell wrote a great book about a major philosopher of the past: his *Critical Exposition of the Philosophy of Leibniz* of 1900. In the preface he distinguishes a purely philosophical from a historical attitude to previous philosophers, 'an attitude in which, without regard to dates or influences, we seek simply to discover what are the great types of possible philosophies, and guide ourselves in the search by investigating the systems advocated by the great philosophers of the past ... In such inquiries the philosopher ... is examined as the advocate of what he holds to be a body of philosophic truth'. He admits that there is still 'what is, after all, perhaps the most important of the historical questions – the problem of the actual views of the philosopher who is to be investigated'. He acknowledges that there can be an *evidential* problem about this. In the case in hand, crucial bits of Leibniz's writing had only recently become available and, Russell claimed, some of what Leibniz actually published was insincere edification in which the true reasons for his doctrines were not to be found. But he does not recognise that there can be the *historical* problem of understanding what the words uttered by a philosopher of the past actually meant to him. In fact his view that Leibniz's official reasoning was insincere is a truly historical claim, to the effect that the real causes of his beliefs were not the ones he produced publicly. But Russell was more interested in the fact that the concealed reasons were the best reasons, philosophically speaking, for Leibniz's conclusions than that they were the reasons that actually weighed with him.

Nearly half a century later he undertook his popular *History of Western Philosophy* in a different, more thoughtful and more historical, spirit. 'My purpose', he wrote, 'is to exhibit philosophy as an integral part of social and political life.' It is generally agreed that he did not bring this off. J.A. Passmore observes, 'the *History* is polemical in style, but the polemics are interlarded with slabs of pure history'. One reviewer spoke of Russell as conceiving the philosophers of the past as fellow-members of a timeless senior common room. He certainly treats questions of the meaning and justification of the doctrines he reviews in almost complete independence of the historical matter he considers. Since that historical matter is largely political and ecclesiastical the result is not surprising. It might have been different if he had tried to set the philosophies of the past within their intellectual environment, the more concrete, localised thinking from which the preoccupations of philosophers are often derived and on which philosophy will have an influence unless hermetically sealed in professional autonomy.

The absence of effective involvement with the history of philosophy from the work of the three great founders of the dominant form of British philosophy in this century has persisted in their successors. Wisdom and Ayer, Ryle, Austin and Strawson have either let bygones be bygones or treated past philosophers as interesting contemporaries, as in Strawson's brilliant, but explicitly unhistorical, book on Kant: *The Bounds of Sense*. 'As any Kantian scholar who may read it will quickly detect', he writes, 'it is by no means a work of historical-philosophical scholarship.' It is, in fact, a proposal for the radical reconstruction of Kant's *Critique of Pure Reason* by the abandonment of a large part of its content and the reinterpretation of the remainder in what Strawson sees as currently defensible terms.

Without suggesting that philosophers with quite enough to occupy them already ought to spend more time on the history of their subject, there are reasons why somebody should study it seriously or historically. Many of the problems of philosophy are permanent, or at any rate recurrent, and it is valuable to consider them in their freshest and most vigorous presentation. Philosophical classics, in other words, are not simply historical curiosities. Furthermore, past philosophers can free us from the mind-narrowing effect of current controversy. Mary Midgley, in the introduction to her refreshingly enterprising *Beast and Man*, writes of 'slipping out over the wall of the tiny arid garden cultivated at that time under the name of British Moral Philosophy'. One great help in breaking down the wall altogether has been the revival of interest in Sidgwick, who, amongst other things, was the most distinguished historian of ethics. Moore says that he learned least from Sidgwick of all his teachers. 'His personality did not attract me', he says, 'and I found his lectures rather dull'. That important but absurd book, *Principia Ethica*, bears the marks of Moore's unfortunate distaste.

Moore was no more interested in the relation between philosophy and other intellectual activities than he was in its past. He did not acknowledge any source outside philosophy itself, narrowly conceived, for the philosophical problems that seized his attention. Russell and Wittgenstein were at least both led into philosophy in the first place by questions raised in their minds by the study of mathematics, but for which mathematics itself had no answer. In his constructive philosophical work Russell was mainly involved, after the publication of *Principia Mathematica*, with the justification of science. He was a superficial, if still philosophical, critic of the pretensions of theology to be a body of knowledge. But he explicitly detached his lively and continuing concern with moral, social and political questions from philosophy. If anything, his philosophy, by denying that there could be any knowledge about values, was an embarrassment to him in his more prophetic or ideological role.

Unlike Moore, who could be described as suffering from the Forsterian complaint of 'undeveloped head', Wittgenstein was a man of serious extra-philosophical interests. But the deepest of these, the theologico-metaphysical ones, his philosophy unequivocally declared to be nothing to do with philosophy. He left behind some memorable, gnomic remarks about ethics, religion, art and psychoanalysis, but almost in defiance of his own principles. By dint of a self-mutilating effort of will he secured a detachment of philosophy from the rest of the life of the mind as great as that Moore had arrived at by sheer lack of intellectual vitality.

In the thirty years since Wittgenstein's death there has been a noticeable effloresence of what may be called applied philosophy, of those philosophies *of* one thing or another – art, religion, science, history – that were perhaps first recognised as specific disciplines by Hegel and were a standard mode of philosophical activity for his followers. A concern with meaning and justification has always been the hard core of serious philosophy and that concern is essentially cognitive. It is therefore appropriate that philosophy should find problems in, and seek to exert an influence on, cognitive, or intendedly cognitive, activities other than itself, on all the fields in which the human intellect works.

Wittgensteinian purism seems to wish to confine the attention of philosophers to true 'metaphysical puzzlement', to the relief of those extravagant doubts about the existence of the external world, other minds, the past and causal connection, which it is a sign of mental imbalance to regard as more than puzzles. Why not use the weapons sharpened on these ancient whetstones to cut through less obviously playful entanglements?

Most of the essays in the first part of this collection are discussions in a philosophical idiom of topics outside the core of the subject as understood through most of this century in Britain. The first three converge on the concept of human nature. The fourth and fifth carry further the themes of this introduction. Those two themes, that philosophy should interact vigorously with other cognitive interests and that it should be historically aware of its past, are linked by the consideration that in the past philosophy did interact more thoroughly with the rest of the intellectual domain than it has for much of this century so far. So to tell its history is inevitably to treat of the whole intellectual scene of which it is a part. Windelband's resolve to bring in the intellectual environment is what makes his *History of Philosophy* still so valuable nearly a century after its publication.

The essays making up the second part of this collection are broadly historical, although the history in question soon becomes very recent history. Hobbes and Hegel were both highly impure philosophers, in what I intend as a favourable sense of the word. Neither is well served by unhistorical inter-pretation. The Victorian philosophy discussed in the third essay was not very professional until late in the century and at no time was it autonomously enclosed in its private concerns. The essay on absolute idealism accounts for its rapid conquest of the British mind by its being aptly available for reasonably conciliatory defences of religious faith and a politics of social responsibility. The essay on evolutionary ethics resists attempts to pretend that a major scientific discovery cannot be allowed to influence moral thinking.

I am grateful to the editors of the various journals in which these pieces first appeared for asking me to write them and for permitting me to reprint them. Full acknowledgement is given at the end of the book, where precise details of original publication are to be found.

Oxford, August 1981   A.Q.

PART I

Thoughts

1

Has Man an Essence?

Much of recent ethics has been thoroughly formalistic in character. In the first place it has confined itself to the investigation of the general logical properties of moral discourse and has largely ignored the broad psychological context of motives and purposes in which that kind of discourse has its life. Secondly, it has sought to distinguish the field of discourse that it takes as its subject-matter in a formalistic way, in terms of such properties as its universalisability, its autonomy and its overridingness, without reference to the concrete and specific human interests with which moral discourse is connected and which it might serve to promote.

For the formalist moral philosopher it is just brute, established fact that people are in the habit of making utterances that contain members of a set of logically interconnected evaluative terms, such as *good, right, ought* and their opposites; that there is a particularly noteworthy and formally distinguishable moral way of using these terms; and that, in so using them, men are making universal prescriptions for conduct. The question why these terms should be used in this way is not raised. It is, no doubt, ambiguous. It could mean: what is the causal explanation of the fact of moral discourse? It could also mean: what is the justification of the practice, what valuable or desirable purpose does it serve? The formalist will remit the question in its causal form to psychology and sociology. In its justificatory form he will probably deny that it arises, unless in what he might hold to be the trivially prudential form in which it invites such answers as that honesty is the best policy.

The most immediately objectionable consequence of this kind of formalism is that it sets no limit to the content of what can be universally prescribed. Such a prescription is adequate or proper provided that it is sincerely affirmed. Sincerity is shown by the speaker's rigid adherence to the principles embodied in his own moral evaluations, his indignation at the deviations of others from them and, perhaps, by the guilt he feels about his own. Ineradicable conflicts of ultimate principle are not merely allowed for, they are positively welcomed. In so far as there is any sort of convergence towards a moral consensus it is, on this view, a happy accident of emotional similarity between moral agents.

It is understandable that dissatisfaction with this body of doctrine should send its critics back to a very different ethical tradition, that which seeks to base the principles of right conduct on human nature. I am entirely sympathetic to this move in general but there is a traditionally well-established concept of human nature, that of the essence of man, which I do not believe will serve for the purpose. It is this that I propose to consider here.

'Philosophical questions of the form ... "what is the nature of x?" ... are all requests for definitions,' Ayer has said (*Language, Truth and Logic*, p.65). On that view if 'what is the nature of man' is a philosophical question it must be asking what are the defining, necessary or essential properties of man. If that is so, human nature is not an exclusively philosophical concept. Many things are true of human beings in general that are not logically constitutive of the concept of humanity. We should, then, distinguish between a strict interpretation of the phrase 'human nature', in which it refers to the essence of man, and a wider interpretation, in which it includes as well properties which are as a matter of fact true of men in general.

It is on the strict interpretation of human nature as human essence that two of the most noteworthy attempts to derive the principles of right conduct from human nature, those of Aristotle and Marx, have been founded and I shall begin by considering them. I shall go on to examine two very different ways in which it has been argued that man has no essence, those of Sartre and orthodox positivism. A curious, indeed paradoxical, feature of Sartre's position is that his claim that man has no essence is an abbreviated version of his account of the fundamental, one hardly likes to say logically distinguishing, characteristic of human existence, of *le pour-soi* or Heideggerian *Dasein*. Man is the being whose essential property is to have no essence. Furthermore Sartre goes on, much in the manner of Aristotle and Marx, to derive moral conclusions from his anti-essentialist account of human essence.

The orthodox positivist objection to human essence brings to light an important ambiguity in the question I have set myself: has man an essence? It can be taken to mean: are there certain properties everything that is a man must have just in virtue of being a man? But it could also mean: are there certain properties which every individual man has? In other words 'has man an essence' can amount either to: 'has humanity an essence?' or to 'have men essences?' The orthodox positivist will presumably regard it as fairly obvious that humanity has an essence. To admit that is to admit only that 'man' or 'is a man' is a significant predicative general term. He would probably go on to allow that the essence of humanity is verbally specifiable since the concept is not a Lockean simple idea or ineradicably ostensive, but could be introduced by a verbal definition, even if it is not usually so defined on its first introduction to language-learners. What he would resist is the idea that the essence of humanity is part of the essence of the individuals who are human. For, on his view, no individuals have essences at all, except relatively to the indefinitely numerous descriptions of which any one of them is susceptible.

In the traditional doctrine of essence these two versions of the question are not distinguished. Aristotle was primarily concerned with the distinction of the essential from the accidental properties of concrete individuals. Yet the ethically fruitful-seeming claims about essence that he makes are couched in general terms. Conclusions about how men in general ought ideally to live are drawn from premises about the essence of man in general. What seems to be involved is the view both that each concrete individual is essentially a thing of a specific kind, while everything else that it is, it is accidentally, and, further, that the essential, real or natural kind of which it is an instance can be defined or elucidated as some set of properties. Individual essence thus conceived will not of course include all the properties of an individual that has it since such individuals will, in general, have further, accidental properties. Furthermore it will not in general be sufficient to individuate the individual in question, to pick it out from other things of the same essential kind as the unique individual that it is.

I shall conclude by considering the defensibility of the notion of essence as applied to concrete individuals, which has been argued for as required for the identification of individual things and by asking whether, it if is defensible, it has any implications for ethics as far as men are concerned.

I. ARISTOTLE: MAN AS RATIONAL ANIMAL

Aristotle's theory of human essence is incorporated in that prime and exemplary specimen of definition *per genus et differentiam:* 'man' = 'rational animal'. As an animal man is, first, a living thing which takes nourishment and reproduces itself and, secondly, moves itself about and has emotions and desires. The specific difference of man is reason or the power to think, what Aristotle calls 'mind', which for him is only a part of the soul. The detailed working-out of this line of thought in the *De Anima* is not altogether clear about the dividing-line between men and non-human animals. The latter are credited with sensation (at least that of touch) and with imagination. The implication is that non-human animals do not have knowledge, which necessarily presupposes the power to think, or, for that matter, the power of judgement, of forming beliefs, true or false.

Aristotle's position is, at any rate, like that of sensible men in general, somewhere between the extremes of Descartes and Hume. For Descartes animals were complex mechanical contrivances, the possession of souls was proprietary to human beings and God. Hume, however, credited animals with the power of 'experimental inference', though with them, as with most human beings most of the time, he did not dignify that kind of inference by describing it as reasoning, seeing it as a matter of custom or habit. 'If there be in reality any arguments of this nature, they surely lie too abstruse for the observation of such imperfect understandings'. (*Enquiry Concerning Human Understanding*, p.106.) The contrast of reasoning with custom and habit seems to imply that the former is a matter of consciously embracing and of applying in conscious processes of inference such general principles as that the unknown resembles the known.

Descartes's view that the distinguishing characteristic of men is consciousness implies that talk of the sensations, desires and emotions of animals is metaphorical. To speak of a cat's noticing a bird on a low branch or of a dog's anger must be analogous to speaking of a thermometer's noticing the increase in the heat of a room or of an old car's agony as it grinds up a steep hill in bottom gear. Why is this absurd? Presumably because of the systematic thoroughness of the analogy between a cat's perceptions and a man's. The cat has closely similar perceptual equipment in its eyes and their cerebral attachments. That equipment operates in the same sort of circumstances and under the same sorts of mistake-engendering hazards as our own. It connects opportunities to actions in the same sort of way as ours does.

There is a marginal imperfection about Aristotle's account of reason, mind or the power of thought as man's specific difference. This is his ascription of that power of thought to both 'man and possibly another order like man or superior to him'. (*De Anima*, 414b, 19-20.) Are these the 55 or 47 unmoved movers required to account for the movements of the planets? They are not animals exactly but they are not pure form, as God, the prime mover, is. The conceptual pigeon-hole hollowed out in the *De Anima* for the other possible order of rational beings was filled in due course by angels.

Apart from 'nature' and 'idea' there are few more elastic words in the philosophical vocabulary than 'reason'. But in taking it to be man's specific difference, Aristotle gives a fairly clear impression of what he means by it. It is the power of thought which is exercised in the attempt to acquire knowledge and whose success or perfection is the achievement of knowledge. To deny it to animals, Aristotle's account of the distinction between sensation and thought must be recruited. Sensation for him is a direct awareness of sensible objects and thought of intelligible objects, concepts or universals. He may be thought of as holding, with Locke and Geach, that 'brutes abstract not'.

There is no need to pursue this demarcation-dispute for the purpose in hand. For there are, fairly obviously, some powers of thought or kinds of rationality that men possess which non-human animals do not. A currently favoured way of marking them out is as those mental operations involved in the understanding of a language. That manoeuvre makes the material in question more palpable, perhaps, but not all that more perspicuous. How is it to be decided that the systems of signalling or communication in use among animals are languages only in a metaphorical sense? The aspect of human communication that seems lacking from its animal correlates is not the conveying of factual information. Bees are not confined to the expression of their emotions and incitements to action. What is lacking is argument or critical discussion, the practice of deliberately attempting to correct beliefs, in other words reasoning in its most elevated sense. We may agree with Hume that animals infer but they do not construct or conduct inferences.

The protracted authority of Aristotle's idea that rationality is the specifically differentiating part of the essence of man is not undeserved. Rationality is not possessed by all the beings we should describe as human but the exceptions are not of a kind calculated to undermine the principle. Babies are not rational in the way that an ordinary adult who is not reasoning at the moment is. But they are potentially rational in a way that dogs are not. It is, presumably, logically possible that a dog should learn to speak, make up stories, get some O levels. These are possible to a baby in a much stronger, more factual sense. If time and the normal opportunities are supplied it will acquire these accomplishments. What of a mental defective who has either lost or never acquired the status of a rational being? It is surely not too mechanical a defence of the principle to say that they are defective human beings, who look and are physically constructed like men, but are only marginally or by a sort of prudent and humane courtesy fully human beings.

On the other hand the only animals we know of, rather than think about, that are rational are human beings. But what would happen if some non-humanly embodied creature, such as the logically possible dog I mentioned a moment ago, were to exhibit rationality? I suggest that we take both rationality and being humanly embodied as essential properties of men. Confronted with a situation in which the two criteria conflict we should most probably disentangle the concepts of human being and of person which, as things are, we can apply to the very same things and in the same way. A contrasted incentive to the same step would be the discovery of a society of creatures that while physiologically not significantly different from ourselves had the intellectual powers, modes of communication and general style of social interaction that prevail amongst dogs.

There are, indeed, other characteristics than rationality which seem to be common and peculiar to human beings, or as much so as it is. Examples would be laughing and cooking. But universal as these largely are among men they do not seem to be *essential* to humanity in the way that rationality is. It would, no doubt, be depressing to come upon a society of man-shaped creatures who neither laughed nor cooked, who met all changes of circumstance with straight or tear-stained faces and nourished themselves exclusively on the nuts and berries of folklore. But it would not inspire the thought that the creatures in question were not really men. After all there are unquestionably human beings here and there, who, perhaps under the influence of Schopenhauer's philosophy or the macrobiotic ideology, neither laugh nor cook. Laughing and cooking, in other words, are factual not conceptual ingredients of human nature.

A further consideration is that laughing and cooking are, properly conceived, forms of rationality. To laugh is not just to go through a particular audible and visible physiological routine. The cachinnations of the hyena would be laughter only if they were the expression of an ability to see jokes. The nearest that non-human animals get to that is in the smiles of glee on the faces of dogs when they hear the paper crackle in a box of Milk Tray. Similarly a dog who dropped an antelope haunch in a bushfire over which he was jumping and eventually retrieved it in a cooked state and ate it would not on that account be regarded as a colleague of Escoffier. The critical appreciation of incongruity involved in laughter and the intention to transform foodstuffs by the application of heat can be credited only to beings whose activities generally testify to rationality in the fairly advanced, transperceptual sense in which I have taken it.

The crucial ethical inference Aristotle draws from his account of human essence is that the perfection of man lies in the maximisation of his specific differentiating feature. An ideal man is one who exhibits intellectual virtue to the highest degree. In doing so he approximates as closely as possible to God, or pure intelligence, whose proper or exclusive activity is to think about himself or pure thought or, to take the widest possible interpretation, matters of abstract theory.

It should be emphasised that Aristotle's prescription for man's realisation of the ideal does not connect it with the whole of man's essence but only with the differentiating part of it. Animality, that is to say self-locomotion and the life of the senses, and, even more, mere livingness, consisting in nourishment and reproduction, are to be played down and as far as possible transcended. Aristotle's human paradigm is not what might be called a well-rounded man. He shows, indeed, a suspiciously close resemblance to Aristotle himself: he is a clever, truth-loving, hard-working metaphysician.

No blanket condemnation of inferences from *is* to *ought* is needed to put in question this particular inference from what a thing essentially and differentiatingly is to what it ideally ought to be. Is the best rose inevitably the one whose roseate characteristics are so emphatic that it cannot be confused from a distance with an anemone or a peony? Is the best island the one separated by the longest and deepest tracts of water from other land-masses?

There is, indeed, one type of entities with regard to whose perfection such an inference can possibly be drawn: entities of functional kinds. A knife is an instrument designed or intended for cutting things with. Any properties it has that are unconnected with its ability to cut things are superfluous. It is, of course, undifferentiatingly, a material body but no one would suppose that the criteria of its perfection are to be sought in that fact. A knife's excellence does not increase with its magnitude and solidity.

But men are not items of intentional construction, although many of them are brought into existence intentionally. Those who bring them into existence exercise negligible control over their design. At best the expectant mother may hope to avoid certain defects in her offspring by avoiding certain habits and indulgences. Christian theism would assign the detailed planning of the human species to God but Aristotle, holding no theory of creation, did not.

Hobbes and Spinoza ascribed to all kinds of being a self-preservative impulse or *conatus*, a drive to maintain themselves in existence. If, with Hobbes, one assumes that going out of existence is the worst fate that can befall a thing then the primary good for a thing must be the continuation of existence, on any terms and overriding all other considerations. As far as men are concerned that assumption is built into the practice of supposing that anyone who commits suicide does so because the balance of his mind is disturbed. Unless things, or, at any rate, living things, to which alone it is literally intelligible to ascribe such characteristics, had some native impulse to stay alive and avoid destruction they would be replaced by other living things which did have the impulse or by the inanimate destructive forces to which the notion of self-preservative instinct does not literally apply.

But if self-preservation, as well as being characteristic of living things, were a prime value for them that would not entail that an ideal member of a species was one in which the specifically differentiating part of its essence was most developed. Aristotle's metaphysicians, his ideal leisure-class of theorists, notoriously required a social substructure of slaves and soldiers to keep them in existence. More generally, it is obvious that a man in whom theoretical rationality is emphasised at the expense of other characteristics is in a precarious situation.

Something of Aristotle's idea that rationality is the perfection as well as the essential differentiating property of man survives in the curious argument in Kant's *Groundwork* which concludes that since the satisfaction of desire would be better served by instinct than by reason it is incumbent on men, equipped as they are with reason, to exercise it in actions that have nothing to do with the satisfaction of desire. In Kant, of course, the exercise of reason, in its legitimate, practical form, is connected much more closely with what is conventionally regarded as moral than it is in Aristotle. But the general structure of the argument is the same: it is reason that essentially differentiates men from non-human animals, so human excellence consists in the domination of the non-rational aspect of man by his reason. The difference between them is that in one case reason is exercised in metaphysics and theology, while in the other it operates through the conforming of actions to rationally universal principles.

I conclude that there is no justification for the view that since reason is what essentially differentiates men from other things it is the criterion of human excellence. Man is not a functional kind. The metaphysics of self-preservation supports no partiality to the differentiating part of man's essence at the expense of the rest of it. The fact that men ought logically to be rational, in so far as they are not really men unless they are, does not imply that the more rational they are the more they are what they morally ought to be. Whatever may be thought of the fallaciousness of ethical naturalism, it is clear that ethical essentialism of this kind is a fallacy.

II. MARX: MAN AS PRODUCTIVE

The most explicit statement by Marx of his theory of human essence occurs early in *The German Ideology*. He says, 'Men can be distinguished from animals by consciousness, by religion or anything else you like. They themselves begin to distinguish themselves from animals as soon as they begin to *produce* their means of subsistence.' He goes on, 'By producing their means of subsistence men are indirectly producing their actual material life', and a little later, 'As individuals express their life, so they are. What they are, therefore, coincides with their production.'

Earlier, introducing the concept of alienated labour in the *Paris MS*, he had written, 'Productive life is species-life ... The whole character of a species, its generic character, is contained in its manner of vital activity and free conscious activity is the species-characteristic of man.' 'Alienated labour ... alienates from man his own body, nature exterior to him and his intellectual being, his human essence.'

For Marx, says Tucker, 'man is universally a being who produces things'.

Animals, of course, are also productive in a marginal way, by their own vital activity they *secure* the means of their own subsistence. But they simply appropriate nourishment that is immediately available. Man's production is a matter of conscious will and design. Developing the point, Acton takes Marx's view to be that man is essentially a tool-maker and tool-user. The making and use of *instruments* of production is a crucial expression of the conscious forethought peculiar to human productive activities. It could be argued that the provision of the means of subsistence is production proper, and not merely acquisition, to the extent that the use of tools is involved in it.

This conception of human essence is Marx's materialist correction of Hegel's idealist and more or less Aristotelian notion of man as an essentially rational being. Man is, indeed, essentially rational for Marx but his reason is actualised in productive activity, first and foremost in nature, of course, but also in the realm of ideas, broadly conceived. Marx allows for the spiritual aspects of human nature, but he conceives these as a sophisticated and developed form of productive activity, and not, in the Aristotelian way, as an activity of contemplation. Aristotle had, in effect, taken the theoretical exercise of reason to be a kind of higher perception, an encounter with the abstract objects of pure thought that is only truly active as a kind of attention. For Marx theories and works of art are literally human productions. Where for Aristotle there is a sharp break between the practical activities by which men satisfy their desires and the sequestered, contemplative life of the mind, for Marx the two are both on a continuum. The two points of view correspond to two conceptions of society: one in which a leisured elite is liberated for its contemplative enjoyments by a labouring mass which provides for its tiresome animal needs, another in which all who do anything worth doing are engaged in some form of production.

Marx does say in *The Povery of Philosophy*, in a variant of a familiar formula, that 'all history is nothing but a continual transformation of human nature'. But that is not a denial of the conception of a human essence. The human nature that changes in history is contingent human nature, the set of needs, habits and beliefs that men have at a particular stage of history. Marx holds that men make themselves in the sense that the historically transitory aspects of human nature are the outcome of the interaction between man, producing his own means of subsistence, and nature, and particularly of the modes of social organisation through which material production is carried on, both man and nature being radically altered in the process.

Marx's account of human essence has some plain superiorities to that of Aristotle. In the first place, it treats man, as Marx would say, as he actually is, that is to say as a natural object and not as a pure intelligence which happens for some unfathomable reason to be embodied. Secondly, his conception of the higher, more spiritually elevated activities of man as being a kind of production rather than a kind of perception at once detaches the acquisition of knowledge from an unacceptable epistemology, which sees it as actually being a kind of perception, rather than as resting, among other things, upon it in a crucial way (one might say that it treats the business of acquiring knowledge as a whole and does not concentrate on the final, gratified phase of luxuriating in its achievement), and also accords a juster place to art than the traditional remission of it to the status of a practical craft for the fashioning of objects of amusement and instruction. In treating art as he does, Marx, one might say, inverts the traditional status of the creator and the contemplator.

An interesting implication of Marx's account of human essence is that it provides the outlines of a criterion for determining the point at which men proper evolved from mere anthropoids. With the invention of agriculture man is undoubtedly on the scene: it involves tools and long-sighted planning. To go one stage further back to herding, it could be reasonably held that the herd itself is an instrument of production which is assembled, preserved and improved by conscious design. To go further back again to hunting, its human could be distinguished from its animal form, not, of course, by its social or co-operative nature, but by its use of deliberately fashioned weapons. Only at the most elementary stage of food-gathering is there nothing in the species' mode of securing the means of its subsistence which exhibits humanly essential productiveness. Thus Marx's doctrine would allow humanity to the aboriginal inhabitants of Australia, though it would be, in the Wellingtonian phrase, a close-run thing.

Marx does not draw as direct an ethically essentialist inference from his account of human essence as Aristotle. He does not conclude that since man is essentially productive the best man is the most productive man. Nevertheless his notion of the ideal life for man is expressed in terms of the character of his production. The good life is a life of free and creative productive activity, a life in which men's productive essence is actualised without alienation. The chief source of alienation, of course, is the institution of private property in the means of production. Under the system where the worker sells his labour he does not decide what is to be produced and he does not control the product of his labour. He is thus alienated both from his labour and its products. But two further forms of alienation do not seem wholly attributable to the phenomenon of wage-labour, namely alienation from other men and from nature. They would seem to result, in the first instance at any rate, from the fact of scarcity, from the fact that men's desires, including those imperious desires that correspond to vital needs, outrun the supply of freely available goods. Men are in consequence alienated from other men in that they are in competition with them for the things they want or need and from nature since it does not directly supply, but has to be compelled laboriously to yield, the things men are in pursuit of. It can be argued that scarcity is intensified and exacerbated in two ways by the property-system. The owners of property by exploiting the mass of wage-earners appropriate goods that go far beyond their needs and which could, otherwise distributed, satisfy the needs of the mass of labourers. Secondly, it is characteristic of capitalism to induce wants in the mass of consumers by advertising, which should be understood to embrace the kind of conspicuous display which excites impulses of emulation. But even in a simple subsistence economy, whose technical and organisational primitiveness does not turn differences in energy and ability into large differences of wealth, there would still be scarcity, competition between men for the goods that there are and a natural compulsion to labour caused by a shortage of freely appropriable goods.

Marx's answer to this is that capitalism, at great human cost, has solved the primary problem of material production, in principle at any rate, by its accumulation and development of a vast array of instruments of production. In due course automation will finally free men altogether from the drudgery of compelled labour for the satisfaction of material needs. Once that has been achieved men will be free to engage in purely self-expressive, non-material productive activities.

One shadow on this rosy picture is the Malthusian one. Excessive population requires a mobilisation of productive resources proportionately greater than itself, if only because the satisfaction of the most elemental needs requires the cultivation of ever more marginal resources. It also seems to embody an oversimple conception of the difference between material needs and immaterial ones. A lot of labour is locked up in a power boat or a piano, but boating and piano-playing are not the satisfactions of primordial, natural desires; they cannot be assimilated to eating as if they were a kind of larger helpings. Even the paradigm immaterial activities of creative art and theorising often have lavish material conditions: linear accelerators and vast chunks of marble, for example.

Marx's ethical essentialism differs from that of Aristotle in an important respect. Aristotle derived his notion of human perfection not from the whole essence of man but from the specifically differentiating part of it. For the specific difference to serve as a criterion of excellence it had to be susceptible of difference of degree. Otherwise all men, just because they have to satisfy the logically necessary conditions of being men, would have to be perfect. Marx's specific difference, productiveness, also differs in degree, but, as I said earlier, he does not make that his criterion of excellence. He is not an ethical Stakhanovist.

What he does in fact is to say that man approaches perfection to the extent that his specific difference is actualised in a particular way, that is freely. And that is to introduce something that is not intrinsic to his conception of human essence at all.

The ethical upshot of Marx's reflections on the ideal nature of man is what Sorel called an ethic of producers. His notion of happiness, fulfilment or self-realisation defined it in terms of activity and not of the self-indulgent, passive, consumption which is intimated as the ideal end by the traditional utilitarian concept of pleasure. That is an interesting idea but it is rather a large and perceptive empirical generalisation about the real conditions of long-lasting human satisfaction than a consequence of his account of the essential nature of man.

A threefold distinction between types of men is crucial to Marx's thinking. There are unproductive owners, compulsorily productive workers (the indispensable correlate of the owners), and the freely productive creators of the future. He does not in any way suggest that leisured and unproductive owners are not really men at all. It might be said that, in their alienating but nevertheless historically indispensable way, owners are productive after all. It is necessary to distinguish here between the managerial activities which bring capitalist undertakings into existence and direct their operations and the merely passive reception by pure, non-managerial owners of the bulk of the fruits of the labour of others. Exploitation is an offshoot of productive activity but it is not a productive activity itself. The purely exploitative owner is, then, wholly non-productive, or is so, at any rate, in so far as he does not do anything else but just luxuriously consumes his wealth. But he is still a man. Marx, no doubt, thinks of him as a morally inferior sort of man, but he does not take him to be totally dehumanised.

Whatever Marx's attitude to merely leisured owners of wealth may be it is plain that there are and always have been some and that they are unquestionably human. So productiveness is not a logically necessary condition of being human. That difficulty can easily be circumvented by interpreting the productiveness which for Marx is the essence of man as the capacity for, rather than actual engagement in, productive activity. But it could be said that, for all his remarks about how to distinguish men from animals, which suggests that it is logical essence he is concerned with, his real purpose here is something different.

Productiveness should be conceived, perhaps, more as man's real essence, in a Lockean sense, than in the Aristotelian way as a logical criterion for the classification of men as men. Essence, on this interpretation, is not the set of defining properties of a kind, but the set of properties that are fundamental, from an explanatory point of view, with regard to a given kind. It is in this sense that it is not essential to fishes that they live in water or to mammals that they do not. The methodological fruit of the materialistic interpretation of history is the injunction to examine men in their productive, indeed in their materially productive, activities if their general characteristics and behaviour are to be understood. It is in that sense that the view that human beings are in essence erotic might be attributed to Freud.

But here too no ethical consequences follow. In his last writings Freud committed no inconsistency in holding that civilisation involved a repressive transformation of essential instincts and for valuing it on just that account. If Marx had based his criterion of human excellence on productiveness pure and simple, and not on the particular free and creative form of production that he did, a corresponding position would have been both consistent and appropriate and it is, in effect, implied by what Marx says. The pursuit of ever more massive productive output, even if it maximises the specific difference of man, is not his highest aim.

As an account of man's logically specific difference, then, productiveness is not an improvement on Aristotle's rationality. Contrasted as it is with the mere instinctive appropriation of the means of subsistence to be found in animals it is a form in which rationality is applied and presupposes it. There can be men who are wholly unproductive. The fact that for Aristotle they are the truest and most perfect of men is not a good reason for turning his view on its head, particularly since, as Marx himself saw in admitting that there is such a thing as non-material production, it is only by misrepresenting abstract thinking as a more or less passive, quasi-perceptual contemplation, that Aristotle assimilated those engaged in the purest exercise of reason with the class of leisured consumers.

III. SARTRE: MAN HAS NO ESSENCE

The freedom, which Marx attaches to his view that productiveness is the specifically differentiating essence of man, to arrive at his criterion of human excellence, occupies an even more central place in the account of human nature given by Sartre. Sartre takes it to follow from the fact that men are free that they have no fixed characteristics which, together with the circumstances in which they find themselves, necessitate their acting in the way that they do. Men, in contrast to mere things, are self-determining beings.

A radical distinction between men and natural objects is the starting-point of Sartre's philosophy, as it had been for Heidegger's *Sein und Zeit*. A natural object is a being in-itself (*en-soi*), existing as a matter of brute and determinate fact, endowed with a set of properties which rigidly fix its behaviour. A man, on the other hand, is a being for-itself (*pour-soi*) which endows itself with such properties as it has by its own choice and which is not bound by its past choices in making future ones. The ability to choose involves both consciousness and will: consciousness of possible future self-determining choices and the will that can select one of these possibilities for action. At any moment, then, man's properties are the result of previous choices as manifested in action, a man is what he has done. But these past circumstances do not circumscribe the range of future choice. Since what I now am I may negate by my choice for the immediate future, I am what I am not and I am not what I am. These defiant formulae are, I suspect, rendered intelligible by those who come across them by the cryptic addition of 'going to be'. So amended they amount to the statement that man is a changing being. That is not necessarily true and is not even contingently true on a universal scale unless it is trivialised by being taken to refer to long tracts of time and to all, and not only radical or important, changes of character.

So, Sartre says, 'there is no human nature ... Man simply is ... he is what he wills ... Man is nothing else but that which he makes of himself.' What that comes to, in humdrum and intelligible terms, is that man is a changing being whose changes are the outcome of his own free and unnecessitated choices. What that is directed against, in the first instance, would appear to be the notion that each man has a fixed and definite type of character or personality, in other words to the old doctrine of humours, where these are conceived as intrinsic and invariable attributes of their possessors. But in defining men as self-determining beings, equipped with consciousness and the power of choice, and by so distinguishing them from everything else that exists it amounts to the assertion of a theory of human essence. It denies that any specific attributes of character are essential to any individual man, but it plainly asserts that men in general, to be men, must have certain abstract or even higher-order properties, which account for the varying concrete characteristics which it is of the essence of men to choose to take on. It is the abstract and essential nature of men to choose and vary the concrete and specific nature they each individually have.

I said that Sartre was setting himself in opposition to the idea that each man is of a fixed character-type in the first instance. The further aim he has in taking this stand is ethical: he wants to emphasise the scope of men's moral responsibility. I cannot escape responsibility for my choices and acts by saying that I could not help doing what I did because I am that sort of man. The sort of man I am is itself something I have chosen and for which I am responsible.

He goes on to draw a further ethical conclusion from his account of human essence, one that is strictly analogous to the ethical essentialism I have attributed to Aristotle and, in a more qualified way, to Marx. As a self-determining being I cannot devolve my responsibilities of choice on to some external provider of moral principles. There is an important ambiguity about this contention. It may mean that I cannot avoid choosing; it may also mean that in submitting my choices to externally supplied moral principles I do not free myself of responsibility.

To guide one's choices by the principles supplied by a church or a political party or, worst of all, the conventional, customary morality of one's social group is to be guilty of inauthenticity. At times he says that that is not, however, to avoid choice, but is, at best, to economise it, since the selection of some mentor or institution is itself a choice. Even if my principles have been formulated by something or someone external to myself they come to govern my actions only by a choice I have made. But that kind of inauthenticity could equally, and in many cases more realistically, be regarded as a failure to choose, as a supine conformity to the prevailing moral assumptions of the community within which I live. In that case, rather than positively choosing a body of externally supplied principles, I have failed to choose a morality of my own and contented myself with passive absorption of the conventional.

The difference between the two interpretations is brought out by considering the case of a man who, after full and searching reflection, positively chooses to embrace the fully-articulated moral system of some group or institution. Is his situation reprehensible because the content of his principles has been externally supplied? Or is he to be praised for authenticity in that his moral commitments have been entered into by a free and consciously reflective act of choice?

At any rate if a man's morality, however external in origin and however passively embraced, is necessarily the outcome of choice, it follows that whatever morality he winds up with is an expression of his essence as a freely choosing being. If, on the other hand, the element of choice in his adoption of a morality can vary in degree, if he can at one extreme positively choose it and at the other slide passively into accepting it, it might be concluded that the morally superior man is the one whose morality by being positively chosen most fully expresses his essence. If Sartre's theory of essence is to have any ethical implications it must be in the latter interpretation. But, as I have said, one may positively choose a morality whose content is externally supplied.

The idea that man is in essence a self-determining being *can* have ethical implications, if his exercise of his capacity for choice can vary in degree. But that is to say that it can have ethical implications *only* under these conditions, not that it actually does have any. It is also true that only a being with the capacity for choice is properly conceivable as a moral agent, as responsible for what he does. But that does not imply that one ought to choose one's moral principles any more than it implies that one should individualistically choose one's beliefs about matters of scientific fact and that one is being somehow cognitively inauthentic if one more or less passively accepts the beliefs of the scientists of one's epoch. One should, no doubt, be able and, when one's experience provides an opportunity, be willing to criticise generally accepted opinions, both in science and morals. But to say that is not to endorse a general free-for-all, in science or morals.

If the essence of man is self-determination by choice, and its exercise can vary in degree, is its maximisation the criterion of human excellence? Here, as in the two previous cases, there seems to be no necessary connection between premise and conclusion. With this conception of man, as with others, there is no inconsistency in taking 'all-too-human' to be an unfavourable description. Aristotle's doctrine of the mean is at least as applicable here as his doctrine that each natural kind has its intrinsic and essential excellence. To acknowledge that there can be too much choice as well as too little is at least as reasonable as the idea that the unlimited maximisation of choice (of choosings, not things to choose from) defines the perfection of man.

Sartre's view that the essence of man is self-determining choice entails either that he cannot help but choose, in which case there can be no merit in his doing so, or that he can exercise his capacity for choice in varying degrees. If the latter is what he means, it is far from obvious that he *ought* to exercise it to the utmost possible extent. It is not clear whether such a maximisation of choice is compatible with the adoption of already established, institutional or conventional moral attitudes, but it is at any rate calculated in fact, if not in logic, to enhance moral idiosyncrasy, perversity and disagreement. While not denying that these can be valuable in periods of great moral stodginess, I cannot see that they are of absolute and unconditional value. Sartre's theory of human essence elevates a Bohemian prejudice of post-Nietzschean urban intellectuals to the whole truth about the ideal life of man.

IV. DO INDIVIDUALS HAVE ESSENCES?

At the beginning I pointed out that the question, has man an essence, is ambiguous. It could mean: is there a set of defining properties associated with the concept of man? That would be answered negatively in one way by those, if there are any, who believe the concept to be simple and unanalysable and in another way by those, and there are certainly some of these, who believe that men are linked not by a common property or properties but rather by family resemblance. But it could also mean: is it essential to the individuals that are men *that* they are men? That this is so is clearly assumed by all three of the doctrines of essence I have considered.

For Aristotle, Marx and Sartre would not deny that the individuals who are men have other properties than the rationality, productiveness or self-determination which they respectively regard as essential to being a man. Certainly both Marx and Sartre suggest that some of men's properties are somehow conspicuously foreign to their essence. In Marx's case these are the properties forced on men by the more or less oppressive social systems in which men find themselves. In Sartre's case there is an emphasis on the spurious, play-acting character of many typical human roles, as in the example of the elaborately investigated waiter. But that disparagement can hardly be applied to non-essential properties in general. To be female or red-haired or a good swimmer or have absolute pitch is neither an oppressive social distortion nor a piece of theatrical make-believe, even if it may have oppressive social consequences, on the one hand, or be exploited in a theatrical manner, on the other.

They clearly believe, then, that for any individual who is, amongst indefinitely many other things, a human being, the fact of being human has some overriding importance. A particular Hungarian postman is essentially a man, but only contingently a Hungarian and an employee of the postal service. Presumably one who holds that to be true would adopt an analogous view about non-human things. A particular Red Admiral would be essentially an animal but only contingently red and a butterfly; a particular television set would be essentially a machine but only contingently dark brown and of 27 inches in screen-width.

It is this assumption that is challenged by what I have called 'orthodox positivism'. C.I. Lewis bluntly observes, 'It is, of course, meaningless to speak of the essence of a thing except relative to its being named by a particular term.' (*Analysis of Knowledge and Valuation*, p.41.) It is plainly implied that things are always capable of being named by a host of non-synonymous terms, each bearing a different essence with it. Ayer denies that individuals have any necessary properties. 'We can significantly ask', he says, 'what properties it is necessary for something to possess in order to be a thing of such and such a kind, for that is a way of asking what properties enter into the definition of that kind of thing ... On the other hand, there is no such definition of an individual.' (*Central Questions of Philosophy*, p.197.)

That position would seem to be strengthened by the existence of non-connotative ways of referring to individuals. If ordinary proper names and the pure demonstratives like 'this', which Russell thought to be logically proper names, are non-connotative and imply nothing about the properties of the things to which they refer and yet serve to identify them it would seem to follow that no denial of a property to a thing thus named could yield a contradiction and thus that no property whatever was essential to such a thing. It is not, indeed, necessary to individuals having no essences that there should be wholly non-connotative ways of referring to them. For it might be the case that there was no common element to the sets of properties connoted by the identifying descriptions that referred to them. But, if there are non-connotative names, the thesis that none of an individual's properties are essential to it seems all the more evident.

It is, indeed, widely agreed that even if not strictly connotative, in the sense of logically implying the possession of certain properties by the things they refer to, proper names and pure demonstratives are associated in their standard identifying use with something connotative. Anyone who uses such a term to identify an individual thing must be able to fix or further determine the reference he is making with some descriptions of the individual in question. But, it is admitted, these associated descriptions are not logically tied to the terms whose use they support. A referring term can be used in communication between people whose sets of associated descriptions are different and perhaps even have no element in common.

There is, however, a problem about the determinacy of identity-statements which might serve to reinstate individual essence to some extent, by way of implying at least a minimal connotation for apparently non-connotative terms. Geach has argued that identity is relative, in the sense that '*a* is the same as *b*' may be true if *a* and *b* are thought of in one applicable way, and false if they are thought of in another, and thus that it means different things in the two cases. 'Is *a* the same as *b*?' is, in Geach's view, an insufficiently determinate question as it stands. It must always be possible, even if it is not always, or even often, practically necessary, to secure understanding, for the questioner to answer the counter-question, 'same what?'

The sort of example that inspires that conclusion may be illustrated by the question put to a sculptor working on a large lump of clay 'is that what you were working on when I called last week?' It may properly receive the answer 'it is the same piece of clay but a different statue, last week I was doing the Archbishop of Canterbury, but this week I'm doing George Eliot'. As defenders of the univocal purity of the concept of identity have been quick to point out, such a state of affairs does not require the admission that the concept of identity is indeterminate, or that it is ambiguous as between different sortal respects in which it may be applied. It would be enough to allow that the reference of the singular terms 'this' and 'what you were working on' is indeterminate.

But, if that is so, then pure demonstratives like the word 'this' and proper names of the ordinary non-connotative sort must implicitly carry some minimal element of connotation with them when they are used to make identifying references. Something of the sort seems to be admitted by Ayer, despite his rejection of individual essence, in his consideration of the question, 'what makes a person the person that he is'. To that question, he says, 'we can, then, answer that certain properties are after all essential; the property of having some human characteristics, perhaps also the property of occupying some position or other in space or time'. (*The Problem of Knowledge*, p.208.) The fact that those properties do not serve to individuate the things whose essence they are, that none of the properties which are uniquely satisfied by an individual are essential to it, may be admitted without prejudice to the conclusion that an individual has an essence, even if not a proprietary one.

One consideration leading Ayer to this conclusion is the apparent existence of logical limits to the changes we can intelligibly conceive an individual to undergo without forfeiture of its identity. I might have been, or he might change into, a female, a Bulgarian, a trapeze-artist, an epileptic. But there seems no sense to the supposition that I might have been or that he might change into an ashtray or a daffodil or a Jumbo jet. Certainly the stuff of which I am composed might be turned into fertiliser or the *pièce de résistance* of a dinner-party in New Guinea. But then I am not identical with the stuff of which I am composed, I am just made of it.

Individuals, then, do have at least a minimal essence if the determinacy of reference without which they cannot be identified is to be secured. And as far as the individuals who are human beings are concerned it appears that this reference-determining essence is their humanity. Any other properties they may possess they can be conceived as losing without loss of identity, provided, of course, that they are not, as Ayer's property of location in time and space may be, logically implied by being human. Or perhaps one should say, being a person. For, as horror films concretely show, it is intelligible that a person should change from being a man, that is from being embodied in the characteristically human way, into a wolf, provided that the wolf is, as actual wolves are not, a person.

In fact, by and large, only all things that have, or are, living human bodies are persons. But in so far as they can be conceptually distinguished it is the personality rather than the human embodiment that is essential to them. Keeping both options open, for the moment, let me raise the question: does the fact that being men, in either or both of these senses, which is essential to the individuals that are men, in a way that none of their other properties is, have any ethical implications?

It is clear that the concept of a person enters into the constitution of many of the central concepts of morality, including the concept of morality itself. Moral principles are logically confined in their application to persons in two distinct ways: they enjoin or forbid the actions and approve or condemn the characters only of persons and, secondly, they are concerned with the actions of persons (and the characters these actions express) in regard to their effect on persons.

But that does not make the concept of a person a moral, and so perhaps especially disputable, concept any more than the fact that the concepts of negation or implication or causation enter into the constitution of such concepts as poison or defeat in war or resentment makes them concepts of chemistry, history or psychology. They are not peculiar to these disciplines and the concept of a person is not peculiar to morality.

I have argued elsewhere ('Two Conceptions of Personality', *Revue Internationale de Philosophie*, 1968 and *The Nature of Things*, pp. 103-5) that we tend to operate with two different notions of personality, one of rational, responsible agency, as exemplified by adult, sane human beings, the other much less exigent and applicable to babies, the insane, the senile and, I would suggest, the higher animals. Both figure in the two modes in which the concept of a person enters into the constitution of the concept of morality that I mentioned. The persons to whom alone moral injunctions are addressed are persons in the narrower sense, rational and responsible agents. But the persons whose interests are relevant to the determination of the moral qualities of action are the wider class of sensitive beings, capable of enjoyment and suffering, and to whom alone the possession of interests can be intelligibly ascribed. In neither case, however, does the fact that personality is the individual essence of those endowed with it have ethical implications. The relation is the other way round: the concept of morality presupposes both conceptions of personality. But that, as I have argued, does not make it a moral concept itself, although it is logically indispensable to the concept of morality.

2

Character in Real Life

The idea of character and the idea of personality are somewhat entangled. In quite a number of connections they amount to much the same thing. Of a grimly factual biography or obituary, that takes the form of a register of posts held, official acts performed, places visited and people met, one could say indifferently that it gives no sense of the character or of the personality of its subject. Nevertheless the two can be distinguished. It is a very different thing to say that someone has no character from saying that he has no personality. To have no character is to be weak, easily led, responsive to immediate pressures of need or desire or importunacy on the part of others. But to have no personality is to be dim, unnoticeable, conventional, to make no distinct or memorable impact as a unique person. It would seem possible to have a good deal of one while having, colloquially, none of the other. Castlereagh, perhaps, had character without personality; Alcibiades personality without character.

Character, fairly narrowly and conversationally interpreted, seems to be a matter of the will. It is a measure of the control a man has over his conduct, of his persistence and consistency in seeking to realise his long-term aims. The character-building that was the primary, perhaps even exclusive, purpose of the late Victorian boarding school (the Latin periods being not so much a gateway into the enjoyment of a various and powerful literature as a training in emotional resilience in the face of an intrinsically repulsive task) sought to impart that kind of resoluteness or energy of will. Personality-building, however, is a more cosmetic art, the service yielded to John D. Rockefeller by the public relations expert Ivy Lee or to a battalion of meaty but appetising young women in the late 1940s by Mr Rank's 'Charm School'. The most celebrated and durable of the graduates of that academy, Diana Dors, could not have retained her place in public attention for so long without a good deal of character in addition to the personality with which she was supplied.

It could be said that character, in view of its connection with the will, is an ethical notion, while that of personality is really aesthetic. Character is intrinsic and deep-seated, a rather central constituent of a person, something that it is not easy for others to influence or for the person himself to change. But personality can be put on and taken off with much less difficulty; there is something histrionic about it, as a role that can be played, or sartorial, as an outfit that can be chosen and worn when the occasion suits. This conception of personality is carried to an extreme in the alleged usage of Hollywood press agents in the great days of that cultural centre: 'this girl has a terrific personality' being a euphemistic formula for conveying the fact that she had large and well-shaped breasts.

Those who like to support claims about meaning with etymology will draw attention to the derivation of the word 'personality' from *persona*, a mask. A less fragile confirmation of the distinction between the two as ethical and aesthetic is the fact that while it is natural to praise or condemn character as good or bad, personality is usually judged as attractive or unattractive. But both, it must be admitted, can be assessed as strong or weak. The idea that personality is somehow more ornamental than constitutional is vindicated by the practice of describing some personalities as artificial. The public figure presents a socially visible surface of unremitting geniality, interestedness and emotional warmth. When the crowds drift away and the television cameras are wheeled back to the vans, he resumes his more comfortable domestic costume of surly indifference. But there seems to be no such thing as an artificial character. If a man by persistent effort overcomes some character-defect we should not describe the boldness with which he has replaced his previous timidity or the despatch with which he has replaced irresolute dithering as artificial, even though we know it to be, in a sense, manufactured. Furthermore we do not think any the worse of it or him because of this fact, if anything we think the opposite.

For all that, the two terms do refer, in general, to very much the same thing: the more or less enduring system of tastes, propensities, desires and aversions, values and habits which constitute the inner causes or determinants of conduct. A possible way of viewing them would be to see character as the system of sentiments and so forth that a man actually has and personality as the system, real or pretended, which his public behaviour implies. If they are markedly different (markedly, since some leeway must be left for the claims of minimal politeness) he can be condemned as hypocritical or insincere; if they are much the same he is a man of at least one important sort of integrity.

The sub-title of David Riesman's *The Lonely Crowd* is 'a study of the changing American character'. The typical American, in his view, was moving from a state of inner-directedness, in which conduct is governed by firm, internalised rules, adhered to without concern for the impression that that will produce in others, to one of outer-directedness, in which the object is not to be oneself but to be what others want, to adjust to, and even resemble, them as much as possible. In my terminology the change is one from a condition in which character and personality do not need to be distinguished to one in which character proper is so attenuated that only personality is left.

Outside imaginative literature the study of different types of character or personality has been traditionally carried on in two ways. On the one hand there are theoretical systems of character-types, developed by a series of inquirers from Galen in the 2nd century AD to Professor H.J. Eysenck at the present day. Galen's theory of the four humours or basic kinds of temperament had a long run, almost as long as Aristotle's logic, for both disciplines were regarded by Kant towards the end of the eighteenth century as giving the last and authoritative words on their respective subject-matters. Indeed Galen's doctrine has done better than Aristotle's. The logician has been irreversibly superannuated, his findings, considerably amended and reorganised, being reduced to a small fragment of what, since Frege, we think of as logic. The psychologist, however, has, if Eysenck is right, fared much better. Eysenck maintains that experimental evidence supports both Galen's two-dimensional array of basic character- or personality-types and his belief that the psychological differences thus classified have a physiological foundation, although not the specific, liquid, one that Galen supposed.

The second mode of investigating human types is also of Greek origin: the delineation of 'characters', initiated by Aristotle's pupil and literary executor Theophrastus, revived by the English 'character writers' of the seventeenth century, Hall, Overbury and Earle, under the inspiration of Casaubon's Latin translation of Theophrastus in 1592, and brought to a higher level of literary accomplishment in 1688 with the publication of La Bruyère's *Les Caractères, ou les Moeurs de ce Siècle*. The character-writing of Theophrastus and La Bruyère has a primarily practical purpose of moral edification. Every one of Theophrastus's thirty exemplary characters is more or less deplorable. Over his whole enterprise stands the unstated rubric: do not be like this. The forms of vice illustrated are not, perhaps, of the most severe and desperate kind. Typical are surliness, arrogance, officiousness, loquacity and cowardice. But the darker vices are not likely to respond to literary therapy. However there is a theoretical, or at any rate a factual, interest served. Nothing remotely systematic is conveyed but there is a pleasing recognisability about many of Theophrastus's types. The 'patron of rascals', for example, ('conceiving that, if he associates with such persons, he will become more a man of the world') was familiar to the Kray brothers. Most of us will have met the Unseasonable Man who 'when he is asked to a wedding will inveigh against womankind … loves to rise and go through a long story to those who have heard it and know it by heart … when he is minded to dance, will seize another person who is not yet drunk'. A strong sense of the essential stability of human nature is communicated.

Galen held that there were four main kinds of character or temperament: the choleric, or vigorous and aggressive, the sanguine, or optimistic and sociable, the phlegmatic, or calm and reserved, and the melancholic, or gloomy and withdrawn. A man's possession of one of these character-systems he attributed to the predominance in his body of the particular secretion mentioned in the label of the type: bile, blood, phlegm and black bile. Eysenck contends that the distinction into four main types does contain an important truth and, even more significantly, that these character-differences have a physiological basis, which, going beyond Galen, he takes to be largely hereditary.

The scientific study of personality starts from measuring the extent to which various traits are possessed. The measurement is carried out in several different ways: by questionnaires, by non-verbal tests where these are applicable, by ratings given by people familiar with the subjects. The correlations between the particular traits; positive, negative and neutral or indifferent, can be plotted as a two-dimensional array. Eysenck's hypothesis is that the two axes of the array, at right angles to each other, signify, in one case, the degree of introversion or extraversion and, in the other, the degree of stability or neuroticism. The two factors are independent of each other so that any amount of one is compatible with any amount of the other. The two pairs of extreme cases can thus be freely combined and the four resulting compounds are pretty well the same as Galen's four humours. The phlegmatic is a stable introvert, the choleric an unstable extrovert and so on.

The next step is to test the hypothesis that psychological types are physiologically based. Eysenck reaches that conclusion by way of arguments to show that being of a given psychological type is hereditary rather than environmental. For if that is so it is reasonable to infer that the bodily constitution, which is clearly inherited, is at the root of the matter. Four kinds of evidence support the claim. Identical twins are more alike in character than fraternal ones. Twins who have been separated at birth and have lived in wholly different environments have closely similar characters. The degree of resemblance in character-traits is greater between people the closer their consanguinity. Finally, as everyone knows, animals can be bred for gentleness just as well as for glossy coats or strong shoulders.

In what he admits to be the speculative margin of his researches, Eysenck connects his two dimensions of character-difference with bits of the brain and nervous system: stability-neuroticism he links to the 'visceral brain' through the automatic nervous system, introversion-extraversion to the reticular formation in the brain stem on which depends the potential for arousal of the cerebral cortex.

One possible implication of this turns out to be actual: the relevant bit of cerebral apparatus can be influenced by drugs. Of course, in a way we all knew that already. Those well-known pharmaceutical products coffee and gin have been quite extensively experimented with in an informal fashion. In fact, since their effect is ordinarily fleeting, they do not really change the psychological type of their imbibers, they merely interfere for a while with the manifestation of character in behaviour.

It is the opposite implication that is, perhaps, more disquieting. Eysenck holds that character or personality, like intelligence, is about three-quarters attributable to heredity. That, if true, would seem to set firm limits to the possibility of self-improvement and, indeed, to character-training by ordinary educational methods. Cold baths and early rising, unless they somehow have a lasting effect on the state of the visceral brain or the reticular formation, cannot really get to the root of the matter. Eysenck, quite consistently, follows through the logic of his argument. He suggests that the predisposition to criminality responds better to doses of amphetamine than to the gallows and the lash.

It is an important fact about the world that people do have fairly fixed characters or personalities. People might, after all, be as various as the English weather. To the extent that they do ever approximate to that degree of unpredictability we tend to think of them as out of their minds. With people as they mostly are it enormously economises our practical dealings with them to come to them with a pretty clear idea of what they will do in given circumstances, how they will respond to given approaches and requests, what, in their cases, is the most effective way of getting them to act in various desired ways. Personal relations have traditionally been obstructed in England by the careful experimental inquiries that have to be undertaken by those who have just met to identify each other's precise social status. How exhausting it would be, every time one encountered someone, to have to start from the beginning and find out of precisely what psychological class he is a member today.

Hume, discussing the ancient problem of free-will, argued that causal determinism is true of men, as much as of non-human nature, on just this ground. 'The conjunction between motives and voluntary actions', he says, 'is as regular and uniform as that between the cause and effect in any part of nature ... this regular conjunction has been universally acknowledged among mankind, and has never been the subject of dispute, either in philosophy or common life'. Of course, there are apparent exceptions. 'A person of an obliging disposition gives a peevish answer; but he has the toothache or has not dined. A stupid fellow discovers an obvious alacrity in his carriage: but he has met with a sudden piece of good fortune'. The apparent exceptions fall under further rules about the effects on behaviour of toothaches and successful bets.

Hume takes it for granted that motives, and the characters they compose, are related to action as cause to effect, as cue to billiard-ball. In recent times many philosophers have rejected the idea that character is a causal determinant of conduct. In brief their argument is that there is no more to character than a certain regular pattern in conduct and a pattern cannot be regarded as the cause of one of its constituents.

There are two answers to that. Consider a rubber ball which has been dropped several times on a stone floor and has bounced. Because of that regular behaviour we shall ascribe the property of elasticity to it. We shall expect it to bounce in future and when asked why it does reply 'because it is elastic'. In saying that it is elastic we are, perhaps, saying no more than that it bounces whenever it is dropped on a hard surface. Nevertheless, given that it is elastic, when it is dropped on a hard surface it has to bounce.

In fact, when we say it is elastic we are saying more, or would like to say more, than merely that it bounces whenever it is dropped. There is something intellectually indigestible about the thought that there could be two rubber balls between which the minutest scrutiny could find no difference in structure or composition and yet one of which bounced while the other stayed put with a thud. Even if we do not know what it is, we cannot but suppose that there is some further difference between the way in which the constituents of the two balls are stuck together. It is that impulse to find a difference of fine structure behind a difference in patterns of behaviour that lies behind Eysenck's more adventurous physiological speculations.

In the chapter of his first *Enquiry* from which I have already quoted Hume further remarks, 'Mankind are so much the same, in all times and places, that history informs us of nothing new or strange in this particular. Its chief use is only to discover the constant and universal principles of human nature'. That is very much at odds with the current view that characters must differ with the differing social circumstances in and by which they are formed. He does go on to water his first statement down a good deal, admitting differences due to age and sex, and even time and place. The admission of age is important as an obvious case where the character of a particular individual can change within his lifetime.   .

How much do people's individual characters change? Gruff and timid children seem to turn into lively and sociable adults. Some dreadful reverse or misfortune may turn a genial and optimistic man into a melancholy cynic. Eysenck's physiological theory allows a substantial influence to environment and circumstance and it is in principle quite compatible with his view that the basic character-determining bits of the body may alter with time, even if a fall on the head seems more calculated to bring that about than a bankruptcy or a divorce. In general people's characters do hold together pretty firmly, allowing for the changes of circumstance, vigour and expectations wrought by the passage of time. It is this that makes people recognisable through time as the particular individuals they are and justifies our habits of continuity in personal relations. There is a price to be paid for that in monotony. Possibly a small side-benefit of the practice of presenting to the world a personality that somewhat conceals one's actual character is that it makes people more interesting than they would otherwise be.

3

The Image of Man in Twentieth Century Literature

> Unreal city,
> Under the brown fog of a winter dawn,
> A crowd flowed over London Bridge, so many,
> I had not thought death had undone so many.

Those lines from what is perhaps this century's most characteristic poem, T.S. Eliot's *Waste Land*, suggest several of the leading elements in the transformation that man has undergone in the last seventy years. He lives in a city but the city he lives in has a certain unreality. It is not a community of true individuals like Periclean Athens or Renaissance Florence. It is merely a container, not a stage; it forms the banks between which the undifferentiated tide of humanity flows.

Transported from the country into the town, man is no longer separated from other men by natural space, he becomes a statistic, an ingredient in a mass. Work and family are separated. Where once work was undertaken by the whole family and to satisfy the needs of the family directly, it is now done within a large and impersonal organisation, at a rhythm and for a purpose determined by other, unknown people, and is a thoroughly indirect means to the satisfaction of the family's ends.

Both the economy and the state concern themselves only with the broadest differences between men. The characteristic techniques of rational management used by these institutions require men's conduct to be definitely predictable: as specialised worker, as consumer, as recipient of public welfare. They are indifferent to, and even impatient of, human variety. Where that variety is an obstacle to the aims of rational management it has to be eliminated. Men's desires are shaped and directed by advertising and by the media of communication. The totalitarian state sets about the moulding of its citizens into the required form more directly, by coercion and by carefully planned uniformity of instruction, in school and out of it.

For the great mass of mankind in the urban, industrial west, in Europe and North America, there has, of course, been a great enrichment at least of material life. Hunger and destitution, infant mortality, illiteracy have been enormously reduced by new styles of social organisation: the massive industrial firm and the bureaucratically complex welfare state. But these advantages have been bought at the cost of a great loss of independence. Social theory has accommodated itself to this change in social fact. Once the institutions that bring men together were thought of as consciously planned means to the fixed ends of human nature. Since Hegel and Marx and the rise of sociology as a science, human nature has come to be seen as determined by the institutions in which men live. What were tools have become limbs, the environment has turned into the skin.

At the same time there has come about a recognition of the precarious nature of human rationality. Christianity, drawing on Greek philosophy, saw man as a divided being: an eternal reason, joined for its career on earth to a body and the bundle of more or less animal desires of which that body was the source. On that view the mature, fully realised human being was one in whom reason was the master of desire, who had, through that mastery, attained real freedom of choice. Psychologists, most notably Freud, and sociologists, most notably Marx, have combined to destroy that conception of man. They have substantiated with a great mass of theory the provocative suggestion of Hume in the eighteenth century that reason can only be the slave of the passions, that it is not an autonomous director of men's conduct but only a device making possible the more complex fulfilment of desire. On that view man is one kind of natural object among others. The laws of his behaviour can be discovered, just as those of other natural objects can, and the ultimate force behind his behaviour is instinctive desire, whether for sexual satisfaction or economic goods.

Men in the west were living in towns and working in factories or offices long before the twentieth century. The greatest of British novelists is an essentially urban writer, although Dickens's characters are clerks rather than machine-minders. Even so man's natural place for Dickens is still rural. The town-dwellers all have friends and relations in the country to visit and the proper setting for a happy ending in Dickens is, as George Orwell observes, 'a quaint old house with plenty of ivy on it'. Nicholas Nickleby retires to Devonshire, Esther Summerson settles contentedly at Bleak House, 'somewhere near St Alban's'. Dulwich must have been a rural spot when Mr Pickwick moved there.

The last major English novelist in whose work the traditional agricultural setting plays an essential part is Thomas Hardy. Many of his heroes work on the land: Gabriel Oak as a shepherd, Giles Winterborne as a forester, Jude Fawley as a smallholder and labourer. The effects of the agricultural depression of the late nineteenth century make themselves evident in his books, the process which has led to the more or less industrial farm of the present day in which the hand-worker has given way to the agronomist and the motor engineer. Many novelists have continued to use rural settings, but only either defiantly, like the brothers T.F. and J.C. Powys, against the current of the age, or else decoratively, like a host of popular entertainers. In D.H. Lawrence there are some incomparably fine representations of the rural scene but his remarkable human creations live their intense lives against a rural background rather than really within a rural setting.

Baudelaire is the most cityfied of great poets.

Le coeur content, je suis monté sur la montagne
D'ou l'on peut contempler la ville en son ampleur ...

Je voulais m'enivrer de l'enorme catin
Dont le charme infernal me rajeunit sans cesse ...

Je t'aime, o capitale infame! Courtisanes
Et bandits, tels souvent vous offrez des plaisirs
Que ne comprennent pas les vulgaires profanes.

(With a happy heart I climbed the hill from where the city can be seen in its
fullness ... I wanted to intoxicate myself with the vast whore whose infernal charm
unceasingly makes me young again ... I love you, O infamous capital! Harlots and
gangsters, you often hold out pleasures that the profane masses cannot
understand.)

There is, indeed, a deliberate perversity about his glorification of the city, his
emphasis on its naturally least appealing features. It is a sophisticated
correlate of the robust judgments of Samuel Johnson: 'he who is tired of
London is tired of life' and 'the country is a kind of healthy grave'.
Baudelaire may be seen as making a virtue of a new necessity of the human
condition.

Organised, industrial, urban life inspires a feeling of powerless anonymity.
Men's activities are controlled by forces that they can hardly identify, much
less influence; they are situated in an environment of other human beings
whom they do not know. The most powerfully memorable presentation in
imaginative literature of this state of dereliction is to be found in the novels of
Franz Kafka, who died in 1924. In *The Castle* K. arrives in the village to which
he has been summoned in his capacity as land surveyor and endeavours
hopelessly and against increasingly complicated obstruction to get in touch
with the authorities at the castle who have sent for him. In *The Trial* the
initiative comes from the other side. 'Someone must have been telling lies
about Joseph K., for without having done anything wrong he was arrested
one fine morning,' is the first sentence of the book. He is interrogated, tried,
sentenced and finally executed but never manages to find out who is accusing
him or what he is accused of.

The Trial is astonishingly prophetic of the style of totalitarian government
that was to prevail over most of Europe from Hitler's seizure of power in 1933
until his defeat and death in 1945 and which has continued in Eastern
Europe from the purges that followed the murder of Kirov in 1934 until the
present day. The great novels of Alexander Solzhenitsyn, *The First Circle* and
Cancer Ward, are the finest representations of the bureaucratically
mechanised barbarism, dedicated to the literal and spiritual extinction of the
human individual, that was perfected by Stalin and has been carried on, in a
slightly less hyperbolical way, by his successors.

For many years Arthur Koestler's *Darkness at Noon* was the most
authoritative account in imaginative writing of the amazing process by which
Stalin liquidated anyone in the ruling apparatus of Russia who might
conceivably be any sort of obstacle to his absolute power. Rubashov, the old
Bolshevik, is a man whose character was formed before the Revolution. He
retains the original humanitarian ideals which led him to join the communist
party and is brought to acquiesce in his rigged condemnation by the

argument that his public destruction will serve the cause for which he has lived. The propounder of this argument is the abominable Gletkin, a being of human form from whom all vestiges of humanity have been removed, an instrument of torture in a uniform. He is the ideal citizen of the communist state, completely submerged in his oppressive function.

The conspiratorial background from which both Rubashov and Gletkin emerged had been the subject of many novels before 1917: Conrad's *Under Western Eyes* and *The Secret Agent*, Henry James's *Princess Casamassima* and Dostoevsky's *The Possessed*. But the most striking anticipation of Gletkin is the Grand Inquisitor of Dostoevsky's *Brothers Karamazov*. Christ appears to him at a grand *auto da fé* in Seville and the Inquisitor orders his arrest as a heretic. During the night that follows the Inquisitor visits the imprisoned Christ in his cell and launches into a brilliant oration on the theme that men cannot be left to live in freedom, bound only by love, but must be ruled absolutely by those who will give them bread to eat and some satisfying mystery to worship. Dostoevsky puts this story into the mouth of a character he regards as evil, but he allows the Inquisitor to make so powerfully cogent a case that it must be suspected that he was at least half convinced of its validity. It certainly gives the most distinguished possible justification for the practices of totalitarian governments.

In the democratic and capitalistic West the pressures on the individual are less direct and brutal but they still work effectively to create the kind of homogenous humanity that is most convenient for large organisations. Commercial advertisement, in a bewildering variety of forms, has with much apparent success taken on the task of determining men's styles of life, as a substitute for ideals: creating assumptions about how and where one should live, how one should spend one's time and money.

Humorous poets have expressed their sense of the intrusiveness of hoardings and headlines. Thus E.E. Cummings:

> my country, 'tis of
> you, land of the Cluett
> Shirt Boston Garter and Spearmint
> Girl With The Wrigley Eyes (of you
> land of the Arrow Ide
> and Earl &
> Wilson
> Collars) of you i
> sing:

And William Plomer:

> Alleged Last Trump Blown Yesterday;
> Traffic Drowns Call To Quick And Dead;
> Cup Tie Crowd Sees Heavens Ope;
> 'Not End Of World', Says Well-Known Red.

Leopold Bloom, the hero of James Joyce's *Ulysses*, that immensely elaborated reconstruction of a day in Dublin in 1906, is an early and most memorable example of the representation of badgered, trivial, urban man in modern literature. Many earlier fictional heroes were passive victims of circumstances: Tom Jones and Candide, for example, even David Copperfield. But where they were innocents who ultimately escaped contamination by the world for all its rough dealings with them, Bloom and his successors are seen as twisted into an irremediable human imperfection. The political events of the age have fostered the creation of some heroes of classical dimensions, in the novels of Malraux, or, less convincingly, Hemingway. But these are exceptional. Winston Smith of George Orwell's *1984*, preserved from complete mechanisation by love and a glass paperweight, is a more representative symbol of the human condition.

At the same time as complex organisations have been diminishing human autonomy and individuality while fulfilling men's more material desires, ordinary people in the west have achieved a kind of freedom from the broadly moral pressures of the society around them once available only to aristocrats and outcasts. The personally repressive customs and institutions of Victorian society have been dismantled at an ever-increasing rate. Progressive writers like Ibsen and Shaw challenged the assumptions that men were superior to women, the old to the young, the rich to the poor, the respectable to the unrespectable. Along with moral censoriousness with its attendant hypocrisies, the rigidities of class division have been much reduced. Even in the most humane and liberal-minded of nineteenth-century novelists, such as Dickens and Hardy, working-class characters are either comical (like Sam Weller) or exotic (like Fagin). The requirements of the mass market, to put it at its lowest, have brought into a being a population of remarkably homogeneous tastes and pursuits: baths and cars and fitted clothes and jet travel to foreign countries are now within the reach of nearly all. With the approach to classlessness, fiction in England, at any rate, is being deprived of one of its staple themes.

Thus if organisations, pursuing the logic of technical advance, diminish men's freedom and replace genuine action by passive response, many of the oppressive divisions between particular kinds or groups of people have been disappearing. In particular, sexual behaviour, and the discussion of it, have been opened up in a striking way. On one level this has been made possible by the general availability to women of means of preventing unwanted conception. On another the doctrines of Freud, popularly interpreted as tracing all mental ill-health to sexual frustration, have helped to create the appropriate climate of thought and feeling.

The novels of D.H. Lawrence express a more edifying version of that widespread, if none too accurate, interpretation of Freud's ideas with their message about the healing character of primal instinct and of the destructiveness of rational foresight, cautious calculation, the stifling armour of bourgeois prudence. Lady Chatterley's husband and her lover represent the paths of life between which he invites his readers to choose. The greater accessibility of sexual fulfilment has undermined the traditional romantic ideal of literature. Lionel Trilling, discussing Nabokov's *Lolita*, suggests that only by making Humbert Humbert fall in love with a child could Nabokov invest his pursuit with the requisite difficulty; in a love story the object of love has to be somehow forbidden. Thus is an era of amicable divorces adultery loses its old literary magnetism.

If Freud may be seen as having dethroned the heavy Victorian father from his imperial position in society, he has also, less gratifyingly, dethroned reason from its commanding position in the mind. In the world of Trollope people are seen as acting, more or less sensibly, in pursuit of consciously formulated ends. In the world of Joyce and Virginia Woolf, and even more in that of their present-day successors, that type of order no longer prevails. It is not so much that the recognised purposes of their characters are clearly different from those that actually govern their conduct. That has always been the normal structure of comic writing. It is, rather, that the idea of character, as a stable system of individual purposes, has tended to dissolve. The stream-of-consciousness technique was appropriate to a conception of the human mind, which does not pick out the rational pursuit of conscious ends as essential and discard everything else as an unimportant accompaniment to it, but treats the life of the mind, in all its variety, as a world in itself, with all its constituents having an equal right to notice. Carried to its limits this idea yields Joyce's *Finnegans Wake*, which is made up of the vast, chaotic dream of a single individual who is so inclusive as to stand for anyone. He has a name, Humphrey Chimpden Earwicker. But its initials, as Joyce points out, also stand for Here Comes Everybody.

This century, then, is an age of organised masses and disappearing individuality. The unique, autonomous human person, whose great literary record is the European novel, is ceasing to exist, or is, at any rate, under heavy pressure. There are some, most conspicuously Marshall McLuhan, who welcome this. In *The Gutenberg Galaxy* McLuhan joyfully predicts man's reversion to the anonymity of tribal life. Perhaps it is McLuhan's new tribesmen who confront their still recalcitrantly individualistic elders on the other side of the generation gap.

4

The Lives of Thinkers

'The autobiography of a man whose business is thinking should be the story of his thought.' The opening sentence of the preface of R.G. Collingwood's *Autobiography* lays down what seems to be a reasonable principle. The lives of those who are interesting or important because of what they thought should be concerned mainly, or at least centrally, with the thinking of their subjects. Their love affairs, their travels, their impingements on the public life of their times are unlikely to stand in any but the most accidental relations to the thinking for which the subjects are valued. Furthermore, under the division of labour which has most serious and original thinking done by academic or otherwise rather sequestered people, everything about thinkers but their thinking is likely to be tame and ordinary.

These generalities instantly cry out for qualification. To start with, the division of labour that confines thinkers to the study, laboratory and lecture-room is both a very recent phenomenon and is even now very far from complete. Anselm was not engaged in whole-time work on the ontological proof; he was also archbishop of Canterbury and struggled against Henry I to protect the rights of the church. Hume was a diplomat; Locke was ideologist-in-residence to Shaftesbury; Lord Herbert of Cherbury a swaggering gallant; Newman, and still more John Stuart Mill, the leaders of influential public movements. Even more academic figures than these had a good deal of notable extra-intellectual life. Richard Bentley spent as much of his brilliant powers on enraging and exploiting the fellows of Trinity (the main topic of Monk's engrossing biography) as he did on the scholarly consideration of classical texts. Abelard is a hero of amorous romance as well as the greatest philosopher of his age and his autobiography is a history of his calamities in the former role rather than of his intellectual work. Henry Sidgwick was a pioneer of psychical research and of the admission of women to higher education as well as the most earnest and thorough of utilitarians. Most of those mentioned in this paragraph are the subject of a biography or autobiography that is still widely read. But of these books only Newman's *Apologia* and Mill's *Autobiography* have their centre in the intellectual activity of their subjects.

Even in this century the thinkers who have written most memorably about their own lives or whose lives have been most memorably written about have not much resembled the almost purely academic Kant. Everyone knows a few facts about Kant: that he never left the city of Königsberg, that the citizens of that city used to set their watches by his emergence from his front door for his daily walk. But those facts serve only to underline the impression of Kant as an individual wholly submerged in his function as a thinker.

The result of the vacuity and monotony of his extra-intellectual life is that there is nothing of much interest in the way of Kant biography. In English the only notable item is De Quincey's essay, 'The Last Days of Immanuel Kant' (*Collected Works*, vol. iii, pp. 99-166) which takes the form of, and largely is, a translation of the sublimely trivial recollections of Kant's former pupil, Wasianski, concerned with the minutiae of Kant's domestic regime during his last years. De Quincey introduces the essay with the remark: 'A great man, though in an unpopular path, must always be an object of liberal curiosity.' But he sees that the curiosity is not liberal in the most elevated sense. 'Biographical gossip of this sort, and ungentlemanly scrutiny into a man's private life, though not what a man of honour would allow himself to write, may be read without blame.' It is not quite clear where the translator stands in this refined moral distinction.

Nothing whatever is said about Kant's thought beyond a mention of the hours of the day that were devoted to it and the strategies its creator employed to recover from the effort of it. The alleged gaiety of his dinners sits a little uneasily beside the information that Kant talked 'all the way to the eating-room about the state of the weather, a subject which he usually pursued during the earlier part of the dinner'. There is some mild knockabout material concerning Kant's drunken servant Lampe and the news that Kant 'never perspired, night or day'.

Kant is great enough to survive that kind of treatment. No doubt, from a conventional point of view there is nothing much more to be said about his outward life, although Wasianski's point of view is rather exclusively Crawfie-eyed. But there is an alternative, an account of the development of the system of ideas that it was Kant's particular distinction to produce: the influences, human and literary, that moulded it; the chief difficulties encountered in its elaboration; its author's conception of its deficiencies or incompletenesses. But, even where such a purely intellectual life-story is all that there is occasion for, it is very seldom to be found.

To return to the thinkers of the present century, there are some distinguished autobiographies (Russell's, Santayana's *Persons and Places*, and Collingwood's) and some impressive biographies (that of Freud by Ernest Jones, that of Namier by his wife and that of Wittgenstein by Norman Malcolm and G.H. von Wright). More usual is the pleasant, chatty, comparatively self-effacing memoir such as the unfinished autobiographies of Gilbert Murray and H.A.L. Fisher and the brief autobiography of G.M. Trevelyan.

Now the autobiographies of Russell and Santayana are only very marginally concerned with their thought. Both are about family, interesting friends and acquaintances, travel and, in Russell's case, politics, educational experiment and the ups and downs of his career as an amorist. But Russell did go on to supply the missing element in his *My Philosophical Development*, a much less jerky and cobbled-together affair than his autobiography proper. The title of Russell's book recalls that of the initial chapter, 'My Mental

Development', that he contributed to the volume in the Library of Living Philosophers that was devoted to him. These massive, and, for the most part, useful and successful, volumes have all been edited, since the inception of the series in 1939 with a volume on Dewey, by Professor Paul A. Schilpp. The two volumes (a new departure) of 1,323 pages in all, devoted to the philosophy of Sir Karl Popper that have recently been published brought the number of the series to fourteen and five more are currently in preparation.

A feature of nearly all these books (only here and there excluded by old age or death) is the autobiography of the subject with which each begins and the replies to critics with which (alongside a full bibliography) they close. In the volume devoted to him Santayana made up the deficiencies of his autobiography proper with a long essay called 'Apologia pro Mente Sua', appearing at the end of the book in the place usually reserved for detailed replies to criticisms in the body of the volume. The 82 pages of intellectual autobiography in the volume on Rudolf Carnap (a particularly good one) provide much the best account of Carnap's thought that there is.

Philosophers have been well-served by this series, while in other fields the traditional *Festschrift* prevails with its principle of the non-playing captain. Without that kind of institutionalisation of the intellectual autobiography there is thus a comparative shortage of lives of thinkers since that is really the only sort of autobiography that a professionalised, academic thinker is qualified to write. As for studies of thinkers written by others, they are either not really biographies at all, but at most, chronologically arranged expositions of the thinker's writings, perhaps with a brief biographical note added (Ronald Jager's substantial recent book on Russell and P.M.S. Hacker's *Insight and Illusion* on Wittgenstein are good examples) or they are conventional biographies of the outward-event-recording kind (such as Alan Wood's book on Russell, for example, and a great host of books on earlier thinkers, such as Maurice Cranston's *Locke* and E.C. Mossner's *Hume*).

It has, indeed, always been true that almost the only truly biographical, and not merely chronologically expository, accounts of the development of the minds of thinkers have been written by the thinkers themselves. Roper's life of Thomas More, Izaak Walton's lives of Hooker and Sanderson (a quite productive philosopher who died, according to James I, of not being made a bishop), Dean Burgon's richly comical account of Mansel in his *Lives of Great and Good Men* are almost exclusively concerned with the outward life of their subjects.

Perhaps that is inevitable. A treatise, a body of written theory, it like a set of accounts, so tidied-up that it is impossible to extricate the detailed movements of the mind from which it eventually emerged. The actual process of thought, then, is known only to the thinker himself, so far as his memory is reliable. Someone else writing about him must, unless he was in close and regular intellectual communication during the subject's career (as was the case, to some extent, with Broad and McTaggart or Maitland and Leslie Stephen), rely on his subject's notes, drafts and records. But even then much will be unavailable to him except in the most tenuous way: particular moments of enlightenment, the detailed procedure of working at a problem, the actual experienced effects of influential people and books.

The most propitious kind of intellectual biography is, then, the intellectual autobiography. That genre has to be distinguished, as we have seen, from the autobiography of a thinker. The deficiencies, as accounts of the intellectual development of their authors, of the autobiographies proper of Russell and Santayana have many earlier parallels. One of the more extreme examples is the autobiography of Lord Herbert of Cherbury. Herbert, in his *De Veritate*, laid the foundations of deism, of the theory that there are rationally self-evident first principles of natural religion, in 1624, uninfluenced by the only English philosophical works of importance available to him, Bacon's *Advancement of Learning* and *Novum Organum*, and before Descartes or Hobbes had published anything. His autobiography, however, is mainly concerned with self-inflating accounts of his military prowess and courage, the vindication of his honour as a duellist and his activities as a philandering gallant. The *De Veritate* itself refers explicitly to only two previous philosophers, Aristotle and Cicero, but a mass of influences is discernible, in particular that of a large variety of more or less wildly speculative writers of the preceding century. But his reading and studies are not matters Herbert finds it gratifying to boast about.

On the whole the most perfect model for an intellectual autobiography is John Stuart Mill's. It is, of course, far more than a bare record of intellectual work. Childhood and family life are there, but largely as the scene of the James Mill's extraordinary educational experiment with his son. The emotions recalled are not merely cognitive. Yet the depressive breakdown of Mill's early manhood, from which the poetry of Wordsworth did so much to restore him, is of intellectual relevance, connected as it is with his deviations from the orthodox utilitarian faith he had inherited, his dilution or mitigation of Bentham with Coleridge.

Collingwood's autobiography is close enough in form to Mill's to suggest that it was its conscious model, for all Collingwood's contempt for Mill's kind of philosophy. To the extent that Collingwood's parents appear it is as teachers not as providers of holidays and uncomfortable suits. When he hurts his leg at football it is mentioned because it freed him from the time-wasting demands of compulsory games for studies of medieval Italian history and early French poets, 'unhampered by masters'. (Kant's *Grundlegung* he had already abstracted from his father's bookshelves at the age of eight, he maintains.) There is nothing about his marriages (apart from a bare mention of the first) but the role of the second in his sudden, late acquisition of enthusiasm for Marx, which appears nowhere else in his work, by being left out, leaves the conversion described in the final chapter, on theory and practice, inadequately explained.

If that lack of candour can be put down to a reasonable discretion (dons did not get divorced much in the 1930s), the absence of any reference to Croce must be attributed to vanity. Croce's influence is irresistibly evident in Collingwood's *Speculum Mentis* and in the general bias of Collingwood's interests towards history and art. It was natural enough for any philosopher of broadly idealist sympathies in the inter-war years to draw sustenance from

Croce's *Filosofia dello Spirito* (1902-17), the most imposing recent attempt to salvage Hegelian idealism by a judicious unloading of ballast (in accordance with the policy implied by the title of his book *What is Living and What is Dead in the Philosophy of Hegel.*) Collingwood's complete silence about the size of his debt to Croce looks very like a claim to undeserved originality, though there may have been an element of prudence in concealing an affinity with a figure who was so firmly and unfavourably 'placed' in general British philosophical opinion as Croce.

There are other, more venial manifestations of exaggerated self-esteem in the book. In one the botanical ignorance of a Rugby master is exposed before the class with an apt quotation from Browning. In others grandiose programmes of intensive reading, which were quite probably carried out as described, are mentioned with self-glorifying off-handness. In general, the effect of vanity is that what was in fact largely derived from others is claimed as original and that what was the outcome of an exhausting and personally costly investment of time and energy is represented as easy and effortless.

If vanity may diminish the value and adequacy of intellectual biographies that actually get written, modesty may prevent them from being written in the first place. A thinker who has already confronted the reading public with the objective expression of his thoughts in considerable bulk may well feel that it would be trying that public's patience altogether too far to supply and expect them to read and welcome the subjective background of his primary product.

There are, indeed, two kinds of theoretical justification for this form of self-effacement by thinkers. The first is that there is a difference between the causation of an idea or theory and its justification, between the private sequence of reflections, full of false starts up blind alleys, that preceded it in its proponent's stream of consciousness and the grounds that can be put forward to establish it as true or probable. I mentioned earlier the likeness between a published theory and a set of accounts. Both leave out a great deal, in both cases for the sake of relevance. An argument for a conclusion that proved invalid and had to be replaced is of no more concern to those to whom that conclusion is addressed than the negotiations of a business that did not terminate in a binding contract.

But although that is true as far as it goes the work of thinkers is not of interest exclusively to those who are concerned with those thinkers' findings. Some readers will typically be thinkers, indeed creative thinkers of the same kind as the theorist they are studying, themselves. For them the subjective process of arriving at the theory and finding substantiation for it may be of as much importance as the theory itself. This need is most immediately served by such works as the third part of Blanshard's *Nature of Thought*, Polya's *How to Solve It*, Hadamard's *Psychology of Invention* and other such heuristic works. But to the extent that books of this kind go beyond the direct cognitive experience of their authors, the pieces of thinking that they have done themselves, they must depend for their evidence on items of intellectual autobiography by others.

A second, and more fundamental, reason for thinking that intellectual autobiography is unnecessary, and even undesirable because misleading, derives from the Aristotelian notion that reason, the organ of thought, is universal and only feeling is particular and bound up essentially with the mental life of a particular person.

Curiously enough, Collingwood himself has affirmed that point as forcibly as anyone. Defining history as rethinking the thoughts of past agents, he argued that history can only be history of thought since only thoughts, which are objective, impersonal things, can be truly shared by more than one mind. A similar position is approached from a different direction by Popper who maintains that the kind of knowledge that is important and worthy of theoretical discussion is objective knowledge, as contained in books and formulated theories, not the fleeting and amorphous mental processes of individual thinkers.

A fact that has some bearing on that is the frequency with which a given discovery is made independently by more than one person (Leibniz's and Newton's roughly simultaneous discovery of calculus being only the most famous example of it). It is as if the new thought was not significantly the product of the mental processes of a particular individual thinker but rather that of the general intellectual situation of the age. There is, at any time and in any subject, a certain body of established knowledge, an array of unsolved problems recognised as posed by it and an accumulation of intellectual resources with which to solve them. From this point of view it is pretty much a contingent and accidental matter that one thinker rather than another comes up with a new theory. And that suggests that the particular processes by which the thinker on whom chance lit arrived at it has in the end only the interest of gossip.

To that the same answer can be returned as to the previous argument. Whoever makes the discovery, some particular person has to do so. Even if it is likely that someone else would have made it if he had not, it does not follow that the fact that he made it is purely a matter of chance that could not be influenced by any study he had made of the way in which new thoughts have in fact been arrived at. As well as the 'liberal curiosity' of which De Quincey wrote there is still room for practical concern with the accounts of the development of their own thought which those thinkers alone, it would seem, can effectively provide.

5

Which Philosophy is Modernistic?

The title of this chapter clearly embodies an assumption. It is one that many would be disposed to reject. What is assumed is that the different aspects of culture in any age show a sufficient affinity of fundamental attitude or style for it to be fruitful, or at least illuminating, to classify them together as all manifestations of a common underlying theme or point of view.

Usually, no doubt, this idea of a systematic interconnection between the aspects of culture is the final stage of a process that begins with the piecemeal detection of affinities, in particular with the transfer of a term used to pick out the special character of one branch of an age's culture to another branch. Thus the term 'romantic' starts its career in application to literature but is soon carried over to the music and painting of the early nineteenth century. 'Baroque' begins in architecture, 'Augustan' in poetry. By the time 'decadent' and 'surrealist' come into currency the idea of cultural correlation is so well-established and familiar that it is no longer possible to assign any clear priority of application.

The examples I have mentioned so far are to a large extent confined in their application to the domain of imagination and the creative arts. There seems nothing figurative or metaphorical about describing a piece of music as romantic or a painting as classical. But under the influence of German students and critics of culture more extensive applications have become familiar, even if it still gives a slight poetic shock to the English reader to find Spengler talking of the baroque state. Beyond the domain of the arts the terms of cultural classification have come to be applied to the politics, the religion, the philosophy, the morals and customs, the conception of human nature of epochs in the history of culture.

In his lecture *In Search of Cultural History* Gombrich has associated the idea of cultural correlation above all with Hegel. For Hegel, however, the bare fact, if it is a fact, of correlation is only intelligible as the consequence of a theory. His theory is that the various aspects of the culture of an age are all manifestations of the condition of Spirit or mind in general in that age, expressing itself in different media or forms. More precisely, they are manifestations of the spirit of an age in its most historically developed and progressive form. Since in each historical epoch there is one particular nation whose moment has come and which is the dominant nation of the time, the spirit of an age is the spirit of that people which is the most progressive in that age. The *Zeitgeist*, at any given time, is a particular *Volksgeist*. It further follows that the best route to an understanding of interconnectedness of cultural forms is through philosophy, or its history, which for him is much the same thing, since the philosophy of an age contains within it, even if in a transmuted way, all the philosophy that has gone before. Philosophy is the highest expression of Spirit and to study philosophy is to study Spirit in itself and not indirectly through its expressions and effects.

Gombrich is surely right in thinking that Hegel more than anyone is responsible for the wide diffusion of the assumption underlying the title of this paper. But, as he goes on to point out, aspects of culture other than philosophy can be allotted the central, determining place in the scheme, as with Marx, who substitutes the relations of production for philosophy. Other historians of culture have been content to affirm no more than the correlation itself and to abstain from the theory of causal primacy involved in picking out one aspect of culture as basic or, in a different image, central. But the important place of Hegel in disseminating the theory of cultural correlation makes specially appropriate an inquiry into the correlatedness of that form of culture which he believed to determine all other correlations.

What gives some force to the assumption that there is some kind of philosophy that is connected to the kinds of literature, art and music which we correlate as modernistic in the same sort of way as they are connected to each other is the fact that such a connection does seem to be reasonably discernible, without an undue amount of squeezing and forcing, as far as philosophy up to the middle of the nineteenth century is concerned. The philosophers of Christendom can be characterised with some point and without evident absurdity in terms of the words used to characterise the prevailing forms of creative art in their ages.

Anselm, to start with, can be contrasted as Romanesque by comparison with the Gothic of Thomas Aquinas. Anselm's thought and writing are stark, simple and elemental, where Aquinas's system is elaborate, detailed, intricately developed and specified. The Italian Platonists Ficino and Pico della Mirandola have more than a chronological connection with such painters of the high Renaissance as Botticelli and Leonardo. They share vitality, an emphasis on the concretely human, a concern with symbols.

A less obvious, but still, I think, substantial affinity obtains between the great rationalist system-builders of seventeenth-century Europe, Descartes, Spinoza and Leibniz, and baroque art and architecture. At the level of style there is a close correspondence between the great intellectual structures of the rationalist philosophers and baroque buildings. The philosophical systems sought to replace the complex, haphazard, structurally faulty edifice of traditional Christian theology with altogether sounder constructions, set up on new and firmer foundations. Admirable to contemplate, they were, in their cold remoteness, unwelcoming to inhabit. If there is something of Palladio's Vitruvianism in Descartes, there is plenty of fantasy and grotesque ornament in Spinoza (for example, the infinity of God's attributes) and Leibniz.

The philosophical version of the Augustan classicism of the eighteenth century is plainly the thought of Locke and the Encyclopaedists. Rousseau is generally acknowledged as a literary inaugurator of romanticism as well as of its philosophical correlate the great subjectivist metaphysical systems of the early nineteenth century, in particular those of Fichte and Hegel. Kant, one could say, occupies the same sort of ambiguous position as Goethe, at once a bridge between classic and romantic and, by reason of special pre-eminence, transcending any parochialism of involvement with a particular age, in the manner of Shakespeare and Plato.

It is at this point that the attempt to correlate the philosophers of an age, or, at any rate, those leading figures who give an age its character, with the inflection in the creative arts that is contemporary with them, begins to waver. After Hegel, many would say, philosophy begins really to become what it has so often been proclaimed to be, for example by both Kant and Hegel – a true science.

That influential figure in British modernism, T.E. Hulme, drew a sharp distinction between two ingredients of what is commonly called philosophy.

> Philosophy is not a pure but a *mixed* subject. It results from a confusion between two subjects which stand in no essential or necessary relation to each other, though they may be combined together for a certain practical end. One of these subjects is a science, the other not. The scientific element in philosophy is a difficult investigation into the relations between certain very abstract categories ... Mixed up with this is the function which philosophy has assumed of acting as a pale *substitute* for religion. It is concerned here with matters like the nature and destiny of man, his place in the universe, etc., all matters which would, as treated, fit very well into a personal Weltanschauung. (*Speculations*, pp. 14-15.)

Hulme saw his distinction between technical philosophy and Weltanschauung as something already acknowledged by two leading philosophers of his time, Bertrand Russell and Edmund Husserl. These were creditably prophetic choices, considering that Hulme must have made them some time around 1914. For it is from Russell and Husserl, above all, that the two great streams of technical, objectively neutral, more or less scientific philosophy of the twentieth century have flowed, from Russell that of analytic and linguistic philosophy, from Husserl the 'eidetic science' of phenomenology. (The fact that Heidegger and Sartre have remixed Hulme's two elements, technical phenomology and the dramatic existentialist Weltanschauung, should not obscure the fact that phenomenology can be and has been practised without any attachment to a Weltanschauung.)

Philosophers in the analytic tradition have adhered rather faithfully to the programme of an austerely technical philosophy. For doing so they have been strenuously criticised in various ways. A more or less conservative objection has been that they have abandoned the traditional concern of philosophy with large issues of profound human interest for the minute investigation of a mass of disorganised and abstract trivialities. A somewhat populistic variant of this protest is that by offering analytic stones in response to requests for metaphysical bread they have created an intellectual vacuum or waste-land all too easily filled by irrationalism. The currently favoured charge is that they are, in fact, apologists for the status quo, more specifically for the technological and bureaucratic style of repressive dominance that is characteristic of advanced capitalism.

There is no need to assemble many examples of professions of scientific neutrality by analytic philosophers. Of the philosophy he practised, Russell wrote:

> It is thus able, in regard to certain problems, to achieve definite answers, which have the quality of science rather than of philosophy. It has the advantage, as compared with the philosophies of the system-builders, of being able to tackle its problems one at a time, instead of having to invent at one stroke a block theory of the whole universe. Its methods, in this respect, resemble those of science ... There remains, however, a vast field, traditionally included in philosophy, where scientific methods are inadequate ... Whatever can be known, can be known by means of science; but things which are legitimately matters of feeling lie outside its province. (*History of Western Philosophy*, p.834)

For Ryle the task of philosophy is 'the detection of the sources in linguistic idioms of recurrent misconstructions and absurd theories' (*Collected papers*, vol. 2, p.61). For Carnap philosophy is, a little more constructively, the logic of science, a view reiterated in a slightly different form by Quine, who sees it as the science of science, as 'lore about lore'.

Two tendencies are represented in these quotations. One, exemplified by Ryle's remark and characteristic of both phases of Wittgenstein's work, is negative. It takes the function of proper, enlightened philosophy to be that of dispelling the pretensions to truth or significance of various forms of utterance, in particular of a great deal of what has previously passed for philosophy. The other, more positive, tendency sees philosophy as an adjunct to science or, in one important variant, to the proto-science of common sense. Its function is to clarify the terms and to extricate and criticise the reasonings of scientific and common-sense discourse. It should not be concerned to make, but at most to deflate, large affirmations about the nature of man and his place in the universe.

Husserl had a somewhat more dignified conception of the proper place of philosophy in the system of knowledge as a whole. He saw it as a kind of *a priori* science of mental activity, presupposed by and thus prior to all other kinds of thought and inquiry, logic included. For these other forms of thought were among the mental activities which it was the business of philosophy as phenomenology to examine.

Analysts and phenomenologists were at one in taking philosophy to be objective, impersonal and neutral in the manner of mathematics and physics, the most developed of sciences proper. Now it has been held that even these last austere disciplines reveal in any age the marks of the *Zeitgeist* upon them. But they are the least plausible of candidates for inclusion in hypotheses of cultural correlation. The broad unity of methods endorsed by their practitioners, together with the cumulative character of their findings, itself a consequence of that agreement about method, detaches them from any serious dependence on the characteristic attitudes of any particular age. If the exact sciences, then, are not discernibly time-bound and if philosophy is practised as an adjunct to science and, even more, in a resolutely objective scientific spirit it follows that it will no longer be correlated with the historically variable aspects of culture in the way that it was when it was more inclusive in scope.

Now even if both these assumptions about the timelessness of exact science and the possibility of an exactly scientific philosophy are true it remains the case that by no means all modern philosophy is, or even aspires to be, exactly scientific. In fact, both assumptions are thoroughly questionable. Kuhn's theory of scientific history as the scene of revolutionary replacements of one paradigm of explanation and theorising by another puts the first in question. If it is false, the second assumption cannot preserve philosophy, however scientific, from infection by the general culture of its age. And, despite all the protestations of scientific philosophers about the independence of their technical philosophy from any moral, political or religious attitudes they may happen to adopt in another capacity, as it were, it is far from evident that the independence is anything like as great as they suppose. But, before examining these claims on behalf of scientific philosophy on their merits, it will be reasonable to consider whether there is any kind of philosophy for which no such claims are made yet which could serve as the cultural correlate of modernism.

The best point to start from is the fact that most attempts to give some general characterisation of modernism have a strongly philosophical scent to them, in the traditional sense of the word 'philosophical' at any rate. Perhaps the most persistently recurring term in attempts to describe the general mood of modernism is alienation. At its widest this is a kind of cosmic alienation, a sense of homelessness in a world from which God has departed, as revealed in emphasis on the terrible or degraded aspects of the world and human life. Marginal men and anti-heroes replace saints and heroes in fiction and drama. Human misfortune is seen as the desperate outcome of chance, not as an occasion for tragic affirmation. The glorification of nature gives way to the distortedly agonised human faces of Picasso, the German expressionists and Francis Bacon.

Secondly, there is the theme of social alienation, most conspicuous in the modern artist's sense of himself as standing in an adversary relationship to his society, its institutions and its public values. This is not just the traditional irony of the literary moralist, satirically drawing attention to the gap between profession and actual performance. It is, rather, a rejection of the professions themselves. Consider the difference between Baudelaire's attitude to his social world with that of Molière. Another version of this is alienation from history, what Northrop Frye, in his *The Modern Century*, calls 'alienation of progress'. Fear of historical change, the denial of the true progressiveness of progress, was a feature of the romantic rejection of the ideals of the Enlightenment. It preceded, but was much intensified by, the more monstrous and repulsive consequences of the French Revolution. In abandoning their early revolutionary optimism Wordsworth and Coleridge also returned to orthodox Christian belief and to a reverence for nature that was made more forceful by the destructiveness to nature of the chief economic realisation of the Enlightenment: the industrial revolution. The further dehumanising and denaturing course of mass politics and urban industrialism had evoked an altogether more desperate, less hopefully protective response.

Finally, there is what might be called an alienation from the self, a loss of faith in the unity and consciously rational self-management of the human personality. Freud's account of human nature crystallised into a widespread suspicion that men are driven in action by forces which, since they are unknown, cannot be controlled. The integral conception of human personality bound up with the notion of character, conceived as embodying the resources for its rational self-development, gives way to the idea of the contingent person who does not know or understand himself. Stavrogin, Smerdyakov and Raskolnikov are modernist men, as are, less dramatically, Leopold Bloom, the amorphous, omnicontinent Earwicker, and Sweeney and the other flat, heteronomous personages of Eliot's early poems.

In so far as this kind of alienation, cosmic, social and human, is the characteristic theme of modernist art and literature it is plain that the first modernist philosophers are the great, irrationalistic anti-Hegelians of the nineteenth century, above all Schopenhauer, Kierkegaard and Nietzsche. In general, European philosophy in the nineteenth century consists of a series of massive rejections of Hegel. (That is not true of British philosophy, which did not become aware of Hegel in any effective way until the last third of the century. Spencer, Hamilton and Mansel were the dominant British philosophers of the decade in which Schopenhauer and Kierkegaard died, namely the 1850s, in much the same way as *Madame Bovary* and *Les Fleurs du Mal* are approximately contemporaries with *Idylls of the King*.)

In relation to his successors Hegel occupies a position much like that of Victor Hugo in relation to his. His all-inclusive system was the last, overblown culmination of a tradition that was running out. It was a high romantic take-over of both the language and many of the governing beliefs of the enlightenment. Hegel presented himself as the prophet of Reason, but in a transmuted, metaphysical form utterly different from the analytic type of thinking from which the Age of Reason took its name. He was a progressive, historical optimist, but his theory of progress did not see progress as the inevitable result of the accumulation and application of scientific knowledge, nor did he see it as bound up with the destruction of Christianity, but rather with the metaphysical reinterpretation of that, in his view, 'absolute' religion.

On the social plane, Hegel was as enthusiastic an exponent of freedom as he was, on the intellectual plane, of reason. But the freedom he favoured had nothing to do with liberating individuals from the dominance of church and state. It involved the self-suppressing immersion of the individual in the historically formed institutions of his society, the liquidation of subjective individuality in the great structures of objective mind.

Hegel's consoling endorsement of historical change was rejected with scorn by Schopenhauer and Kierkegaard who, in their different ways, insisted on the reality and value of the subjective individual against the Hegelian system and against the large coercive institutions, political and religious, for which it served as an intellectual apology. Kierkegaard attacked both Hegel's system, and Christendom as a public institution, on behalf of the solitary human individual in his confrontation with God. Schopenhauer saw the human individual as alienated from his cosmic as well as his social environment, conceiving both as hostile or indifferent to him; denying all possibility of salvation, religious or political, he took art to be the only palliative of the forlorn human condition.

Despite the fact that Kierkegaard did and Schopenhauer did not believe in God, they gave comparably bleak accounts of the place of man in the universe. Kierkegaard's omnipotent, rationally inscrutable Jehovah, the God who told Abraham to sacrifice Isaac, is little more comforting an absolute reality than Schopenhauer's blind, impersonal Will. If Schopenhauer found man's situation to be irremediably desperate, Kierkegaard found it absurd.

The anti-Hegelianism of Schopenhauer and Kierkegaard, their rejection of historical optimism, their hostility to the public forms of religion and politics were carried to greater lengths by Nietzsche. Like Schopenhauer he proclaimed that reality is will and that God is dead. Disdaining Schopenhauer's pessimistic aestheticism of renunciation and sequestered self-cultivation, he endorsed Kierkegaard's view that man must express himself through decision. He went further than both of them in an irrationalist direction. He saw all thought as the instrument of will and took that to imply that values are purely relative and that science is just a device for the service of desire. His rejections reached back to embrace all the melioristic elements of the European tradition of thought that had been absorbed into Hegel's system, whether they came from Christianity or from what he saw as a pallid echo of Christianity, the Enlightenment. Against the slave-morality of Christians or the herd-morality of the Enlightenment, as expressed in socialism or the faith in democracy, he asserted the claims of the heroic individual, doomed to destruction but capable of tragic glory.

Nietzsche is separated from his great irrationalist forerunners by the emergence in the meanwhile of Darwinism. The doctrine of evolution was unpalatable to orthodox Christians because of its implication that man is wholly a part of nature, simply the highest product so far of the struggle for existence through natural selection. But for secular optimists of the Enlightenment variety Darwinism appeared as a grand confirmation on a larger scale of the law of progress that they discerned in the history of human society. What struck Nietzsche in the evolutionary narrative was not its apparent upward and improving tendency but its brutality and wastefulness, its identification, as the driving force of change, of the crude will to life and power. In particular, by representing mind as an evolved instrument of biological survival, it fortified his scepticism about the products of human thought.

There was, of course, a fourth great anti-Hegelian in the nineteenth century: Marx. But he differed from the others in the limited and selective character of his repudiation of Hegel. He had no quarrel with Hegel's method which he saw as constituting a major and vitally important advance on all previous ways of thinking about man, history and society. Furthermore Marx accepted a crucial implication of the dialectical method, the idea that history is the unfolding of a law of inevitable progress. Where he differs from Hegel is in his materialism, which, by way of the earthy, unmetaphysical conception of fundamental human needs that it embodies, brings Marx closer to the Enlightenment than Hegel was. In his own way Marx endorses Hegel's view that history is a process in which men attain self-realising freedom through the overcoming by reason of contradictions. And if his notion of reason is more that of Hegel than that of Voltaire, his notion of freedom is much more the traditional, literal, 'negative' notion of eighteenth century liberalism than what Hegel used the word to express. For Marx, after all, the state is bound to wither away, not, as with Hegel, to absorb wayward, various, subjective individuals into its service almost without trace.

For Marx, finally, alienation is not a necessary and unalterable feature of the human condition. It is a social dislocation which can and will be cured. Despite the dialectical method and historicist optimism he got from Hegel, then, and a certain amount of romantic upholstery, notably his insistence on the necessity of violent revolution, Marx is, more than anything else, a late Enlightenment figure, dressing up his faith in the perfectibility of man in romantic and Hegelian idioms.

Formal experiment has been a persistent feature of modernism in literature and the arts. Free verse, the stream of consciousness novel, ritualised or pantomimically informal plays, abstract painting, surrealist departures from naturalistic representation, atonal music are familiar ways in which the characteristic alienation of modernism has been carried from the content of literature and art to their formal and stylistic traditions. There is something of this in the irrationalist philosophers I have picked out as modernistic. Schopenhauer, indeed, is no more of a formal innovator than Baudelaire. In the circumstances in which he wrote, in fact, the extreme elegance and polish of his writing, together with its comparative lucidity, was a break with the prevailing traditions of German philosophical prose in which the vile example of Kant had been generally followed, if with less aridity and desiccation, by his successors. But it was continuous with Voltaire and Hume.

Kierkegaard, however, did not, for the most part, produce impersonal academic treatises in professorial jargon. His favourite form of expression was through pseudonymous irony. *Either/Or*, for example, purports to be published by Victor Eremita. Its first volume consists of various works ostensibly by 'A.': aphorisms, essays, a speech, a review of a comedy by Scribe, and *Diary of the Seducer*, edited by A. but written by 'Johannes'. The work continues with the letters of 'Judge William' to A., taking a position nearer to Kierkegaard's own than do the writings of A. *Fear and Trembling* appears as the work of 'Johannes de Silentio', *Concluding Unscientific Postscript* as that of 'Johannes Climacus'.

Kierkegaard's literary practice conforms to his principle that truth is subjectivity. His philosophical works are related to incidents and problems in his personal life. Thus his account of Abraham's sacrifice of Isaac in *Fear and Trembling* is a metaphor for his own sacrifice of Regina Olsen. The variety of literary forms and mouthpieces he uses goes with a variety of moods and attitudes. In his writings against Hegel sarcasm and rhetoric play at least as large a part as straight argumentation. The different personalities he adopts allow him to give full expression to all the views that tempt him and to express his own conclusions from a multiplicity of points of view. No philosopher has so consciously and consistently disdained the ideal of neutral, impersonal objectivity.

Nietzsche, too, is formally experimental, although in a less varied and interesting way than the more sophisticated Kierkegaard. *Thus Spake Zarathustra* is a quasi-scriptural incantation; *Beyond Good and Evil* consists of nearly three hundred loosely connected chunks of more or less aphoristic prose, some of properly aphoristic brevity, others running to two or three pages. Nietzsche's variously sibylline procedures are consistent with his radical scepticism. Inspired *aperçus* cannot consistently be couched in the language of logically articulated theories.

The three great irrationalist anti-Hegelians were not, except in the most short-lived and glancing way, academics. But respectable, professorial philosophy continued in spite of them. Lotze and the neo-Kantians kept the conventional style of philosophising alive in the German-speaking world in a way that was by no means merely imitative and inertial. But after 1918 the philosophy of the German universities, and after the late 1930s that of the French, came to be increasingly dominated by their disciples. Heidegger and Sartre, philosophically brought up in neutral, scientific phenomenology (Heidegger was both Husserl's pupil and his supplanter) achieved their broader celebrity by expressing the themes of Kierkegaard and Nietzsche in the idiom of phenomenology. After his early *Being and Time* Heidegger's attachment to phenomenology wore increasingly thin. The close scrutiny of essence gave way to undirected musings inspired by idiosyncratic Greek etymology. The abstract elusiveness of his later work makes him something of a philosophical Mallarmé.

Sartre gives his philosophy direct expression in treatises of fairly standard form but supplements them with novels and plays. In recent years his favoured method of communication has been the curious form of metaphysical literary-cum-psychological interpretation exemplified by his books on Jean Genet and Flaubert. His incomplete but nevertheless very considerable submission to institutionalised Marxism, in which while boggling at the punitive suppression of Czechoslovakia he manages to endorse Russian endeavours to destroy Israel, invite comparison of him with those fellow-travellers like Brecht who are prepared to forego autonomy in their chief field of activity because of commitment to the Marxist faith.

What one can surely conclude, then, is that if there is a philosophy which is the cultural correlate of modernism, as that term is primarily understood, in its application to literature and the arts, it is existentialism in the broad sense, covering the tradition of thought that runs from the irrationalist reaction to Hegel in the nineteenth century up to Heidegger and Sartre in recent times That conclusion raises three points for further examination, about the temporal and spatial extent and the comparative excellence of the two correlates.

It seems to be generally agreed that existentialism, having come to the forefront of informed consciousness in the interwar years, flourished well on into the 1950s, but has since been somewhat shouldered aside. In its spiritual home in western Europe it has been supplanted at the height of fashion by the altogether more scientistic doctrine of structuralism and by various admixtures of Hegelianism and Marxism. At the same time phenomenology continues, in much diminished involvement with the high metaphysical dramatics of existentialism. But that, it might be said, is as it should be, if existentialism really is the cultural correlate of modernism in literature and art. For modernism is not what it was. It is now more an achieved background to creative activity in art and literature than a particular point of view or manner of approach. Populism and variously playful kinds of aestheticism (Borges, even Nabokov) are forms of post-modernism rather than direct continuation of modernism.

Secondly, there is the problem posed by the fact that while modernism in art and literature has dominated the culture of civilised societies for about a century, existentialism has been more spatially confined. There are hardly any existentialists in the English-speaking world, although there has been some, fairly casual, interest in it and, in the United States, occasional propagandists for it. Creative modernism has been as vigorous and fruitful there as in the western European heartland of existentialism (mainly France and Germany, to some extent Italy and Spain).

It is tempting to respond to this consideration by saying that in its western European home existentialism is not so much the philosophical correlate of modernism as a particular form of literary modernism. A less desperate measure would be to say that different societies do not have to be in the front line of progress in all dimensions or aspects of cultural activity, but this is still something of a dilution of the thesis of cultural correlation. It could, finally, be suggested that there is a marginal element of existentialism lurking in the seemingly inhospitable framework of analytic philosophy, a matter to which I shall return.

The third point, about the comparative excellence of existentialism and modernism, may be put with a quotation from William Barrett. In his admirable broad survey of existentialism he writes:

> Through modern art our time reveals itself to itself ... In our epoch existential philosophy has appeared as an intellectual expression of the time, and this philosophy exhibits numerous points of contact with modern art. The more closely we examine the two together, the stronger becomes the impression that existential philosophy is the authentic intellectual expression of our time, as modern art is the expression of the time in terms of image and intuition. (*Irrational Man*, pp. 55-6)

Barrett here asserts the correlation for which I have been arguing and goes on to infer, making the implicit but surely reasonable assumption that the great art of our epoch is modernist, that the best philosophy of our epoch must be existentialism. For his implication is that analytic and other varieties of non-existential philosophy are inauthentic and that is plainly a term of dispraise.

But it need not be taken to be so. A defender of analytic philosophy could well reply that authenticity of the kind Barrett has in mind is not something that his philosophy does, or perhaps any philosophy should, seek to achieve. A philosophy is authentic in Barrett's sense if it concerns itself with and is permeated by the most active and responsive spiritual interests of its time, what I have called 'spiritual interests' being the values, preferences, emotions and anxieties of reflective people, underlying their morality, politics and, as one might put it, 'cosmic attitude', whether religious or unbelieving. For the analytic philosopher the proper, or, at any rate, prime, task of philosophy is strictly intellectual or cognitive in character, the critical examination of our thought and language with regard to its meaning, truth and logical consistency or validity. He does not have to maintain that this logically critical activity has no bearing whatever on what I have called spiritual interests. But he need not suppose that it is his professional duty to serve or express them.

This brings us back, finally, to the claim of analytic philosophers that their philosophy is strictly technical or scientific and that it embodies no Weltanschauung. Many such philosophers have had things to say about morality, politics and religion but they frequently hold that these are outside activities, extra-professional forays into domains of common concern. Russell, convinced that scientific method could not settle questions about value, always insisted on this disjunction between his technical work and his libertarian doctrines in morals and politics. There is, indeed, a certain incongruity between the internal moral implication of his theory of knowledge and his practice as a moralist. His view that nothing substantial can be known for certain and that there is no such thing as truth in the domain of values implies that substantial, and, even more, evaluative assertions should be tentative and qualified. Yet his own evaluations became ever more strident and dogmatic.

There is a rather high correlation between the endorsement of analytic philosophy and the adoption of the liberal, secular, melioristic ideology of the Enlightenment. On the ideological plane Russell occupies much the same position as H.G. Wells, and his followers are for the most part spiritually at home with the *Guardian* and the *Observer*, a little to the right, one could say, of Kingsley Martin's *New Statesman*. They tend to share Russell's cheerfully dismissive attitude to religion, believing that traditional Christianity is an exploded superstition and that there is no need for anything to take its place. Politically they are social democrats of a non-revolutionary kind. Their morality is thoroughly secular and practically but undogmatically utilitarian. Even if their moral philosophy convinces them that utilitarianism is just one possible choice of basic moral outlook amongst others, in no way demonstrably correct by comparison to them, they incline to think it is a choice that any reasonable and benevolent person will make.

But this correlation is far from complete. One of the most distinguished of American analytic philosophers voted for Goldwater. Plenty of analytic philosophers are more or less orthodox Christians. There is also the case of Wittgenstein, deeply preoccupied with the religious questions his philosophy required him not to talk about and the exponent of a more or less Tolstoyan morality of simplicity and self-denial.

In general analytic philosophers confine themselves to the study of man as a knower of empirical or conceptual fact. By doing so they for the most part steer clear of large issues about man considered as a whole and in relation to his human and cosmic environment. This makes any attempt to correlate their professional activities with the work of creative writers and artists fairly nebulous. In so far as they do touch on these larger issues it is usually by accident or, as it were, in their spare time. In the most notable case where an analytic philosopher insists on the relevance of his philosophy to these larger issues, that of Popper, the resulting ideology is Enlightenment liberalism in its classical form. But Popper, it should be added, is a passionate opponent of at least one form of modernism, namely modernism in music, and in his most recent reflections about objectivity, which he sees as a necessary condition for good work in any form of human activity and not just in science, he has, in effect, generalised this hostility. If analytic philosophy is correlated with any broad cultural mood, then, it is that of the Enlightenment. But nearly as good a case could be made for saying the same of contemporary physics.

There is just one central analytic doctrine which has a faintly existentialist flavour. That is the non-cognitivist ethical theory which sees value-judgments not as genuine statements, either true or false, and thus possible items of knowledge, but as universal imperatives of conduct chosen more or less autonomously by their affirmers. This acknowledgment of the non-rational character of ultimate moral choice seems to occasion no anxiety or vertigo in those who make it. Radicals would ascribe this to unreflective bourgeois confidence. To existentialists analytic moral philosophers must look like Walt Disney characters walking blithely into thin air off the edge of a plank.

6

Philosophy and Literature

'The cow is there', said Ansell, lighting a match and holding it out over the carpet. No one spoke. He waited till the end of the match fell off. Then he said again, 'She is there, the cow. There, now.'

'You have not proved it,' said a voice.

'I have proved it to myself.'

'I have proved to myself that she isn't,' said the voice. 'The cow is *not* there.' Ansell frowned and lit another match.

'She's there for me,' he declared. 'I don't care whether she's there for you or not. Whether I'm in Cambridge or Iceland or dead, the cow will be there.'

It was philosophy. They were discussing the existence of objects. Do they exist only when there is someone to look at them? or have they a real existence of their own? It is all very interesting, but at the same time it is difficult. Hence the cow. She seemed to make things easier.

That opening passage from Forster's *The Longest Journey* shows one way in which philosophy can have an influence on imaginative literature and suggests another, much more important, one. What it shows is philosophy serving as a subject-matter for the imaginative writer. In this case it is philosophy at a modest and rudimentary level, seen as a complex and soul-stiffening experience undergone at a certain stage in their lives by favoured young men.

The subject figures in a somewhat more arduous and dignified way in *To the Lighthouse*, by Virginia Woolf, a fellow-member of Forster's intellectual world. There it is conceived as a solitary torture undergone by Mr Ramsay, to the detriment of his temper and sociability.

A fiction-reading philosopher is bound to notice such references to his profession in the novels he reads, even if he regards it as displaying the influence of philosophy on literature in the most obvious and uninteresting sense. It is not surprising, given the fact that Iris Murdoch was a teacher of philosophy for a number of years, that references to it should turn up in her first book *Under the Net*. One of the characters there is described as the author of an article on the Kantian topic of 'the incongruity of counterparts', the problem posed by the fact that a pair of gloves are spatially identical as far as the relations between their parts are concerned and yet remain irresistibly different as spatial things. Here the shaping spirit or esemplastic power was at a slightly low ebb, for Miss Murdoch must have been drawing on a well-known article by D.F. Pears in *Mind* for 1952.

The only philosophical scene comparable to Forster's debate about the cow that I know of in recent fiction occupies a comparably commanding position at the start of Veronica Hull's *The Monkey Puzzle*. Catherine, the bemused and distressful heroine, is found at a philosophical seminar run by the easily recognisable Mr Marble.

> He was well under way now. He was always in good form at the first seminar of a new year. He had disposed of individuation and the problem of identity which was now chalked up in tidy and indecipherable symbols on the blackboard; and was launching into negation with ten minutes to go.
>
> 'What is "failing to find"?' he said again in a bright excited voice. 'What is failing to find my cigarette-case? Is it finding my paper the books the ashtray *plus* the rider that these are all the things on the table? How do we verify "my cigarette-case is not on the table"? Was it this that worried Bradley?' ...
>
> 'What could Bradley mean by this?' said Mr Marble looking at the open window. He liked it stuffy. 'What's the man talking about? "All negative judgments affirm that the quality of the real excludes a suggested ideal content, so all are existential." ' He tipped his chair back precariously, then swung forward on it. 'Analytic or synthetic?' he said triumphantly He leant back again smiling and fiddling with a box of matches. He was always fiddling with matches.

At the beginning of the book Catherine, an unsatisfactory Catholic, is simply suspicious of the austere kind of analytic philosophy with which she is being hit over the head by Mr Marble and his claque. 'She supposed she would understand one day, in the meantime the whole business seemed unimportant. This hypostatisation of the word appeared to be only another religion, and a religion not always more humane than those that had preceded it.' By the end, when Marble and Co. have failed to respond to the demands of the Suez crisis, one of the characters is more forcefully critical:

> 'To believe equals to behave. O.K.? Then they don't believe, these liberal philosophers you admire, because they haven't behaved, the buggers. Haven't got time, just going out to dinner, got a lecture to prepare ... There's your liberal philosophers for you. The ones whose facetiousness you in the end accepted and excused saying they were good socialists anyway. No doubt they will continue to write their little articles, continue to spread their true facetious little philosophy *but* when the barricades go up, it's not that they're on the wrong side, they aren't there at all. And d'you know why? It's awfully easy. They're snobs.'

I said earlier, about Forster, that the passage about the cow suggested a more important way in which philosophy could affect literature than as a kind of human activity capable of being part of an imaginative writer's subject matter. It can also, of course, be a source of ideas. Forster was at least an associate member of the Bloomsbury circle and there is the authority of Keynes for the view that the creed of Bloomsbury was provided in essentials by the *Principia Ethica* of G.E. Moore. This is obliquely confirmed by the Moorean topic and also style, one of inarticulate directness, of Ansell and his interlocutors.

Keynes's essay, *My Early Beliefs*, reports that he and his friends derived their religion without morals from the concluding chapters of Moore's book, a chapter called, 'The Ideal', in which it is held that human states of mind are the only things in the universe that are of value in themselves, that the more intense and passionate they are the better and that of such states the supremely valuable ones are those arising from affectionate personal relationships and the contemplation of beauty. Keynes was indeed right to say that this system of values has little to do with morality as ordinarily conceived: for it provides no justification for Oxfam or the movement for the abolition of the slave trade. As a set of ultimate values it recalls Russell's observation about Aristotle's ethics: a doctrine for someone with limited sympathies and a secure private income. Yet, as mediated through Forster's sensibility and with some of its respectable trappings removed, it did take on the character of a genuine morality. In opposition to the iron moral authoritarianism of his dreadful clergymen and the worship of material utility of his gruff men of action, Forster speaks up for impulse, open-heartedness, the instinctive and uncorrupted wisdom of the natural man; most memorably perhaps in the clash of Gino with Philip Herriton in *Where Angels Fear to Tread*, Italian genuineness used to show up the English undeveloped heart.

Moore's influence on an influential group of writers was exercised largely through the last and least philosophical chapter of his chief book on moral philosophy (also, I suspect, through the crystalline purity and unworldliness of his personality). The elaborate conceptual preliminaries to the final exposure of his ultimate values – the doctrine of non-natural qualities, the refutation of naturalism – have little to do with his literary effect. Even less have Moore's other philosophical preoccupations influenced imaginative writers: his sixty years of slow-motion all-in wrestling with sense-data and the nature of philosophical analysis.

Imaginative writers are concerned with human beings, from the standpoint of introspection or else as members of a society. British philosophy in this century, in so far as it has been concerned with human beings at all and not with the truths of logic and the nature of material objects, has considered man in almost exclusively cognitive terms, as a detached spectator, conceptualising his physical environment. Even if modern philosophers reject most of Descartes's principles it is still Cartesian man that they study. Only very recently has the idea of man as essentially an agent, a central tenet of existentialists, figured at all noticeably in the local product, most conspicuously in Stuart Hampshire's *Thought and Action*.

In its intellectualism, then, recent philosophy has failed to provide material worth appropriating by the imaginative writer. Its image of man is a deliberate abstraction, it has steered clear in principle of the formulation of systems of values or ideologies. At the other end of the relationship imaginative writers have for the most part resolutely avoided any kind of didacticism. Tennyson, however ill-fitted he was for the task, felt himself under a responsibility to pronounce on the intellectual perplexities of his age, earning in the process the label 'the modern Lucretius' from T.H. Huxley. In our time only the brief efflorescence of Marxist enthusiasm among literary intellectuals in the 1930s produced anything in the way of committed civic prophecy. Powerful talents like Auden's blithely survived this ideological conscription. Looking back on his earlier poems from our present vantage-point, his early Marxism seems little more than an involvement with a source of quaint imagery: 'the flat, ephemeral pamphlet and the boring meeting' and 'the research on fatigue and the movements of packers'. In less confident and dexterous hands the Marxian contraption exploded into farce. The closing passages of Edward Upward's *Journey to the Border* are irresistible:

> He would begin tutoring again, but with a difference. Perhaps in the evenings he would be able to do propaganda work in the village, among the agricultural workers. He would make a point of meeting the village schoolmaster, would have a talk with Stokes. Perhaps he would be sacked from his job as a tutor. If so he could try to get another job – next time preferably in an industrial town. His decision to join the workers' movement would lead to difficulties. But he would at least have come down to earth, out of the cloud of his cowardly fantasies; would have begun to live. He had already begun.

It would require an extravagant fertility of interpretation to discern any didactic element at all in the poets most active at the present time, in Ted Hughes or Thom Gunn, for example.

Philosophy, then, in its currently analytic form, the staple brand of academic instruction in the subject, deals little in what could catch the interest and attention of the imaginative writer. Here as elsewhere the last century has seen a steady increase of specialised technique and professionalism; there are no serious philosophers nowadays who are not looking forward to the pension to which their involvement with the subject entitles them. For the most part philosophers write for each other and, although the students who pass through their hands may be hoped to acquire a greater facility in abstract thinking from the fact, they are no more likely to remain alert to the forward movement of the discipline than a Victorian undergraduate would have been caught up for life with the latest refinements of classical scholarship. For better or worse, philosophy is only vestigially part of the public intellectual domain. Even where an imaginative writer is concerned with issues of a broadly philosophical kind, such as William Golding, preoccupied with evil, causation and the freedom of the will, his reflections will show no sign of exposure to current philosophical debate about these issues.

In these circumstances, if any relationship is to be discerned between philosophy and imaginative literature, either the relationship sought must be conceived in more inclusive and hospitable terms than those of direct influence or the concept of philosophy must be allowed to apply to regions falling outside the surveillance of the University Grants Committee.

It is to Hegel as much as to anyone that we owe the fruitful if abusable practice of applying adjectives, that are first introduced to make distinctions within a specific field of human activity, over the whole range of human interests and manifestations. Many people must have learnt this art from Spengler, with his references to baroque music and the baroque state, or from Marx, with his talk of bourgeois economics and bourgeois religion. These extensions of terms must be justified by underlying analogies and affinities, even if they are first suggested by the mere fact of approximate contemporaneity.

Kingsley Amis, speaking, I think, on behalf of that generation of new writers of the Attlee period of whom he has proved to be the most fertile and successful, claimed an affinity between the outlook of himself and his friends and three bodies of doctrine: the literary criticism of F.R. Leavis, the social criticism of George Orwell and analytic philosophy. There undoubtedly are analogies between the fiction and poetry of his particular generation and the ordinary-language kind of analytic philosophy which, dominated by Ryle and Austin in Oxford, radiated out in the first postwar decade over the whole philosophical scene. Both movements were robustly suspicious of all varieties of established pretension, unwaveringly alert to the spurious, unwilling to entertain large hopes, addicted to the plainest of colloquial language, espoused concrete satisfactions (for Jim Dixon a nice girl and a good job, for Austin getting some muddles cleared up) in preference to expansive ideals (heroic achievement in life or an all-inclusive system of the universe).

The prevailing attitude both of 'the Movement' and of the philosophy of ordinary language that was contemporary with it was deflationary, disenchanted, somewhat self-consciously philistine (compare 'filthy Mozart' with 'Descartes' howler'). It was an attitude altogether congruous with the historic situation of the country, nominally victorious in a war that had extinguished its last pretensions to great-power status.

Since the mid-1950s both literature and philosophy have become a little more colourful. Both are less wedded to the russet-clad virtues of plain vernacular statement. In poetry the intensity of Sylvia Plath has secured the admiration formerly given to the conversational wryness of Philip Larkin. Fiction, with William Golding, Iris Murdoch and Anthony Powell, has become more imaginatively ambitious and enterprising or, failing that, more formal, autonomous and mannered.

The posthumous publication of a long sequence of ever more fragmentary writings by Wittgenstein has likewise done something to relieve the sensible, dun-coloured uniformity of the philosophical landscape. A recurrent feature of his later thought is an insistence on the uniqueness of man; for him man, as a language-using creature, must be marked off very sharply from the other animals, to whom emotions can be ascribed, for the most part, only in a figurative way, and as an agent, who acts on reasons, he must be distinguished from all other objects, since his activities, unlike their behaviour, cannot be explained in a casual way. Wittgensteinians are deeply critical of the whole idea of social science and so are natural allies for the novelists who fear the erosion of their own craft by sociology.

There is, then, in very general terms some sort of correlation of underlying attitude between recent literature and philosophy, in its standard academic form. Can anything more like a genuine exercise of influence be discerned if philosophy is conceived in a less strict and exclusive way? Between 1944 and 1948 Cyril Connolly's *Horizon* published a series of thirteen articles under the general heading of 'novelist-philosophers'. Since the series included in its later phases articles on Hemingway and Cervantes it is clear that novelist-philosophers were not required to be very philosophical. Four leading French novelists of this century figured very naturally in the group: Gide, Malraux, Sartre and Camus. But the only representatives of this country were George Eliot (who did after all translate Strauss's *Life of Jesus*) and, very curiously, R.L. Stevenson and George Douglas Brown (of *The House with Green Shutters*).

The plain fact is that general ideas have never been a central preoccupation of British novelists. Straightforward reforming propaganda is an occasional supplementary feature, most notably, of course, in Dickens, but the nearest thing to a modern British novelist of ideas that comes to mind is Aldous Huxley and in his case the ideas are presented in a very externally attached, conversational, not to say brains-trust, form; their development is not the bone-structure but rather the obtrusive surface of his fiction.

One admirable recent novelist, John Fowles, has published a volume of aphorisms, *The Aristos*, which is certainly philosophical in the large sense of the word. His ideas are humane, thoughtful and fresh; he effectively makes explicit attitudes that would seem to be widespread among his contemporaries but not to have been clearly formulated by them. On the whole the book did not get a very good press; even the friendliest reviews treated its author as if he were guilty of the offence of Lord Finchley (who, it will be remembered 'tried to mend the electric light himself ...'). It would seem that our society is firmly wedded to the principle of the division of labour in the field of abstract thought as well as in more literally industrial activities.

7

The Organisation of Knowledge

The eleventh edition of the *Encyclopaedia Britannica* did something to counteract the alphabetical miscellaneity of its contents by including in its index volume a classified table of contents. (That was the last British, or, at any rate, all-British, edition. The mild cult which sees it as the last real Britannica is not merely chauvinistic. Despite the fact that that well-known group 'ninety per cent of all the scientists who have ever lived' began work after it came out, it had an authoritativeness and, even more, a standard below which its entries never fell, which have been missing from its successors.)

The list was an unassuming affair. Its twenty-four main headings were themselves alphabetically arranged, apart from the systematiser's white feather of its final section: 'miscellaneous'. Art lies next to astronomy in it, education to engineering, religion and theology to sports and pastimes. Within the sections, too, no very officious ordering hand was discernible. A handful of large general entries was listed first; then particular entries; finally biographies.

The succeeding, Chicago-based, editions presented their contents to the world without any such guide. On the whole the technique of revision they embodied was that of finding space for new-fangled subjects such as 'aeroplane' ('aeronautics' in the eleventh edition had been largely illustrated with steel engravings of Jules Verne-like balloons), finding more room for such topics as 'philately' (from half a page to five pages) and dropping or condensing items of humanistic interest to make the space available.

The new, fifteenth, edition of the Britannica, under the influence of its director of planning, Dr Mortimer J. Adler, has firmly reversed this tendency. The first of its thirty volumes, the *Propaedia*, or Outline of Knowledge, or Guide to the Britannica, devotes nearly eight hundred of its nine hundred or so pages to a massively detailed articulation of the whole, all-inclusive field of the encyclopaedia's concern under something like fifteen thousand headings, themselves arranged in seven levels of taxonomic stratification. Thus 'forced labour in modern states', e.g. the Third Reich, the Soviet Union, is item ii under 'servitude and slavery in the late nineteenth and twentieth centuries', itself item c under 'social immobility: slavery, servitude and forced labour'. The latter is item 6 under 'social stratification and social mobility', which is part B of 'social status', the 523rd of the consecutively numbered main sections, itself the third ingredient of 'social organisation and social change', which, finally, is Division II of 'human society', Part Five of the whole system.

Beside each of these headings in the *Propaedia* is a list of the places where the topic may be investigated in the rest of the work, or rather, in the nineteen volumes of the *Macropaedia*, which contains over four thousand longish articles (the longest, literature, western, runs to 174 pages). The ten volumes of the *Micropaedia* contain brief factual entries of not more than 750 words.

In his preface, the editor, Mr Warren E. Preece, sets out the reasoning behind this division into macro and micro parts. The ten volumes of the *Micropaedia* are for quick reference, a source of information; the nineteen-volume *Macropaedia* has a more educational purpose, its aim is to provide understanding. But there is no essential connection between this division in the main body of the work and the systematic outline of knowledge set out in the *Propaedia* with which we are concerned here. Such a systematic outline could have been derived from, or, as here, have guided the composition of, an encyclopaedia whose contents were not divided, so long, at any rate, as it contained a fair proportion of longer, survey articles.

Dr Adler's introductory remarks about the system over whose construction he has presided are brief and conciliatory. 'Does not the Outline of Knowledge here presented' he asks 'reflect, perhaps even conceal, a commitment to one set of organising principles rather than another? Does it not embody biases or preconceptions that are not universally acceptable?' Dr Adler's long association with the movement in Chicago, whose most prominent representative is Robert M. Hutchins (chairman of the board of editors of the *Encyclopaedia Britannica*), which has sought to restore to learning unity of a kind exemplified in the work of Aristotle and with a pronounced neo-Thomist inflection, might indeed inspire such questions. The goal implied by the second question, of working from a set of organising principles that are universally acceptable, seems almost too heroic a resolution to avoid *parti pris*.

The suspicious reader will be on the look-out for the assignment to theology, whether interpreted in a conventional way or, with Aristotle, as 'first philosophy' or metaphysics, of a commanding place. But in so far as anything is given special dignity, or, at any rate, special treatment, it is the collection of disciplines which comprise the tenth and last part of the whole system: 'the branches of knowledge'. What is to be found here is knowledge about knowledge or knowledge of the second order, knowledge of the intellectual activities of man. The five divisions of this strategically crucial part are logic, mathematics, science (conceived as a knowledge-seeking activity, not as a set of findings about nature, man and society), history and the humanities, and philosophy.

There is nothing very tendentious in separating consideration of the methods by which a particular segment of first-order reality is studied, and the history of the process of studying it, from consideration of that segment of reality itself. It is natural to go on to add to the methods and history of the pursuit of knowledge in particular disciplines the logic, which is an instrument of all forms of inquiry, and the mathematics which is an instrument of most. To include philosophy as well is perhaps to understand it rather as a kind of general methodology, in other words as epistemology, than more speculatively and traditionally as a form of inquiry whose subject-matter is reality as a whole, in other words as metaphysics.

Their second-order character, the fact that they pursue knowledge about knowledge rather than knowledge about what is not itself knowledge, is a safer and less controversial ground for linking the disciplines of Part Ten together than another that might occur to mind. Many theorists of knowledge would hold that logic, mathematics and philosophy, and also the methodologies or philosophies of particular first-order disciplines, physics, psychology, history and so on, consist of assertions of a nature logically distinct from the theories and statements by which other bodies of knowledge are constituted. Where the latter are empirical or factual, the former are *a priori* or conceptual in character. That criterion would not endorse the inclusion of the history of human intellectual activities, which is as much a matter of empirical fact as the history of card-games or cosmetics. Even so, when assembling the facts about the human conceptual activities whose formal properties the *a priori* disciplines investigate, a case could be made for putting them in the place where the *Propaedia* puts them. But the *a priori*-empirical dichotomy has been a matter of philosophical dispute for the last few decades, ever since Quine began to argue that the contrast between the necessary and the contingent is a matter not of kind but degree, that logic and mathematics are just the most general of sciences and that philosophy is simply the science of science, 'lore about lore', in effect a branch of psychology.

Dr Adler, at any rate, does not appeal to a tradition that begins with Plato's contrast of *episteme* and *doxa*, was revitalised with Leibniz's distinction between truths of reason and truths of fact, and until recently took the form, in the minds of theorists of knowledge, of an instinctive conviction that all thoughts or propositions could be divided without remainder into the analytic and the synthetic.

To repel the accusation that his system accords an especially elevated status to knowledge about knowledge, Dr Adler lays much stress on the conception of learning as a circle. With some earnestness he draws attention to the fact that if the parts of the circle of learning are conceived in the manner of slices of a cake none, in view of the symmetry of their arrangement, is implied to be more important or fundamental than any of the others. This egalitarian conception of the parts of knowledge, however, gives way to one in which the tenth, second-order part forms a little circle at the middle, while the other nine parts ray out from it. Here an old-fashioned pie, with a bit of crust held up in the middle by an egg-cup, replaces the strictly symmetrical cake. One would have to be very suspicious to think that this concealed some deep, ideological design and that perfectly sound and straightforward reasons had not been given for it.

What of the other nine parts? The first five follow a more or less evolutionary sequence: matter and energy; the earth; non-human life; human life; human society. So far nothing for Auguste Comte to raise an eyebrow at. The scheme coincides pretty well with what he took to be the

totality of true sciences, although he added mathematics at the beginning
and divided the *Propaedia*'s 'matter and energy' part into three: mechanics,
physics and chemistry. There then follow art, technology, religion and
history. The placing of technology seems a bit odd. Is it a measure of
subliminal Marxism that leads one to feel, once we are on an evolutionary
track, that what that influential library classifier Melvin E. Dewey called the
useful arts should precede the fine arts?

History gets its penultimate place as a bit of a catch-all. It has a firmly
traditional background in political events, as far as one can tell from the
detailed subdivisions of the part, but this is decently relieved with mention of
society, economy and culture. Thus 'Muslim, Norman and Magyar
invasions and the debilitation of central authority' in the Carolingian empire
after Louis the Pious is swiftly followed by 'the Frankish world: society;
institutions; economic life; the church; literature and the arts'; 'the Armada'
by 'cultural developments in Spain's Golden Age'.

It would, no doubt, have been possible to allocate everything in the
exclusively historical Part Nine under various other headings. Most of it
would have had to go under human society. One effect of this would have
been that human society, instead of being the second largest of the ten parts
but only twice as large as the smallest, would have become more than twice
as large as the next largest. More to the point is the fact that it is natural to
look some things up, things that are not confined to one place or one topic, in
a chronological way.

There are two kinds of need which systems that classify sciences or fields of
learning are called upon to serve. The first is sternly practical. Librarians are
required to do more than arrange the books in their care by alphabetical
order of title or author or by date of publication. Classification by subject-
matter is essential to the reader with access to the shelves to show him what
there is on the subject he is interested in. It is also economical of the time and
effort of library assistants.

More or less independently of this way of approaching the problem of
classification there also exists a theoretical interest in attempting to find
some ideal, or at least proper, order for the various fields of knowledge. This
theoretical interest is slightly smaller in scope than that of the librarian, for
he has to accommodate works which are not primarily or at all containers of
knowledge, principally works of imaginative literature, but also such things
as astrological predictions. (In the *Propaedia*, incidentally, magic, astrology
and alchemy figure under religion, more specifically under religious
phenomenology, Section 2, natural objects or forces viewed as bearers or
manifestations of the sacred.) In the Dewey decimal system, still much used
in libraries, fiction is extruded into a limbo of its own, poetry is tucked in
with criticism, plays and humour under the 800s, and magic and the occult
generally jostle for position with psychology and some more appropriate
things under 100, philosophy.

Library classification is, no doubt for institutional reasons, a fairly
autonomous undertaking, although some of its more heroic recent exponents,
particularly Bliss in the United States and Berwick Sayers in this country,

have sought to nourish their work by attention to a more theoretical or philosophical tradition of classification. The accounts that both of them give of that tradition owe a good deal to the *History of the Classification of the Sciences*, brought out in 1904 by Robert Flint, the author of the first serious survey in English of the philosophy of history and of the first serious English book on Vico (a quietly proud footnote in his *History of Classification* points out the understandably gratifying fact that the latter was translated into Italian).

Berwick Sayers made some discoveries of his own. He makes much of Konrad von Gesner (described, it appears, by Cuvier as 'the German Pliny'), a Swiss who, at the time of his death aged forty-nine in 1565, had already published 72 books and left 18 unfinished. He anticipated the *Propaedia* in distinguishing primary sciences (including discourse and mathematics) from fundamental or substantive ones. But for the most part his account follows Flint, as does Bliss almost exclusively.

There are intimations of a classificatory system in Plato's fourfold division of kinds of knowledge and belief, but this subject, like so many others, gets properly launched only with Aristotle. There are various drafts of systems in his writings, two of which are particularly noteworthy. He explicitly distinguishes the theoretical sciences of physics, mathematics and metaphysics (in ascending order of dignity), first, from the practical sciences concerned with the regulation of actions (pre-eminently ethics and politics) and, secondly, from the productive sciences concerned with the making of things (exemplified in his writings only by his *Poetics*, but presumably including technology). Logic he saw as a preliminary to all scientific inquiry. More influential, perhaps, was a casual remark in the *Topics*: 'some propositions are ethical, others physical and others logical'. This tripartite division was taken over by the Stoics and Epicureans and prevailed until the medieval scheme of seven liberal arts and three philosophies was established by Cassiodorus, Capella and Isidore of Seville.

In the present age this second Aristotelian trinity of logic, physics and ethics has experienced a revival among theorists of knowledge. All assertions, it has been held, can be classified as (a) necessary and conceptual, such as those of logic and mathematics, and also philosophy, in its analytic mode; or (b) factual and empirical, as in natural and social science and history; or (c) evaluative, as in morals, politics and the criticism of art. Anyone who is enough of a pragmatist to suppose that knowledge is, broadly speaking, for the sake of action, and not merely for detached, Aristotelian, world-renouncing contemplation, will be inclined to conclude that every non-practical science has some kind of practical outcome. Thus the logical disciplines can be seen as supplying rules for the conduct of empirical inquiry and the empirical sciences as yielding corresponding technologies or applications.

Now in view of the generality of the logical disciplines, the fact that they apply indifferently to all the other branches of knowledge, it would be proper to accord them separate treatment in an encyclopaedic ordering. But the factual sciences would seem on the whole to be correlated, one to one, each to its own practical art, craft or technique. So, it might be inferred, investment advice should be included in the treatment of economics, medical therapy with anatomy and physiology, political ideology with political science.

But there are limits to this procedure. Should the art of cookery be placed under chemistry of which it is an application? (In the new *Britannica* it comes under Human Life, division V: aspects of man's daily life.) Should technology, as it does in the new *Britannica*, have a whole part to itself and not be included, along with the physics and chemistry it applies, under Matter and Energy? Abstaining from the full rigour of subordination of practical arts to their corresponding sciences is reasonable enough in these cases. Most cooks know no chemistry and do not think of themselves as chemists; technology is so large and diverse as to merit consideration on its own.

In the middle ages a rather different tripartite organisation of knowledge (and of university curricula) prevailed. To start with there were the verbal sciences of the *trivium* (logic, rhetoric and grammar); next the mathematical sciences of the *quadrivium* (arithmetic, geometry, astronomy, music); and finally the 'three philosophies' (natural, moral and metaphysical or theological). Isidore substituted for these last the professional disciplines of medicine and law and added chronology or history. Hugh of St Victor, at the beginning of this millennium, reverted to Aristotle's more considered scheme of theory, practice and production, imitatively in the first two categories, in the new guise of the mechanical arts (weaving, navigation, acting etc.) in the third.

The most influential knowledge-organiser of the modern age must surely have been Bacon, both because of the elaboration of his scheme in the *De Augmentis* and because a century and a half later it was still taken by D'Alembert and Diderot to be, if not the last, at any rate the best word on its subject. In Bacon's scheme for the first time there is a a clear separation of the theory-practice distinction from the nature-mind distinction. For him philosophy and history both have their natural and civil forms. At much the same time Descartes was putting the distinction between mind and matter at the centre of philosophy in place of Aristotle's near-continuum of forms.

A comparable enthusiasm for the organisation of knowledge occurred in the nineteenth century, related, no doubt, to Darwin's work as Bacon's carnival of minute classification was to the new physics of his time. In between there had been largely verbose extravagance such as that of Bentham in the fifth appendix to his *Chrestomathia*, in which, for example, arithmetic turns out to be gnostosymbolic alegomorphic pososcopic somatic coenoscopic ontology.

With Ampère and, rather less quaintly, Comte and Spencer, and down, at least, to Karl Pearson, schemes of a more or less evolutionary character, in which the field of knowledge was confined to positive sciences, were the predominant form. Like some kinds of social gathering their real interest lay in those who were not invited. Comte left out logic, philosophy and psychology. Spencer, opposing Comte's idea of a natural serial order of sciences, was rather more hospitable.

Today the kind of optimism about the growth of real knowledge and the routing of old error that inspired the evolutionary positivists of the last century has largely disappeared. There was still a flicker of it in the Vienna Circle with their notion of the unity of science and the somewhat Comteanly exclusive encyclopaedia of unified science they produced at the end of the 1930s. We are, of course, aware of the massive churnings of the knowledge industry but its principal output is taken to be an accumulation of detail. If recent molecular biology has enhanced the connection of the life sciences with the sciences of physical nature, there is a feeling that nothing in physics proper since the mid-1920s has matched in significance the theoretical advances of those years.

If bold novelties in the classification of the sciences require a buoyant intellectual atmosphere, the present is not, then, a time to expect them. A widely used encyclopaedia bringing out a new edition, furthermore, is not the proper place for them. Dr Adler lists three main outstanding problems about the organisation of knowledge. First, do the different branches of knowledge stand in a hierarchical order? Secondly, are the various branches of knowledge consistent with each other? Finally, how deep-seated is the line of division between the sciences and the humanities?

The first of these questions poses a problem for any encyclopaedia-compiler who aims at some point to classify his material in respect of its content, and not just the alphabetic position of the letters of its name. In the new Britannica it is solved by the resolutely eirenic device of taking the main branches of knowledge to be arranged in a circle. The second question would embarrass a compiler if he believed that the answer was in the negative and that in his work of summarising the present state of knowledge he was endorsing its status as knowledge proper and not as an accumulation of more or less reasonable knowledge-claims. In practice he can afford to let the contributors fight it out among themselves. It is not the task of the toastmaster to keep the conversation going. But the compiler is also the host in this kind of banquet and must exercise some discretion in his choice of entry-writers for contentious topics. Professor Eysenck would be too tendentious a choice for the article on psychoanalysis, as would Ivan Illich on schools or R.D. Laing on schizophrenia.

No fixed view about the answer to the third question is implied by the mode of the new *Britannica*'s arrangement. If history had been subsumed under human society a scientistic bias could have been imputed. But the fact that it has a part of its own does not imply insistence on the duality of the two cultures, for it rests, as was shown above, on non-methodological grounds, those of keeping together what will be consulted together and of keeping the main parts comparable in size.

One up-to-date piece of classification deserves particular notice. Language, which had a part to itself in the system of the eleventh edition, and in libraries, as in universities to a considerable extent, is attached to literature, is included towards the end of the part on human life, between human behaviour and experience and aspects of man's daily life (viz. the means of subsistence and leisure and play). This reflects the most recent developments in the study of language and puts it where, for instance, Chomsky would presumably put it, at the upper end of psychology and at the entrance to social science.

The organisation of knowledge of the new *Britannica*, then, as set out in the *Propaedia*, is an immensely thorough and detailed piece of work. It embodies in its general form no striking innovations and does not conceal within it any principles likely to provoke controversy. Free from architectonic Procrusteanism it seems, for all its elaboration, a practical answer to a practical problem. Only the most exquisitely fastidious could think that they are somehow being got at.

8

Authority and Autonomy in Knowledge

I. THE INDIVIDUALISM OF EPISTEMOLOGY

Ever since Descartes brought it into the centre of philosophical attention epistemology has been a thoroughly individualistic discipline or, as it is more usually put, a thoroughly subjectivistic one. The individual knower or subject is represented as setting out on his cognitive career with nothing more than the senses and the reason that he stands up in. He gets to work on the virgin territory of the unknown with this rudimentary survival kit and in due time, through his industrious activities of construction and inference, he accumulates a substantial body of general theory and a somewhat less stable stock of singular beliefs of a broadly historical and geographical character.

All theorists of knowledge agree that men enter the world endowed with sensory receptivity. But rationalists assert, while empiricists deny, that they are also equipped with innate principles of inference, an instinctive skill for working up what is given to the senses. Rationalist believers in innate knowledge of this kind do not generally regard it as a social product. Innate knowledge is taken to be something characteristic of the human species as a whole. It is a divine or natural gift to the entire human community from some beneficent agency wholly external to it. The only familiar exception to this general rule is Herbert Spencer. He explained our knowledge of the necessary truths to which fundamental principles of inference correspond as an inheritance of the more entrenched theoretical certainties laboriously accumulated by our ancestors, as literally, if biologically, a patrimony. An initial, logical, weakness of this position is that it leaves unexplained the inferential skills deployed by our ancestors in their accumulative task. This could perhaps be circumvented by the theory that the first men went in for a random variety of inferential practices and that only those whose practices accorded with the way things actually hang together survived to become ancestors, thus justifying the logic and methodology we accept by way of their endorsement by natural selection. As it stands, however, Spencer's doctrine would seem to collapse with the general principle of which it is an instance: that of the inheritance of acquired characteristics. Logic and methodology must be a social, not a biological, inheritance, if they are an inheritance at all. Apart from Spencer, then, theorists of knowledge all agree that man is cognitively self-made.

This individualistic account of the growth of human knowledge is an analogue of the received picture of early capitalism as theoretically embalmed in the more simplified expositions of classical economics. The individual comes into the world with the brute labour-power of sense and, perhaps, with some measure of innate inferential craft. He goes in for sensory fact-gathering and some inferential processing of the facts he has gathered, storing his cognitive products in memory and applying his stock in the guidance of his actions. In due course he builds up a cognitive technology (logic, mathematics and methodology), productive capital in the form of general theory, durable goods (his name, his height, the distance of London from Birmingham), a connoisseur's collection of logically singular bric-à-brac, and a rapidly changing stock of passing, forgettable singular items (where he parked his car this morning, whether he put the cat out).

To emerge from metaphor, epistemologists commonly account for the growth of human knowledge by reference to four principal sources. The first of these is sense-perception. Next there is memory in which the findings of perception, and, in due course, of other cognitive operations, are stored. (As a store, of course, it should not really be described a *source*, a point emphasised by Ryle.) Thirdly there is inference, very broadly conceived, so as to include, besides deduction, induction, if there is such a thing, the formation of hypotheses and the development of various kinds of theoretical construction. These first three sources are all individual, in the sense that the knower has recourse to them on his own and such recourse appears to imply no dependence on other people. Perception yields knowledge of the current physical environment of the subject. Its slightly questionable associate introspection provides knowledge of the current state of the subject's mind. Memory contains knowledge of past environments and states of consciousness. Inference, in its most substantial employment, provides the generalities which make explanation and prediction possible, as well as the practical operations of production and prevention, and thus gives knowledge of the unobserved part of the physical world, of other minds and of the future.

It is only with the fourth of the conventionally accepted sources of knowledge, testimony, that knowledge explicitly takes on a social character. Once the existence of other minds has been established it becomes possible to take the noises uttered by the bodies with which they are associated as expressing potential items of knowledge. Access is thus achieved to the cognitive property of others. This is not exactly trade since items of knowledge, like colds, can be given to others without being lost to the original owner.

II. THE SOCIAL CHARACTER OF KNOWLEDGE

If taken as a historical or genetic account of the way in which we acquire our knowledge this Crusonian story of initially solitary knowers building up their private stores of knowledge and only then entering into exchange relations is plainly unacceptable. It utterly fails to recognise the extent to which we are cognitively members of one another. As Popper says: 'quantitatively and qualitatively by far the most important source of our knowledge ... is tradition', that is to say the store of knowledge in the possession of the people around us which they communicate to us. (*Conjectures and Refutations*, p.27.) My private or personal knowledge, what I have discovered by my own observations and stored in my memory, together with what I have inferred from this, constitutes a quantitatively minute fragment of the whole range of what I claim to know. And, if quality is a matter of scope and importance rather than of certainty, all but a vanishingly small proportion of my general, theoretical knowledge is derived from others.

Not only is this the case now, with me or any other mature cognitive subject, but it always has been so. Indeed dependence on others is even more extreme at the beginning of one's cognitive career than it turns out to be later, when one has at least accumulated quite a substantial body of personal knowledge and has acquired the skill of critically sifting the testimony of others. One thing that obscures this fact is the use of the word 'testimony' to describe the nature of our cognitive dependence on others, for it misleadingly over-intellectualises the relationship in question. To talk of the acquisition of a belief from another person as the acceptance of his testimony represents what is usually a passive and largely unconscious process in terms of the deliberate, critical scrutiny of evidence that is typically found, because institutionally arranged for, in law courts, where the liability of witnesses to lie, to be simply misinformed or to use words in an unusual way is explicitly presumed. Epistemologists, in their comparatively rare discussions of testimony, overintellectualise the relationship still further. Perception acquaints us with the existence of certain noises, emanating from human bodies. We have to infer that these are meaningful utterances, that they express the actual beliefs of the minds that lie behind them and that the beliefs in question are likely to be true.

In fact I am taught my observation-language by others who, in the process of doing so, get me to accept a good many observation-statements as true. On the basis of this understanding I am gradually taught the non-observational part of language, together with a good deal of logic and methodology, that is to say the rules of evidence which govern the acceptance of theory on the evidence of observation. Once I am equipped with the linguistic means to articulate my perceptions and with the knowledge of logic and method which enables me to criticise my perceptual beliefs and to draw various sorts of inference from them I am in a position to achieve a measure of cognitive autonomy by using these acquisitions to criticise the authorities who present me with beliefs for acceptance. But at all stages of my career very much the greater part of what I believe has been derived from witnesses whose testimony I have not checked directly. At most I have carried out a very few sample checks on their reliability and have checked their deliverances against those of others. Indeed a certain amount of what I believe, or think I believe, I do not know properly how to check; I know at best what I would have to do, in broad outline, to come to be in a position to check it, for example, my 'knowledge' of quantum physics, cosmology and molecular biology.

We enter the cognitive economy, in other words, in a pretty impoverished condition. Others equip us with the indispensable techniques of knowledge-gathering and knowledge-processing, with consumable items of singular information and with more durable theory. All of this but our initial sensory labour-power (the cognitive analogue of Locke's primary property in one's own labour), together with any innate skill we may possess, is on credit. The epistemologist turns the authorities on whom we depend into providers of testimony, into criticisable witnesses who are kept at a distance until from the sounds we hear or writing we read we infer another mind at work, interpret the meaning it wishes to convey and assess its reliability. But this type of response to the utterances of others is a sophisticated achievement, hard to acquire and hard to maintain. In the ordinary course of events, and exclusively during the earlier stages of one's cognitive career, other people just cause one to believe certain things. It is only later that we fully recognise the external source of the beliefs so imparted and acquire the capacity for critical assessment of authorities to which such recognition makes them accessible.

III. BELIEF AND JUSTIFICATION

Is the fact of the predominantly and ineliminably social character of our knowledge incompatible with the individualistic assumptions customarily made by theorists of knowledge? Such a conclusion has been drawn in Popper's British Academy lecture *The Sources of Knowledge and Ignorance* from which I quoted earlier. But there is a familiar distinction which can be used to show that this conclusion is not inevitable; that between belief and knowledge or justified belief. What is socially originated and acquired by passive acceptance from uncriticised external authorities is simply belief. Many or most of the beliefs acquired in this way may be justifiable and many of the authorities who cause them to be believed may have a justification for them. But in general our beliefs in the early stages of our careers, before we have achieved cognitive autonomy, are not justified beliefs, and thus not really knowledge, for us.

What the epistemologist does is to set out the conditions for the justification of beliefs which we in fact acquire before we are in a position to justify them. In arguing that certain things have to be known or rationally believed before other things are known or rationally believed he is not committed to the view that the former are as a matter of fact acquired as beliefs before the latter. It is fair to say that epistemologists have not usually drawn attention to the conclusion that does follow which is that to start with very few of our beliefs are justified, at all times many are not and many again are justified only precariously and indirectly. Belief is historically, as well as logically, prior to knowledge.

There is a measure of analogy between the individualism of epistemology and the social contract theory of government. It is not a relevant objection to the latter that as a matter of fact men did not create political institutions in the state of nature by means of jointly entering into a system of mutual obligations. The social contract theorist holds that a state *deserves* the allegiance of its citizens, that it *ought* to be obeyed by them, only if they have promised one another to submit to it or, more plausibly, if it operates in such a way as to make such a promise reasonable. He does not maintain that political institutions in fact first originated by promissory agreement or even that men's submission to them is to be explained causally in terms of the recognition of obligations so generated.

The individualistic epistemologist, then, can admit that for much of the time much of what we believe is derived by uncritical acceptance from external authorities. What he affirms is that the acceptance of such authority can be justified and only by the application of the non-social faculties we have of perception, memory and inference. We have to perceive the means by which authorities communicate with us as real events in the common world, attach a meaning to them and proportion the measure of acceptance we give to the beliefs thus identified to the critically assessed reliability of the authorities in question. So however primary testimony may be in the historical order of our beliefs it is still secondary in the logical order of knowledge.

There is, therefore, no real collision between the individualism of epistemology and the fact of the social character of our beliefs. We cannot acquire knowledge or justified belief until we have achieved cognitive autonomy and we do not achieve it until we have acquired a good many beliefs without justification. But most of these initial beliefs are no doubt both justifiable and justified for someone and in due course we do, after all, achieve cognitive autonomy. In achieving it we become able to discharge the debts we have incurred, that stock of borrowed beliefs which enabled us to get started.

If this line of argument is correct it would seem that Popper's claim that individualistic epistemology is altogether on the wrong track is unwarranted. He goes on to conclude that epistemology should not concern itself with the justification of beliefs at all but should, rather, examine the methods by which beliefs are criticised. He associates the study of justification with the assumption that truth is manifest, an assumption whose pervasiveness and undesirability he convincingly demonstrates. But it is with certification rather than justification that the assumption that truth is manifest is connected. To take it that some of our beliefs can and should be justified is an altogether more modest supposition than that any of them are intrinsically and self-evidently certain or, in other words, that in some cases at least truth is manifest.

Popper also advances an argument against the idea that epistemology should concern itself with the sources of knowledge. It would be pointless, he says, in attempting to assess the merits of a newspaper report to try to seek out the actual sources of the reporter's belief or assertion. It would itself rest on further testimony and also on a mass of background knowledge which would ramify out indefinitely. In such circumstances we should occupy ourselves not with origins but with validity. Now it is no doubt true that the soundest check on the reliability of a witness is to investigate the content of his report for oneself. If this is practically impossible one still does not have to examine the actual, historical sources of his belief. One can assess his general reliability in various ways or check his testimony against that of others. But, in any case, if we ignore the actual sources of *his* belief this does not mean either that we are not concerned to justify the claim in question or that we do not do so by recourse to sources of knowledge in the epistemologist's sense. To make his argument work Popper has to circumscribe the concept of a source of knowledge in an irrelevantly narrow way.

IV. A PROBLEM OF CIRCULARITY

But although this prima facie incompatibility between the individualism of the theory of knowledge and the social determination of belief is only apparent there is a further difficulty lying beneath the surface of the problem. This is that the instruments of criticism in whose possession cognitive autonomy consists are themselves provided by authority. We acquire from other people (1) the observation-language which makes what might be called theoretically usable perception possible, (2) the logic with which bodies of beliefs are criticised and developed and (3) the methodology which specifies the degree of support given to theory by observation. This would seem to introduce a vicious circularity into the growth of knowledge. The claims of authority can be justified only by means which authority itself has provided. We can weigh the purported pound of sugar only on the scales the grocer himself supplies.

The essential point on which this problem rests is one that has generally been ignored in the comparatively small number of epistemological discussions of testimony that there are; external authority is the original source not only of items of information, singular and general, but also of language, logic and method, the indispensable means for the formulation and critical assessment of our beliefs. When this is recognised the problem of justifying the acceptance of testimony moves to a new level and is intensified since the genuineness of the cognitive autonomy which is supposed to solve it is put in question.

I am going to argue that testimony must, broadly speaking or on balance, be reliable. The argument will be transcendental in character. Like H.H. Price (*Belief*, Series 1, Lecture 5, pp. 117-19) I do not regard the principle that testimony is broadly reliable as an inductive generalisation. But I do so for a different reason. His position is that the principle is too weakly confirmed to derive the degree of confidence we place in it from the inductive evidence in its favour, which he takes to be very limited and sketchy. My point is that the rules of inductive reasoning which would be involved in establishing it as an inductive generalisation are themselves derived from the external authorities whose reliability is in question. Therefore to argue for that reliability on inductive grounds would circularly involve its assumption at least with regard to the inductive lessons they teach.

I shall approach my argument for the principle that testimony is broadly reliable by way of a related argument of Russell's which appeared first in his *Outline of Philosophy* (p.178) and again in his *Human Knowledge* (p.206). Despite the facts that he presented the argument twice at an interval of twenty-one years and that it is of a mathematical nature I am bold enough to assert that it is fallacious. 'If twelve men', he says, 'each of whom lies every other time that he speaks, independently testify that some event has occurred, the odds in favour of their all speaking the truth are 4,095 to 1.'

In fact, in the circumstances described, the odds are evens. Admittedly there are 4,096 distinguishable distributions of truth and falsity between twelve utterances as to the P-hood of S. Furthermore in only one of these do they all agree in saying what is false. But equally in only one of these do they all agree in saying what is true. In the other 4,094 cases the witnesses disagree, some say what is true, some say what is false. And these are irrelevant to Russell's calculation since it is one of the conditions of the situation as he describes it that the twelve witnesses all say the same thing about the event in question.

But now consider the somewhat less bleak assumption about the reliability of witnesses that for every three statements a witness makes two will be true and one false. In that case the probability that whatever the majority of a group of five witnesses agrees about is true is 0.79 (roughly odds of 4 to 1 on). If the group of such two-thirds truth-tellers is thirteen in number the probability that what the majority agree to is true goes up to 0.89 (roughly odds of 9 to 1 on).

Under this more cheerful assumption about human credibility the chances that what is *unanimously* testified to by a group is true go up very rapidly. If the group of five is unanimous the odds on what they agree about being true is 32 to 1 on. If the group is twelve in number the odds are very near to Russell's being 4,096 to 1 on. For a group of a dozen two-thirds truth-tellers there are 3^{12} (=531,441) relevant distributions of truth and falsity (not all distinguishable, as in the former case, since truth has to appear twice as often as falsity). Of these, however, only 4,097 have all the witnesses saying the same thing, 4,096 all true, 1 all false. It is conceivable that Russell was working from this assumption of two-thirds veracity but it somehow seems more likely to me that he got the number right and the application wrong than the other way round.

In the light of these arithmetical considerations it is plain that, if we can reasonably assume that witnesses are more likely to say what is true than what is false, if we can assume more than Russell's perfect evenhandedness about their veracity, what the majority of them agree about will carry a great deal of weight. There is a practical factor that must be emphasised, however. For the arithmetic to apply the witnesses must be independent of one another and must not be simply passing on each other's testimony, conditions it is not in practice always easy to be sure are satisfied.

V. WHY MOST TESTIMONY MUST BE RELIABLE

The reason why most testimony must be reliable, or at least that part of it which relates to the current environment of witness and client, is that unless it were predominantly true what witnesses say could not be understood, and thus identified as testimony, at all. How do we come to understand the sentences that other people utter? In the first instance, at any rate, only by becoming aware of a regular correlation between a given repeated pattern of utterance and a repeated kind of observable situation which usually accompanies it. Unless we become aware of such a regular correlation between utterance-pattern and situation-type we cannot take that pattern to be an observation-sentence. Until we have identified the observation-sentences of those who speak to us we cannot make sense of that large remainder of their utterances which do not refer to the immediate, perceptual environment. For the non-observational statements of other people have to be explained in terms of antecedently understood statements of observation.

I do not think that this argument presupposes either that there are pure observation-statements or that there is any precisely demarcated boundary between observation-statements and others but it would be too laborious to try to make this out in detail. It is enough that there should be in everyone's learning of language a class of sentences whose use he learns in the presence of what they refer to, without reliance on the sentences already understood, and that members of this class should play an indispensable part in the learning of all other sentences.

To make the point in a slightly different way: suppose you are confronted with a collection of people who have a practice of coming out with articulate utterances, many of which recur. Any such recurrent pattern that is fairly regularly associated with a recurrent type of observable situation can at least be taken to be a more or less reliable sign that a situation of the correlated type obtains. The next step would be to take it as a report which is true just in case the situation is of the type with which instances of the pattern in question have been predominantly associated hitherto. There are only two possibilities: either a language we do not know is intelligible to us, in which case most of what it is used to say must be true, or it is not intelligible to us at all.

This conclusion applies as much to our relations with our primary linguistic community, the one from we acquire our native language, as it does to our relations with any external linguistic community whose language we are trying to find out how to translate into our own. I acquire membership of my primary linguistic community by imitating the practices that I find going on in it. I attach that meaning to the utterances I imitate which is determined by the assumption that they are true of those circumstances in which they are predominantly produced by other speakers. I am then either received into the community with praise and reward of my utterances or I am not. If not I try to modify my utterances in a praise-yielding way. If I succeed and hit on a habit which observably conforms to the practice of others and secures their endorsement well and good. If not I simply fail to master the language. There could be several reasons for that: the tendency to utterance I observe might conceivably not be a language proper at all; I may be too dim, in my intellect or my senses, to pick up the prevailing rules; it is even possible that the community of established speakers is malicious, that its members, behaving as counter-inductive demons, allow or encourage me to acquire an understanding of their utterances which is different from their own. Whether they teach me their rules but then consistently speak falsely or instil rules that are not theirs but then speak truly I should end up in a state of hopeless confusion. So either most of the statements I hear are true or I cannot attach any sense to them.

In one of his discussions of testimony Russell says: 'that we learn to speak correctly is a testimonial to the habitual veracity of our parents.' This is perhaps too fulsome. Unless they were habitually veracious on the whole, at least in their dealings with the other members of the linguistic community, into which they recruit us, there would be no such community, because there would be no language and therefore no such goal as understanding for us to achieve.

It will not have escaped attention that what I have tended to present as a ground for the acceptance of testimony generally applies directly only to observation-statements. Can it be extended to apply to non-observational beliefs as well? For this purpose a distinction between two ways in which, in principle, a belief may be non-observational should be drawn. Some beliefs are non-observational, as regards particular individual believers, for circumstantial reasons, in that, although they relate to observable situations, these situations are not part of the present, or remembered, perceptual environment of the believer. Only someone who is prevented from moving about can be systematically deceived about the observable, but by him unobserved, state of the world, someone who is unable to bring the situation itself within his environment, in the case where it is persistent (for example, 'there is a cathedral in Salisbury') or its causal consequences, where it is not (for example, 'there was an explosion in Belfast last night'). Such cases come, then, a little insecurely, under the rule.

Other beliefs are non-observational in a non-relative or formal way: beliefs that are logically general, whether explicitly or not, and beliefs about unobservable, theoretical entities. To deal with these we need to consider those instruments of criticism whose derivation from others constituted a prima facie argument against the genuineness of cognitive autonomy; language, logic and method. I have argued that an understanding of language is necessarily connected with the predominant truth of a good deal of testimony. It also implies the grasp of a certain amount of logic. It is part of my understanding of 'this is red' that it implies both 'this is not green' and 'this is not not-red'. But if elementary logic and the observation-language are given then at least the means are at hand for the falsification of theories. One does not understand 'all A are B' unless one recognises that 'this A is not B' contradicts it. For some methodologists, pre-eminently Popper, this is enough. Others would claim that we need and possess a positive logic of inductive confirmation which would determine which of the unbounded host of possible theories compatible with a body of observational evidence is best supported by it. But even without that somewhat controversial endowment we have, in elementary deductive logic and an understanding of the observation-language, means for the critical assessment of theoretical testimony which are sufficient to eliminate definitely false items and at the same time are not dependent on an ungroundable assumption about the reliability of authorities for their acceptance. In other words the justified acceptance of observation-statements and logic is not dependent on an independent check on the reliability of the authorities from whom we take them.

It is true that a great deal of authority and testimony is false or unjustified. To deal with that we have to develop specific principles of credibility of the form: what A says about subject X is in most cases probably true, where A can be an individual or a type of individual. Everyone gradually builds up a complex body of such specific principles under the impact of disconcerting experiences with secondhand car dealers and Irishmen. In every case of apparent testimony we must at least be ready to ask: is he honest, is he well-informed, does he use words in the ordinary way, did he actually say something, is he really there? But the general principle ensures that such questions will receive negative answers only in exceptional cases. The very possibility of our being deceived by witnesses presupposes that there is enough true testimony about to support the language which is used to deceive us.

VI. EPISTEMOLOGY, AUTHORITY AND AUTONOMY

Epistemology is the critical examination of the ways in which beliefs are arrived at. Because of its primary concern with *justified* belief it has always treated the belief-system of an individual as a strictly personal construction and emphasised the ultimate sources of knowledge – perception, memory and inference – which are personal rather than social. But since most of our beliefs, and indeed most of our justified beliefs, are in fact derived from authority it should perhaps pay more attention than it traditionally has to the criticism of authorities.

Cognitive autonomy is achieved when the capacity for the criticism of authorities and of personally-formed beliefs, which epistemology studies as a matter of explicit theory, has become an operative skill. Although the basic instruments of criticism are in fact causally dependent on authority, since we do not invent our observation-language and logic for ourselves, they are not dependent for their acceptability on the particular credentials of the source from which they are acquired. Thus cognitive autonomy is genuine, despite an appearance of circularity.

An absolutely minimum conception of cognitive education sees it as the authoritative communication of knowledge. Everyone would agree that this is quite inadequate by itself; cognitive autonomy has to be fostered as well. The pupil learns to acquire knowledge on his own: both for its own sake, because he needs it for use, and as a basis for the critical assessment of authorities. In particular he needs to learn how to assess the reliability of authorities indirectly, for he can never, in practice, dispense with them altogether. The philosophical theory of knowledge approaches the critical practice which is the exercise of cognitive autonomy from a theoretical point of view; it makes the instruments of primary criticism accessible to criticism themselves. It can also show that these instruments do not owe their acceptability to the very authorities to which they are applied even if they are, in fact, initially supplied by them.

9

Social Objects

I. WHAT IS A SOCIAL OBJECT?

By a social object I mean a group or institution which contains or involves a number of individual human beings, such as a people, a nation, a class, a community, an association, a society, even, perhaps, Society itself. There are other kinds of social entity, involving a plurality of people, besides what I am calling social objects. First, there are large-scale historical events: the Thirty Years' War, the French Revolution, the economic depression of the 1930s. Secondly, there are social forces or movements, such as the French Enlightenment, romanticism, the liberal tradition, even, possibly, the *Zeitgeist*.

I shall confine my attention to social objects proper as I have described them, since I think it is reasonable to assume that all statements about the other kinds of social entity can be recast as statements about social objects, that is, groups or institutions. To say that the war of 1939 was the real cure for the depression of the 1930s is to say that the countries that had been economically depressed in the 1930s recovered when and because many of them started to go to war with each other. Similarly to say that the French Enlightenment drew its inspiration from Locke is to say that the progressive thinkers of eighteenth century France derived their leading ideas from the writings of Locke.

It would be convenient if this assumption were correct since we have a firmer logical grasp of objects than of events and processes. We have a clearer notion of the criteria for individuation and identification of the former than we do of the latter. I am not assuming that events and processes in general are reducible to objects in this way, only that events and processes of a social or historical kind are. Nor have I any very precise criterion for distinguishing social entities that are objects from those that are not. A rough and ready verbal or grammatical test is available. Objects can be naturally and properly said to exist and to come into or go out of existence. Events and processes, on the other hand, occur, happen or take place. On this basis the name of a social entity such as 'the French Enlightenment', can be the name either of an object or of a process. When we say that the French Enlightenment ceased to exist with the advent of Napoleon, we are talking about a social object, a particular human group. But when we say that the French Enlightenment came to an end with the advent of Napoleon we are talking about a process, the intellectual activity characteristic of that group of people.

Social objects are the theoretical entities of history and social science.

They are, I suggest, the form of generality that is proper to history, as contrasted with laws, the form of generality proper to science. They are, furthermore, what distinguishes history proper from chronicle, although even in the latter some mention is likely to be made of such obvious and, at least intermittently, visible groups or institutions as the Witan or the host. The names of social objects are the characteristic subject-terms of the laws of social science: classes and reference-groups in sociology; governments, parliaments and parties in politics; firms and industries in economics. In so far as individual people are mentioned in the laws of social science it will be as the occupiers of particular social rôles, and to occupy a rôle is to stand in a certain relation to other people within a group or institution.

On the whole, the natural sciences of man treat him in isolation, for example, physiology. Where, as in evolutionary biology, these sciences treat man in relation to other people, the relations involved are natural relations of biological parenthood or competition for food supply. What is characteristic of the relations studied by the social sciences is that they involve consciousness of each other in the people related. Two men can be in biological competition for food if one gets to it first, unaware of the fact that the other was planning to eat it. If they start fighting over it or try to outwit each other in securing it the relation becomes social. There is, of course, no precise demarcation between natural and social relations between people (or other animals).

II. COLLECTIVISM AND INDIVIDUALISM

Two broad kinds of interpretation have been given of the nature of social objects. The individualist view is that there is no more to a group or institution than the individuals who compose it and the collectivist view is that there is more. These are, in the first instance, ontological doctrines which can be expressed in the idiom of philosophical analysis as the theses that statements about social objects can or cannot be reduced, are or are not logically equivalent to, statements about the individuals who are the members of the groups or institutions in question.

What I have described as ontological individualism and collectivism are ordinarily called methodological individualism and collectivism. The aim of this qualification is entirely virtuous. It is to mark off the point at issue from that in dispute between ethical individualists, who take the ultimate good to be the good of individuals, and ethical collectivists, who hold that the needs and interests of the group ought to prevail over those of its members. It is these ethical positions that are commonly described as individualism and collectivism *tout court*. The ethical versions of these doctrines are usually associated with the non-ethical versions and it seems generally to be supposed that some relation of implication holds between them, an implication that can hold only if its two terms are conceived as distinct.

I believe that there is also a distinction on the non-ethical side between ontological individualism and collectivism and methodological individualism and collectivism properly so called. The ontological theses concern the reducibility of objects or the definability of terms. The methodological theses, on the other hand, concern the derivability of laws. It is, *prima facie*, one thing to say that statements referring to social objects can or cannot be translated into statements referring to individual people, another to say that all laws in which social objects are mentioned can be derived from laws in which only individual persons are mentioned. In view of this I shall reserve the term 'methodological' for the doctrines about explanation or the derivability of laws, and describe what I take to be the more fundamental issue of the reducibility of social objects as ontological. (The distinction between ontological and methodological forms of the opposition between individualists and collectivists has been recognised by Nagel, in *The Structure of Science*, who marks it with the terms 'connectibility' and 'derivability', and by Popper, in *The Open Society*, who distinguishes the dispute between ontological individualism and collectivism from that between 'psychologism' and 'sociologism' and goes on to support individualism as an ontological thesis about reducibility while supporting collectivism as a methodological thesis about explanation.)

The ontological problems of social objects is closely analogous to the problem of the status of theoretical entities in natural science. The latter, things like atoms, molecules, cells and viruses, are at once the main items referred to in the laws of natural science and also share with social objects the property of being theoretical, that is to say, in some way or other, unobservable. The two main theories about the nature of theoretical entities in the physical world are realism, which takes them to be distinct from straightforwardly observable common objects, and instrumentalism or positivism, which maintains that statements about them are reducible to statements about common objects.

Realism about physical things can be affirmed in two different ways. More moderately it can take theoretical entities to be the literal parts of common objects. More radically it takes such theoretical entities to be the real constituents of the physical world while the common objects of everyday observation are more or less illusory appearances. The more radical kind of physical realism infers its Lockean conclusion from the greater scope and precision of physical theory in comparison with the findings of ordinary observation and from the inconsistencies it discerns between such findings and those of physical theory. What common observation finds to be coloured, continuous and stable, physical theory, it is held, shows to be really colourless, discontinuous and in rapid motion.

The version of ontological collectivism about social objects put forward by Hegelian idealism is comparably radical in maintaining that social objects are somehow more real than the individual human beings involved in them. This principle is ordinarily derived from a very strong interpretation of the thesis that man is essentially a social being. It is often associated, furthermore, with the idea that a social object, a group or institution, is itself a mind or person, of a higher, more 'objective' sort than an individual mind or person.

Moderate ontological collectivism about social objects need amount to no more than the negative thesis that they are not analysable in terms of the individuals who compose them. In that form, like its physical analogue, it need not hold that individual people are any less real than the social objects of which they are members.

Physical reductionism usually takes theoretical entities to be *less* real than the common objects to which statements about such entities ultimately refer. It regards them as logical constructions or abstractions, as useful *façons de parler* or symbolic conveniences. Its social analogue, ontological individualism, adopts the same attitude to social objects.

I shall expound and defend a position about the nature of social objects which is intermediate between the extremes of holding them to be more or less real than individual people. I am an ontological individualist in believing statements about social objects to be statements about individuals, interrelated in certain ways. But I do not take the relation of a social object to its human constituents to be that of a logical construction to its elements. It is, rather, that of a whole to its parts, both of which are equally real and objective.

To reconcile these two positions I shall aim to show that although social objects are in a way constructed out of people, the mode of construction is not one that carries any ontological implications. It is, I shall argue, a categorical construction, like that involved in arriving at the conception of the solar system from observation of the lawfully regular behaviour of its components, and not a hypothetical construction, like the average man, or material things and mental states as understood by phenomenalists and behaviourists.

III. SOCIAL OBJECTS AS CONCRETE UNIVERSALS

The idea that social objects, in particular the state, but also class and family, are more real than their individual members is first explicit in Hegel's theory of objective mind. 'The consciously free substance', Hegel says, 'has actuality as the spirit of a nation. The abstract disruption of this spirit singles it out into *persons*, whose independence it, however, controls and entirely dominates from within.' The state, he goes on, 'is the self-conscious ethical substance' and 'as a living mind the state only is as an organised whole'. Its rational, universal will is opposed by Hegel to the idea of 'a common will as the sum and resultant of atomistic single wills', 'an idea which has on it "the mark of unreality of an abstraction" '. History, in Hegel's view, 'should not concern itself with individuals but with the state, or, which is the same thing, with mind or spirit in history'. 'The self-consciousness of particular nations is a vehicle for the contemporary development of the collective spirit in its actual existence: it is the objective actuality in which that spirit for the time invests its will'.

The state, although the highest, is not the only ethical substance, which may be immediate or natural, as in the family, or relative, as in the estates or classes that make up civil society. In marriage, persons, with their exclusive individualities, 'combine to form a single person'. Civil society is a multiplicity of people engaged in the satisfaction of their wants. Through the division of labour that leads to their allocation to classes or estates. 'As belonging to such a definite and stable sphere', Hegel says, 'men have their actual existence'. The system of estates is politically significant as relating the individual to the state. 'It is not in the inorganic form of mere individuals as such (after the *democratic* fashion of election) but as organic factors, as estates, that men enter upon that participation'. Hegel condemns individualistic notions of liberty and equality for their abstractness.

Hegel's theory of objective mind clearly affirms three propositions mentioned earlier as central to the radical form of ontological collectivism. First, man is essentially social, he is always a member of groups and institutions and is made what he is by that fact. Secondly, the group is more real, more concrete and substantial than its members. Thirdly, groups are themselves minds or persons, they are self-conscious and have minds and wills of their own.

Bosanquet makes the same points more clearly and unequivocally. He praises Rousseau for being the first to see that 'the essence of human society consists in a common self, a life and a mind'. Society, he says, is a 'moral person', not 'an abstraction or fiction of the reflective mind'. It is a mistake to accept 'the absolute and naturally independent existence of the physical individual'. It follows that 'the common self or moral person of a society is more real than the apparent individuals'. The reality of groups and institutions is not the particular people they comprise but 'an identical connection between minds'.

The starting-point of the theory of objective mind is that man is essentially social. Men are truly men, and not mere anthropoid animals, to the extent that they are rational, self-conscious and moral. Rationality, and the language which is its indispensable vehicle, is social. Self-consciousness requires that consciousness of others which is the defining condition of the existence of social rather than natural relations between them. Morality is of its nature a social phenomenon, a concern with the bearings of one's actions on others. There is, it is then inferred, an asymmetrical dependence of individuals on society and the groups and institutions in which it is articulated, a dependence analogous to that of attributes on substances, states of mind on conscious subjects or creatures on God. Society is concrete substance; the individual is abstract attribute. Finally, societies or social objects are themselves self-conscious subjects or persons, with minds, wills and interests.

IV. SOCIAL OBJECTS AS LOGICAL CONSTRUCTIONS

The standard empiricist theory of the nature of social objects is that they are logical constructions. This is as often assumed as explicitly argued for, since the state and other social objects are often called in as paradigm logical constructions in order to explain the application of that concept to more controversial cases such as material things and minds. Thus Ayer, giving an account of contextual definition in general, says 'the English state is a logical construction out of individual people' and Wisdom explains that 'to say that a chair is a logical construction out of appearances of a chair is to say that a chair is related to its appearances ... as (amongst other things) a family is to its members'.

There is, however, a straightforward argument for the thesis. It is that social objects can be significantly referred to and described but their names are neither ostensively definable nor explicitly definable in terms of ostensively definable expressions that can be uniformly substituted without alteration of meaning for all occurrences of the name in question. The only other way of endowing the names of social objects with meaning is by contextual definition, the provision of rules for replacing statements in which they occur with statements that refer only to unproblematic entities, the significance of whose names gives no trouble.

The names of social objects are not ostensively definable because social objects cannot be observed. I can observe a member, or several members, of the class of unskilled workers, but I cannot observe the class of unskilled workers as such. They are not, in general, explicitly definable since it is very often the case that the predicates ascribed to them either cannot be significantly applied to the unproblematic entities from which they are held to be constructed, or, where they can be significantly applied to them, may well not be true of them although they are true of the social object involved. The German people is numerous but no individual German can be significantly said to be so. The Japanese nation is larger than the Swedish nation, but, on the whole, individual Japanese are smaller than individual Swedes.

It must be admitted that the unobservability of social objects is not very absolute. Relatively small ones – the Cabinet posing for a group photograph, the Jones family at its Christmas gathering, even an army division – are sometimes so arranged as to be straightforwardly observable. But that is the exceptional case. We refer significantly to and make true or at least justified statements about social objects that have never been observed in that sort of way. Our understanding of the names of, and our knowledge or well-founded beliefs about, the great majority of social objects is not directly observational. These things are linked with observation by way of our perception of the activities of individual people who are members of the social objects in question. If not strictly unobservable, then, social objects are not, on the whole, effectively observed.

The theoretical entities of natural science owe their characteristic unobservability to the fact that they are too small. Those of social science elude observation because they are too large and, even more, too scattered. However, there are some parallels to this in physical science, above all in astronomy. The conception of the solar system is a potentially observational one in that we know what it would look like from a rocket very much further from the earth than any rocket has yet travelled. But this conception has been constructed from observation of particular elements of the solar system of the relations between them. The same is true of social objects like nations and classes.

In some cases, which may be called summative, statements about social objects are equivalent to statements otherwise the same that refer explicitly, if at some level of generality, to individual people. To say that the French middle class is thrifty is to say that most French middle-class people are. Quite often to say that the A group is F is to say that all or most or the most influential people who are A are F. But the predicate F is often either not significantly or not truly predictable of A people, although significantly and truly predicable of the A group. The British aristocracy is hierarchically arranged and the Unitarian church is getting smaller but British aristocrats are physically organised much as other men are and individual Unitarians have not shrunk. Carelessness about this can have quaint results. After the General Election of 1964 *The Times* said that the British electorate had been unable to make up its mind. Yet more people voted in 1964 than in the more decisive election of 1966.

Apart from this, predicative, obstacle to explicit definition of the names of social objects, there are many non-summative, primarily institutional, statements about such objects, for example 'Holland has declared war on Belgium' or 'the Acme Company has laid off half its labour force'. The ultimate reference here is to some identifiable collection of decision-making people, the rulers or management of the institution in question, but, so described, they still constitute a social object and to express the facts in terms of individual people will require more complex and specific predicates than 'declared war' or 'laid off workers'.

The names of many social objects are notably ambiguous, particularly, but not exclusively, those of nation-states. To speak of France may be to speak of all or most Frenchmen *or* of the French government *or* of a portion of the earth's surface. The same variety of reference is possible with 'the Bank of England' or 'the Athenaeum'.

For the reasons given, separately or in combination, it turns out more often than not that the sense of a statement about a social object cannot be conveyed by a statement which differs from the original only in substituting an explicit, if general, reference to some collection of individual people for the name of the social object.

But if the names of social objects cannot be ostensively defined, or, at any rate, are not in practice so defined, and cannot be explicitly defined in ostensive terms, they must, if they are to be endowed with empirical meaning and the statements in which they occur are to be brought under empirical control, be defined contextually. And to say that is to say that social objects are logical constructions.

What that is taken to imply is that social objects are not concrete things but abstractions, convenient devices of abbreviation for thinking about the social actions and relations of individual human beings, even, in the hyperbolic term favoured by Hume and Russell, fictions. The defensible empiricist thesis that social objects are not distinct from the people involved in them, are nothing but their members, appropriately related, is taken to amount to the proposition that they do not really exist in their own right at all. I shall argue that the reducibility of social objects to people does not have such an implication since it is of a different kind from that of the average man to individual men or of the phenomenalist's material thing to appearances. It is rather that involved in the relation of a whole to its parts, of a wood, for example, to its trees. A wood is nothing but the trees that compose it, suitably arranged, but it is as real and concrete a thing as any of them is. The standard version of ontological individualism seems unable to acknowledge the wood for the trees.

V. METHODOLOGICAL IMPLICATIONS

The two ontological doctrines I have set out have methodological implications. Collectivism in its moderate, negative form, where it holds that social objects are irreducible to individuals, seems to imply that observation of the acts and relations of people must be insufficient by itself to establish the truth or falsity of statements about social objects. The radical form of collectivism makes the point more strongly. How can beliefs about what is not real determine the truth or falsity of our beliefs about what is?

One theory of our knowledge of social fact that proceeds from this assumption is that which distinguishes *verstehen* from *erklären*, the empathetic understanding that is proper to the apprehension of facts about social beings from the merely external perception we bring to the constituents of physical nature. A variant of this theory is the Wittgensteinian view that our understanding of human action as done for reasons is something quite distinct from the explanations we give of natural happenings in terms of their causes.

In a less articulate way, what Popper calls 'sociologism' asserts that the laws of social science cannot be derived from laws of individual psychology, the error, as he sees it, of 'psychologism'. Psychologism is the type of general social theory propounded by Hobbes, by Hume and other thinkers of the Scottish Enlightenment, by the classical economists and by Mill in his account of the logic of the moral sciences.

Idealist social theory, stemming from Hegel, is opposed to the element of intuitionism in the doctrine of *verstehen*, but it would agree that psychologism is mistaken, on the ground that it assumes the existence of an abstract, universal and timeless human nature, when in fact human nature is a historical variable. Positively it contends that the understanding of social fact is confined to abstract appearance if it is no more than the inductive assemblage of observable facts about individual people. A true understanding of social fact may start with the inductive accumulation of such material but it must go on to a philosophical grasp of the inner, rational nature and relations of what is observed.

Ontological individualism simply denies that any special mode of access to social facts is required for knowledge of them to be obtained. Since statements about social objects are equivalent and reducible to statements about individual people, it must follow that every law expressed in social terms is expressible as a law about individuals. For this reason some critics have failed to see how Popper can consistently claim to support what he calls methodological individualism and, at the same time, reject psychologism.

In general, the ontological individualist recognises no fundamental difference of method between physical and social science. Both begin with ordinary perceptual observation, seek to arrive at causal laws and to articulate these causal laws into a theoretical system. Both are at liberty to introduce new theoretical notions, but these notions must be somehow definable in terms of the objects of ordinary observation.

VI. ETHICAL IMPLICATIONS

As well as these methodological implications about the nature of our knowledge of social fact, the two ontological doctrines also have implications of an ethical kind. Ethical collectivism takes two forms. The first and more important is the view that the interests and well-being of the group are more valuable than those of the individual and ought to override them. In some sense, no doubt, anyone would accept that. If the interests involved are more or less commensurate, the interests of the great majority, it would be agreed, should override the interests of a few. What gives this principle of ethical collectivism its controversial force is the theory that the common good of the group is not simply the sum of the interests of its members. Just as, for the ontological collectivist, the group is not merely the whole or aggregate of its individual members, so, for the ethical collectivist, the welfare of the group is not an aggregate of individual welfares.

For the ethical individualist social objects, groups or institutions, have no intrinsic value that is not constitutive of the welfare of individual people. He sees social objects either as sums of individuals or as institutions and in the latter case any value they possess is purely instrumental. The point was put with memorable vigour by that untypically individualistic idealist McTaggart: 'Compared with the worship of the state, zoolatry is rational and dignified. A bull or a crocodile may not have great intrinsic value, but it has some, for it is a conscious being. The state has none. It would be as reasonable to worship a sewage-pipe, which also possesses considerable value as a means.'

The sharp distinction between common and individual good assumed by the first form of ethical collectivism starts from Rousseau's distinction between the private, self-regarding, more or less competitive satisfactions of individuals and the more public-spirited and selfless satisfactions they can enjoy as citizens. But both Rousseau's kinds of satisfaction exist only to the extent that individuals actually experience them. They are, as it were, essentially located in individuals.

But when the idea that the group is more real than the individual is superimposed on the distinction between common and individual good, the ethical collectivist conclusion naturally follows: that the good of the group, as real, is more important than, and should therefore override, the good of its individual members, which is only abstract appearance.

If the further thesis of ontological collectivism, that the group is itself a person, of a higher kind than its component individuals, is embraced, the supremacy of the common good is only further entrenched. If a group really is a person, then the idea that it has a good of its own is more effectively established and, to the extent that it is a superior kind of person to ordinary individuals, it follows that its good is of a higher and more important kind.

A second form of ethical collectivism holds that the group is more authoritative than its members with regard to what is right and, therefore, that the moral convictions of the group are more worthy of acceptance than the deliverances of the individual conscience where the two conflict. This point of view is expressed in Hegel's elevation of *Sittlichkeit*, or social ethics, above *Moralität*, or the morality of the individual conscience. True moral wisdom, on this view, consists in the individual's subordinating his spontaneous moral impulses to the prevailing prescriptions, and, in particular, the positive law, of the community of which he is a member.

Ethical individualism simply denies both these propositions. It takes value to be realised only in the experiences of individual human beings and takes the common good to be no more than the sum or aggregate of such experiences. Furthermore, it takes individuals to be morally authoritative. Although it can allow that some individual moral convictions are likely to be better founded than others, it attaches no special importance to the prevailing moral sentiments of the community at large.

VII. CRITIQUE OF THE THEORY OF OBJECTIVE MIND

The principle that man is an essentially social being, on which the theory that groups and institutions are more real and concrete than the individual people involved in them rests, is not seriously disputable. What makes human beings human, or, more precisely, persons, is their rationality and their moral capacity. There is, indeed, a comparatively trivial mode of dependence of men on other human beings, their biological parents, for coming into existence at all and, in all but the most exceptional cases, for nurture. To become rational beings men need to become incorporated in a linguistic community and to become moral agents they need to be brought up as members of a social system of rights and duties. However, the most minimal and rudimentary of social groups, the family, is sufficient for both accomplishments.

There are, of course, true human beings who have withdrawn from society, hermits and castaways, but they have first been socially formed. Robinson Crusoe and Ben Gunn (once his passion for cheese had been satisfied) did not have to start again from the beginning when they rejoined the society of their fellow-men. Wolf-children, on the other hand, nurtured from birth by non-human animals, are not fully human persons when they come into human society.

But if men are essentially social, societies are even more essentially human. A memberless society is logically inconceivable, a contradiction in terms. A wholly unsocial man, one who has not passed at least an extended, humanly formative, period in social relations with other human beings, is at most a contingent or empirical impossibility. It is not logically necessary that all human beings should have human parents (indeed it is logically impossible if the human species had a beginning), that they owe their survival to other human beings and not self-preservative instinct, and that they did not invent language for themselves.

This distinction between kinds of impossibility may be questioned. It is widely held that self-consciousness necessarily presupposes consciousness of others and that a private language is not just unactual but inconceivable. For the purpose in hand this can be conceded. All I am trying to show is that there is not an asymmetrical dependence of men on society. For that it is sufficient to establish that there is as much dependence in one direction as in the other.

As a last resort a defender of the original thesis of asymmetry might argue that, although memberless societies are uncommon, they are not impossible since there actually are some. A college might have an archery club all of whose members leave and which, after an interval, is started up again. It could still be said to exist during the interval. It might still be listed in the college handbook, with blanks or the word 'vacant' beside the words 'president' and 'secretary'. This is, at any rate, a pretty fragile sort of existence, an existence by courtesy, based on the fact that it has had members, will probably have members in the future and may have property, archery equipment, say, in the hands of some such ontologically reliable custodian as the college bursar. It would be at least as natural to say that there is no archery club during the interval.

Individuals are, then, certainly no more, and arguably less, dependent on social objects than the latter are on them. Men are essentially social but, since societies must have members, there is no ground for the claim that societies are in some way more real and concrete than the individuals who compose them.

Is there any other ground for this central proposition of the theory of objective mind? A social object is, in a way, larger and more comprehensive than its human components. But that does not make it more real. The Galaxy is larger and more comprehensive than the solar system. It is no more, and no less real than the groups of heavenly bodies, or particular heavenly bodies, that go to make it up.

The elusive idea that societies are more real than their members is encouraged by three comparisons with supposedly parallel relationships in which one term is held to be more real or concrete than the other. The first of these is the relation of substance and attribute. Substance, conceived in the Aristotelian way as formed matter, and not as bare *substratum*, is certainly the paradigm of concreteness, as attributes, in themselves and uninstantiated, are of abstraction. But individual people cannot seriously be considered to be attributes of social objects. A society will always have attributes, such as vitality, integration or stability, but its human members are not among them. Individuals can, indeed, be shared by different social objects, as attributes are shared by different substances. This differentiates the members of social groups from such proprietary parts of things as limbs, which can be part of only one body at a given time. As capable of sharing members social objects resemble logical classes, although as will be seen there are crucial differences between the two. But classes are taken to be more, not less, abstract than their members. In general, sharing does not relate its terms asymmetrically. A tomato and a carpet may share the attribute of redness; but redness and roundness may also share a tomato that is an instance of both.

The second parallel case of allegedly asymmetrical dependence is that of mental states on a mind or subject of consciousness. Philosophers have usually taken it to be an indubitably self-evident truth that every mental state must be the state of some conscious subject. In their own way mental states are essentially social. But among those who have affirmed this, two of the most influential, Descartes and Berkeley, have asserted the opposite dependence as well, that the mind always thinks, is conscious, is in some mental state or other. Locke, of course, took that to be refuted by 'every drowsy nod'. The Lockean mind is something like the intermittent archery club I mentioned earlier. Sometimes it is active, is characterised by what is, for Descartes, its essential attribute; sometimes it is not. Whatever view is taken of the dependence of minds on mental states the parallel still breaks down. Individuals can, like Robinson Crusoe, withdraw from society. A mental state cannot, according to the original principle of dependence, exist in detachment from a mind at any time. The strictness of the dependence in the mental case is much greater.

Finally, there is a measure of analogy with the relation between God, the *ens realissimum*, and his creatures. In the social case this relation cannot be conceived in the manner of theism, with God as distinct from and prior to what he creates. It must be taken pantheistically, with God being identified with the totality of what exists. But in that case the relation is between a whole and its equally real and concrete parts, whatever else it may be.

If men, then, are essentially dependent on society, social groups are at least as dependent, and arguably more so, on men. There is, therefore, no ground here for the claim that social groups are more real and concrete than the men who compose them.

The comparison of the relation between a society and its members to that between a mind and its states encourages the inference that societies *are* minds, of a higher and more objective kind, an important support for ethical collectivism. We do, of course, speak freely of the mental properties and acts of a group in the way we do of individual people. Groups are said to have beliefs, emotions and attitudes and to take decisions and make promises. But these ways of speaking are plainly metaphorical. To ascribe mental predicates to a group is always an indirect way of ascribing such predicates to its members. With such mental states as beliefs and attitudes the ascriptions are of what I have called a summative kind. To say that the industrial working class is determined to resist anti-trade-union laws is to say that all or most industrial workers are so minded. Where groups are said to decide or promise the statements in question are institutional: the reference is to a person or persons authorised to take decisions or enter into undertakings on behalf of the group.

VIII. CRITIQUE OF THE LOGICAL CONSTRUCTION THEORY

Just as I have acknowledged that men are essentially social while rejecting the inference that social objects are on that account more real and concrete than their members, so I agree that social objects are logical constructions while rejecting the inference that they are on that account merely abstractions. Social objects are logical constructions because they are not, in practice, or effectively, observable, so that their names cannot be ostensively defined, and because their names cannot be explicitly defined, by reason of the fact that statements about them either involve institutional reference or contain social predicates that cannot be significantly ascribed to individuals.

Now philosophers who try to show that certain things, usually problematically unobservable things, are logical constructions are very insistent that the relation between a logical construction and its elements is not that between a whole and its parts. Ayer, for example, says that 'when we speak of certain objects b, c, d ... as being elements of an object e, and of e as being constituted by b, c, d ...,, we are not saying that they form part of e, in the sense in which my arm is part of my body, or a particular set of books on my shelf is part of my collection of books'. Furthermore, it is 'a mistaken assumption' that, in being taken to be a logical construction out of sense-data, 'a material thing is supposed to consist of sense-data, as a patchwork quilt consists of different coloured pieces of cloth'. Carnap insists that a social or cultural object is not literally composed of psychological or physical objects, but that social objects form what he calls an 'autonomous object-sphere', in other words that they are, as it were, on a higher level of abstraction than their constituent elements.

It is clearly true that some logical constructions are not wholes with their elements as parts. The average man is not the totality of men. Similarly a material thing, if it were a logical construction out of sense-data, as phenomenalists believe, would not have sense-data as its parts, but other, smaller material things such as molecules and atoms. A mental state, likewise, if it were a logical construction out of items of behaviour, would not have such items as parts. The parts of X's anger at Y, to the extent that it can be said to have any, are other mental states: his desire to injure Y and his belief that Y has done something to injure him.

The crucial thing about the philosophically interesting examples, the phenomenalists's material thing and the behaviourist's mental state, is that they are *hypothetical* constructions. In the first case, to say that there is a tree here is to say that, *if* certain conditions are satisfied, certain sense-data will be experienced. In the second, to say that this man is depressed is to say that, *if* such-and-such circumstances arose, he would react in such-and-such ways. Categorical statements about material things and mental states, so interpreted, can be true although no relevant sense-data at all actually occur or no relevant behaviour takes place. Such things and states are conceived as systematic *possibilities* of experience or behaviour. But possibilities cannot be parts of an actual thing.

Carnap, in the only extended treatment of social objects as logical constructions that I know of, maintains that they are latent and manifest themselves, thus imputing the same hypothetical status to them as phenomenalists do to material things and behaviourists to mental states. But the example he relies on does not establish the point. To say that there is a custom of hat-raising is, as he says, to say that individuals have a disposition to raise their hats to one another as a greeting. But the custom is not a social object proper; only the group in which it prevails is. Furthermore, the custom is no more dispositional than its elements. It is, in fact, an aggregate of individual dispositions.

Logical constructions, then, are not as such abstract and in some way less real than their constituent elements. That is arguably true of hypothetical constructions and perhaps of others as well. What I am concerned to show is that something can be a logical construction out of other things and, at the same time, be a whole of which the elements out of which it is constructed are parts. It is in this sense that the solar system is a logical construction out of certain systematically related heavenly bodies and a massive geographical feature like Australia or the Rocky Mountains is a logical construction out of observable bits of terrain or mountain-peaks. Is there any good reason to reject the view that social objects are related to the individuals who constitute them in the same way?

IX. SOCIAL OBJECTS AS WHOLES

One fact that might have suggested the idea that social objects are not wholes whose parts are individual people is that their membership changes through time. But it is plain, in reflection, that most wholes survive the replacement of their parts, provided that it is not too drastic. A replacement that is both sudden and comprehensive, or nearly so, makes the identity of the whole precarious. The masonry of a mediaeval castle can be steadily replaced, a small proportion each year, until none of the original material is left, and it will still be the same castle. Locke, who favoured identity of parts as a criterion for the identity of inorganic material things, felt constrained to abandon the requirement in the case of living bodies.

We do sometimes identify aggregates by way of their component parts. When the beach party is over, Anne's clothes are just those very garments that Anne arrived in and took off in order to swim. But Anne's clothes, conceived now as the customary occupants of a particular group of shelves and wardrobes, will have a temporally variable composition.

This point should be distinguished from the superficially similar consideration that I can know something about a constructed whole without knowing anything much about its specific individual parts. To know that France is a food-loving country is to know that most French people care about food. I can have good reason to believe that, without knowing much in particular about the majority of Frenchmen who are indefinitely referred to in my summary statement. This fact is sometimes, but invalidly, brought up as an objection to the view that statements about groups can be reduced to statements about individuals. But, even if the reference in the reducing statement is indefinite, the reduction has still been accomplished.

A more substantial reason for denying that social objects are wholes with human parts is that they are, in all but very exceptional circumstances, scattered and radically discontinuous in space. Many of them, indeed, such as children or vegetarians or motor-cyclists, who are not the proprietary occupants of a particular tract of the earth's surface in the way that nations tend to be, are intermingled in space with the membership of other social groups. Carnap, in the spirit of this objection, contrasts a forest with the present vegetation of central Europe, which he describes as 'a conceptual assemblage'.

This property of social objects is a good reason for denying that they are material objects. Material objects are ordinarily spatially continuous, or, to take account of physical theory, are at any rate perceived as such, even if only in the way that a net is, where there is a perceptibly continuous path from any point in the thing to any other. The reason for this is that our standard concepts of material objects involve a characteristic, definitive shape, whose boundaries mark the object off from others and make possible identification and counting.

We may prefer, therefore, to call a spatially scattered entity a collection or aggregate, for example, a library that is not all in one place, or even a forest. But an aggregate or collection of objects is still a perfectly good whole of which those objects are parts, even if we are unwilling to describe it as a material object itself.

A more striking peculiarity of social objects, which might be thought to count against their being wholes with people as parts, is that every human being is at any moment a member of a great number of distinct groups. These may, indeed, overlap only in respect of his membership of them. A man can be the only member common to his family, the local fire-brigade and a wine-tasting society. Ordinary material objects can share parts only at different times. *A* cannot be at a given moment part of both *B* and *C*, unless *B* itself includes or is included in *C*.

An interesting limiting case of member-sharing which could and perhaps occasionally does occur in the field of social objects is that in which two groups have exactly the same membership. It is possible that the parish council of a given village should have as its members all and only those who are members of the church bell-ringers of that village. From that it follows that a social object, even a social class, is not a logical class, whose membership is the criterion of its identity.

But although simultaneous sharing of parts, and, *a fortiori*, complete identity of parts, is impossible for distinct material objects, that is not true of aggregates or collections. John's books, the books in the thatched house and the paperbacks in this street may have one or many or even all their members in common and yet these book-collections are perfectly good wholes with individual books as their literal parts, held together in these distinct collections by different aggregating relations: ownership, location, physical character.

Wholly distinct material objects cannot simultaneously share parts because in the case of such wholes the aggregating relation is spatial. The strands of wool that make up a sweater in the morning and, when unpicked and reknitted, a scarf in the afternoon have to stand in different and logically incompatible spatial relations in their sweater-forming and scarf-forming rôles. The collection-forming relationships between the parts of the book-collections in the example are, however, logically independent. The same is true of social objects. In the case of the identically-membered parish council and bell-ringers there is no incompatibility between Smith's subordination to Jones as regards parish administration and Jones's subordination to Smith as regards bell-ringing. Smith and Jones are, in a way, in two different social places at the same time. But there is no inconsistency in that. To continue the metaphor: Smith and Jones exist, like other men, in a number of distinct social spaces.

There is, then, no good reason for denying that social objects are wholes with individual people as their literal parts, as real and as concrete as their members. They are, in a way, 'conceptual assemblages', in Carnap's phrase, but only in the sense that that is true of every object of reference. They do not thrust themselves so obtrusively on perception as the generality of ordinary material objects since the aggregating relations that form the collections in question are comparatively elusive and theoretical and do not involve the spatial proximity, joint movement and sharp demarcation from the spatial environment that is typical of material things. But some of these are a bit elusive themselves: the Gulf Stream, the electrical wiring of a house, or a person's cardio-vascular system. And that kind of perceptual elusiveness does not entail that its possessors are abstractions.

X. METHODOLOGICAL IMPLICATIONS OF THIS THEORY

At first glance it seems that if ontological individualism is true the main methodological issue about social objects is easily settled. For if every statement about a social object is equivalent to and can be replaced by a statement in which only individuals are referred to and in which the predicates, whether the same as or different from those of the original statement, are predicates of individuals, then it rather trivially follows that every law about social objects is derivable from a law about individuals since it must implicitly be such a law itself.

Can such a reduction be carried out in fact? Consider an example: in every society the lower middle class is the most patriotic. That implies and would be tested by analogous assertions about particular lower middle classes. In order to establish any such assertion a sample of lower middle class people from a given society would be compared in respect of patriotism with aristocrats and proletarians. Direct reference to individuals would be reached with statements of the form: X is lower middle class and patriotic. Neither of these properties of X is a simple, natural property of an individual. It is a relational property and, in the case of patriotism, at any rate, the other term of the relation is itself a social object. To say that X is patriotic is to say something like 'X is much concerned for the welfare of his country'.

This apparent ineradicability of social terms from the most elementary statements we can make about human beings is emphasised in Mandelbaum's account of 'societal facts', in which he draws attention to the large difference between describing someone as cashing a cheque (with its implicit mention of money, a banking-system and so forth) and as giving someone an oblong piece of paper and receiving some smaller oblong pieces of paper from him. Such implicit reference to social objects enters into our most everyday remarks about the character and activities of individuals, particularly those which are going to serve as the basic empirical evidence for the propositions of history and social science.

Powerful as this consideration is, I think the individualist can meet it. It is true that reference to social objects is implicitly present in ordinary social judgments about particular individuals, since social predicates like 'is patriotic' and 'cashes a cheque' express complex relational properties among whose terms are social objects like nations and banks. But that does not make such references in principle ineliminable. It is just that there is seldom any occasion to eliminate it; the use of the predicates is too familiar. An indirect way of bringing this out is to contrast a child's conception of what cashing a cheque is, which would amount to little more than the visible exchange of oblong pieces of paper, with an adult's grasp of the notion which would involve a conception of the attitudes and customary practices of the very different kinds of people involved in a transaction of this kind.

It would be extemely laborious to spell out Mandelbaum's example in wholly individual terms, but it could be done. In the case of 'X is patriotic' an approximate translation is fairly easy. It might run: 'X is one of a nationally related collection of people and is much concerned for the well-being of that collection of people, conceived as so related'. Even here we are not individualistically home and dry if a common government is held to be essential to nationhood, but that could be coped with my means of something along the lines of Austin's definition of sovereignty. It should be noted that a patriot's state of mind is partly constituted by his possession of the concept of a particular kind of social object, but that does not imply the irreducibility of that concept.

In practice our ascription of social predicates to individuals is unreflective. It is one of the functions of social science to clarify our social concepts in individual terms and thus to make it possible for empirically rigorous evidence to be substituted for unreflective impressions in the making of social judgments.

But even if this reducibility in principle is admitted there is still an important point to be made by explanatory collectivism, methodological collectivism proper, what Popper calls 'sociologism'. To maintain that laws about social objects are in principle reducible to laws about individual people is not to say that there is a single psychology of human beings in general, a comprehensive theory of human nature, from which all social laws can be derived. Popper is right to question Mill's remark, 'men are not, when brought together, converted into another kind of substance'. When they are brought together in a national, rather than a tribal or merely familial, way they do become different. In other words, the psychology that Mill thought of as the master social science will, as far as we can tell, be a social psychology. New social objects, new social systems or schemes of social relationship between men, not only make it logically possible for new things to be true of men, for instance patriotism, they also causally promote new states of mind and styles of conduct, for instance thrift or snobbery. There can be, that is to say, emergent properties of people in particular kinds of relationship to each other.

In practice a rigidly psychologistic social science is often unsatisfactory, in Pareto, for example, or Russell's *Power* or the vulgar Marxism, largely avoided by Marx, which emphasises individual acquisitiveness rather than the influence of the social and economic structure. Hobbes's social theory is an impressive example of rigid psychologism. Classical economics is even more impressive but, despite the psychological look of the postulate of utility-maximisation, is not wholly psychologistic. The maximisation postulate allows for indefinite variation between different assessments of utility, as between, for example, income and leisure, which are, no doubt, socially determined. Furthermore it assumes an initial allocation of controlled resources which implies the institution of ownership, and thus some law or custom of property, and also some institutional scheme for the exchange of factors and resources.

I believe, then, that all statements about social objects are statements about individuals, their interests, attitudes, decisions and actions. But the predicates of these statements about individuals will essentially, if only implicitly, mention social objects in a way that is not practically or usefully eliminable, even if it is eliminable in principle. Social objects are involved from the beginning in our every-day characterisations of individuals. To say that Smith owns the house he lives in presupposes a property system, although it can be translated into something like 'Smith is one of a collection of people who recognise the right of certain of their number to protect Smith from any interference in his use and disposal of the house he lives in.'

It could turn out that the socially determined variations in human nature are themselves explainable in terms of a universal psychology. The idea is analogous to Einstein's belief in a unified theory of gravitational and electromagnetic forces. But it does not follow from ontological individualism. All that does follow is that the social determinants of human variety are themselves no more than observable relationships between individual human beings.

XI. ETHICAL IMPLICATIONS OF THE THEORY

The view that I have defended about the nature of social objects denies, on the one hand, that they are, in Hegel's phrase, the true 'ethical substances' and, at the opposite extreme, that they are mere abstractions. Both denials have ethical implications, which I can treat only very sketchily here.

The idea that social objects are mere abstractions encourages the belief that personal obligations are more important than institutional ones. That belief is expressed with some force in E.M. Forster's remark that if he had a choice between betraying a friend and betraying his country he hoped he would have the courage to betray his country. This is, in fact, to adopt an unreasoned and unreasonable preference for one kind of social object, an intimate and informal one, to another, which is more comprehensive and formal. It is, in a way, a sophisticated version of the kind of moral barbarism which regards fellow-tribesmen as moral beings but looks on everyone else as game in the open season.

No doubt this personalist moral outlook is a reaction called into being by the excesses of its collectivist opposite, which shares the extravagance of its counterpart. For when the collectivist denies that the good of the community is simply the aggregate of the goods of its individual members he is treating that community as a kind of person, or at least as something with a life of its own. If this conception is, as it should be, rejected, it should be acknowledged that what collectivists regard as the overriding common good, the preservation of the power and vitality of a scheme of social relationships, is of no intrinsic value but has value only through its contribution to the welfare of its individual members. That contribution will be most evident in the form of what may be called convergent, as contrasted with competitive, goods; goods, that is to say, which are available to any only if available to all, like peace or a stable currency or a pure water supply. As the chief provider of convergent goods however, social objects have very great value as means. And they do not have this in quite such a contingent fashion as McTaggart's sewage-pipe. The scheme of social relationships in which a person is placed is not simply a set of mechanical arrangements for the pursuit of individual ends. It is much more intimately involved in an individual's personality than that, above all in his sense of himself. It is the framework of his settled expectations and often the object of his direct affections. The common good is indeed an aggregate of individual goods, but the individuals in question are still essentially social beings.

A comparable middle position is possible with regard to the problem of authoritative moral knowledge, one that falls between the contrary extremes of taking the convictions of the community, conceived either as those of the majority or those of some ruling group, or the convictions of the isolated individual conscience as the final arbiter. Neither the prevailing convictions of the majority of the community nor those of some ruling group within it are immune to individual criticism. On the other hand, the individual's capacity for criticism and innovation, in morality as in science, rests on the foundation of established opinions and, at a higher level, on a method of critical reasoning which the individual has derived from society. The individual can criticise the moral traditions of his community. But he can do so only with the critical weapons with which that tradition has equipped him.

10

Tragedy

There are two points of view from which tragedy can be of interest to philosophers. First, there is the task of defining or elucidating the concept: a problem of logic in an inclusive, if familiar, sense. Secondly, there is the metaphysical problem of tragedy, an examination of the tragic view of life and the world that is held to be implied and perhaps recommended by tragic drama. I shall be concerned with both of these problems in what follows and I shall try to show how it is that the concept of tragedy implies or at least suggests a metaphysical view of the world. First of all, in Part I of these remarks, I shall argue that there is a genuine concept of tragedy to be investigated; an indispensable preliminary in view of the assault of Croce on the reality, the more than merely labelling character, of all literary and aesthetic classification. In Part II, I shall propose a distinction between natural and institutional concepts, locating tragedy in the latter group. Institutional concepts, I shall argue, pose special problems of definition, and in Part III I shall consider various theories of tragedy to see what kinds of definition they offer. Finally, in Part IV, I shall try to give an account of the 'tragic view' and to distinguish it from some metaphysical doctrines of comparable scope.

I. THE REALITY OF LITERARY CLASSES

In chapter 4 of his *Aesthetic* Croce asserts that 'the greatest triumph of the intellectualist error lies in the theory of literary and artistic classes.' He does not deny that works of art can be and have been brought together in classes in the light of resemblances between them; but he insists that these classifications are no more than labelling devices, convenient perhaps for the historian of art, but of no real significance. They are pseudo-concepts and belong, not to aesthetics, but to psychology. Creative artists should not let themselves be imposed upon by these fictions, they are concepts that anyone may define as he pleases. In general the tragic 'is *everything* that is or will be so *called* by those who have employed or shall employ this *word*'.

This sweeping contention has both a reason and a purpose. The reason is the essential uniqueness and individuality of works of art: the purpose is the rejection of a rigorous classicism, the aesthetically insupportable view that works of art must conform to and can be conclusively judged by a collection of fixed rules. I suggest that one might well accept both the reason and the purpose, both the principle of individuality and the view that there can be no adequate system of aesthetic canons, without committing oneself to Croce's extravagant connecting link between the two.

Let us consider first the principle of individuality. Some people might be disposed to accept it on the ground that it is a truism that applies not merely to works of art but to everything. 'Every individual work of art is unique,' they might argue, is a not particularly interesting special case of the tautology, 'every individual thing is unique'. To argue in this way, however, is to insist that there is no distinction between uniqueness and individuality. If one were to reply that a thing is unique only if qualitatively distinct from everything else, but individual provided that it is numerically distinct the identity of indiscernibles might be appealed to as showing that all numerical diversity is in the end qualitative. Although I think that there is or could be merely numerical diversity, that there are or could be things whose spatio-temporal distinctness is not reducible to qualitative terms, it is fortunately not necessary to argue the point here. It will be enough to draw a provisional distinction between the unique as that whose *important* or *significant* features are, as a group, peculiar to it, and the individual as that whose features as a group, whether important or not, are peculiar to it. Here the word 'feature' is being used to include quality and position with no assumption as to the reducibility or otherwise of the latter. Now on this distinction a person will ordinarily be unique (even of an identical twin it can be reasonably presumed that his memories will differ in some fairly notable respect from those of his brother) but a mass-produced article of manufacture is not. Similarly *The Tempest* is unique in a way that two particular copies, side by side on the bookseller's shelf, of a particular printed edition of it are not. As Strawson has shown (*Individuals*, p.231) this distinction between a work of art and its 'instances' is not really confined to literature and music. 'The things the dealers buy and sell are particulars,' he says of painting and sculpture, 'but it is only because of the empirical deficiencies of reproductive techniques that we identify these with the works of art. Were it not for these deficiencies, the original of a painting would have only the interest which belongs to the original manuscript of a poem.'

There is, then, a sense in which works of art are non-trivially unique, the same as that in which persons are unique, which is different from the necessary individuality of any individual whatever, even if this difference between forms of individuality should turn out to rest on nothing more definite than the importance of individuating features. This fact is not exactly an accident. That all the individuating features of a work of art are important, that they all contribute to its effect upon us and are thus relevant to our evaluation of it, is simply a more explicit rendering of the requirement that a work of art should be original or creative. A purported work of art that is not distinct from an earlier work in respect of its important, aesthetically relevant, features is an imitation or a piece of plagiarism, for such things do not seem to happen by accident, and is despised as such; it is a work not of creation but transcription.

It is this requirement of novelty in works of art that underlies reasonable hostility to the regularian obsession of an ossified classicism. The historical variety of the forms of art gives us a sense of unexploited creative possibilities and this encourages us to feel that we cannot lay down in advance the specific, formal conditions which new art must satisfy. There can be no set of aesthetic canons which is sufficient for the appraisal of new creations. Joyce with *Ulysses* is inventing a new form for fiction rather than doing badly what was done well with *David Copperfield* and *Madame Bovary*. Again, we may admire Richardson in spite of, rather than because of, the laborious epistolany convention which he chose to adopt. Certainly if an artist declares his formal intentions, reference to the canons of that form will make it possible to judge his intentions' success. But the success of his intentions neither entails nor is entailed by the excellence of his work.

But the fact that the formal intentions and achievements of an artist cannot conclusively settle the critical, evaluative problem posed by his work does not mean that different works of art do not possess common features nor does it imply that these common features, whether intended or not, are critically irrelevant. The plain fact is that artists are influenced in their work by the formal characteristics that they and critics and appreciators of art generally have discerned as common to the work of other artists; that to elicit these characteristics in a new work is an essential part of the interpretative task of criticism, and that such interpretation is indispensable to any judgment or evaluation of art that is to make a rational claim to our attention. Briefly, to apply classificatory terms to a work of art, to discern features in it that it can share with other works, cannot be the whole of criticism; but *any* such classification may be relevant and *some* such classification must be made if criticism is to be more than merely demonstrative, more than quotation and excitement.

The uniqueness of persons lies behind the idea of romantic love in much the same way as the uniqueness of works of art lies behind the romantic emphasis on the essential place of originality and creativeness in art and it may be instructive to compare the two cases a little further. Although our ideas about personal relations presuppose the non-trivial uniqueness of human beings they do not entail that human beings are unclassifiable. When people protest against classifications of human beings, when they say that one should not think of men as negroes or members of the bourgeoisie or foreigners but rather as unique individuals, they are not denying that the classification can be made; they are insisting, rather, on its inadequacy as a basis for evaluation. Nor need they hold that no classification of men can be used to support our moral or personal judgment of them. In place of a superficial and well-established classification in terms of social groups they may be recommending one based on personal character that is less obvious, harder to apply and less familiar, one that classifies men as honest or 'alive' or genuine. Likewise, to protest at literary classification may be to object to the critical superficiality of classifications in terms of content (novels of the sea, novels of hospital life, etc.) or in terms of verbally formal features (sonnets, triolets, ballads) in the interests of attention to more elusive likenesses. In each case we have to be warned against our predilection for obvious external similarities and the temptation to ignore on account of it the more important features on which a responsible and rational judgement must rest if it aims to work from the genuine sources of satisfaction.

With works of art as with people there are different levels of classification. At one extreme is the merely verbal or morphological and its equal and opposite counterpart the merely sociological. At this level are found classifications of poetry by metrical pattern and rhyme-scheme, of fiction by length and, to turn to the counterpart, all classifications in terms of subject-matter: nature poetry, detective novels, ghost stories. These have only the most modest critical utility, mainly that of suggesting a possible field of comparison. The more serious literary categories, such as tragedy, comedy, epic, romance, satire, fable, in applying to less superficial properties are harder to apply and their criteria of application are harder to formulate. That is the price of their critical importance.

There are two opposed errors that can be made about literary kinds. At one extreme is the platonism that regards the whole body of literary forms as already known and fixed. For only on the assumption that all possible forms are known and their value assessed is it possible to lay down binding rules. The opposite error is to infer from the inexhaustible character of the formal possibilities of literature that any formal resemblances there may be amongst existing works are of merely historical interest. Literature is a traditional affair, the body of existing work exercises an influence, conscious and unconscious, on the creative writer. If the tradition constituted by his immediate predecessors is exhausted he turns to a larger, more embracing tradition: either to the remoter past (as with Pound and Eliot) or to art of a 'lower', less deliberate and respectable kind (as with Auden). Literary kinds exist and, when not too superficial, are significant for criticism but they are not immutable. Historical things, they depend on the relation of writers to their literary tradition. The reasons for this continuity and dependence are plain if vague. Persisting literary forms reflect persisting needs for expression: there will be satire as long as society offers material for complaint. Again the use, even in a modified way, of an established form helps communication and intelligibility. Finally, and perhaps vaguest of all, there is the attraction to the writer of a finite task; a creative undertaking is too vast if every element of it has to be a new creation. The greatest literary achievements, it is worth noting, are not usually those of the most adventurous formal innovators.

II. INSTITUTIONAL CONCEPTS

We can never be sure that our conceptual apparatus is going to be adequate to our future experience. To take extreme cases first: if the human race went permanently blind the concepts of colours would soon fade away into disuse, and if we acquired new kinds of sensitivity, either by the extension of an existing range in becoming visually aware of ultra-violet colours or by the growth of a wholly new sense, new concepts would be needed and found that would be indefinable in terms of our current conceptual equipment. On a more plausible level: animal species become extinct, the summers of our youth never return, and, on the other hand, new species arise from selective breeding, new diseases and new kinds of artefact spring from civilised life. In short, concepts have histories. But in many cases the history of a concept is monotonous enough to be ignored. Such as these I shall call natural concepts and contrast with what I shall call institutional concepts. Prime examples of the natural are the adjectival concepts of colour and of sensible properties generally. Their durability derives from that of the sensory organisation of our species. Among substantival concepts, those of natural objects and stuffs (trees, stones, water, smoke) fall in this class as do those of animal and plant species (always allowing for the work of the big game hunter, the dam-builder and the selective breeder) and of such things as conditions of weather. Natural concepts are the friends of the translator. They remain the same under variations of time, place and language. A good reason for this invariance is the fact that the things to which they apply are comparatively immune to the meddling Prometheanism of man.

Institutional concepts, on the other hand, are those that apply to the fruits of human contrivance. First and foremost artefacts (tools, machines, houses, furnishings); then institutions proper (marriage, property, the state); the social roles associated with them (priest, king, creditor); customs and practices (manners, games, meals). Amongst this class are to be found the concepts of literary kinds. The history of these concepts is not monotonous and because of this the more specific of them have only a chronologically local application (it is absurd to describe a Druid or the Roman *pontifex maximus* as a clergyman) while the more generic undergo substantial changes of meaning (Druid, *pontifex* and clergyman can all be described as priests). The elements of art, technics and society are pre-eminently subservient to the human will. They are functional in the sense that they serve human purposes more or less, and often also in the sense that they are believed to serve these purposes or others. To the extent that the purpose of art-forms, instruments and social institutions becomes recognised and explicit the way in which they serve this purpose becomes accessible to criticism and from this criticism reformed and improved means to the end in question can be derived. It is to institutional concepts, incidentally, that Stuart Hampshire's theory about the dependence of our descriptive concepts on our needs and interests (*Thought and Action*, chapter 1) most adequately applies. Our colour-classifications, for example, depend on our physiological endowment and not on our purposes, unless these are thought to stand in some evolutionary relationship to that endowment.

This account has been over-simple in assimilating social and aesthetic concepts to technical ones, for it is in the case of technical concepts that the relevance and effect of purpose are most noticeable. Kinds of artefact are commonly brought into existence for the sake of an explicitly formulated purpose; though there are accidental inventions, a man idly playing about with something suddenly finds it, or realises it, to have an unexpected use. But social institutions, it is reasonable to assume, generally antedate any conscious recognition of their functions and although their subsequent modification may be carried on with a view to formulated purposes, these will ordinarily be rather numerous in any particular case and for the most part extrinsic to the institution itself. Bentham and his followers never, at the best of times, had an entirely free hand. The social reformer, to be effective, has to compromise with the reservations of the unconvinced. On the other hand there are utopian communities and private variations on the approved pattern of marriage where the institution is separated, sometimes at a disabling cost, from its normal social surroundings. Yet again the sphere of technique can be invaded by political considerations in such large and expensive matters as the designing of a supersonic aircraft. The model of the individual technician contriving with a clearly formulated purpose fails to apply to the arts for different reasons. Here there is ordinarily only a single human will involved but in the nature of the case the purpose will be highly indeterminate. The dramatist says to himself, 'I am excited by the idea of a man ready to sacrifice anything in the pursuit of power': the result, after a multitude of redirections and modifications, perhaps *Macbeth*. However, works of art are not usually, and not if they are any good, the outcome of blithe inconsequence. Even if the ostensible purpose undergoes change throughout the process of creation and even if the artist may only fully comprehend his purpose, if at all, when he contemplates his finished work, he nevertheless has some more or less statable purpose throughout. The amendments that the technical model requires before it can be applied to the work of the writer or artist are not such as to rule out the institutional account of the concepts of literary or artistic kinds. In literature, tragedies do not just happen, they are intended. To get started at all a writer must propose some form or other and unless his dislike of the prevailing tradition induces him to invent one he will take it from his tradition. But the inner, progressively revealed requirements of his particular task may lead him to modify it in a wholly original way.

Institutional concepts, then, are historically mutable and, in a wide sense, purposive. Both of these properties have a bearing on the problem of their definition. For both contribute to disputes about the proper range of their application. By contrast the definition of natural concepts is a comparatively straightforward matter. A collection of more or less universally agreed instances can be assembled and inductively inspected for common properties or resemblances. Critical scrutiny of the assemblage is required only to ensure that the applications of the concept it contains are informed, serious and careful. With institutional concepts, on the other hand, the task of assembling recognised instances presents serious difficulties. Only a proportion of the informed, serious and careful applications will be universally agreed upon. There will, therefore, be no secure starting-point for the inductive comparison. To take our particular case of tragedy: no-one is going to make a fuss about the inclusion of the *Agamemnon*, *Hamlet* and *Phèdre*, but there will be large and serious minorities protesting against the inclusion of *Romeo and Juliet* and the exclusion of *The Mayor of Casterbridge*. The members of any small set of paradigm tragedies that we select will be complicated things exhibiting a mass of similarities and dissimilarities to other literary works, above all because of the inevitable historical mutation of literary forms.

It is tempting at this point to say that in fact there is no single determinate concept of tragedy and to renounce, in consequence, the attempt at definition. Different people, impressed by different resemblances, use the word in different ways as they have a perfectly good logical right to do. One might enumerate the prevailing uses and extract some such common core to them all as 'plays about disasters befalling important people which end unhappily'. That, it might be felt, is as far as the search for a definition can usefully go. But something more can be done with the concept, all the same: whether it be described as the proposal of a new, improved concept or as the definition of a concept already implicit in the present field of overlapping uses. The most reasonable way to proceed would be by a kind of critical induction which would extract a preliminary criterion from a central group of unquestionable paradigm cases and test it against marginal ones. To admit a marginal case would require a restatement of the criterion and consequential admissions and exclusions. Now such an activity is not to be described without qualification as the definition of an existing concept, for one thing because its result might well not coincide with any existing use. On the other hand, it is not a mere proposal, not the mere selection of an existing or brand-new concept for preferred status over all others. For the modification of the criterion is a critical process whose standards will derive from the critics' ideas of the purposes of writers of tragedy. Its aim is not mere tidiness but rather the fulfilment of existing aims. It involves, of course, the assumption that there is some unity of purpose to be found in the area loosely covered by the indeterminate, merely empirical concept of tragedy. But such an assumption is not an unreasonable one: its chief justification is the part played by tradition in the work of those who write, or seek to write, tragedies.

The same point can be made about two institutional concepts from the social field: those of democracy and marriage. The application of these to widely differing modes of political organisation and of human relationships is afflicted with the same dissensions as is that of tragedy. But it is surely intellectual defeatism to maintain that anything is a democracy or a marriage that somebody firmly wants to describe as one: the Athens of Pericles and the East Germany of Ulbricht being just as much democracies as Asquith's England; the concubines of Solomon being just as much wives as the equal partners of modern Western monogamy.

Of the two salient properties of institutional concepts, that of historical mutability poses a problem to which that of dependence on human purposes suggests a solution. In describing critical induction as a solution there is no need to quarrel with those who would prefer to call it an activity of concept-formation rather than one of definition. The ambiguity that it aims to remove is not of a fruitful kind; the very fact that in this area of discourse a single word is used with an indeterminate and contention-provoking meaning is sufficient reason to arrive, by proposal or discovery, at a single and determinate concept. And since the concept of philosophy is an institutional one the objectors are in no position to assert that the undertaking is anyway no part of the business of philosophers. In particular it does not follow from the characteristic indeterminancy of institutional concepts that any such rectification of their outlines must be an arbitrary business. For the dependence on comparatively inexplicit purposes that is part of the explanation of the historical variation of institutional concepts, can be used as a standard to guide the critical sifting of their historical variety.

III. DEFINITION OF TRAGEDY

'A tragedy, then, is the imitation of an action that is serious and also, as having magnitude, complete in itself: in language with pleasurable accessories, each kind brought in separately in the parts of the work; in a dramatic, not in a narrative, form; with incidents arousing pity and fear, wherewith to accomplish its catharsis of such emotions.' Aristotle's statement is the inevitable starting-point. It is presented as, and can reasonably claim to be, a direct induction. But Aristotle's situation was peculiar and not to be repeated; unlike the modern investigator of the concept of tragedy his field of instances was, as groups of literary works go, notably determinate. His examples were all in one language, had all sprung from a fairly unitary literary tradition and had done so within a comparatively short space of time. All the same his procedure had its critical elements. One departure from mere induction is his progressive refinement in the course of the *Poetics* of his conception of the seriousness of tragedy's content. At first he is prepared to allow the plot to run from misery to happiness as well as from happiness to misery. But in the end he defends the unhappy endings of Euripides as 'more tragic'. Another example is provided by his account of the tragic hero, who must be neither simply good nor simply bad; yet another by his view that the tragic sequence of events must flow, not from the depravity of the hero, but from an error of judgement.

Most of the elements of his definition need explanation and some need revision. A tragedy is *the imitation of an action*: this means that it must be a literary representation of human activity, not that it must be a strictly accurate historical record of real occurrences. It is *serious*: it must represent things in the way that they actually happen and not as we might more or less idly wish that they would happen, the plot must consist of events that stand in probable or necessary relations to one another. It must have *magnitude and completeness*: this demand for a beginning, middle and end is not specific to tragedy, it is an obvious requirement for any seriously intended piece of imaginative literature. It must be expressed in *language with pleasurable accessories*: this demand for 'rhythm, harmony and song' is inductively correct but critically irrelevant; the claims of Ibsen and Eugene O'Neill cannot be ruled out by such a comparatively trivial consideration. It must be *dramatic not narrative*: this again is a morphological and so superficial requirement. To eliminate *Anna Karenina*, *Madame Bovary* and *The Mayor of Casterbridge* we must consider what is said in these books and not the manner of saying it. A dramatic *version* or *adaptation* of a novel is not on that count alone a different work. It must contain *incidents arousing pity and fear*: any reasonably engrossing and believable narrative or drama may contain *incidents* of this kind, a picaresque novel, a political thriller or an unclassifiable work like *War and Peace* (consider the death of Anatole Kuragin). What is requisite to tragedy is that the work as a whole should be calculated to arouse these emotions. It does so by being a story of human misfortune, suffering and disaster. It must bring about a *catharsis*: it would seem that Aristotle understood by this, the most disputed part of his definition, to mean that the spectator of tragedy should derive his satisfaction from it by being purged, in a more or less medical sense, of his emotions of pity and fear, that he should leave the theatre emotionally evacuated. Lessing's rather pious view that *catharsis* is 'purfication' cannot be accepted. As a psychological account of the mechanism by which tragedy has its effect this part of the theory is both irrelevant to the matter of definition and highly dubious on its own account. To be moved by a tragedy is to be exalted rather than exhausted.

The acceptable and intelligible residue of Aristotle's formula, then, is that a tragedy should be the representation of a single and rationally connected series of events that involve misfortune and suffering and end in disaster. He later adds that the action should centre on a single person, the tragic hero, who should be impressive and admirable (or at least important, perhaps as a symbol of these qualities) and whose error of judgement, rather than depravity, should contribute causally to the disastrous sequence of events in which he is engulfed. In this revised formula the elements of form (verse and drama) and psychological effect (the *catharsis*) have been removed; what remains is a preliminary account of the purpose of tragedy. Preliminary because the question arises: why represent the misfortunes and sufferings of admirable people? A trivial answer to this question, like Hume's, takes it to ask: how is it that we enjoy the spectacle of such misfortunes? The more serious romantic theorists of tragedy of the nineteenth century – Hegel, Schopenhauer and Nietzsche – imply that the point of tragedy is that it is an image of human life, a condensed, heightened and telling representation of man's place in the universe, of his situation and of the possibilities of action open to him. The pre-eminence of tragedy, in their view, derives from its being the most metaphysical of literary forms. The differences between them are essentially metaphysical, they arise from their different opinions about the place and possibilities of man in the world. The chief virtue of Aristotle's formula is that by clearly specifying the essential character of tragedy it suggests, even if it does not explicitly raise, the question of its ultimate and underlying purpose. The answer to this question is that tragedy gives a literary, an imaginative, solution to the most humanly interesting of metaphysical problems. Where Aristotle's romantic successors differ is in the precise account they give of the nature of this solution, in their expositions of the tragic view of life. Through their dependence on the idea of purpose these theories at least approximate to the ideal of critical inductions, though they are more critical, perhaps, than inductive.

The immediate form of their disagreement concerns the causation of the tragic sequence of events. In very summary terms: Hegel requires it to develop from moral excess in the hero; Schopenhauer looks for its cause in the inexorable indifference of blind fate; Nietzsche makes no such limited demand, all he requires is that the hero's individuality should be gloriously destroyed. These three points of view imply corresponding pictures of the place of man in the world. For Hegel man is subordinate to an omnipotent and infallible principle of cosmic justice; for Schopenhauer he is the inevitable victim of a mindless, merciless cosmic will; for Nietzsche he is the creator of value in an indifferent universe. These three doctrines must be examined more closely.

For Hegel the misfortune, with its capacity of arousing pity and fear, that is characteristic of tragedy is the outcome of a conflict or collision, in particular of a collision of right with right. A conflict of right with right can only be apparent: what happens is that the 'ethical institution' to which the hero is committed is given by him an improperly commanding and important place to the exclusion of other equally important ethical institutions. Thus Antigone, in Hegel's favourite and paradigmatic example, by pressing too hard the claims of the family comes into destructive conflict with the claims of the state. This situation, 'the self-division of the ethical substance', a lop-sidedness in the scheme of values, can only be set right by the destruction of the initiator of the conflict and a reaffirmation of eternal justice as a whole over the pretensions of its constituent parts. Hegel's view rests on a questionable interpretation of the *Antigone* (Creon is too tyrannous a monarch to be regarded as a representative of the moral claims of the state); in requiring the moral responsibility of the tragic hero for the disasters that befall him, in seeing his destruction as the reaffirmation of absolute morality, it is fundamentally a demand for poetic justice and as such inapplicable to by far the greater number of the works about whose status as tragedies there would be little disagreement. A.C. Bradley amended the theory to include amongst conflicting elements not merely ethical institutions but also 'universal interests', moral values that had no determinate social institution as their expression, and even 'personal interests', such as Macbeth's ambition. So adjusted the theory can accommodate the tragedies of Racine, with their characteristic battle between love and duty, and to some extent the tragedies of Shakespeare, in which personal goals collide with the demands of that overriding order and harmony without which all human arrangements come to ruin. But this amendment really evacuates the Hegelian position: it allows for the reality of unrecompensed, unreconciled evil, it abandons the demand for the moral responsibility of the hero and for an essentially retributive view of his sufferings. The significance of Lear's or Othello's suffering is trivialised by seeing it as a just return for their moral offences. Certainly their follies contributed to the disasters which overtook them but only against the background of a world which allows the persistence and effectiveness of evil. Schopenhauer's protest against poetic justice is exaggerated and quaintly phrased but it makes an appropriate point: Hegel's view, he says, expresses 'the dull, optimistic, Protestant-rationalistic, or peculiarly Jewish view of life'. It can be said, at any rate, to have a flavour of complacent pharisaism.

Schopenhauer's position is the exact opponent of Hegel's. For him the purpose of tragedy is to represent the terrible side of life; the response it seeks to evoke is resignation, an abandonment of the will to live. The tragic hero 'atones for the crime of existence', he shows us how even those most fitted to triumph in the world are really weak and powerless. Behind the world of phenomena, which, as amenable to our understandings, seems amenable to our desires, stands the thing-in-itself, the cosmic will. In the end this is the source of all tragic sequences of events, whether these are immediately initiated by chance or fate, by the will itself, or by evil men or by what Schopenhauer none too consistently preferred as a tragic initiator 'the ordinary morals and relations of men'. (His preference here stemmed from the belief that the third type of tragedy brought home to us the closeness of disaster to ordinary life. On the other hand misfortunes with ordinary causes are more easily thought of as preventable by human thought and effort, only the obvious workings of chance and fate can enforce an attitude of resignation.) Schopenhauer's theory derives some strength from the mild satisfaction and comfort that can be got from looking directly at the worst possibilities. This consolation, however, in so far as it does not consist in the pleasure of mere knowingness and disillusion, of having overcome the sentimental follies that afflict others, can only occur if the resignation is not total. Complete resignation that can console us and so contribute to life shows the limitation of our powers, the inexorable obstacles that we have got to recognise, and not that we have no powers at all. The resignation that tragedy does produce is not of Schopenhauer's all-engulfing kind: if, as he claims, it is the summit of art it is not because it leads to total collapse and admission of defeat. What conclusively refutes Schopenhauer's theory is the outcome of its concrete application. On his specifications *Jude the Obscure* would be far more of a tragedy than any work of Shakespeare's.

Nietzsche's *The Birth of Tragedy* is an extraordinary rhapsodic affair full of *a priori* cultural history, the mysterious combat of Apollo and Dionysus and resonant hymns to the music and metaphysics of German romanticism. In general he accepts the outlines of Schopenhauer's view, the dualism which sees the world as composed of a clear, definite, rational, harmonious order of phenomena (the world of Apollo and of plastic art) and of a dark, inchoate, irrational, ecstatic order of things-in-themselves (the world of Dionysus and of music). Tragedy is the master-art that brings these two worlds together and in which the Apollonian individuality of the hero is destroyed by the wild, depersonalised forces of the Dionysian abyss. It is as if the conflicting elements in tragedy were the fixity of the intellect on the one hand and the unformed creativeness of the emotions or the unconscious on the other, as if, that is to say, the two sides to the conflict were both somehow contained in man. The tragic hero is not destroyed by impersonal forces quite external to humanity but by the more vital features of humanity. It is in these terms that Nietzsche tries to explain our delight in the tragic annihilation of individuality. We derive a metaphysical comfort, he says, from tragedy's affirmation of the power and pleasure of life that underlies the flux of phenomena. As it stands this theory seems to be of very limited application.

In the tragedies of Shakespeare and Racine it is impersonal *order* and not disorder that seems to be affirmed and the individuality that is destroyed is more Dionysian and emotional than Apollonian and intellectual.

The value of Nietzsche lies in his suggestion that even if the misfortunes and sufferings of the tragic hero are real and, as unrecompensed and undeserved, not to be argued away as parts of some larger, consoling design, they can still be glorious and exalting. The words he uses of the experience of tragedy such as *joy* and *delight* seem more to the point than Aristotle's emotionally hygienic *catharsis*, Hegel's smug concept of *reconciliation* or Schopenhauer's *resignation*. The values that men create are somehow more than the men who create them and can survive the destruction of their creators. In tragedy this destruction is represented and here above all the valuable qualities of men are most strikingly revealed. The necessary impressiveness of the tragic hero is provoked to its fullest expression in the face of imminent destruction and stands out all the more noticeably against the background of disaster. Leavis, although he disowns Nietzsche ('the Nietzschean witness had better be dispensed with; at the best it introduces a disturbing vibration'), admirably states this side of Nietzsche's doctrine. 'The sense of heightened life that goes with the tragic experience is conditioned by a transcending of the ego – an escape from all attitudes of self-assertion. "Escape," perhaps, is not altogether a good word, since it might suggest something negative and irresponsible ... Actually the experience is constructive or creative, and involves recognizing positive value as in some way defined and vindicated by death. It is as if we were challenged at the profoundest level with the question, "In what does the significance of life reside?" and found ourselves contemplating, for answer, a view of life, and of the things giving it value, that makes the valued appear unquestionably more important than the valuer, so that significance lies, clearly and inescapably, in the willing adhesion of the individual self to something more important than itself' (*The Common Pursuit*, pp. 131-2). It is this Nietzschean point of view, midway between the extremes of Hegel and Schopenhauer and asserting the reality and attainability of human excellence in a world that neither guarantees the triumph of good nor the fruitlessness of human effort, that I shall consider in the final section.

IV. THE TRAGIC VIEW OF LIFE

'Tragedy,' says I.A. Richards, 'is still the form under which the mind may most clearly and freely contemplate the human situation, its issues unclouded, its possibilities revealed. To this its value is due and the supreme position among the arts which it has occupied in historical times and still occupies ... [It] is too great an exercise of the spirit to be classed among amusements or even delights, or to be regarded as a vehicle for the inculcation of such crude valuations as may be codified in a moral.' It is, he says elsewhere, 'the most general, all-accepting, all-ordering experience known'. And again, 'the central experience of tragedy and its chief value is an attitude indispensable for a fully developed life'. To accept this view of the metaphysical import of tragedy is not to accept the speculative psychology of aesthetic satisfaction as a balance of nervous impulses that Richards associates with it. My final object is to state more explicitly the character of this form under which the human situation may be most clearly and freely contemplated.

Its central theme, I suggest, is *the contingency of value*. Whatever is of value in the world, it asserts, is due to men. Not merely in the sense that without human purposes and satisfactions nothing would be of value at all, though that may be presupposed, but rather that the achievement and maintenance of value in the world can be brought about only by the efforts of men. There is no extra-human guarantee of the persistence and eventual triumph of value, no God or Reason, in the light of whose infallible purposes all evil, error and suffering is revealed as apparent and illusory. On the other hand, the extra-human world is not merely destructive or malevolent, men are not powerless to achieve value, their failure is no more guaranteed than their success. (I use the somewhat despised word *value* here to prevent concentration on the exclusively moral aspects of the good, whether these be taken in a conventional, negative sense related to the performance of duty, or more inclusively in relation to the collective interests of humanity. One type of moral value is realised by the dutiful man, another by the saint who goes beyond the claims of duty. Distinct from both is the value achieved by the hero, a category that must be understood to cover Shakespeare and Newton as well as Cromwell and Lincoln.)

Tragedy asserts, then, that value is contingent for its realisation on the agency of men. The tragic view of life rules out both the kind of optimism represented by Hegel, which asserts the necessity of value, and the kind of pessimism represented by Schopenhauer, which asserts its impossibility. Cosmic optimism holds that the good must triumph, that what seems to be bad will cease to seem so when viewed in its place in the whole scheme of things; cosmic pessimism holds that the good cannot triumph, that indeed what appears to be good is only an illusion which sharpens the suffering that must accompany its inevitable exposure. Neither of these views is easy to express too consistently, for each seems uncomfortably to combine an absolute thesis, to the effect that evil (or good) does not really exist at all but only seems to (which provokes the question whether the seeming of evil or good is not itself evil or good), with a temporal thesis to the effect that present evil or good will lead in the end to the complete triumph of their opposites. Now whether present evil or good are considered as necessary to the realisation of the ultimate state or not, they conflict with the idea that the final triumph of good or evil can be properly described as total. Whether the evil there is must or merely does precede the final triumph of good, it is real and the total situation is less good than it might conceivably have been. For our purpose it is not the state of the cosmic account that matters so much as the responsiveness of its items to the human will. Absolute optimism and pessimism make human activity pointless: since everything that happens is necessarily good or evil it makes no difference in point of value what in particular it is. Similarly those versions of temporal optimism and pessimism that hold the inevitable final state *necessarily* to require the realisation in preceding states of their opposites, rule out justifiable or rational choice. If evil must exist so that good may find its ultimate and necessary realisation it is something we are powerless to prevent. The other versions of optimism and pessimism take the world as it apparently is, as a mixture of good and evil: they add to this the consoling or depressing assurance that good or evil will triumph in the end but since the present state of things is logically independent of this final state there is no good reason to suppose that there is nothing men can do about it.

These highly schematic possibilities can now be given a more concrete form. Redemptive religion, and its secular analogue the theory of progress (in its liberal or Marxist form), are versions of optimism; what might be called desperate materialism, which emphasises human mortality, the coming death of the earth and the universal impossibility of life that follows from entropy, is a version of pessimism. How are these to be interpreted? Are they inconsistent with the tragic view of life? Richards remarks, 'Tragedy is only possible to a mind which is for the moment agnostic or Manichaean. The least touch of any theology which has a compensating Heaven to offer the tragic hero is fatal.' Is the tragic view of life consistent with Christian belief? It is certainly not compatible with possibly over-simple but nonetheless familiar theological interpretations of that belief. If mystically, in the manner of absolute optimism, Christianity contends that evil is unreal or if again the present and temporal evils of the world are necessary to the final triumph of good, if God's best is not the best, then human action can make no difference to the value realised in the world. But if temporal evil which does not contribute to the final triumph of good is admitted to be real, evil that God could eliminate without prejudice to his final aim but in fact does not, then there is a tragic version of Christianity. I must leave others to decide whether such a theology is orthodox. A readiness to countenance such a view, at any rate, might seem to be present in the view that the reality of evil is a mystery that we cannot fathom; though in fact such reverent suspense of judgment looks like an uneasy oscillation between two equally unpalatable alternatives: on the one hand an admission of the limitation of God's power or benevolence, on the other the squalidly comfortable view that the evils of the world are nothing to worry about since they are the indispensable preliminaries to the final triumph of good. The kind of cosmic gloom represented by Joseph Wood Krutch's *The Modern Temper* can be briefly considered. If science makes it reasonable to suppose that the death of the individual is a final extinction and that the human race is also destined to pass away that does not entail that nothing of positive value can exist in the meanwhile nor that human effort is irrelevant to its achievement.

The tragic view of life, with its assertion of the contingency of value, is necessarily presupposed by the idea that human action has any point. It entails that no reasonable optimism or pessimism can be universal or cosmic in scope. I can be optimistic or pessimistic about a particular project of my own, about the possibilities of my own life, about the prospects of a particular human society and even about the long-run prospects of the human race. But there is no reason to submit passively to these expectations.

11

Spaces and Times

We are accustomed to thinking of space and time as particulars or individuals – even if we should hesitate to describe them as things or objects or substances. We say 'space has three dimensions', 'material things occupy space', 'the debris has disappeared into space' and we talk in a comparable fashion about time. Not only do we think of space and time as individuals but, in many connections at any rate, we think of them as *unique* individuals. When we talk about spaces and times in the plural, when we say 'fill up the spaces on the form', 'it could go in the space between the lamp and the door', 'there were peaceful times in the early years of their marriage' we think of these multiple spaces and times as parts of the unique all-encompassing space and the unique all-encompassing time. Kant believed that we could not help thinking of them in this way. We do, at any rate, in fact think like this and it is this conviction that I want to examine. What, I shall ask first of all, does the belief that space and time are unique individuals come to? Secondly, is the belief in either case true? Finally, if it is true in either case, is it necessarily true or is it simply a matter of fact?

I

What, to start with, does it mean to say that space is a unique individual? We could say instead that all real things are contained in one and the same space. Two things are in the same space if they are spatially connected, if there is a route connecting them, if each lies at some definite distance and in some definite direction from the other. The relation of spatial connection is clearly symmetrical. If I know the route leading from A to B, I must also know the route leading from B to A. It is also transitive. Given the route from A to B and the route from B to C the route from A to C is unequivocally determined. Now it does not follow from these properties of the relation of spatial connection that everything is in one and the same space, that everything is spatially connected to everything else. What does follow is that if A and B are spatially connected then everything spatially connected to A is spatially connected to B and vice versa. Spatial connection is analogous in form to identity in colour, which is also symmetrical and transitive. Provided that A and B are identical in colour everything identical in colour with A is identical in colour with B. But there are, of course, many distinct colours and so many pairs of things which, while identical in colour with some things, are not identical in colour with each other. So far, then, it is an open possibility that spatial things should be arranged in spatially connected groups – just as coloured things can be arranged in colour-identical groups – all of whose members were spatially connected to each other but none of whose members were spatially connected to any of the members of any other group. To say that everything is in one space is simply to deny this possibility and to assert that all things are spatially connected. Naturally this assertion applies only to things that are in some sense spatial, things to which spatial predicates can intelligibly be ascribed. But that qualification does not affect the situation. The unity of space is not involved in the conception of a spatial thing. To say that a thing is spatial is to say either or both of the following: (a) that it is extended, that its parts are spatially connected to one another and (b) that it is spatially related, that it is spatially connected to something distinct from itself. It does not follow from either of these or from both of them taken together that it is spatially connected.to everything. It does not follow, then, from the mere conception of a spatial thing that space is a unique individual. So far the formal possibility of a plurality of spaces remains open.

The.same thing holds for time, as can easily be shown. Let us call two events temporally connected if there is a time-interval between them or if they are simultaneous. This relation, like that of spatial connection, is clearly symmetrical and transitive. So it allows for self-contained and exclusive groups of temporally connected events. Nor does the unity of time follow from the conception of a temporal thing or event. A temporal thing is something that occupies a lapse of time, that has temporally connected parts or phases and/or is something that is temporally connected to something else. From neither of these conditions does it follow that a temporal thing is temporally connected to everything.

But although the unity of space and the unity of time are not formally deducible from the concepts of spatial and temporal connection or the concepts of spatial and temporal things we do appear to believe that space and time are unities. Our direct information about the spatial and temporal connection of things is comparatively local. We observe the spatial disposition of things – the tree beside the barn, the mountain on the other side of the river – and we observe their temporal succession – the egg-white turning into a meringue, the bruise following the blow. Cartographers and chronologists piece these facts together in a single system of spatial and temporal positions. Provided that they can be answered at all, questions as to where things are or were and when they happened can always, it seems, be answered in terms of a system of positional references in which all positions are connected. As things are if a thing cannot be found a home in this unitary system of positions we conclude that there is no such thing.

The belief in the existence of one all-embracing space and one all-embracing time has not gone unchallenged. Bradley, in his determination to show the merely apparent character of space and time, addresses himself to the question at various points in his writings (*Appearance and Reality*, chapter 18, pp. 186-9). He argues that the unity of space and of time is not only no necessity but that it is not even a fact. Why, he asks, should we take time as one succession and not as a multitude of series which are altogether temporally disconnected and separate although the members of each such series are temporally related to one another? In support of this proposal he draws attention to the relation between events in dreams and stories. In these imaginings events occur that are indisputably temporal entities since they are temporally related to other events in the same imagining. Yet these events cannot be located in the framework of public or historical time. Bradley rejects the suggestion that they should be dated by the time of their appearance in the mental history of the imaginer which can, we may assume, be located in ordinary public time. His argument is characteristically summary: it would be absurd, he says, to date the events of a novel by the date of its publication. The point he is making can be more persuasively developed. We can understand having good reason for saying that a dream lasted for thirty seconds or less of the dreamer's mental history while the content of the dream occupied a much greater tract of time. Here the events of the dream and the process of dreaming it are at least in the same order though the intervals between the things ordered are different. But we could also have reason for saying that the things I dreamt about on Monday were subsequent to the events I dreamed about on Tuesday. For on Monday I might have dreamt about myself as I am now and on Tuesday about myself as a child at school. Similarly it is quite possible for novelists to think up and for novel-readers to read what would naturally be called the later part of a story before the earlier part. Isherwood's *The Memorial* and Fitzgerald's *Tender Is The Night* are familiar examples of the latter possibility. Bradley goes on to suggest that even if all the events of which I am aware do fit into one all-inclusive temporal scheme it does not follow that there could not be events entirely unrelated to my time-series. But this is an empty proposal since he does not suggest any circumstances in which we could have any reason to think that there were such series. He attempts to dispose of the unity of space in a more cursory way. At first glance the order of extension seems to be one whole. But if we reflect we can see that extension is manifested in dreams: the trapeze I dream that I am swinging on is an obviously spatial thing but it is connected by no spatial route whatever to the familiar spatial contents of the common world.

Bradley's arguments for plurality all derive from the spaces and times of imagination. But since Russell's first works on the theory of knowledge we have become familiar with another source for arguments of the same kind – the spaces and times of sensation. My visual sense-data are extended, spatial entities, occupying positions and spatially interrelated to other things in the space of my momentary visual field. To the extent that my sense-data are veridical and have been obtained under normal conditions of observation they will at least correspond to the contents of common, public space. But they are not located in it. For I am the only person in the world who is even tempted to suppose that they are to be found there. And I need not give way to this temptation. If I look at a mountain and then close my eyes I do not suppose that anything at all has happened in the part of public space that is occupied by the mountain. To the extent that my sense-data are not veridical they do not usually even correspond to anything in public space. At best they have some sort of causal determinant within it. To take an example whose existence at least is uncontentious: my after-image is plainly a spatial thing, it occupies at any one moment a definite position in my visual field, but it has no real location in the public world.

There is a short but not entirely convincing answer to Bradley's arguments from the spaces and times of imagination. It could be said that imaginary objects and events, the contents of our dreams and fantasies, are nowhere at all. The contents of our imaginings are simply unreal. They can raise no problems of spatial and temporal location because they just do not exist. But to this it could be replied that although the trapeze I dreamed about last night has never hung in any actual, publicly observable circus tent, there really was something, a private entity, an image or dream-element, of which I was aware shortly before I woke up this morning. The remarks I produce at the breakfast table are not free and spontaneous creations, mere playing with words. I make earnest efforts to get my descriptions right, to leave nothing out, to set out the events dreamed of in the exact order in which I dreamt them. Bradley's argument can be countered in this way only if one is prepared to adopt a theory of dreaming like Professor Malcolm's which takes them to be no more than the utterance of sentences which, though just like the sentences we use to give genuine descriptions of our past experience, are not in fact being used for this purpose and are not intended to be understood as if they were. If this is accepted we do not have to worry about the spatial and temporal character of whatever it is that the report of a dream describes because such reports do not describe anything.

The most straightforward way of bringing out the implausibility of this theory is phenomenological: one has only to point to the experienced difference between making a story up out of one's head and reporting a dream or an earlier product of the imagination. There are two sides to the activities of the imagination: the story and the experience. The story is the words, written or spoken, in which a dream is reported or a piece of fiction is told. The experience is the body of images or private elements that the dreamer was aware of while he was dreaming, that the novelist was aware of while he was working out his book and that the reader is no doubt intermittently aware of as he reads. Only if we can eliminate the experience, by regarding it, for example, as no more than the disposition to produce a story, can Bradley's argument be summarily disposed of. Even if we do eliminate experience from our account of imagination there is still the spatial and temporal character of sensation to be dealt with. Bradley's argument for a plurality of spaces and times can be said to rest, then, on the spatial and temporal character of private experience – of images, dreams and sense-impressions. In private experience we are aware of things that are spatially extended and temporally enduring. These things are spatial and temporal in virtue both of the spatial and temporal relations between their parts and of the fact that they are spatially and temporally related to other spatial and temporal things. The dream-trapeze has ropes stretching away above the bar and the whole thing hovers above the sawdust surface of the dream arena. If we cannot show private experience to be the disposition to speak in a peculiar way we must either accommodate its contents in the unitary space and time of the common world or concede Bradley's point – that there is in fact a plurality of spaces and times.

We should perhaps reconsider this first alternative that Bradley so rapidly brushed aside. Can the tiger I am now picturing in my mind's eye be accommodated in public space? It cannot be accommodated at the place at which it looks as if it were. In the first place it may not look as if it were anywhere in particular. The background against which I am now experiencing it may be too dim and vague to provide any clue to location or it may be entirely unfamiliar. In these circumstances there can be no such activity as trying to find out where it is imagined to be. All I can do is to imagine it to be definitely somewhere, perhaps on the steps of the Albert Memorial and thus against a definite background located in public space. But in doing this I have not so much found out where it was as moved it there or, should one say, imagined another, no doubt very similar, tiger to be there. The situation is no better if the tiger does definitely look as if it were at some known and familiar place. For even if I dream of a tiger on the steps of the Albert Memorial, the real steps of the real Albert Memorial are not occupied by the tiger I am aware of in my dream. I can perfectly well have such a dream and accept reliable testimony that no tiger has been seen anywhere near the place I dreamt of. Even if, by some wild chance, there was an escaped tiger on the actual steps at the moment I was having my dream, we do not have to say that it is the very tiger I was dreaming of, however close the similarity. If my dreams turned out to be consistently correct representations of what was currently going on in the places I was dreaming about we might come to regard them as visions or cases of long-distance perception. But in that case they would no longer be dreams and it is characteristic of dreams that they do not exhibit any reliably attested correspondence of this kind.

The only other alternative is to locate the dreamed-of or imagined tiger at the place where I am, as, for example, quite literally, in my head. But this is an obviously hopeless manoeuvre. When I dream of tigers there generally are no tigers anywhere near where I am, my head is not large enough to contain tigers, the possible pattern of electrical activity in my brain associated with dreaming of tigers is not identifiable with the tigers I dream of since I know that I have dreamt of tigers but the electrical activity is an unstable compound of hearsay and guesswork. We cannot literally identify the places *in* my experience with the places *of* my experience.

II

Is the same thing true of time? Earlier, developing a rather sketchy argument of Bradley's, I suggested that the lapse of time someone dreams of might be much greater than the interval between the time at which he began to dream of it and the time at which he stopped doing so and I also suggested that one could dream of events happening in an order opposite to that of the events of dreaming of them. It might seem that these suggestions could be resisted. Could we not say that the estimate of time made in the dream is just a mistaken one, that the dreamed-of fall from the top of the building and the dreamed-of splash into the river are really only a fifteenth of a second apart even though they seemed in the dream to be separated by an interval of several seconds or even minutes? Again if I dream on Monday of taking off bandages to find my wound almost healed and on Tuesday of receiving the wound with a great deal of associated connecting tissue to link the two dreams together am I not compelled to say that the time in the dreams is in reverse order to the time of dreaming then? The wound I dream of on Tuesday could be said to be a new wound in the same place, if we felt compelled to link the two dreams together. In the first example the determination to identify the time of the dream with the time of dreaming is rather gratuitous. The correlation of dreams with their manifestations in the public world is tentative and infrequent. My audible cry of 'help' does not have to be taken as simultaneous with my dreaming of a fall from the building nor my visible shudder with the splash. In most cases there is nothing even to suggest to us that the time of the events dreamed of is anything but what it appears to be. In the second example the situation is not so clear. In the first place the temporal propriety being defended is of a more fundamental kind. The topology of time-order is more sacred than the geometry of time-intervals. All the same it would seem unreasonable to deny that there was a difference between the time of the dream and the time of dreaming it if on a series of twelve nights one dreamt and remembered in precise detail a series of occurrences whose content could only be naturally arranged in exactly the reverse order to that in which they were dreamed. My general conclusion, so far, then is that we do have reason for admitting the existence of a plurality of experiential spaces over and above the space of the common world and that we could have reason for a similar admission about experiential times. There is no obvious contradiction in saying that there is such a plurality and, given the implausibility of strictly verbal accounts of private experience, better reason for saying that they do exist than that they do not. However if we consider the character of these experiential spaces and times more closely it will appear that they are so different from physical space and time that the concession we have made to Bradley's line of thought involves only a small modification of the common conviction of spatial and temporal unity.

III

There are two fundamental differences between physical and experiential space and time. Where the physical is vast and systematic, the experiential is small and fragmentary; where the physical is public, the experiential is private. These are not exactly contingent features even though comprehensiveness and publicity could vary in degree. Consider the space of dreams. There is ordinarily no ground for saying that the space of Monday night's dream has anything to do, or is any way connected, with the space of

Tuesday night's dream. We often have several spatially disconnected dreams in one night. And in the course of one more or less continuous dream it is only the comparatively momentary spatial relationships of the dreamed-of things, the spatial relationships revealed in a temporal cross-section of the whole dream, that are at all definite. First I am on the trapeze. Below me I see a familiar face. Shortly afterwards my friend and I are seated side by side in a boat. Such continuity as there is is provided by the familiar face but it is not sufficient to establish any spatial relation between the trapeze and the boat. Many dreams are more coherent than this, of course, but it would seem that the constructibility of non-momentary spaces, spaces that endure as the scenes of comparatively protracted change, is the exception rather than the normal case in the experiential realm. We do have dreams where temporally successive incidents occur against a fairly definite and persisting background and there can be enough correspondence between the spatial contents of two quite distinct dreams for it to be reasonable to regard both as relating to one and the same spatial order. But as things are this is about as much in the way of system and coherence as our dreams ordinarily yield. It is plain that the same thing holds for our imaginings which, being so much more interrupted, so much more exposed to the solicitations of the external world, are perhaps even less coherent than dreams. It is also to some extent true of our sensations which become coherent only as a result of a good deal of suppression and filling-in. Privacy is as obvious a feature of the experiential realm as fragmentariness or incoherence. Nobody, as things are, can tell what our dreams or imaginings are unless we tell them. In the case of sensations reliable inferences can be made on the basis of well-established correlations between sense-experience and the condition and environment of the observer. If such correlations were available for inference to the other domains of experience they would have to rest in the end on the admissions of observers. We can imagine circumstances in which the correspondence between the dreams of two or more people was so extensive as to lead us to say that they were dreaming the same dream, especially if in the event of some marginal disagreement between two corresponding dreamers one of them subsequently admitted that he was mistaken. If there were many more blind people than there are the remarks of the sighted about clouds and sunsets might well appear to be the by-products of a widely-shared dream. This is not altogether unfamiliar ground. The raptures of mysticism and musical appreciation incite, in rather different ways, just such a response amongst the less respectful of the unititiated. Only if the correspondence becomes general enough to count as normal can dreaming come to be accounted as observation.

These differences between physical and experiential space and time are substantial enough as things are for the thesis that space and time are unitary to survive Bradley's arguments almost intact. Instead of saying that there is only one space and only one time the defender of unity must say that there is only one space and only one time that is coherent or public or both. Coherent and/or public space and time are, he might say, the only real space and time. Other spatial and temporal entities are fragmentary and private, a sort of ontological litter to be bundled into the wastepaper basket of the imaginary. He could argue that we count only those things as real that can be fitted into the one coherent and public space and time, that such locatability is a criterion of being real. For what is a dream or a fantasy or an illusion of the senses but an experience that fails to fit into the unitary spatio-temporal scheme? From this it follows that Descartes' hypothesis that perhaps everything is a dream is illegitimate. It cannot be significantly affirmed since to call a tract of experience a dream is to say that it fails to conform to the standard of coherence and publicity exhibited by the greater part of our experience. So to say that all our experience is a dream is to say that none of it comes up to the standard of most of it, a straight self-contradiction. Here is one case, at any rate, where the paradigm-case argument works. It does not entirely dispose of the Cartesian hypothesis. A man might have acquired a standard of coherence from somewhere else, perhaps a religious experience, though this would not show that the present distinction between waking and dreaming was improper, only that it should be differently named. More important is the fact that even if life hitherto cannot all have been a dream it does not follow that the whole structure will not come to pieces in the next few minutes, that from then on none of our experience will attain the standard we have come to expect and all will be as incoherent as what we have hitherto regarded as dreams.

IV

The position we have arrived at, then, is that even if it is not true that absolutely everything can be located in one space and one time, everything real, provided that it is spatial and temporal at all, can be so located. If the suggestion that such locatability is a criterion of being real is correct, it follows that the thesis of unity in its revised form is a necessary truth. Now this is essentially the opinion of Kant (*Critique of Pure Reason*, A25, B39). Space and time, he said, are not discursive or general concepts of the relations of things in general but pure intuitions. In other words they are not universals but particulars and unique particulars at that. His argument is that we can conceive limited spaces and times only as parts of one all-inclusive space and one all-inclusive time. These unique particulars are not literally composed of perceptually observed spatial extents and temporal durations, are not constructions from these extents and durations as elements, because they are somehow presupposed by these elements.

The logical status of arguments from conceivability is always insecure and in this type of case especially so, for we are concerned with a very primordial feature of our experience. Our habits of thinking about space and time are so early acquired and so deeply ingrained that their extreme familiarity can easily look like logical indispensability. It is clear anyway that we do in fact take all real spatial extents and temporal durations to be parts of the one space and the one time. But Kant is claiming more than this and to assess his claim we must ask whether we are compelled to think in this way. We can even concede that on our present interpretation of 'real' the statement 'everything real is in one space and in one time' is analytic. The question still remains whether there are any conceivable circumstances in which it would be reasonable to modify this interpretation. For it can be maintained that there are, in a sense, degrees of analyticity. That we have a certain concept at all can often be explained by referring to facts which might not have obtained. With any one concept there may be a number of such explanatory facts which can be arranged in some order of importance. The essentials of the concept would remain if some of the less important facts did not obtain and if, therefore, the conventions that depend on them did not exist. Let us take a very simple example, that of brotherhood. Our existing concept of brotherhood is determined by facts of biology and sociology. Men are borne by women, as a result of sexual intercourse between those women and other men, and pass the helpless years of infancy in a group commonly led, protected and provided for by their parents. Now imagine a society in which women were elaborately promiscuous or in which all conception came about through artificial insemination by anonymous donors. Suppose also that the family group consisted of the mother and her children alone. In these circumstances we should presumably count children of the same mother as brothers and the statement 'all brothers have both parents in common' would be no longer analytic but contingent and false. It is too narrow to describe this situation as one in which we should use the word 'brother' to mean what we now mean by 'maternal half-brother'. For what is really important about the concept of brotherhood, that it relates persons who share both a biological inheritance and certain fundamental loyalties and affections, is still retained by the revised concept. Now suppose that children were taken from their mothers at birth and brought up in institutions. Even here there might be some point in having the concept if the institutions in which children were brought up had something of the emotional structure of the ordinary human family as it now exists.

Let us look at a more complicated and perhaps more. philosophically interesting example considered by Professor Ayer, which concerns the privacy of pain (*The Problem of Knowledge*, chapter V, section iii, pp. 228-9). As things are, the causal conditions of pain are commonly found in the body of the sufferer. If I am in pain it is not usually the case that anyone near me has a similar affliction and I cannot generally get rid of the pain by moving about. Now suppose that circumstances were different, that everyone whose body is in a certain region of space during a certain period of time feels a pain of much the same sort, that the intensity of this pain uniformly diminishes as they move away from a determinable point in the region and that it disappears altogether when they are at a certain distance, roughly agreed upon by all, beyond this central point. In these circumstances, Ayer suggests, we might well cease to think of pains, as we now do, as being private and might come to accord them much the same sort of status as we now give to material things. 'Look out', we might say to a man walking in a certain direction, 'there's a pain there'; and we might say this with good reason even if there were at the time no one in the region in question and therefore no one suffering the pain. If this were to come about people might cease to speak of 'my pain' and 'your pain' and there would be no question that different people could feel the very same pain. In other words the statement 'no one but me can feel the pain I am feeling' would no longer be analytic. The same thing would happen to the statement 'all pains are felt by somebody'.

It would still, of course, be open to philosophers to talk about pain-data and they might well be encouraged to do so if there were perceptible differences of sensitivity between people or if some people felt pain in places . where nobody else did. They would have the same reasons for talking about pain-data and pain-hallucinations as they now have for talking about sense-data and hallucinations of the senses. Ayer's supposition reveals the contingencies on which our current convictions about the concept of pain rest. If it came true it would be reasonable to alter these conventions and to regard many statements as synthetically true or false which we now regard as analytic or contradictory. The essentials of the concept have not been tampered with; under his supposition there are still experiences which people generally and instinctively dislike having.

Can we construct a myth that will reveal the ultimately conventional character of the Kantian thesis that real space and time are unitary? Do our current convictions about the unity of space and time rest in the end on contingencies which we can conceive as ceasing to obtain? I believe that there is an important asymmetry in this respect between space and time and I shall argue that a coherent multi-spatial myth can be envisaged but not a coherent multi-temporal one. So I shall begin with space.

V

Now suppose that your dream-life underwent a remarkable change. Suppose that on going to bed at home and falling asleep you found yourself to all appearances waking up in a hut raised on poles at the edge of a lake. A dusky woman, whom you realise to be your wife, tells you to go out and catch some fish. The dream continues with the apparent length of an ordinary human day, replete with an appropriate and causally coherent variety of tropical incident. At last you climb up the rope ladder to your hut and fall asleep. At once you find yourself awaking at home, to the world of normal responsibilities and expectations. The next night, life by the side of the tropical lake continues in a coherent and natural way from the point at which it left off. Your wife says 'You were very restless last night. What were you dreaming about?' and you find yourself giving her a condensed version of your English day. And so it goes on. Injuries given in England leave scars in England, insults given at the lakeside complicate lakeside personal relations. One day in England, after a heavy lunch, you fall asleep in your armchair and dream of yourself, or find yourself, waking up in the middle of the night beside the lake. Things get too much for you at the lakeside, your wife has departed with all the cooking-pots and you suspect that she is urging the villagers to sacrifice you to the moon. So you fall on your fish-spear and from that moment on your English slumbers are disturbed no more than in the old pre-lakeside days.

There are some loose ends in this story but I think they can be tidied up. What, first of all, about your lakeside life before the dream began? Either the lakesiders will have to put up with the fact that you have lost your memory, and we can leave it open whether they are in a position to fill in the blank for you or not, or you might find 'memories' of your earlier lakeside career spontaneously cropping up. The most immediately digestible possibility is perhaps a version of the latter in which your lakeside past gradually comes back to you after an initial period of total amnesia. But complete loss of memory is the easiest to handle. Next, how are the facts that you are awake sixteen hours and asleep eight hours in each environment to be reconciled? How can sixteen hours of England be crammed into eight hours of lake and vice versa? Well, why not? As long as there is some period of sleep in each day in each place there is room for the waking day in the other place. We often say, after all, that dreams seem to take much longer than they actually do. The same principle could be applied to our alternative worlds. To make the thing fairly precise we could correlate hours in England with hours by the lakeside, on the basis of nocturnal mumblings and movements, so that midnight to eight a.m. in England is eight a.m. to midnight at the lake and vice versa. This would have mildly embarrassing consequences but not contradictory ones. If I stay up till 4 a.m. in England I cannot wake up beside the lake until 4 in the afternoon. If an alarm clock wakes me two hours early in England, i.e. at 6 a.m., then I shall find myself dropping irresistibly off at eight p.m. by the lake. One embarrassment is common to both hypotheses: if in either place I stay up all night I must sleep all through the day in the other. Some of these embarrassments can be avoided by supposing that the lakeside day is normally eight hours long and the lakeside night sixteen hours long. To imagine such a comatose manner of life is perhaps easier than having to put up with the embarrassments of rigid correlation.

Now if this whole state of affairs came about it would not be very unreasonable to say that we lived in two worlds. So far it may seem that only one of the properties of physical space as we understand it has been added to the space of dreams, namely its coherence. But it only takes a small addition to equip it with publicity, an addition already implicit in the fable as I have told it. For I am not alone at the lakeside, there is my wife and the moon-worshipping villagers, whose statements and behaviour may confirm all the spatial beliefs I form at the lakeside, with the usual minor exceptions. It might be argued that this sort of publicity is bogus, that it is only dream-publicity. But as it stands that is just prejudice. At the lakeside, on my hypothesis, we have just as good reason to take our spatial beliefs as publicly confirmed as we have in England. However, a less questionable type of publicity can be provided if we suppose that the dreams of everyone in England reveal a coherent order of events in our mythical lake district and let everyone have one and only one correlated lake-dweller whose waking experiences are his dreams. (In this case we should have to correlate the clocks of England and the lakeside, either by the rather embarrassing proposal of elastic time-intervals or by that of the eight-hour lakeside day. For otherwise I could drop off at the lakeside on Monday, wake up before you go to sleep and tell you a whole lot of things about Tuesday in England before, from your point of view, they had happened.) There are various ways in which we can suppose that people who know one another in England could come to recognise one another at the lakeside, for example, by the drawing of self-portraits from memory or by agreeing, in England, to meet at some lakeside landmark.

I shall not pursue the hypothesis of a dream that is public in this strong sense since it becomes imaginatively too cumbrous, though not, I think, self-contradictory. One special difficulty is that in such circumstances some measure of causal interpenetration by the two worlds would be natural. Even if physical causation cannot, *ex hypothesi*, operate from one region into the other, psychological causation presumably would. The injury I do you at the lakeside may be revenged not there but in England. I think, in fact, that my original one-man hypothesis is sufficient for the purpose in hand. But we can publicise this a bit further without going all the way to publicity in the strong sense. It might, for instance, be the case that everyone's dream-life was coherent but that no one person's dream-life corresponded with anyone else's. In this case everyone would inhabit two real spaces, one common to all and one peculiar to each. This residual asymmetry can, of course, be eliminated by requiring that the same be true of all the lakesiders. On this supposition the worlds we have some reason to believe in fray off into infinity. Each of my lakeside acquaintances has his other life, in which he comes across people, each of whom has his and so on. But this infinity does not seem to be a vicious one.

It might be said that if this myth were realised we should either have to say that the dream-place was somewhere in ordinary physical space or else that it was still only a dream. Both of these alternatives can be effectively disputed. Suppose that I am in a position to institute the most thorough geographical investigations and however protractedly and carefully these are pursued they fail to reveal anywhere on earth like my lake. But could we not then say that it must be on some other planet? We could but it would be gratuitous to do so. There could well be no positive reason whatever, beyond our fondness for the Kantian thesis, for saying that the lake is located somewhere in ordinary physical space and there are, in the circumstances envisaged, good reasons for denying its location there. Still suppose we do find a place, in New Guinea let us say, exactly like the lakeside. I, the dreamer, lead the expedition into the village, brandishing trade goods. Friendly relations having been established with the elders of the place, we are led to the longhouse to meet the populace and there, to my amazement, is the face I have often seen in my dreams while bending over the pools at the lake's edge in pursuit of fish. Now if the owner of this face is fast asleep and cannot be woken up until I go to sleep this village and the place of my dreams can be identified. But suppose he is wide awake and we get into conversation. He turns out to have coherent dreams about my life in England and in fact to have dreamt last night of my progress towards the village on the preceding day, just as I dreamt last night of what he was doing the day before. The natural conclusion will be that we are connected by a kind of delayed cross-telepathy and that what the Kantian insists are still only dreams are at any rate in the same order of reality as dreams. If, then, we do find what is to all intents and purposes the place of my dreams, the Kantian's dilemma – either in the one real space or just a dream – does apply. But if we do not there is no reason to insist upon it.

If, failing to find the scene of my coherent dream in ordinary physical space, we insist that it is, then, only a dream we are neglecting the point of marking off the real from the imaginary. Why, as things are, do we have this ontological wastepaper basket for the imaginary? Because, approximately, there are some experiences that we do not have to bother about afterwards, that we do not, looking back on them, need to take seriously. Dream-events, where they have consequences at all, do not have serious consequences. If I dream of cutting somebody's throat my subsequent dreams will in all probability be entirely unrelated to him and to my act. Even if they are, when I am haled into court I am as likely to be given a bunch of flowers as a death-sentence. But beside the lake there is a place for prudence, forethought and accurate recollection. It is an order of events in which I am a genuine agent. There is every reason there for me to take careful note and make deliberate use of my experience. Reality, I am suggesting, then, is that part of our total experience which it is possible and prudent to take seriously. It is, of course, because I am ultimately interpreting reality in this way that I can envisage dispensing with locatability in one physical space and time as a criterion of it. My conclusion so far, then, is that it is a contingent matter that the experience we can and prudently should take seriously can all be assigned to one space. Kant's unity of space is not an unalterable necessity of thought.

VI

Let us turn finally to the case of time. Can an analogous myth be constructed here? Can we conceive of living in two distinct orders of temporal extension? The lakeside story did present some peculiar temporal features, in some of its versions a sort of time-stretching, but at least the proprieties of temporal order were respected. And, with the eight-hour day, it was possible to do without time-stretching. Another avoidable difficulty was the temporal status of the events 'remembered' by me at the lakeside after I have started, *nel mezzo del cammin*, consciously living there. Here again temporal order is all right. The trouble arises about the correlation of my 'remembered' twelfth birthday and initiation ceremony at the lakeside with events in my English life. However this is not a serious problem. Either we can say the date of my initiation in English terms is unknown, apart from being before such-and-such a date on which my lakeside experiences started, or we can extrapolate with the help of rules of correlation we have established in the directly experienced parts of my lakeside life. Our multi-spatial myths are not, then, also multi-temporal myths.

So for a multi-temporal myth we must begin again from the beginning. What we are in search of, in general terms, is this: two groups of orderly and coherent experiences where the members of each group are temporally connected but no member of either group has any temporal relation to any member of the other. Such a search seems doomed from the start. How can these experiences be my experiences unless they constitute a single temporal series? This will become clearer if we consider some examples of possible multi-temporal myths.

Consider first the myth that results from a small complication of the original myth about England and the lakeside. Suppose that my memories become, so to speak, disconnected, that I can remember the relative temporal situation of English events and the relative temporal situation of lakeside events but not the temporal relations of any English events to any lakeside event. I can remember that I got on the bus after I had spoken to Jones about our favourite television programme. I can remember taking part in the fertility-rite after setting the fish-traps. What I cannot remember is whether getting on the bus occurred before or after setting the fish-traps. The trouble with this obstacle to unitary dating is that it is too easily circumvented. At the beginning of day 1 in England I write down in order all the lakeside events I can remember. On day 2 in England I cannot remember whether the events of day 1 follow or preceded the lakeside events in the list. But the list will be there to settle the matter and I can, of course, remember when I compiled it.

A desperate shift that might suggest itself at this point is the supposition that I cannot remember lakeside events at all when I am in England nor English events while I am at the lakeside. But this is self-destroying. For unless I have memories of one series of events while experiencing the other there can be no reason for saying that I am involved in both of them, that both are experienced by one and the same person. *Ex hypothesi* the lakeside can have no physical, observable traces in England, so my memories of it in England are the only reason there can be for me, in England, to think that the lakeside exists.

Another line of approach requires us to suppose that the experience of dreaming coherently about the lakeside is general or at least widespread. It might be thought that we could all pass in and out of the coherent dream-world, or the alternative reality, at different times. But suppose the salient events of the day for two people in England are kipper for breakfast and steak for lunch, while the salient event for the approximately corresponding day at the lakeside is a distant volcanic eruption. The two people breakfast together in England, so their kipper-eating is simultaneous. After breakfast one of them drops off and witnesses the volcanic eruption. He awakes for lunch and over their simultaneous steaks tells his partner about the eruption. After lunch the second man falls asleep and witnesses the eruption for himself. At first glance this might seem to suggest that the eruption cannot be fitted at all into the English time-sequence. But on reflection it is clear that we can fit 'the eruption' in only too well. For it happened, to A, before their simultaneous lunch and, to B, after it. What happens before an event, happens before everything that happens after that event. Therefore the eruption happened before itself. The only consistent conclusion from the data is that two eruptions took place and for each of these there is a perfectly unequivocal position in the English time-series.

The moral of these unsuccessful attempts to construct a multi-temporal myth is the same in each case. Any event that is memorable by me can be fitted in to the single time-sequence of my experience. Any event that is not memorable by me is not an experience of mine. This second proposition is not equivalent to a Lockean account of personal identity which holds my experiences to be all those experiences that I can remember. For the memorability to which it refers is memorability in principle not in practice. All that is required for an experience to be mine is that I should be logically capable of remembering it. But from the fact that, at a given time, I am logically capable of remembering a certain experience, it follows that the experience is temporally antecedent to the given time, the time of my current experience, and so is in the same time, the same framework of temporal relations, as it is. Thus if an experience is mine it is memorable and if it is memorable it is temporally connected to my present state. The question we are raising – is it conceivable that we should inhabit more than one time – answers itself. For what it asks is: could my experience be of such a kind that the events in it could not be arranged in a single temporal sequence? And it seems unintelligible to speak of a collection of events as constituting the experience of one person unless its members form a single temporal sequence. This view of the concept of a person's experience is supported by another consideration. It is possible to imagine that our experience might not be spatial. As Strawson has shown, if our experience were all auditory, although it might contain features and differentiations which could be used as clues to spatial position with the aid of correlations with the deliverances of other senses, these features would have no spatial import on their own (*Individuals*, chapter 2). On the other hand it is not possible to imagine an experience that is not temporal. We should, of course, have no sense of the passage of time unless our experience exhibited change. But an unchanging experience is no more intelligible than a non-temporal one. An experience of one unvarying sound, or even of an unvarying mixture of sounds, would not be an experience at all. A high, thin, metaphysical whistle sounding in one's mind's ear from birth to death would be in principle undetectable, like the impression of the self that Hume rummaged unsuccessfully around in his consciousness for.

I conclude, then, that we can at least conceive circumstances in which we should have good reason to say that we knew of real things located in two quite distinct spaces. But we cannot conceive of such a state of affairs in the case of time. Our conception of experience is essentially temporal in a way in which it is not essentially spatial.

12
Elitism

The present [197] Labour Government in Britain is committed to removing selection by ability from the school system, or at least that part of it which is supported by public funds. Some time ago, the then education minister announced that in 1976 the winding up of the direct grant system would begin. The direct grant schools, among which are many of the best British urban day schools – for example, Manchester Grammar School and Dulwich – reserve a substantial number of places for able children from poor families whose fees are paid by the local government authority. The National Union of Teachers welcomed the announcement in the following words: 'the decision marks a big step towards the removal of elitism from British education.'

This is a typical occurrence of one of the most used words of political disapproval at the present time. Elitism is said to be exemplified by private schools and private medical arrangements. It is held to be present in school curriculums that emphasise high culture and neglect folk or pop culture. The word tends to be applied to any institution in which plans are drawn up and decisions made by any sort of inner circle of experienced professionals, indeed where decisions are reached by anything short of a mass meeting. Someone must by now have applied it, or soon will, to the division between officers and other ranks in the armed forces, to restaurants or clothing or cars of high quality, to grammatical rather than demotically colloquial speech and writing – to any form of human activity, in short, in which an effort is made to rise above a level of achievement accessible to the weakest performer.

In very general terms, what elitism is is clear enough. It is the loathsome opposite to comprehensive egalitarianism, the principle that all good things – in particular power, wealth, and status – should be equally distributed. In these very general terms, elitism seems to be the belief that there are often good reasons for unequal distribution of the things to which human beings attach value. But if one tries to arrive at a more detailed and specific conception of elitism, the matter becomes less straightforward. Is there really a theory or doctrine of elitism? If so, who are its theorists? Is the competitive pursuit of status and other desired ends by the superior always elitist? Are there to be no more competitive sports and games, with their associated apparatus of league tables and orders of merit? Is the bestowal of licenses to practice medicine or drive cars on the basis of examinations, which some will pass and some fail, unacceptably discriminatory?

The word *elitism* gets some of its pejorative force from association. In common speech, the élite used to be that socially select circle, united by mutual admiration and contempt for those outside, who frequented nightclubs and race meetings and stayed up in dress clothes into the small hours. More recently, we have become familiar with the elite guard of the SS; and the best known of the sociological elite theorists, Vilfredo Pareto, was, by and large, a supporter of Mussolini's fascism. The older association makes the idea of an elite both fatuous and rather offensive. The newer one makes it evil and menacing.

I am inclined to think that the fundamental elitist text is Plato's *Republic*. There are several instructive features about the choice. In the first place, the work is not as antiquated as the date of its composition might suggest. It was, after all, the operating manual of Benjamin Jowett, master of Balliol in the mid-nineteenth century and the most influential determiner of the style and purpose of British higher education from the time of its major reform in the 1850s and 1860s. In Jowett's interpretation, Plato's guardians became a public service elite of competitively selected and highly trained people, a ruling class not recruited by birth but by competitive examination, an intellectually superior mandarinate. It is by the products of this system, for the most part, that Britain has been ruled for the last century. The higher administration of the country – Parliament, the civil service, the upper management of the larger public and private corporations – has been manned by people selected and trained in accordance with Jowett's prescriptions. At the highest level, that of prime minister, there have been some feudal residues, such as Salisbury and Churchill and one or two men of the people such as Lloyd George and Ramsay MacDonald, but the norm has been Jowett's version of the Platonic guardian: Balfour, Asquith, Attlee, Heath, Wilson.

A second point about Plato's elite is that it is selected by merit or ability, on the basis of its members' possession of the talents appropriate to their elevated position. Elitism, that is to say, is not just inequality, but meritocratic inequality. The more traditional kind of inequality was largely a matter of inheritance. It thus seemed to be, like such other inherited advantages as good looks or good health, a matter of chance; a possible object of envy, no doubt, on the part of the less favoured, but not the outcome of any deliberate, and thus readily alterable, social arrangement. The spectacle of inherited advantage seems to be less exasperating to those who do not have it than the kind of advantage that has been achieved by an individual's own efforts and gifts.

A final point is the closed or sequestered nature of the Platonic ruling class. To start with, its membership is to be supplied largely, though not exclusively, by the children of preceding members. Once in the class, a person receives a special kind of education and lives a special kind of life. Its mode of existence has often been seen as the paradigm of monasticism. It is more of a caste than a class.

The egalitarian opponents of elitism react to all three of these features of the Platonic ideal. They believe it to be exemplified by the social structure of

Britain at the present time. They are offended by its insistence on fundamental differences of capacity between human beings, for it assumes that the fostering and rewarding of superior ability are essential to the well-being of society as a whole. They see it as picking out and secluding a small number of allegedly superior people from the rest of the community, the masses that are the proper counterpart of the elite, and endowing them with a monopoly of the power and status and the first and largest call on the wealth that all men desire.

Now, although I am opposed to comprehensive egalitarianism, I am far from willing to endorse the entire Platonic package. I am an elitist to the extent that I believe excellence should be recognised, fostered, and rewarded, but I am not in favour of an elite that is closed, either with regard to the selection of its members or with regard to its style of life and activity. I do not want to see society divided into a minority of highly educated manipulators and a manipulated mass, sharing neither language nor interests, almost two distinct human species. I believe that much of the rhetorical force of current egalitarian anti-elitism depends on linking the recognition of excellence with the idea of the elite as a caste, sharply separated from the masses, a link that involves the former in the deserved disrepute of the latter.

How far does the recognition of excellence imply the emergence of an elite that is a closed caste? Before answering that question, something has to be said about the meaning of the word *recognition*. In its most literal and restricted sense, to *recognise* excellence is to admit that there is such a thing, hence to concede that this person has it and that person does not. But one can admit the existence of a distinction without going on to do anything about it. We all know that people are of different heights and weights, but little in the way of policy depends on the fact, aside from allocation of beds and car seats.

In the more inclusive sense in which I intend to use it, recognition of excellence involves, beyond the acknowledgment that it exists, the belief that it should be fostered and encouraged to develop, largely by appropriate education; that it should be provided with opportunity for its effective exercise; and that its exercise should be encouraged by rewards. All three of these things are going to be more or less costly, so that in one way or another a larger than average share of the community's resources will be diverted to the possessors of excellence.

The educational fostering of ability requires a longer educational process, which is itself negatively productive: it requires smaller classes and it requires superior teachers, whose services can be secured only by larger than average rewards. Those teachers who carry out conspicuously valuable services for the community need to be relieved of the everyday practical nuisances that are calculated to use up time and energy that could be more valuably employed. (I do not imagine that Fidel Castro goes to work by bus.) More positively, they need the power and resources without which their abilities cannot be actually exercised at all. Finally, they need some direct inducement to apply themselves to the tasks, responsible or arduous or both, that in everyone's interest they should perform.

Many who would be prepared to recognise excellence in the minimal sense of admitting that it exists, and who would also agree that it ought to be fostered and provided with opportunities for effective expression, would deny that any further reward needs to be given. Responsible work supplies the satisfaction of power. Interesting work, in particular where it makes full use of the qualities people most prize in themselves, is its own reward. Insofar as excellence is recognised in the minimal sense it will inevitably attract status to itself – that is to say, respect and a measure of deference that goes beyond what is directly entailed by the formal possession of power. What need, then, is there for any further reward of an economic kind?

Sterner egalitarians argue that once you allow a minority, whether excellent or not, to acquire power and status, its members will enevitably use their position to secure an economic advantage for themselves. And once that happens, you have the makings of a closed caste. Greater wealth, beyond what is needed simply to make it possible for socially valuable tasks to be carried out, will lead to a special style of life. What is more important in the long run is that the members of an elite that is notably better off than the mass of the population will try to confer on their children the advantages they themselves have enjoyed. In a way, provided they carry out the ordinary duties of parents, they are bound to do so.

There are, in fact, three different kinds of advantage that children can derive from their parents. The first is simply genetic. Any beneficial characteristic that is biologically inheritable – most notably, if controversially, intelligence – must pass from one generation to its descendants. Second, there are the benefits received from being brought up in spacious and comfortable circumstances: at the very least, those of being well fed and housed; more elusively, those of growing up in an intelligent, stimulating, interesting atmosphere. No doubt in the case of many ostensibly privileged children this advantage is neutralised by the opportunity wealth gives to indifferent parents to neglect their children, by handing them over to the care of more or less inadequate child-minders. But such a sharing of the load of upbringing may equally enhance the quality of parental affection and interest, and there seems no reason to suppose that there is any great variation in parental inadequacy at different social levels. It would seem, if anything, to be one of those great human constants – like irritability, or a sense of humour, or enthusiasm for sex – that are randomly distributed and not significantly correlated with other human differences. Third, there is the inheritance of wealth.

Now, if wealth is inherited by those who have neither inherited the ability of those who acquired it nor, for some reason or other, derived any advantage from the circumstances of their upbringing, elite positions will be secured by those who do not have the qualities, whatever they may be, by which those positions were obtained in the first place. The elite, in other words, will decay. That, according to Pareto, is the natural course of development. An effective elite bequeaths its position to its less effective descendants. Elites, then, must be replaced, either by a revolutionary supersession if they are very exclusive or, more peaceably, by a continuous exchange of personnel with the masses, whose abler members are constantly recruited into them.

It might be thought that if ability is biologically inheritable – as intelligence, which is certainly a part of ability, seems to be – the children of a capable elite ought to qualify as a capable elite themselves. But that argument leaves out a good many factors of dilution. First, the element in ability for whose inheritability there is considerable support, intelligence, is only a part of it. Energy is needed just as much, and also perhaps good sense or, at any rate, a certain mental stability and balance. Second, no one would claim that the children of intelligent parents will certainly be at least as intelligent as they; at best there is only a substantial probability that they will be. But a large proper fraction multiplied by itself a number of times becomes quite a small proper fraction: a superimposition of probabilities becomes an improbability. Third, a point that is not often raised in this connection is that children have two parents, who may be quite different from one another. I have often wondered whether the Paretian decay of elites could not be reconciled with the inheritability of intelligence by the tendency of successful men to marry very pretty women.

Egalitarians often argue that the liberal ideal of equality of opportunity – the arrangement by which power, wealth, and status are available in open competition – is self-contradictory. If the second generation enters the competition from what may be described as irrelevantly different starting points, it will undermine itself. That will be the case only where those children of the successful who have inherited wealth, but have not also inherited, genetically or by upbringing, the relevant qualifications, are enabled to secure high positions.

Plato, of course, recognised this danger. In order to make sure that his guardians should not bestow the rewards of ability on their children who did not deserve them (according to his no doubt elitist notion of deserving), he decreed that there should be no fixed marital unions among his ruling class. As a result, fathers would not know their children or have any regular relationship with them, and would thus be immune to the claims of paternal affection.

The conclusion is that equality of opportunity is self-destroying to the extent that there is both substantial inheritance of wealth and a liability of elites to decay. The total withdrawal of the right of bequest would remove the former; a much more unattractive stratagem, that of selective breeding, might largely rule out the latter. As things stand, few would now deny the right of communities to limit bequests by estate duties so that able people of moderate means could advance to leading positions unimpeded by the inherited wealth of their less able competitors.

Elitism, in the moderate, sub-Platonic sense in which I would defend it, is not quite the same thing as the sociological elite theories that emerged as a reaction to Marxism around the turn of the century. Against the Marxian claim that the inevitable next stage in human social and economic development is the classless society, Pareto, Mosca, and Michels argued that no society, and certainly no complex industrial society, could exist without an elite. What they meant by an elite was a minority of determined and resourceful people who monopolise power and thus secure for themselves wealth and status.

A comparatively weak argument for this thesis is that human societies have always been stratified into the rich and deferred-to rulers and the poor and deferential ruled. That argument is menaced by the wheel, the steam engine and the aeroplane; unprecedented novelties do crop up in human affairs. Pareto's reasoning was psychological: some people stand out from the general run of mankind because they want power and its fruits more than others do, and have the skill and resolution to get what they want. Mosca's reasoning, on the other hand, was organisational: concentration of power in a few hands is essential for the effective running of complex organisations, political or economic. Organisations without such central direction will either be competitively weeded out or will drift into conformity with the oligarchic norm.

Sociological elitism presented itself, with suspicious intensity, as a purely scientific doctrine, as an account of the factual necessities of social life. But plainly it is, as Marxism more candidly acknowledges in its own case, both science and advocacy. Its exponents believe, not merely that society must be oligarchical, but that it ought to be; that policies designed to eliminate the intervals between the upper and lower reaches of the social structure are damaging to attempt as well as impossible to carry through. Since an elite is inevitable, the rational aim of social policy should be to ensure that it is as stable and efficient as possible. Stability and efficiency go together. A vital elite that succeeds in recruiting the bulk of the pre-eminent ability in the community need not fear revolutionary displacement.

Marx himself, at times, spoke contemptuously of egalitarianism. The formula 'to each according to his needs' is not 'to each the same', and fairly substantial inequality could be required by the special needs of those carrying out socially important tasks. Marx's aim was the elimination of classes. These, in the circumstances that concerned him, were defined by whether or not their members had the means of production as their private property. Once the means of production were socialised, division into classes would disappear. But, as is clearly shown by the history of the Soviet Union, inequality in power, wealth, and status need not do so.

The opposite of elitism is egalitarianism, not socialism. Despite the late Hugh Gaitskell's best-known remark, 'Socialism is about equality', the type of democratic socialism to which he was attached is only marginally egalitarian. In the abstract, socialism is not so much a view of how valued things ought to be distributed, even if greater equality is one of the ends it is designed to ensure. It is, rather, a view of how society should be organised. That view might be called statism, since it seeks to remove all the major institutions and organisations of society – banks, factories, large landholdings, schools and universities, hospitals, and so on – from private control and incorporate them in the state. As experience shows, this can easily be done without noticeably changing the internal hierarchical structure of the institutions in question. Public ownership of the means of production no doubt removes one kind of inequality, that based on invested wealth, but it can leave the other kinds intact. To the extent that public ownership is brought about by compensation rather than outright confiscation it will still leave partly standing the one kind of inequality it is designed to remove.

In practice, democratic socialism of Gaitskell's variety – the official doctrine of the numerically dominant moderate wing of the British Labour party – aims to diminish inequality rather than to eliminate it. It countenances a mixed economy in which only certain strategic industries are nationalised and within which the ordinary capitalist mode of organisation persists. Steeply graduated taxation is invoked to finance large welfare programmes, but well-off geese are still seen as the principal source of golden eggs.

As for totalitarian socialism, the notoriously unequal social structure of the Soviet Union was brought home to me by the innocent remark of a physicist who returned from a trip to Russia full of praise for the esteem in which physicists of his eminence were held there. In Russia, he reported, he would be receiving seventeen times the wage of a manual worker, not merely four or five times as in Britain.

The social development of the Soviet Union is not, of course, a direct realisation of Marx's hopes and predictions. Marxism is put into effect in Russia in the special elitist form given it by Lenin. His view that the revolution had to be made by an elite, a vanguard party, could be extenuated as a concession to the fact that Russia had a very small industrial proletariat in 1917, and was intended to be no more than a temporary expedient. As things have turned out, despite the development of a vast industrial proletariat, the party has become the crucial and indispensable elite institution.

The most purely egalitarian of all the great political theorists, Rousseau, recognised that equality could be achieved only under very special social circumstances. In his view, it is possible only in a small, technically unsophisticated, and essentially isolated community of peasant proprietors, living in a simple way on the produce of their own land. Such a community would be independent of cities, industrial manufacture, and trade – a state of affairs approximated in the early stages of European colonisation of North America and Australasia, but seldom elsewhere. This amounts to implicitly acknowledging the truth of the main thesis of the sociological elite theorists: only if men are almost wholly independent of one another can natural differences in ability and energy fail to result in social inequality. In communes and *kibbutzim*, only the most resolute egalitarian enthusiasm, normally peculiar to the founding generation, can prevent it from breaking out.

There are, it must surely be admitted, irreducible differences in ability and energy between human beings. It is not just that one man is best at doing one thing, another best at another. Almost anyone can adequately remove garbage, load and unload trucks, work on an assembly line, clean the floors of office buildings. Rather few people can effectively perform brain operations, manage large industrial enterprises, play *Hamlet*, judge complex legal cases, investigate the fine structure of matter. How are we to make sure, in the words of a sociological essay on stratification, 'that the most important positions are conscientiously filled by the most qualified persons'? The usual method is to pay people more for doing them, so that there is active competition for the kind of work in question, giving scope for the selection of the best-qualified candidates.

This brings us back to a question left unanswered at an earlier stage. Positions that carry power or status or are inherently gratifying should be sufficiently rewarding in themselves, just because of these characteristics. What need is there to superimpose an economic advantage on top of these intrinsic benefits, at least any that goes beyond making it possible to discharge the duties of the position effectively? If a Shavian equality of income were established (mitigated perhaps by allowances for house-bound spouses and children), would the quality of the occupants of high-status, presumably important positions be notably reduced?

In many cases, surely, it would be. Not all high-status work is intrinsically gratifying. Power is nice, of course, but the responsibility that usually goes with it is not. Anyone who has held a few unpaid chairmanships in virtuous organisations will know how difficult it is to secure an adequate successor. Still, the thing could perhaps be done. The quality of people in high-status positions in Britain, for example, does not seem to have deteriorated very noticeably over the past fifty years, during which time their economic position relative to the average wage earner has deteriorated greatly.

To the extent that incomes are determined by market forces, they will turn out to be highly unequal. The community, through the simple voting procedure of its consumption pattern, indicates the value it attaches to the services it receives. Furthermore, the income attached to a position is not always the most obvious determiner of its status. Poor artists and clergy are deferred to; rich bookies and brothel owners are despised. But, by and large, income and status go together, and to remove one reward is to undermine the other. What you get for little or nothing you are likely to attach little or no value to.

In Britain the salaries of university teachers are determined by the state and to a large extent, even if indirectly, paid by the state. Whenever the question of a pay-raise for academics comes up for public discussion, some contented member of the profession writes to the papers saying his job is so rewarding in itself that he is prepared to settle for less, rather than more, pay. Is he not engaged in intellectual work in the field that most interests him? Does he not have the company of ardent young searchers for knowledge? Does he not have long periods, free from teaching, for leisurely study?

It would be possible to treat the academic profession in the same way as the clergy (of which it was, after all, a part until a hundred years ago). There are academics, often quite able ones, who are fit for no other high-status work, but they are not very numerous. There are zealots who are so attracted to the academic life that they would stay in it, however meagre the economic reward. But most academics fall in neither of these classes. Grateful, like the zealots, for the advantages of the profession, they are mindful too of the long stretches of instructional and administrative drudgery. One thing they might try to do is to move into the higher civil service. There salaries have gone up 50 per cent over a two-year period during which academic stipends have risen by only 7 per cent (a singular vengeance on their own pasts by such ex-academics as Harold Wilson and Anthony Crosland). Alternatively, there are the possibilities of moonlighting, the recourse of the underpaid academics of Latin America, or of emigration – not impossible even in these depressed times, given that Britain has only a sixth of the population of the English-speaking world.

Social changes that involve a sudden and radical disappointment of habitual expectations are both practically and morally objectionable. The practical objection is that they create a group of violently embittered people with seditious inclinations – at least if the change is brought about by deliberate policy and not by the natural course of events. The moral objection is that the pains of loss to the disappointed are not compensated for by the delights of gain to the beneficiaries of the redistribution. Frustrated expectations on a large scale are more disagreeable than unexpected benefits are gratifying. Except at the extremes of super-abundance and destitution, large and sudden redistribution brings about a net loss of welfare.

In Britain, as in most countries, there has been a steady movement toward greater equality over the last hundred years. If there has been a tendency in past economic depressions for the better-off to regain some ground at the expense of the less well-off, the present depression is a startling exception. The disposable income, after taxes, of a family doctor or senior university professor is now not much more than twice that of a worker in an automobile factory.

Even more noticeable has been the movement toward what may be called equality of condition. The British class system has always been tenacious and intricate. R.H. Tawney, writing in the 1930s, said that no other country was so sodden with servile respect for money and position. Thomas Paine put the peculiar rigidity of the British class system down to the Norman Conquest. He saw the habits of self-effacing deference, constitutional in the lower classes of British society, as originating in the oppression of defeated Saxons by conquering Normans, and called on his fellow countrymen to undo the eleventh-century work of William I.

To a great extent that has now been done, by gradual, peaceable, largely commercial means. When I was a child in the 1930s, there were three main classes in Britain, each susceptible of further, more refined division: first, gentlemen – that is to say landowners, bankers, industrialists, professionals, and officers; second, the lower-middle class of shopkeepers, office workers, and salesmen; and, finally, the lower classes. The most immediate mark of distinction between them was auditory, for they spoke quite different kinds of English. The gentry and the lower-middle class used much the same words, although the latter assembled them with greater grammatical gentility and revealed themselves by the use of a small set of specially refined expressions conveniently listed in that poem of John Betjeman's that begins 'Phone for the fish knives, Norman'. The chief phonetic indicator of the distinction was the vowel sound *ou* or *ow*. In Aldous Huxley's *Antic Hay*, the revolutionary tailor tells Gumbril that he will be executed, when the time comes, for saying 'towel' instead of 'teaoul'. Lower-class speech was much more distinctive, with its elided aspirates, abstention from the neuter pronoun, indiscriminate use of the nominative and accusative forms of the pronouns that were employed, and above all by accent.

This linguistic stratification has very much lessened in the last forty years, especially among people young enough to have grown up in that time. Radio and television have presumably been the chief linguistic homogenisers. Regression toward the mean has taken place from both ends of the scale. The kind of piercing, self-satisfied drawl that emerged from the mouths of Conservative parliamentary candidates during the Baldwin epoch (and some Labour ones, for that matter) is now hardly to be heard from anyone under sixty except Mr Anthony Wedgwood Benn, formerly Viscount Stansgate, the current hero of the militant ultra-Left.

Another obtrusive distinguishing mark was dress. The collarless flannel shirt and stiff creaseless trousers of the old-fashioned workingman and the shapeless black garment of his prematurely aged wife have disappeared almost without a trace and are now to be seen only on the very old. The great agent of change here has been the mass production of cheap, attractive, even fashionable clothing, above all by the firm of Marks and Spencer from whose counters come the clothes of practically every child in Britain. Cheap and expensive clothes still exhibit differences to the attentive eye, but they are no longer utterly different kinds of clothes. There is nothing now that could be thought of as a kind of class uniform.

Similar erosions of caste are to be found in the universal ownership of cars, in styles of home furnishing, in leisure activities such as travel by air to the sunnier parts of Europe, in habits and tastes of eating and drinking. In its modest but solid way, this general equalisation of condition is wholly to be welcomed. Simply as an equalisation it much increases free and unconstrained communication among people. Fraternal civility replaces the complexities and pretenses of ritual deference. What is more, the process has not been merely an equalisation; it has been, for the great majority of those affected, an upward movement.

But if the process is to continue, there has to be an 'up' to move toward. If false deference to the outward and physical indicators of high status can be abandoned without regret, this does not mean that no human qualities are worthy of respect. The near-elimination of hereditary caste in Britain has been the work of a creative minority. If the process of equalisation is carried to a point at which it is impossible for a creative minority to develop and flourish, the result will be stagnation and mediocrity. It is one thing to eliminate the inequalities that are, because excessive or unjustified, either unproductive or counter-productive. It is another to eliminate the inequalities on which vitality and progress depend.

That extravagant kind of egalitarianism is most evident in the field of education, where there is widespread hostility to any sort of selectivity or competition. Schoolchildren and university students should not, it is held, be exposed to the risks of discouragement involved in any sort of competition, whether for entry to a school or university or for examination of the quality of what they have achieved there. The most influential egalitarian theorist of recent years, Raymond Williams, proclaims 'the substitution of cooperative equality for competition as the principle of social and economic policy'. Against that I would assert, with John Stuart Mill, that 'to be protected against competition is to be protected in idleness, in mental dulness, to be saved the necessity of being as active and intelligent as other people'.

All but the most rudimentary social groups known to history have contained elites, few of them so ruthless and determined as the monolithic parties of those communist societies ostensibly dedicated to the removal of social distinctions between man and man. In the past, securing membership in an elite by merit has been obstructed by the hereditary principle, with its irresistibly ossifying influence. The selection of an elite in circumstances of fairly thoroughgoing equality of opportunity – hitherto confined to periods of revolutionary turmoil, as in mid-seventeenth-century England and late eighteenth-century France – has now taken on something of an institutionally stabilised form. The attempt, energetically pursued by the British Left, to do away with the rational residue of traditional inequality – which was the saving, justifying element in that inequality – can lead only to stagnation or, quite probably, the installation of a new, purely political elite that will use its absolute power to determine for the future, in terms of its immediate political purposes, what is to count as excellence.

A final point is that the demand for comprehensive equality in Britain is not made by those in whose interests it is ostensibly called for. Workingmen support their union leaders in obdurate strategies whose real aim is the revolutionary transformation of the social order, not on that account but for the sake of the extravagant wage increases that are the means to this end. It is significant that no kind of strike seems to evoke more enthusiasm from union members than one intended to preserve their 'differentials', the traditional superiority of their reward to that of other workers.

More generally, there is no movement to equalise the few but gigantic main prizes in the football pools, which are now often on the order of half a million pounds. No government has suggested making winnings from bets liable to taxation, no doubt on a reasonable calculation of the popular response to such a proposal.

There is a question about the moral sincerity of the small group of actual enthusiasts for comprehensive egalitarianism. If equality is right, it is right not just between one English person and another but between everyone. The average British worker has an income at least twenty times as large as his opposite number in India. If the incomes of the two nations were pooled and distributed equally between all the citizens of both, there would be about ten dollars per head per week left, or an average weekly wage of about twenty dollars for each wage earner. This would double the per capita incomes of Indians and save enormous numbers from starvation or the kind of malnutrition that leads to early death. Only a tiny, millenarist minority of egalitarians are ready to carry their reasoning to this consistent limit. For most egalitarians, equality begins at home.

13

Is a Cultural Elite Necessary?

Of course, the only necessity to which the institution of a cultural elite can aspire is relative. What it is necessary for is high culture. In a way that hardly needs arguing. A cultural elite is almost part of the definition of high culture. But it needs to be explained and the best way of giving an explanation is through an account of the meaning of the phrases *high culture* and *cultural elite*. There is a point that I must make before doing this. Even if a cultural elite is necessary to high culture the question still remains: do we have to have high culture? Well, high culture is no more historically inevitable than its accompaniment, a cultural elite. The important question is whether high culture is something that it is desirable to preserve and that is the issue that really underlies the subject of this essay.

There is a difficulty here in the fact that high culture might be thought, in a loose and inclusive way, to be a culture, a body or production of literature and art, that is humanly satisfying, that answers adequately to the real cultural needs of mankind. No-one who supposed human beings to have any cultural needs at all would deny that high culture in this very inclusive sense is something that it is desirable to preserve. But I want to use the expression *high culture* in a more restricted sense, the sense in which, in fact, I think it is ordinarily taken.

The most convenient way of defining this more restricted sense is by contrasting high culture with its most familiar opposite number: folk culture. (One has to say folk culture rather than popular culture. The latter is a more generic thing of which folk culture is a species, along with mass culture and perhaps pop culture.) Folk culture is the culture of comparatively primordial and undeveloped human communities, societies that are technically and economically unsophisticated, that live by food gathering or subsistence agriculture, have not gone far with the division of labour, do not segregate their members in distinct social classes. Its typical forms are songs, heroic or epical narratives, decorations of boats, buildings, domestic utensils, liturgical objects, music for work or dancing or religious ritual.

The salient features of folk culture are the anonymity of its producers and what I shall call the immanence of its products. There are several reasons for the anonymity of the folk artist, but the most important is that his activity is not professionalised. The songs and ballads with which comprehensive anthologies of poetry begin are not anonymous simply because they were composed before the invention of the printed book, the publisher and the literary agent. If anyone has a place as an individual in folk culture it is the performer or executant, the bard or singer, who presents his version of material that is not associated with any particular person. Indeed his material is likely to be more or less common property, which could have been produced by anyone and will often have been contributed to by many people. Everyone will know how to decorate a boat or a spear; everyone will sing the songs of the tribe.

What I mean by the immanence of the products of folk-culture is that they are not pure art-objects, meant to be attentively considered for their own sake. The song is for work or worship, the epic is a treatise on history or theology, visual art is always the decorative completion of something with a practical or ritual purpose: a cooking-pot on a sacrificial altar. Broadly speaking, in folk culture art is a way of doing something else. The conception of a class of objects which are intentionally created for the purpose of detached contemplation has not yet got a foothold.

High culture, in the post-classical west at least, is a renaissance innovation. Bellini's altar-pieces and Bach's cantatas may have had religious and thus communal themes and uses but they are the work of named and definite individuals. At the same time that the individual artist comes to be recognised the pure art-object also makes its appearance. Even if at first many of these pure art-objects have an immanent, religious function, like the altar-pieces and cantatas I mentioned, many do not. The poetry of Dante is written to be read, attentively, for its own sake. Bach's preludes and fugues are composed with a comparable, purely contemplative, end in view. The attitude of pure contemplation which such works solicit can then be transferred to objects which, even if produced with no such intention, are just as accessible and rewarding to a strictly aesthetic consideration. High culture, then, is a matter of the creation of pure art-objects by fully individual, self-conscious, more or less professionalised artists.

It follows from these two differences that high culture will be more complex than folk culture. At one level this greater complexity is formal, at a deeper level it is psychological. The individualisation of artistic work fosters experiment and innovation, the exploration of new themes and new techniques. Some attempt at originality becomes a criterion of the genuineness of a work of art. More fundamentally it makes works of art harder to understand and appreciate. A picture that simply decorates a boat, making it more pleasant and recognisable, and perhaps also has the task of warding off evil spirits, can afford to be conventional and unelaborate in a way that a picture that is meant to be attentively considered in itself and as the expression of a particular individual can not. The musical accompaniment to a victory celebration or harvest feast or the hauling in of a fish-net does not have to offer the same degree of interesting complexity as the song one listens to in uncomfortable clothes in a stuffy concert-hall.

It is clear that a necessary social precondition of high culture is a leisure class with the time and mental energy to devote to it. Furthermore self-conscious artistic creation that aims to be individual and original will generate discourse about art among practitioners while the centring of attention on the pure art-objects they produce will generate it among the audience. Because high culture is more ambitious it is exposed to greater risks of failure and to a greater risk that achievement will be dismissed as failure. In folk-culture where all are potentially artists and where the forms of art are customary there is no need for experts in interpretation and criticism. But once the art-object, freed from immanence, becomes a complex object of interest in itself, discussion of it becomes natural and necessary.

The highest claim that the critical profession can make for itself is that it is needed for the preservation of standards. Works of high culture demand effort from those who seek to enjoy them. But there is always a countervailing force at work, exerted largely by the audience, which comes into conflict with the individual artist's resolve to create something personal and new. It is less taxing to enjoy a more or less elegant variant of a familiar artistic mode than to develop adequate responses to something in some way radically novel. Thus the audience tends to require from artists, individually or collectively, the repetition, with minimal changes, of proved successes. Professionalisation makes the artist economically dependent on his audience and gives him a motive for complying with its demands.

The result is a kind of cultural ossification, a repetition-compulsion that has appeared under numerous guises: as classicism, in a derogatory sense of the word, as academicism, as middlebrow culture. In the last of these there is a special emphasis on the commercial aspect of the relation between artist and audience. High culture needs a leisure class but the greater part of a leisure class may have little taste for high culture. The cultural use to which it puts its leisure may be essentially passive: a matter of amusement, relaxation, passing the time pleasantly. What is required for this purpose is a diluted, often sentimentalised version of the high culture of a preceding period. Emily and Charlotte Bronte are succeeded by Daphne du Maurier and Mary Stewart; Gauguin by Tretiakoff; Tchaikovsky by Ivor Novello. The industrial rationalisation which expels aesthetic elements from the practical activities of man comes to be applied to the culture that it has detached from these activities. The culture of passive amusement becomes an industrial enterprise. The demand for undisturbingly imitative art on which it rests easily elicits suppliers. It is easier to imitate than to create and those with the capacity to create may be economically compelled or induced to settle for the security and comfort of a career of imitation.

The serious creative artist is constantly anxious about the danger of being absorbed into middlebrow culture. He is therefore concerned to establish the autonomy of high culture by acts of principled revolt against the styles, forms and themes of the preceding generation which middlebrow culture soon comes to exploit and devitalise. This process is most obvious in the modern movement of the end of the last and the beginning of the present century. It is at least an aspect of the cultural revolution that preceded it – the romantic movement.

I do not want to suggest that all the revolutions that have occurred in the history of western high culture – the conflict between ancients and moderns, the romantic movement, the modernist avant-garde – have been no more than efforts by the creative producers of high culture to dissociate themselves from high culture's middlebrow surrogate. That would be an anachronism except in the most recent case of the modern movement at the end of the last and the beginning of the present century. Cultural revolutions have more generally been expressions of a sense of constraint, of limited opportunities for the exercise of creative powers, in whatever form the source of the constraint may be identified. The source can be a tradition, now ossified, established by a preceding stage of high culture, just as much as the prevailing middlebrow culture. But where there is an operative middlebrow culture it will add its weight to the other forces that work to preserve a seemingly exhausted tradition.

The cultural revolutions of the past have not all been explicit defences of high culture against its middlebrow parasite, but they have still been elitist in the sense that they have not repudiated the defining elements of the concept of high culture. They have insisted on the importance of the individual artist, for it is his creative liberation that they have sought, and also on the importance of the art-objects he produces. It is this that differentiates the revolutions of the past from the revolution which now, in the last decade or so, seems to have come upon us.

Some of its ingredients are those commonly to be found in cultural revolutions. There is an insistence on the need for a radical break with the past, for an escape from the stifling pressure of a cultural tradition. Only an occasional lonely, magical, prophetic figure like William Blake is excepted from the general condemnation. There is an insistence on the ecstatic, on violent immediacy and emotional shock and an associated hostility to reason, order and purposiveness. The dizzying patterns of Op art and psychedelic lighting, the numbing clatter of amplified rock music present pure sight and sound, without content and with a visual or auditory vehemence that floods the senses to the exclusion of any kind of consecutive thought. There is exoticism in recourse to the I Ching and the sitar, primitivism in the reverence for soul music and the self-expressions of schizophrenics and very young children. There is the familiar Bohemian stand-by of narcotics, used to induce higher or at any rate more intense states of consciousness. But the use of drugs is more widespread than ever before and it is now complacently gleeful, where it was formerly solemn and sacramental, if not guilty.

What is new about the current cultural revolution is the large step it has taken toward the elimination of the two essential elements in high culture: the traditional art-object and the traditional artist. The most direct assault on both of these elements has been the technique of randomisation. The most publicised instance of this was the paint-throwing of Jackson Pollock, a procedure carried to greater lengths by the man who bicycled over his spread-out canvasses to distribute the heaps of paint on them in an interesting way. Analogous methods have been introduced into music by John Cage through the use of mechanical formulae and by Stockhausen, who offers little bits of music that can be played in any order that happens to take the executant's fancy.

The nearest approximation to random composition in literature has been the kind of writing inspired by Henry Miller in which the contents of the writer's mind are tumbled unselectively on to paper in their pristine immediacy and disorder, as in the novels of Jack Kerouac and the poetry of Allen Ginsberg. A more consistently random effect demands a more deliberate strategy. The suddenly liberated consciousness proves to retain a good deal of low-grade order. The purposive, organising habits of the ego can be circumvented only by the kind of principled resolution that lies behind the novels of Beckett and Robbe-Grillet. Somewhat paradoxically, the elimination of the traditional art-object can be achieved only by reinstating the traditional, consciously controlling artist. However, William Burroughs's device of randomly juxtaposing bits of undeliberate writing done at different times comes near to securing both of the ends in view. Here mechanical randomisation is used to offset any lingering consequentiality in the productions of the fully liberated impulsive writer. Accident, with its intended effect of shock, is combined with the anonymity of unorganised cooperation in the Happening, a new form which has the further merit of instancy or disposability, like a paper handkerchief.

The search for impermanence, exemplified by the Happening, can be seen as an attempt to achieve complete expressive purity. In a way this pursuit reaches its culmination in the self-destroying machine of Tinguely. But here, as with the anti-novel, the elimination of the traditional art-object is achieved only by rather prodigious contrivance on the part of the artist. A somewhat similar effect is produced in art that does persist by ensuring that it is static and can be approached from any direction, having no complex internal order that requires it to be taken in one way rather than another. Marshall McLuhan, who describes his albums of highbrow advertising man's patter as 'mosaics', applies this principle in the domain of expository writing.

There are other, more oblique ways of undermining high culture's assumptions about art and the artist. One is the choice of specially anti-aesthetic or anti-cultural themes and subjects. Pop art concentrates on the most banal and insistently everyday objects, as with Oldenburg's vast vinyl hamburger, Liechtenstein's magnifications of segments from comic strips, Warhol's signed soup cans. At the hither end of this continuum, namely Oldenburg's entertaining celebrations of everyday objects, this can be seen as a less solemn version of Wordsworth's project, announced in the preface to *Lyrical Ballads*, of making art speak in the language of common life. Further along the continuum Wordsworth gives way to Marcel Duchamp. But the ridicule of established artistic conventions that Duchamp used to express fastidious exasperation, is now, in the hands of a crafty entrepreneur like Warhol, only a camp trick. In either case this sort of thing is inevitably parasitic on the persistence of traditional assumptions about art. It is no more an autonomous artistic mode than grenade-throwing is a style of architecture.

The new art, then, is in varying degrees accidental, instant, disposable, farcical, pre-rationally and unselectively expressive. The product of art becomes an event rather than an object. The artist ceases to be an autonomous, heroic creator and turns into a humble provider of pretexts for chance or the whim of the audience to assemble an aesthetic experience.

The most searching theoretical account of the phenomenon is Susan Sontag's. She launches herself enthusiastically against interpretation, against what she calls the Matthew Arnold idea of culture, against the burdening of art-works with a content or significance that requires the attention of the intellect. The new free art that she endorses is a matter of immediate sensory gratification, of exciting surfaces, of bodily rapture.

There is a close connection between this notion of art and the celebration of the pleasure-principle by such utopian neo-Freudians as Norman O. Brown and, in his happier moments, Herbert Marcuse. In his later, meta-historical musings, particularly *Civilization and its Discontents*, Freud maintained that the price to be paid for civilisation, for achievement, rationality and social order, is the renunciation of instinct. Unless we learn to direct a good deal of our instinctive aggression on ourselves in the form of moral restraint we shall lapse into barbarism and mutual destruction. The more optimistic American revisers of his gospel believe that we can dispense with the heavy armour of moral and social control and that an Eden of play and polymorphous perversity is within our grasp in which all the psychic wounds inflicted by civilisation are healed. The new art, whether consciously or not, is in prophetic service to this ideal, this metaphysic of permissiveness.

In the light of this the fundamental point of conflict between high culture and the new counter-culture that seeks to replace it can be identified as turning on the value of effort, the prime manifestation of Protestant virtue. The art of high culture requires effort from its creators and also efforts of appreciation from its audience. Only a minority of the population is both qualified and disposed to make the effort demanded. The widespread hostility of the present age toward elites of any kind thus implies a rejection of high culture.

There is a possible objection I had better consider here. I have some sympathy for it but I shall argue that it is not really relevant to the matter in hand. It can be argued that the idea that high culture can be accessible only to a minority expresses too narrow and dismal a conception of human possibilities. No doubt most high culture hitherto has been restricted to an elite but that is not an immutable law of nature. High culture requires effort from its audience, effort requires leisure. Hitherto only a minority has had the amount of leisure needed but that is ceasing to be true. We are constantly being alerted to the problem posed to advanced industrial societies by the impending onset of universal leisure. Thus, when the 20-hour week has become the norm, why should not high culture be accessible to everyone?

The general argument can be supported by historical instances in which the possibility it envisages has been more or less realised. In Periclean Athens, after all, the tragedies of Euripides had the same width of appeal as Hello Dolly in our own day. It is not wholly satisfactory to answer that the audience for Athenian tragic drama was still a minority of the population as a whole since it excluded most women and all slaves. Another instance is Elizabethan drama and another again the English novel of the mid-nineteenth century. Here again there is a not very persuasive counter-argument which holds that the universally gratifying works in question exercised their appeal on different levels, that Shakespeare and Dickens provide jokes and melodramatic excitement for the groundlings as well as more sophisticated pleasures for the discriminating elite.

But even if the historical instances of universal high culture are inconclusive the possibility that the large adult majority of an advanced and highly leisured post-industrial society could in principle be qualified and disposed to appreciate high culture is not ruled out. The point is, however, that the young adults who establish the cultural tone of the approximation to post-industrial society that we have actually got do not answer to the specifications of this ideal. With their sartorial extravagances, their facile political extremism, generously catered for by Pelican books about Che Guevara, their footling preoccupation with obscenity, they constitute a lumpenintelligentsia, a pitifully flawed realisation of the hopes entertained by late nineteenth-century progressives, under the inspiration of Ruskin and William Morris, about the results of universal enlightenment.

The fact is that although leisure is necessary for universal high culture it is not sufficient to produce it. Something else is required, a recognition that high culture is not just passive enjoyment, that independence of mind does not consist in the reiteration of conventional formulas of absolute dissent, that riots, whether political or aesthetic, liberate and encourage not the highest but the lowest qualities of those who take part in them. In saying that something else is required and that it is essentially mental effort I am, of course, denying that the new liberated, universally accessible culture of the lumpenintelligentsia is either a new form of high culture, which its admirers would no doubt be quite content to admit, or any sort of adequate substitute for high culture, let alone an advance beyond it, which they would not.

I agree, then, that it is not by an immutable necessity that high culture as traditionally conceived, the complex and original artistic production of creative individuals, is confined to a cultural elite. But that admission is irrelevant since neither those who favour nor those who condemn the new developments I have been discussing suppose that these developments amount to a realisation of that possibility. The new culture at once rejects high culture and proclaims its own universality. It thus concurs with the view that, in practice and as things are, traditional high culture, with its complexity and individuality, must be confined to an elite. It is not welcomed by its adherents simply because it is universally accessible but in the prevailing egalitarian atmosphere that is a factor in the enthusiasm for it.

The crucial issue, then, is whether the new instant, ecstatic, anonymous culture is an adequate or preferable alternative to the traditional high culture which it seeks to replace. And that is a question of the quality of the experiences it provides. I believe that it is radically deficient in four main respects. The objects, events and experiences it provides are boring, wasteful, parasitic and, in a peculiar way that is no part of the intention behind them, unstable. The boringness of purely expressive poetic ramblings, contentless painting and accidental music is simply that of any intense stimulus that is easily obtained. That which at first surprises and excites by the violence of the shock it administers soon numbs the response to itself and anything like it. There is nothing to explore in an art of sensorily exciting surfaces, no possible enriching accumulation of experience. Like Peacock's garden-designer who introduced an element of surprise into his garden layout, it can give no answer to the question: what happens the second time round?

This leads inevitably to the second fault of wastefulness. Immediately exciting aesthetic gestures become rapidly obsolete and have to be replaced. Crude innovations soon pall and as one momentarily engrossing style passes from the scene another has to be feverishly contrived in its place. The rate of superannuation exhausts and confuses; the sensibility of the audience has to be bludgeoned by continually more abrupt and powerful stimuli. The new anonymous, formally unconstrained artist is in a peculiar condition of bondage to his audience: he has become confectioner to a glutton.

Thirdly, much of the new art is parasitic in being a kind of mocking defiance levelled at traditional art. A signed soup tin on a pedestal has a point only if signed objects of greater interest are customarily displayed in that way. A man in dress clothes sitting at a piano for five minutes with his hands in his lap owes any claim to our attention that he possesses to the fact that men so situated usually play something that is meant to be listened to. These little jokes work only against a background of familiarity with traditional art and music as presented in schools, museums and concert halls. So to the extent that the new culture succeeds in supplanting its traditional rival it removes the conditions which are needed for a good deal of it to have any point at all. If children learn, not to write or draw or play musical instruments in the traditional, disciplined way, but simply to express themselves, if visual art becomes no more than striking ornamentation of the environment, if music is made only in a chaos of improvisation to tranced and gyrating revellers, these satirical gestures will lose their reference. Mere expressiveness alone will survive.

Finally there is the special kind of instability that I mentioned. What I mean by it is that a style of artistic production which is controlled only by the requirement of making a strong immediate impact is exceedingly liable to commercial exploitation. As soon as some novelty strikes a spark the methods of industry grind into action. The technology of popular entertainment responds to the Beatles by fabricating the Monkees. Op art is quickly mobilised to restyle the plastic ashtrays and waste-paper baskets on sale in canny little shops and the decoration of eating-places that dispense cheap chemical food and drink. So what is begun with the aim of removing all fetters from the purest and most untampered-with creativeness is swiftly transformed into a lubricant of commerce. The paintings of Titian and Rembrandt can survive reproduction on Christmas cards. But the simple and trivial nature of the products of the new culture makes them easy to imitate for the purposes of mass-production with no discernible loss of their modest original properties.

The new culture does have a kind of elite associated with it. Its audience is unrestricted but there is an inner elite of expositors and commentators. Some of them, like Susan Sontag, are thoughtful and highly, even deadly, serious. More representative, however, is the incoherent rhapsodist of the new like the ineffable Tony Palmer, so rightly and regularly a feature of Pseuds Corner in *Private Eye*. The art-objects of the new culture do not really lend themselves to discussion in ordinary critical prose. The dialect in which they are most effectively celebrated is that breathless flux of interjections and superlatives that falls from the lips of the more enraptured kind of disc-jockey. The objects are too impoverished in themselves to be described and interpreted; the commentator must report and embroider on his own sensations under their impact. But a disc-jockey is not a critic; he is a master of ceremonies, part of the performance itself, not an external observer of it. This lively order of hierophants is not an elite for the new culture: it is what would be the elite if the new culture allowed for such a thing.

Some time ago there was an interview in the *New Left Review* between two of the paper's staff and Noam Chomsky, the current culture-hero who is perhaps most deserving of the reverence accorded him. Didn't he think, they asked him, that the rules which are characteristic of all language are somehow oppressive and dominatory. He was very polite to the fantasy of infantile omnipotence underlying the question but quite firm in his negative answer. A human activity that aspires to any kind of excellence, he said, must be a matter of working against the resistance of some refractory material and under the constraint of formal restrictions. He offered art as a prime instance of the principle. The exchange conveniently summarises the conflict between the new culture and the traditional high culture it aims to displace. The self-conscious, autonomous human individual is at once the creator and the product of high culture. That culture has constantly to reaffirm itself against powerful countervailing forces: the natural inertia of artist and audience that encourages repetition, the commercial impulse that would exploit that inertia and now an egalitarian frenzy that seeks to eliminate anything that is not available on equal terms to all. High culture needs an elite of informed and reflective appreciators if it is to be preserved from these dangers. Fashion and dogmatic moral enthusiasm may be depleting the ranks of this elite but it must persist if the creative human imagination is not to be frittered away in mindless emotional excitement.

14

Egalitarianism and a Just Society

It is often said that there is now, as never before, an almost universal belief that the elimination of economic inequality is a primary moral imperative. Two things are clear enough at any rate. In the first place the language of egalitarianism is now very freely invoked in the struggles by interest groups for greater income. Secondly, there has, at least within the advanced industrial societies, been a steady diminution of gross economic inequality over the last hundred years. Nothing shows that more obviously than the virtual disappearance of private domestic service. A family in which servants outnumber the served by ten to one, a state of affairs not all that uncommon a hundred years ago, must be a good deal more than ten times as rich as the people who serve it.

What makes the claim that most people are now committed in principle to the elimination of inequality a suspect one is that the emphasis is nearly always on reducing the gap between the egalitarian and those richer than he. Much less is said about closing the gap at the other end of the system. This is most obvious when economic inequality is considered on an international scale. The average British worker has an income about twenty times as large as his Indian opposite number. There is a certain appropriateness in taking Britain and India, the most populous and, so to speak, imperial bit of its old empire, together.

If the total incomes of the two nations were pooled and redistributed equally between all the citizens of both there would be about £4 per head per week left or a weekly wage for each wage-earner of about £8. That calculation is, perhaps, unfair: there are so few of us and so many of them. But if the incomes of the whole world were redistributed with perfect equality, although the British wage-earner would go down by only 60 per cent, his American counterpart would go down by the 80 per cent of the original calculation.

A mildly comical instance of this asymmetrical egalitarianism is provided by Mr Michael Foot. He said on a TV programme, when he was only an opposition MP, that nobody ought to have more than £7,000 a year, which may well have been, given his parliamentary stipend and the extracurricular earnings he then had the opportunity to make, just about what he was receiving in the way of income. After he became a minister he returned to the subject but put forward a new figure, that of £10,000, at least implicitly by setting up an inquiry into incomes above that level.

Let me mention a few more instances. A great deal of industrial action in pursuit of higher pay is not directed towards increasing equality but to preserving or increasing inequality, under the euphemism of differentials. Certainly Mr Jack Jones has repeatedly urged that an increase of old-age pensions is one of the conditions of the unions' adhesion to the 'social contract'. But such a concern for the unorganised and economically powerless is at once fairly exceptional and, one is inclined to suspect, in practical terms, largely decorative. It is not a cause that is likely to bring anyone out on strike.

Another mildly significant fact, as far as the state of general opinion is concerned, is the institution of the football pool. There are, of course, all sorts of bets you can lay by way of a football coupon. But what really draws in the stakes is the very long odds bet which may carry a prize of several hundreds of thousands of untaxed pounds. At anything like present rates of interest a big pools winner is provided with the capital for an income up in the top quarter of a per cent of incomes received. The point about big pools winnings is that there is no damned nonsense about merit in the treble chance. The biggest dividends occur when the draws are few in number and unlikely, when, that is to say, teams do not play to form. So the only skill rewarded is that of filling in the form correctly, with the right number of the permitted symbols in the places set out.

The particular relevance of the pools to ideas about equality is that their existence and almost universal acceptability casts doubt on the more moderate egalitarian notion that while different rewards are justified where different services have been performed there can be no justification for inherited wealth. But inherited wealth is, like the pools, a lottery and differs only in being a taxed one.

I suggest, then, that very few egalitarians really believe that absolutely everyone should have the same amount of income and wealth. At most they believe the much less morally vibrant proposition that no-one in Britain should have significantly more than anyone else. In practice, I suspect, the most common form in which egalitarianism is actually held is that no-one should have significantly more than I do, whoever I may be.

From the fact that very few people really believe in the abstract egalitarianism they tend to profess, when excitedly engaged in struggles for increased income by methods other than that of earning it, it does not, of course, follow that abstract egalitarianism is not the correct principle to adopt. But in pointing to what I take to be a widespread discrepancy between profession and actual belief I am not being merely mischievous. What lies behind the actual belief in question, that Englishmen are not morally obliged to give up three or four fifths of their incomes to secure equality as between Britain and India or as between Britain and the rest of the world as a whole, seems to me quite reasonable.

What does lie behind it is the principle that the pains of loss are not, in general, compensated for by the delights of gain. Frustrated expectations are more disagreeable than unexpected benefits are gratifying. Consider a rich old woman living in a Bournemouth hotel. By cutting her down to the level of octogenarian widows in general what would be achieved? She would sustain a terrible, cataclysmic blow; a band of other old ladies would get another 50p a week.

That, of course, is to take very nearly the most unfavourable type of case for the anti-egalitarian argument. There are, after all, even now, old age pensioners who die of cold and malnutrition. The most unfavourable case of all is to be found in the comparison between Britain and India. If everyone in this country were brought down to the level of the average industrial worker there would be no really major transformation of the conditions of life of the beneficiaries. It would be a matter of a few pounds a week. But if half the British national income were redistributed to the population of India it would just about double the per capita income in that country and save enormous numbers of people from starvation or the kind of enfeeblement by malnutrition that leads to early death. Surely a redistribution that makes the difference between life and death is more imperative than one that makes the difference between colour or black and white TV or between whisky and beer? Even arithmetically the British industrial worker is richer than the average Indian worker to the same extent as only the very, very rare person with an after-tax income of £30,000 is richer than he. But in real terms the first gap is much larger than the second. Successive doublings of disposable income do not produce successive doublings of benefit from it. Equality, unlike charity, should not begin at home.

So far, you may feel, I have not come to grips with the central issue. I have argued that much egalitarian profession is at any rate hollow, although not on that account consciously hypocritical. But positively I have not done more than suggest that the real beliefs of professed egalitarians are not unreasonable to the extent that they take account of what people have got into the habit of expecting. However that would really count only against some more or less dramatically instant levelling. It would not rule out gradual approximation to greater equality in which the victims of the process were given plenty of time to accustom themselves to it.

So could it not be held that an ideally just society is an equal one, and that equality should at least be the ultimate goal? What, after all, is justice? In its simplest form justice is a matter of treating people, particularly in the matter of distributing burdens and benefits between them, in strict accordance with the understood rules of the activity in question, whether it be military service or taking up a certain kind of employment or carrying out some family chore like washing up. But, as generations of theorists have said, giving ceremonial form to the children's protest 'why is it always us who have to go to bed while you stay up as late as you like?', the justice of the rules themselves can always be put in question.

Many rules, particularly legal ones, seem to create inequalities rather than to forbid them. The law prescribes that a man can do, within limits, what he likes with a thing that he has made. But it treats him quite differently if he has picked up an exactly similar thing in his neighbour's garden when no one was looking. Attempts to arrive at some general principle for determining the justice of rules are unsatisfying. A just rule, according to Aristotle, treats equals equally and unequals unequally. In much the same vein many have held that a just rule is one that treats people in the same way unless there is a relevant difference between them. But who are unequals and what is relevance? It does not get one much further to say that a just rule is one whose observance contributes more to general welfare than any alternative. The general welfare is not something that can be uncontroversially measured.

All the same this last formula does point us in the right direction. It suggests the sort of considerations that should be taken into account, without appeal to intuitions of intrinsic inequalities between people or, again, relevant differences between them.

To confine ourselves to the kind of equality that is most at issue at the present time, equality of income and wealth or economic equality: what alternatives are there to the absolute equality which Bernard Shaw preached for with such vivid eloquence and from whose practice he so resolutely abstained? Historically there have been two main procedures for the distribution of wealth: force and the price system. Neither, perhaps, has ever existed for long in its pure form; sometimes there is more of the one, sometimes more of the other. Under the force method those with some form of power – religious, military or political – take what they want of what there is, leaving to the producers, unless they are very nomadic or very foolish, enough for those producers to be able to go on producing. Under the price system, voluntary exchange, naturally for a consideration, takes the place of forced levy, the return for which is at best some kind of protection.

As things stand in England the distribution of income and wealth departs in two major ways from the ideal price system of textbooks of classical economics. On the one hand there are accumulations of inherited wealth, the oldest and grandest of them initially acquired from brigandage or something like it, which it is hardly plausible to argue can now be seen as reward for services rendered. On the other, there is large-scale redistribution of wealth from those who have first acquired it to those, unable to acquire it for themselves, who are in serious need of it. I shall have more to say about both of these things in a little while.

The two great arguments for the price system are that it is, in a rather elemental way, just and that it is efficient. Its elemental justice is that it does reward people in accordance with their deserts, in accordance, that is to say, with the service they actually give to the community at large, as measured by the purchasing decisions of the members of the community in their capacity as consumers. Of course, that is only valid to the extent that the system works according to the book, which it never wholly does. And one does not have to be very paternalistic to suppose that the aggregate effect of consumption decisions is an imperfect measure of service to the community. People spend foolishly much of the time. Like Odysseus tying himself to the mast, they recognise this by allowing others to decide for them how much of the national income should be spent on defence or social services. But the imperfections of the system do not entail that centrally-made decisions about everything that is now left to market forces and the rather patchy sovereignty of the consumer, however high-minded and public-spirited the central deciders might be, would be better.

In talking about the elemental justice of this arrangement I was referring to the fact that our instinctive responses as regards justice seem to rest on the principle of desert. This is shown by the child who says 'I carried the shopping home so I should have first choice among the fancy cakes' and again by the labourers in the vineyard who could not see why they should receive no more, when they had worked all day, than those who had put in only an hour at the end of it. (The point of that story, of course, was that since the reward being symbolised was infinite, eternal life, it could not be divided. But theological ingenuity reintroduced elemental justice with the conception of purgatory.)

The argument from efficiency is just that this system gets things done. It supplies motives for some people to provide what other people want. So, in its way, does the force system, but more unpleasantly, through threats and fear, and more fitfully.

However, plenty of other methods are conceivable than the historically familiar reliance on force or the price system. A way of approaching these is to be found in a massive book by John Rawls, *The Theory of Justice*. Very roughly, Rawls' view is that a set of rules is just if they would be chosen by a rational man for a society of which he is to be a member, provided that he did not know what position he was going to occupy in that society. In such a state of ignorance about his fate and with such a fundamentally important matter as his economic status at issue, a rational man, Rawls thinks, would choose that system of rules in which his chances of a bad result were minimised, or, a bit more precisely, that system in which the worst possibilities open were the least bad of all possible systems.

A natural inference, though it is not one that Rawls himself draws, is that absolutely equal shares for everyone is the arrangement a rational man, bent on minimising the chances of disaster, would opt for. For in no other system, it might seem, would the smallest share distributed be so large. In fact, as Rawls sees, that does not follow. The absolute size of the shares depends on the amount there is to share and that, in its turn, depends on the encouragement people get to contribute to the resources available for distribution. To opt for a system in which there is no incentive to effort, for oneself or anyone else, is not only irrational, as likely to reduce the size of everyone's share, but dismally passive and lazy.

I want to come back now to these two, so to speak, alien elements in the system of distribution we actually have: inheritance and provision for need that is unrelated to services rendered. Only a very Neanderthal adherent of the free-enterprise system could urge that the latter ought to be done away with. What I want to question is the assumption that making provision for the victims of natural misfortune, of age and sickness and congenital deficiency of body or mind, has anything much to do with justice. What it does express is humanity or, as people rather too often say, compassion. A society could very well be just and at the same time very inhumane. But why should we suppose that justice is the whole of virtue?

The device by which social compensation for natural disadvantages is made out to be a matter of justice is by the exploitation of the metaphorical description of people's intrinsic disadvantages as pieces of natural injustice. Nature is unjust, we say, in the way it distributes ability, perseverance and, in general, earning power. But to say that indemnification for such disadvantages is to augment justice is to take the phrase 'natural injustice' with superstitious literalness. Nature is not a moral agent and where there has been no injustice, the correction of a bad state of affairs cannot be just, it is simply kind or humane.

At this point an egalitarian might well reply: 'I don't care about words, you can call equality what you like, but whether it is just or humane I am still for it.' But the words in this case, as quite often, do make a difference. There is a stringency or imperativeness about justice which is not attached to humanity. Justice is a right and its infringement justifies indignation. A failure of kindness or humanity merits moral disapproval but that is not quite the same thing. Furthermore the demands of humanity are met so long as serious needs are provided for and major distress is alleviated. They cannot imply that everyone should be absolutely equal, for the pain of knowing that someone else is better off than you are cannot plausibly be regarded as a major source of human suffering nor its elimination as a serious human need.

The prevailing tendency to identify economic equality with justice seems to be the result of one of those verbal slides by means of which a highly controversial preference is invested with a special moral force through association with some uncontroversially favourable term. What has, in my view, happened to *justice* is familiar in the case of the word *democracy*, which is appropriated by any style of government that professes to pursue the common interest. In each case, of course, there is a connection. One reasonable argument in favour of democracy, it was forcefully put by James Mill, is that in it the rulers have the most inescapable motive for actually pursuing the public interest. But that does not make all pursuit of the public interest democratic. Similarly, justice requires that everyone be treated equally in accordance with the rules and, at a higher level, that the rules themselves involve equality of consideration of those affected by them by taking into account the interests of all. But that does not mean that the rules themselves must actually impose equality. The result of that could well be the opposite of justice.

To turn now to the other alien element: inheritance. In resisting the identification of justice and equality I do not want to be taken to be supposing that all existing inequalities are just. In particular those arising from the inheritance of property are open to question. The right of free testamentary disposition of the wealth that a person has himself earned is sometimes defended on the ground that it provides an incentive to effort. There may be something in this. But it is by no means the strongest incentive and it is calculated to enfeeble the appetite for productive work in the passive beneficiaries of inheritance. In a way it is something of an anachronism. When agricultural land was the main kind of inheritable property, the practice of its passing from father to son had all sorts of advantages:

continuity of cultivation, powerful incentives for keeping the land in good condition, even a convenient provision of training for the next generation of cultivators. But none of these considerations applies to the inheritance of large blocks of income-bearing capital, the fruits of which can be enjoyed without having to work on it.

The only basis on which it could be argued that justice requires the protection of inherited capital is the principle I mentioned earlier, that habitual expectations should not be frustrated. This is a consequence of the simplest and least controversial requirement of justice, namely that people should be treated in accordance with the generally recognised and established rules. If the rules themselves are objectionable, then they should be changed slowly enough for the victims of change to accustom themselves to the new rules of the game.

It might be objected at this point that I ought, in consistency, to take the same attitude to inherited abilities as I have done to inherited property. Someone with able parents is as likely to inherit their ability as someone with rich parents is to inherit their wealth. To argue in this way is to ignore the difference between a literal and a metaphorical bequest and between what a person is and what, in the way of literal property, he has. The bequeathing of property is a voluntary act and a fit topic for moral appraisal; a genetic bequest is not and contains a large random element anyway. More important is the fact that a person cannot be distinguished from his distinctive personal characteristics in the way that he can be from the property in a literal sense that he inherits.

There is an intermediate possibility here, between the natural inheritance of abilities and the artificial inheritance of wealth. Well-off parents may prefer to spend on the better education of their children money they would otherwise have left them. How does that stand in the light of the principles I have been proposing? The first thing to say is that an academic education of high quality is not a ticket to comfortable, unproductive idleness in the way that the simple inheritance of wealth once commonly was and still may occasionally be. The recent remark by the education secretary that it would be too expensive for the state to abolish independent schools at present is worth reflecting on. It implies that parents who pay for the education of their children are freely choosing to make a socially valuable investment.

More generally, as long as children are brought up in families and not by the state in the kind of creches that Plato prescribed for the offspring of his ruling class, parents will, and will be expected to where they do not, do everything they can for the benefit of their children. And as long as parents differ, not simply in wealth, but also in concern, generosity, even in mere vitality and imagination, the children whose parents have more of these good things will have an advantage over others. If parents are to be forbidden to provide a better education for their children than the statutory minimum, the aim of the election document *Labour's Programme for Britain*, are they also to be forbidden to supply them with above-minimum holidays or meals or attention?

As long as the things people want are allowed to be bought by free personal choice, and not paternalistically doled out to them, the principles by which that choice should be restricted are reasonably clear. People should not be allowed to buy things that are intrinsically harmful and dangerous. Few would endorse the free availability of poisons and lethal weapons. Secondly, when some good is in such short supply that the universal need for it can be satisfied only by rationing, as with certain basic foods in wartime, then it should be rationed.

But neither of these conditions applies to education. The very style of the animus against the kind of education provided by the fee-paying independent system shows that it is universally recognised as a good in itself. The old idea of the independent school as a nursery of snobbish, repressed, conventional automata is neither applicable nor believed in. Nor is the commodity in question one to which rationing is appropriate. If the independent system were abolished by the state its resources would be largely wasted: many of its teachers would leave the profession altogether, many of its buildings, untransportable to the urban areas where they would then be needed, would moulder uselessly.

Even if I thought that the existence of independent schools was unjust I should still favour their retention. At the present time the method of education in the state system is in two ways becoming increasingly indifferent to academic excellence, increasingly concerned to erode differences in ability and to foster a kind of communitarian uniformity. Institutionally there is the movement towards comprehensive schools and the associated elimination of streaming by ability. On the individual level, young recruits to the teaching profession are animated by an ideology that is hostile to the notion that some people are abler than others. The supply of ability is not available to the independent schools in the way that those who teach in them would wish. Economic pressures mean that it must come almost wholly from the well-off part of society. But to eliminate such explicit provision for it as there is would be disastrous. It is worth noticing that in the eastern European societies that are officially dedicated to egalitarianism, whatever their actual practice in the distribution of social rewards, the educational system is highly academically selective.

I have been arguing for three main points. First, that most professions of egalitarianism are hollow, concerned as they are to impoverish the rich rather than enrich the really poor. Secondly, that although there is a connection between equality and justice this does not mean that the only just society is an equal one. It is humanity, not justice, that egalitarianism carries to an extreme limit. Finally, I have argued that the existence of independent schools is not an injustice and that, even if it were, in the present condition of things it serves a vital social purpose.

PART II

Thinkers

15

Hobbes

The ideas of Hobbes have never ceased to be a source of annoyance since their first bold and pugnacious presentation to the world in 1640. But even those most offended by Hobbes's bleak account of human nature and of the most a reasonable man will hope for must admit his utility. No leading article of the more reflective sort about the current political life of Africa is complete without a reference to his state of nature, the war of all against all. Hobbesian man, in whom vainglorious illusions about himself are kept in check only by the influence of fear, is an indispensable type of anti-hero. So there is one achievement that cannot be denied to Hobbes: he has provided, in language of incomparable force and directness, a full account of one extreme possible view about the human condition. Those who would insist that it is nothing like the whole truth must at least accept it as a magnificent incarnation of an eternally recurrent form of error, and must admit that in some times and places it looks disconcertingly like the truth.

To his contemporaries Hobbes was above all a dangerously destructive theologian. As Samuel Mintz has shown in his valuable book on seventeenth-century reactions to Hobbes, *The Hunting of the Leviathan*, the main hostility of his more serious critics was to his atheism, together with his denial of the primacy of mind or spirit in the general scheme of things. A good deal is said about God in Hobbes's writings but it is nearly all negative. The only rational knowledge we can have of him is that he exists, from which it must follow that he is some kind of vast material object. Beyond this he is incomprehensible. The traditional epithets that are ascribed to him must be seen as honorific, and we may attach a specific sense to them only in accordance with the articles of belief laid down by the political sovereign.

Most obnoxious in his own time for his dismissal of religious liberty, whether the Protestant freedom of faith and conscience from any sort of organisational control or the freedom of the Church from control by the State, Hobbes has been deplored by later ages for his contempt for liberty in general. He has been mainly considered as a social theorist, deriving a series of insufferable prescriptions for Church and State from an exaggeratedly low view of mankind.

Yet it is clear that Hobbes himself wanted to be seen as being as much an epistemologist and philosopher of nature, even a natural scientist, as a social theorist. What is more, he professed that his doctrines about human nature and society were not only deducible from his theories of knowledge and nature in general, but essentially presupposed those theories, as the basis for whatever claim to being demonstrably certain his ideology might have. Such a claim to certainty was a crucial feature of the total Hobbesian project. As J.W.N. Watkins shows, Hobbes regarded the chaos of baseless and fantastic ideologies by which Englishmen were intoxicated in the period preceding the Civil War as the main cause of that lamentable event.

The most important conclusion of Hobbes's theory of knowledge is the distinction he draws between science or rational knowledge and what he calls prudence, which is the passively acquired, almost animal, habit of expecting things to go on much as they have always been. True science, for him, is the awareness of necessary conceptual relationships. But he does not interpret necessary truths in the manner of traditional, Aristotelian rationalism; they do not record the results of a purely intellectual scrutiny of objective essences. The function of these truths is, rather, to set out the consequences of the conventions of language that men have adopted. For Hobbes all thought above the animal level requires language, and language is a free human contrivance in which what is present to the senses is named: it is not the depiction of an objective order in things. Science is the product of reasoning, reasoning is 'reckoning with names', and names are conventional labels for what is sensed. This forcefully instrumental view of language made Hobbes very alert to the possibilities of insignificant speech.

Hobbes's metaphysics is an unusually obstinate effort to interpret everything there is in terms of the mechanically caused motions of matter. The triumphs of Galilean physics led other seventeenth-century philosophers, most conspicuously Descartes, to go some way in this direction, to the conclusion that the non-mental world, at any rate, consists of material bodies, endowed only with the mathematical properties of shape, size, mass, and motion, causally influencing one another by impact. Hobbes, impressed by Harvey's mechanical theory of the circulation of the blood, went a good deal further. For him mental processes were also mechanically caused material motions, although on a very small scale. From this it followed that all mental activity is causally explainable and that every conceivable subject-matter is amenable to one scientific method of investigation. Hobbes is a complete determinist and a believer in the unity of science.

There are several reasons why Hobbes's unequivocally systematic professions should have been ignored. In the first place, his political and religious ideas are more interesting, emotionally, to all but a small minority than his mechanical materialism or his nominalist theory of knowledge. Secondly, among the few people concerned with logic and metaphysics there has been a tacit convention that the materialist view of the world, of which Hobbes is among the handful of major exponents, should be ignored as unworthy of serious discussion. Plato, according to Diogenes Laertius, would have liked all the works of Democritus to have been burnt. Epicurus, despite the version of his system given in the poem of Lucretius, is thought of as a handy personification of hedonism and not as the propounder of an empiricist theory of knowledge (his 'canonic') and of a variant of the Greek atomists' philosophy of nature. The critics of idealism, which has, after all, been the main gift of formal philosophy to religious belief, have remained, from Hume to Russell and beyond, unshakeably loyal to fundamental idealist presuppositions, in particular to the principle that all we directly and certainly know is the contents of our own minds.

Thirdly, Hobbes himself did much to undermine the claims of his metaphysics to serious attention. As a mathematician and scientist he was an overweeningly combative amateur and came off very much the worse in a noisy and protracted battle of words over squaring the circle, mainly with John Wallis, a really professional mathematician. Finally, there is the influence of *Leviathan* itself. There is hardly any of his materialism in it and only a brief sketch of his theory of knowledge, tucked into the middle of Book I. Published in 1650, five years before *De Corpore*, his main metaphysical work, it was produced out of order because of its direct relevance to the events of the time. Hobbes justified this premature delivery of the final part of his system: 'I saw that, grounded on its own principles sufficiently known by experience, it would not stand in need of the former sections.' From a literary point of view *Leviathan* is Hobbes's masterpiece. That helps to explain why it should generally have been supposed to contain the essentials of his thought. Various recent commentators have attempted to give a rational justification for this habit of ignoring Hobbes's non-social philosophy. In 1936 Leo Strauss published his ingenious development of a stray remark by Croom Robertson, Hobbes's excellent nineteenth-century biographer, a remark, incidentally, that Robertson in effect withdrew in a footnote. Hobbes's political doctrine, Robertson wrote, 'doubtless had its main lines fixed when he was still a mere observer of men and manners, and not yet a mechanical philosopher.'

Out of this Strauss excogitated a view of Hobbes, the admirer and translator of Thucydides, as being mainly original as a tough secular moralist. For Strauss, Hobbes's materialism is an irrelevant fad with which he became obsessed after forming his moral and political ideas and which merely obstructed their exposition with paradoxes and inconsistencies. In other words, Hobbes's metaphysics is historically posterior to his social philosophy and is logically incongruous with it.

An even more influential tradition of interpreting Hobbes against his own apparently systematic and naturalistic intentions was started by the distinguished historian of philosophy, A.E. Taylor, in an article published in 1938. In Taylor's opinion Hobbes's references to natural law must be taken at their face value. Hobbes's fundamental law of nature is that 'every man ought to endeavour Peace'; his second law, that every man should be prepared to give up all his natural rights but self-defence, provided that other men do so as well; his third, that 'men performe their Covenants made'. Hobbes says that a law of nature is 'a Precept, or generall Rule, found out by Reason, by which a man is forbidden to do that which is destructive of his life'. He dissents pretty plainly from the idea that natural laws are in a conventional sense divine commands. 'There be some that proceed further,' he says 'and will not have the Law of Nature, to be those Rules which conduce to the preservation of mans life on earth; but to the attaining of an eternall felicity after death.' Holders of this view are crisply disposed of.

Nevertheless Taylor does proceed further. He takes Hobbes's account of men as preoccupied with self-preservation to be an answer to the question of why men can be expected in fact to obey natural laws, and he professes to find a quite different answer to the question of why men morally should obey them. Men in the state of nature, and sovereigns among them, have moral duties which are imposed on them by God. That doctrine, shorn of such excesses as the view that Hobbes is a Kantian moralist, proclaiming duty for duty's sake, is the basis of Howard Warrender's impressively thorough interpretation of Hobbes's political philosophy, which was published in 1957.

Both J.W.N. Watkins in *Hobbes's System of Ideas* (London, 1963) and M.M. Goldsmith in *Hobbes's Science of Politics* (New York, 1966) defend what would appear to be Hobbes's own view about the logical unity and connection of his thought. They pursue their common aim by very different paths. Watkins's book is brief, lively, polemical, and replete with interesting and original ideas. It is an excellent guide to the present condition of Hobbes studies, but there is much more to it than that. Goldsmith's book is a considerably more pedestrian affair which conducts, rather self-effacingly, a guided tour through the whole range of Hobbes's thought. Watkins meets those who would carve Hobbes up with head-on counter-argument and turns the tables on them by tracing some illuminating connections among different parts of Hobbes's work. Goldsmith largely remits controversy to footnotes and a few brief appendices.

Watkins deals concisely but firmly with Strauss's view that Hobbes's metaphysics are causally independent of and logically at odds with his social theory. Hobbes's *Short Tract on First Principles*, the first but unequivocal draft of his materialism, was written in 1630, only a year after the publication of his translation of Thucydides, his only earlier piece of political writing. Furthermore, in the Introduction to his Thucydides, Hobbes employs a merely empirical and comparative method which is replaced in all his mature political works by deduction from the first principles of a mechanist psychology. The main political preference expressed in the early work is for monarchy, and this, though present in *De Cive* and *Leviathan*, is emphatically stated by Hobbes to be no part of their demonstrable content but to rest on merely persuasive arguments.

To the thesis of Taylor and Warrender that Hobbes's theory of obligation rests on theistic foundations, Watkins brings a series of powerful objections. By resting natural laws, the basic rules of conduct, on individual conceptions of God's will instead of on their scientific self-evidence, the Taylor-Warrender thesis forfeits the claim that natural laws are certain and not rationally disputable. According to Watkins, their thesis arises from the mistaken idea that the alternative to interpreting natural laws as full-bloodedly and conventionally moral, and thus as divine commands, is to take them to be merely factual descriptions of the general tendency of human behaviour, without any prescriptive implications about how men should conduct themselves. But there is a third possibility: natural laws can be seen as principles of practical wisdom, specifying what it would be reasonable or sensible or prudent for men to do. Watkins compares them to doctor's orders. He agrees that for Hobbes all laws, strictly so called, are commands and that Hobbes does describe natural laws as divine commands. But this, he argues, is a largely ornamental addition to Hobbes's theory of natural law. As Goldsmith neatly puts it, Hobbes's description of the laws of nature as divine commands does nothing to explain our knowledge of their content (for we have no rational knowledge of God beyond the fact of his existence) or to explain our obligation to obey them (for Hobbes nowhere invokes the characteristically divine sanctions of salvation and eternal punishment; his prescriptions always rest on the altogether this-worldly sanction of the fear of violent death).

Watkins goes on to elucidate three major ways in which aspects of Hobbes's non-social philosophy are indispensable to the fully developed form of his social doctrines. First, Hobbes's treatment of politically organised society as a mechanical artefact is the result of applying to the analysis of society the 'resoluto-compositive' method of the Paduan philosophers of science. The point is made by an effective comparison between Hobbes's analysis of society and Galileo's analysis of the trajectory of a projectile. Galileo showed how certainty could be attained about the laws of motion of ordinary gross material objects; Hobbes believed the same could be done with the behaviour of men in society.

Secondly, Watkins shows Hobbes's account of human nature, his egoistic psychology, to be an application of his metaphysical principle that all causation is literal impact. For him all mental activity is minute or incipient motions within the body. Animal motion, ordinary voluntary behaviour, is the effect of invisible but nonetheless material motions or 'endeavours' within the agent. In circumstances favourable to the organism, external stimuli are felt as pleasant and give rise to endeavours to persist in those circumstances, in other words to desire. In the opposite case, displeasure is felt and contrary endeavour or aversion is set up. Hobbes wanted to show, according to Watkins, that men are more or less uniform and that they are egocentric. Egocentricity explains why they come into collision and what motives they have for avoiding conflict. Uniformity explains why the mutual forbearances of citizenship are the only sure protection against the danger of sudden death, for it entails that every man is naturally vulnerable to every other man. Men are uniform because they are all mechanisms; they are egocentric because the ultimate determinant of all their actions is the overall endeavour toward self-preservation, a speculative adaptation by Hobbes of Harvey's theory of the role of the heart in the economy of the human body.

Finally, Watkins goes on from a short but suggestive examination of Hobbes's nominalist theory of meaning and insecurely conventionalist theory of truth to argue that, since for Hobbes there are no objective moral characteristics in the nature of things, all moral utterances must have their meanings fixed by the fiat of the sovereign. Thus Hobbes's mechanical conception of society is derived from his Galilean theory of scientific method; his egoistic psychology is derived from his materialism; and his moral and legal positivism is derived from his logic.

There are several reasons for dissatisfaction with Hobbes's apparent derivation of prescriptions for conduct from an egoistic psychology and, beyond that, from a materialist view of nature. The first is that the derivation commits the 'naturalistic fallacy' of purporting to extract an *ought* from an *is*. Even if this were a fallacy, as Watkins agrees that it is, it would not follow that Hobbes must be interpreted so as not to have committed it. It is an anachronism to suppose that he would have been in the least disturbed by this piece of Edwardian philosophical chic. Secondly, there is a difficulty about providing a ground for the obligation to keep promises on which men's duty to obey the sovereign rests. It cannot be the sovereign's command that justifies keeping promises, since the sovereign's commands have no rational force unless some men, the police say, admit an obligation to obey him. At least, Hobbes's apparent view – that keeping promises is justified by its natural consequence of safeguarding one's self-preservation – is a better solution to the problem than is the invocation of an incomprehensible God wielding inscrutable sanctions.

Yet, finally, Hobbes does constantly refer to God, and that cannot be brushed aside as verbiage insincerely scattered about to obstruct potentially dangerous opponents. In Goldsmith's book there are hints of interpretation of Hobbes's theology which would close the gap between his main naturalistic drift and his religious vocabulary. For Hobbes, God is knowable as the first cause of the natural order. Goldsmith observes in passing that to believe in him is, for Hobbes, simply to believe in the causal orderliness of the world. That idea could be developed into the thesis that Hobbes is a kind of deist, much in the way that Descartes and even Berkeley are, but one who, less cautiously than Descartes and less irrelevantly than Berkeley, saw that a purely rational deity of his kind was not the proper object of personal attitudes of devotion and submission. On this view, natural laws are based on the causal fact that our primary aversion is to violent death and on the causal laws which specify the necessary conditions of its avoidance. But these are also divine commands because natural causality is the only language in which a Hobbesian God can speak to men.

For those who wish to pursue these and other problems in the continuously fascinating business of the interpretation of Hobbes, K.C. Brown's collection *Hobbes Studies* (Oxford, 1965) is a most convenient aid. It includes a stylish essay by Strauss in which the main theme of his monograph of 1936 is conspicuously absent, Taylor's influential essay, the first sketches of Watkins's book and of the part of C.B. Macpherson's *Political Theory of Possessive Individualism* that concerns Hobbes, an excellent historical critique by Keith Thomas, equipped with no fewer than 405 footnotes, of the view, held by Macpherson, Strauss, and others, that Hobbes's ethical preferences were of an essentially bourgeois character, and an exchange between John Plamenatz and Warrender about the latter's book. It is no criticism of the editor that his selections nearly all focus exclusively on Hobbes's social philosophy (though it is odd and perhaps symptomatic that in his prefatory apology for the selectiveness of his selection the editor does not mention this bias). The fact is that Hobbes's metaphysics (apart from Brandt's great treatise) and, even more, his epistemology have received nothing like the critical attention given to his social doctrines. Goldsmith's early chapters on this neglected area are the weakest and most summary of his book, and it is a particular virtue of Watkins's treatment of Hobbes that he has thought enough about Hobbes's non-social philosophy to raise the question of its connection or lack of connection with the rest of his thought in a genuinely illuminating way.

The two sides of Hobbes's general philosophy do not rest their claim to attention on the mere fact that they exist; both raise live issues. His linguistically oriented theory of thought and knowledge is a uniquely thorough anticipation of a leading theme in the analytic philosophy of this century. He was the first philosopher in history to give to language that first place in the study of the powers of the mind that would now be widely accepted as proper to it. Even if his conventionalism is exaggerated, it has the merit of giving an account of the capacities of human reason that was not improved upon until Wittgenstein's *Tractatus*. As for his bold extrapolation of materialism from inanimate nature to the human mind, this was rejected in his own time as both morally and intellectually monstrous, and has been ignored until very recently by all but a handful of more or less isolated and marginal thinkers, usually reflective scientists unable to break through the protective barriers of the philosophical profession. But developments within science have rendered increasingly insecure the dualistic presumptions of even the least spiritually minded of philosophers. Darwinism in the last century, molecular biology and cybernetics in this, have undermined the Cartesian immunity of spirit to the kind of investigation the rest of nature has been exposed to. There is now an active body of dissenting philosophical opinion which argues that mental events are in fact occurrences in the brain and nervous system, and which tends to deduce from this many of the major features of Hobbes's system: his deterministic view of human conduct, his account of value in terms of desire and aversion, his belief that there can be a science of society.

Hobbes's political prescriptions depend for their more unattractive qualities on his poorly argued principle that there is no fate worse than death. We can reject this without making the very large remainder of what he has to say otiose. By no major philosopher has the intention of interpreting the world systematically with the smallest possible number of clear ideas and obviously true assumptions, the attitude behind the progress of science, been more boldly and resolutely pursued. At the end of a period in which brilliance and dexterity of argument have been achieved at the expense of fragmentation and inconclusiveness, his Elizabethan intellectual pride is a timely reminder of what is possible to the human mind.

16

Hegel

Hegel's reputation in the English-speaking world was at its lowest ebb in 1945. That was the year of Russell's *History of Western Philosophy*, with its genially dismissive treatment of Hegel, and of the stormy invective of the Hegel chapter in Karl Popper's *The Open Society and Its Enemies*. In Britain the last embers of resistance to analytic philosophy, itself inaugurated at the turn of the century by Russell and Moore in total rejection of British neo-Hegelianism, had been stamped out. Collingwood had been dead for three years and had left no visible disciples. Idealism had, indeed, one distinguished exponent, the immaculately courteous and stylish Brand Blanshard at Yale. But his loyalty was not so much to Hegel as to F.H. Bradley, the most original and Hegelianly unorthodox of late-nineteenth-century British idealists, who, in fact, respectfully disowned Hegel. Like Bradley, Blanshard was more a critic of empiricism than a constructive practitioner of speculative philosophy. In all branches of philosophy Hegel's ideas were not thought worth consideration even as an exemplary form of error, except in political philosophy, a field which analytic philosophers avoided and whose controversies thus proceeded, to the extent that they proceeded at all, in the idiom of an earlier age.

Hegel had fallen from grace in Europe by 1840, a decade after his death and long before he was known at all in the English-speaking world. But the chief initiators of the post-Hegelian philosophies of the nineteenth century, Schopenhauer, Kierkegaard, and Marx, critical as they were of Hegel, all agreed with him that philosophy should be done in the grand manner. Schopenhauer preserved his all-inclusively systematic aims; Kierkegaard followed his antiscientific concentration on the higher spiritual activities; Marx, claiming to be a scientist, understood by science a Hegelian, dialectical form of thinking. So although his European supplanters voted against Hegel, they accepted his agenda. But the brief interruption of idealism in Britain had no lasting effect on the national tradition of conceiving the philosopher, in the words of Locke and the practice of a host of others, as an underlabourer to the scientist, or, with Moore and the linguistic philosophers, to the common man.

What has done most for the restoration of Hegel's fortunes, both in continental Europe and the English-speaking world, has been an increasing sense of the need for a new Marx. The official Marx of the interwar years, discredited as the theological ornamentation of Stalin's slave state, was the late, scientistic Marx of *Das Kapital*, as interpreted by the naïvely positivist

Engels, whose task it was to generalise Marx's theory of history and society into the comprehensive philosophy of dialectical materialism. The recovery, by 1930, of Marx's more Hegelian and philosophical early writings of the 1840s, from the Paris MS to *The German Ideology*, drew attention to a Marx altogether more libertarian and less deterministic than the sage of Highgate, and, in its emphasis on man as the creator of himself and the world, much more attractive to ardent reforming spirits.

In Europe the revival of Hegel came about at much the same time as the philosophical revision of Marx and in much the same way: by attention to the earliest writings, which had for the most part been newly discovered. The *Realphilosophie* of Hegel's Jena period provided a new approach to *The Phenomenology of Spirit* as did Marx's *Economic and Philosophical Manuscripts* to *The German Ideology*. Kojève's *Introduction to the Reading of Hegel*, now available in English (ed. Allan Bloom, tr. James H. Nichols, New York, 1969) is a version of his famous and influential lectures of the 1930s. These awakened an interest that was further fed by Hyppolite's translation of the *Phenomenology* (1934), his long commentary on it (1946), and the essays of 1955, now available in John O'Neill's translation as *Studies on Marx and Hegel* (New York, 1969).

In the English-speaking world the process began much later and was less dramatic. Starting from J.N. Findlay's presidential address to the Aristotelian Society of 1955, 'Some Merits of Hegelianism,' the revival was inspired less by an interest in the proto-Marxian aspects of Hegel's social and political thought than by a desire to reinstate metaphysical speculation after its long prohibition by positivism. In his substantial, if somewhat idiosyncratic, *Hegel: A Re-examination* (1958), Findlay, indeed, dismisses Hegel's political theory with an air of embarrassment. 'Hegel's theory of the state,' he says, 'is an unedifying piece of writing, largely lacking in thought and argument.' But against Hegel's more strenuous detractors he protests, in a Wittgensteinian turn of phrase: 'there is nothing *vile* in his political philosophy. At its worst it is small-minded and provincial, at its best it achieves the level of inspiration of an average British back-bench conservatism.'

In the United States the revival of interest in Hegel was initially the work of Walter Kaufmann, first in the Fifties in a series of articles, of which the most notable is 'The Hegel Myth and Its Method' (included in Alasdair MacIntyre's useful compilation, *Hegel: A Collection of Critical Essays*, New York, 1972), an analysis of Popper's attack that is all the more effective for the general sympathy it shows to Popper, and later, in 1965, in the slightly inchoate mixture of translation, commentary, and general discussion that makes up his *Hegel*.

Kaufmann's interest in Hegel is part of his general project of rescuing post-Kantian philosophy in Germany from the largely unsubstantiated charge by Anglo-Saxon philosophers that it is intellectually grotesque and morally outrageous. Hegel took second place to Nietzsche in this project, Kaufmann's aim being to dissociate the intellectual transition in which they stand at either end from the Heideggerian philosophy, which in his view really merits the blanket reprobation given to all German philosophers since Kant (cf. chapter 18 of *From Shakespeare to Existentialism*, 'German Thought after World War II').

As the books reviewed here suggest, these first springs of reawakened interest in Hegel in Britain and America have now swelled. Indeed the preparation of this article has been delayed by a kind of Tristram Shandy effect. The influx of new material has steadily outstripped the reviewer's ability to cover it. As a result the reviewer has attempted to select from the output on Hegel of the past five years.

Even if much of the current interest in Hegel derives from his proximity as a social philosopher to the original and allegedly essential Marx, only in Europe did the Hegel revival begin from that interest. In Britain and America it is Hegel the systematic metaphysician that was first exhumed. How far can the social philosopher and the cosmic metaphysician in Hegel be separated? Lenin took a strongly negative line on this issue: 'You cannot completely understand Marx's *Capital*, and in particular its first chapter, without having studied and understood *all* the *Logic* of Hegel.' While the battle of the Marne was in progress in the autumn of 1914 he settled down to this agonising and perhaps impossible task himself.

Certainly Hegel's social and political theory can be considered almost without reference to his metaphysics and still be treated in an informative and intelligible way, as is done by Shlomo Avineri in *Hegel's Theory of the Modern State* (London, 1972). But Raymond Plant, whose excellent *Hegel* (Bloomington, Indiana, 1973) appears in a series of books on political thinkers, says that 'an understanding of these [central metaphysical] doctrines is ... a necessary condition of making his writings on political philosophy intelligible.'

An argument for separating the two aspects of his work might be drawn from the fact that Hegel's metaphysics was not worked out until he had devoted much philosophical attention in his early years to politics and to religion, conceived as a decidedly social phenomenon and not, in the manner of Whitehead, as 'what the individual does with his own solitariness'. But that argument would be cogent only if the metaphysics inspired by his early concrete studies of religion and politics had not influenced his subsequent handling of society, politics, and history. Much systematic philosophy has been inspired by more detailed investigations. From Plato to Russell many distinguished philosophers have started out from mathematics. Aristotle was a biologist, Locke a doctor and political theorist. But, in general, philosophies produced in this way are not mere epiphenomena of the more specific interests that inspired them. Hegel's metaphysics and social philosophy are at any rate congruous and each presents so many obstacles to understanding that it is only sensible to make use of either to help make the other more intelligible.

All the same I am inclined to think that the two ought to be separated in what might be regarded as Hegel's own best interests. The reason is that it is only the epistemological or methodological part of Hegel's metaphysics that has a direct bearing on his social philosophy. The substantive, cosmological part has no more than a general affinity of style with the social philosophy. It is also extremely ambiguous because of the desperate vagueness of its foundations and in either of its more natural interpretations it seems pretty absurd. I am inclined to believe that Hegel's theory of method was first derived from the consideration of human and social questions, the subject of his *Phenomenology* and of the concluding part of his *Encyclopedia*, the *Philosophy of Mind*, a field to which it is plausibly applicable, and that he then projected this theory on to the even larger concerns of cosmology, namely the relations of nature, man, and God, to which it is not plausibly applicable. If I am correct, the extraordinary character of the resulting substantive theory of the cosmos is neither surprising in itself nor necessarily damaging to the dialectical account of the human and social world on which he based his reflections.

I

Hegel saw his own work as the culmination of the whole history of Western philosophy, and with that in mind one should perhaps start any attempt to place and account for it with the pre-Socratics. One must at least go back to Kant's uneasy critical synthesis of the seventeenth-century rationalism that culminated in Leibniz and the British empiricism that achieved its fullest development with Hume. The rationalists held that the real nature of the world, the existence and characteristics of God, nature, and the soul, could be ascertained by pure reason, working deductively from self-evident first principles. Sensation for them is only 'confused thought' and its mangled deliverances provide no more than illusion-riddled appearances of the reality that reason alone can penetrate. For the empiricists knowledge of what really exists can be acquired only from the senses; pure reason is competent to discover only the formal relationships between concepts.

Kant agreed with the empiricists that the senses are necessary to knowledge of reality, but denied that they are sufficient. The intellect has an essential part to play: not as an alternative and superior mode of access to reality, the task of reason as the rationalists conceived it, but *in conjunction with* the senses as a source of organising principles which order and arrange the initially chaotic 'manifold of sensation' yielded by the senses into a world of persisting substances, causally related to one another.

In this more modest, organising employment the intellect is called by Kant 'understanding', not reason. It enables us to construct a common world from our respective sensations because the apparatus of forms, categories, and principles with which it operates is common to all men, a 'consciousness in general' whose identity in all minds Kant takes to follow from the indisputably universal necessity of formal logic. The world of the human understanding is thus objective, in that it is the same for all; but it is not transcendent, not something lying beyond our sensations, since it is composed of them. We can have no knowledge of things-in-themselves, according to Kant, apart from the fact that there are some; both physical and mental it would seem.

Half of Kant's chief work is taken up directly with the project of its title: the critique of pure reason. Thought alone, or reason, gives no real knowledge. Its purported proofs of the existence of God, the immortality of the soul, and the infinite extent and divisibility of nature are all invalid. These seductive forms of intellectual self-deception Kant calls, with pejorative intention, dialectic. But when thought is applied to the raw material of sensation, on the other hand, it gives us real knowledge of a phenomenal but nevertheless objective world, a world described by pure mathematics, Newtonian physics, and, it would seem, although Kant does not work this out much, empirical psychology.

In a famous phrase Kant described himself as limiting knowledge to make room for faith. Even if theoretical reason is powerless to prove the existence of God and the freedom and immortality of the human soul, these attractive beliefs can still be reinstated, if less securely, as presuppositions of our experience of moral obligation. Even if God and the soul are not theoretically knowable they can still be proper objects of *belief*, at least as regards their existence, although we can know nothing of their properties. On the one hand, then, Kant rejects things-in-themselves or noumena, at any rate as objects of philosophically demonstrable knowledge. On the other hand he lets them back in: God and the soul as presuppositions of morality, material things-in-themselves, more tentatively, as the unknowable source of the sensations that our understandings work up into a common world.

Kant's German successors – Fichte, Schelling, and, above all, Hegel – accepted most of what he has positively to say as a starting point but fastened critically on his uncomfortable doctrine of things-in-themselves. In a way that they reasonably argued to be more consistent with his basic assumptions than his own conclusions were, they rejected noumena, conceived as entities altogether beyond the reach of experience, and contended that the reality which reason apprehends with its dialectic is the infinite and all-inclusive whole of which the analytic understanding grasps only the parts. The reality that reason dialectically explores is not, therefore, something wholly distinct from experience. It is the organised totality whose separate and abstracted details are known by the understanding. The work of the reason is not a leap from the level of the understanding into a scrutiny of the inaccessibly transcendent: it is the comprehensive completion of that work. Thus 'reason' and 'dialectic', which had been terms of disapprobation in Kant's mouth, came to be re-equipped with their ancient Platonic dignity.

This counter-Kantian revaluation of reason and understanding is the fundamental principle of Hegel's theory of knowledge or method. For him the understanding, conceived much as Kant conceived it, does not yield true knowledge but, rather, practically useful rules of thumb: abstract, partial, but convenient for practice. Understanding is the analytic, abstractive order of thinking to be found in the sciences and in everyday practical thought. Reason, on the other hand, as Hegel conceives it, does give true knowledge of reality by apprehending things in their concrete interrelatedness with other things. The understanding extracts items of particular interest from the systems of relationships that make them what they are so that they may be more readily manipulated in thought and action. Reason, however, seeks to grasp things in their unitary wholeness: its aim is totality, not artificially abstracted parts. For Hegel, as for the law courts, the only real truth is the whole truth.

As applied to human society this presumption has some interesting consequences. The domain of politics cannot be circumscribed and confined to an investigation of the machinery of government; its ingredients cannot be conceived as conscious human artifacts with clear, antecedently assigned purposes. A state is more than a set of formal institutions. Such institutions interact so thoroughly and intimately with the whole social existence of a people as to be inseparable from it. Again the tendency of all traditional social theory, culminating in that of the Enlightenment, to see institutions as quite distinct from an eternal human nature considered in the abstract, fatally ignores the fact that the institutions of an age are an expression of the human nature of that age. Thus the totalities that reason studies are essentially historical in character.

This body of doctrine is not a complete novelty. Selected elements of the thought of Rousseau and Burke are to be found in it: the idea that human nature is formed by society from Rousseau; the idea that the present condition of men crucially embodies the historic past of society from Burke. But Hegel arrives at something quite different from Rousseau's democratic primitivism and from Burke's reverent conservatism: a kind of historical realism about state and society, which, while committed to the inevitability of change, acknowledges that such change can occur only within well-defined, if hitherto little understood, limits. Hegel is as much of an anti-utopian as Marx, as much convinced that most men's notions of what is socially possible are ludicrously and wishfully exaggerated.

The substantive cosmology produced by the method of reason is a much less digestible affair. The all-inclusive whole of reality is *Geist* or Spirit, which some would prefer to translate as 'Mind'. For Hegel ultimate reality consists not of individual minds or spirits, but of Spirit in general. And how can this reality be apprehended by reason? It presents itself to philosophical reflection (and, by implication, in fact) first in the form of the abstract categories of logic: 'spirit in itself'. Spirit in this form then 'externalises' itself as nature, in which, so to speak, the bare bones of logic take on spatio-temporal flesh: 'spirit for itself'. Finally, mind proper comes on the scene, 'spirit in and for itself', first as individual consciousnesses, then as social institutions, lastly as art, religion, and philosophy, and, in the end, spirit reappropriates the world of nature which it has mistakenly regarded as external but which is really its own unconscious product.

These mysterious, if suggestive, assertions pose two main problems of interpretation. First, what is to be understood by 'Spirit', and, in particular, is it to be identified with God? Secondly, what are we to understand by the 'externalisation' of the Idea in Nature, and, in particular, is it some sort of creation?

The more conventional view is that Hegel's Spirit is a kind of world-soul, of which particular finite minds are fragmentary, and thus not wholly real or self-subsistent parts, but which goes beyond them. Interpreted in this way Spirit is pretty much like God, although it is the God of pantheism not of theism, since this God is not distinct from the world but *is* the world, truly conceived as a unitary whole. Furthermore, this God is not a person since it is not, to start with, self-conscious, but becomes self-conscious only through diversifying itself into the plurality of finite minds. If the sequence Idea-Nature-History is taken in a literal, chronological way this position approximates to the idea that God proper is not so much the originating source as the ultimate, evolutionary goal of the history of the world.

An alternative, more secular interpretation is that Spirit is no more than the integrated totality of all actual finite minds, past, present, and future. This, which is more or less the view of the young or left Hegelians, departs a good deal further from ordinary religious belief than the more conservative interpretation. It also implies a measure of naturalism, an abandonment of the idealist principle that the constituents of material nature can exist only as objects of some mind. For the greater part of what everybody (including Hegel) would acknowledge to exist in nature is not the object of any finite mind. So either nature has to be reconstrued as a grotesquely patchy and fragmentary residue of what we ordinarily take it to be or the dependence of nature on mind for its existence has to be given up.

The crucial passage comes at the very end, section 244, of Hegel's *Logic*. He says of the Idea, 'in its own absolute truth it resolves to let the "moment" of its particularity ... the immediate idea, as its reflected image, go forth freely as Nature.' The natural interpretation of this is that the Idea actually makes Nature, or a bit more offhandedly, lets it go by some metaphysical process of secretion. Somehow or other Spirit, in its raw, original form, produces Nature.

It seems to me that this kind of more or less literal reading of Hegel's account of the relation between Spirit and Nature must represent what he really had in mind. Nothing else is consistent with the radically idealistic starting point of his philosophy, in particular his rejection of Kant's transcendent thing-in-itself, conceived as a reality independent of mind and yet somehow causally underlying the sensations out of which our beliefs in an external nature are constituted.

But it is unattractive to two classes of Hegel's admirers: to those who wish to disentangle what they see as the humanly and socially valuable parts of Hegel's thought from involvement with religion, the left Hegelian party in general; and also to those philosophically purer spirits, like J.N. Findlay, who simply find it unintelligible that a God as flimsy, sketchy, and potential as the Idea, or Spirit-in-itself, endowed with neither consciousness nor will, could create anything. Findlay's alternative is to say that Hegel meant no more than that Nature exists *for* Spirit. But this is no help. For either it means no more than that Nature is the indispensable condition for the emergence of Spirit, which every naturalist would happily affirm and only the most mystical kind of spiritualist would deny, or it means that some intelligent being produced nature as part of a project the completion of which is the production of actual minds, and that brings us back to conception of the Idea as creative, however passively and unconsciously, with which we started.

I conclude, then, that Hegel's substantive metaphysics is essentially religious in character, a watered-down, and on that account less persuasive, version of the Christian theory of an omnipotent personal creator. By diluting the naïveté of the traditional conception of the creator as a person, he turns it into a system of abstract logical notions whose power to create anything is hard to understand. If this residual religious element is interpreted out, Hegel's substantive metaphysics gets turned into a kind of evolutionary naturalism like the philosophy of Samuel Alexander, a matter of redescribing ordinary empirical facts about nature in a misleadingly spiritualistic and teleological idiom. But that does not affect Hegel's social philosophy or his doctrine of method, in so far, at least, as it is confined in its application to the human and social domain.

II

Most of the books I am concerned with here deal with Hegel not as a substantive cosmic metaphysician but as a philosopher of mind and society, the author, that is, of the *Phenomenology of Spirit*, the *Philosophy of Mind* (the third part of the *Encyclopaedia*), the *Philosophy of Right*, the *Philosophy of History*, the *Philosophy of Art*, the *Philosophy of Religion*, and the *History of Philosophy*. The most notable of the exceptions is Ivan Soll's *Introduction to Hegel's Metaphysics* (Chicago, 1969). This seems to me by far the best introduction that there is to the metaphysical side of Hegel's work. It is brief, lucid, and sympathetic to its subject. It is not critical on a large scale; hair-raising Hegelian claims do not cause Soll to raise even an eyebrow. But there is a critical element in the selection of topics, and from time to time some mild internal criticism is voiced, as when Soll observes that Hegel's identification of absolute knowledge with knowledge of the absolute is not much of an argument. (One might as well identify inadequate knowledge with knowledge of the inadequate.)

He considers four main topics. First, the forms of alienation or estrangement from the world enumerated in the section on Consciousness in the *Phenomenology*: the master-slave relation, stoicism, skepticism, and the unhappy consciousness. Secondly, Soll examines the Kantian notion of the thing-in-itself, the philosophical expression of this estrangement, and Hegel's particular objections to it, as an object, something that exists, that is nevertheless not an object, something that is unknowable. In the third chapter he investigates Hegel's view that philosophy must seek to overcome the duality of subject and object. Finally, he presents Hegel's resolution of the duality in which subject and object both turn out to be the absolute. The resolution occurs in the activity of true philosophising, where the philosopher who has transcended his particularity by recognising his identity with infinite Spirit takes infinite Spirit as his object of thought.

Throughout Soll's exposition large questions arise that demand a critical consideration that they do not receive. But it is quite clear what the questions are. Soll seems to assume here Hegel's fundamental premise as beyond question: that there can be such a thing as absolute knowledge of the truly, all-inclusively infinite. But given this assumption, Soll succeeds in presenting Hegel's main metaphysical theses as a coherent sequence of thoughts.

Hegel's Idea of Philosophy, by Father Quentin J. Lauer (New York, 1971), seeks to introduce readers to its subject by translating and commenting on Hegel's introduction to his *History of Philosophy*, from the Hoffmeister edition of 1940, and not Michelet's of 1831, the original of the standard translation by Haldane and Simson. Hegel's history of philosophy, says Lauer, is great philosophy, even if no longer great history of philosophy; and its introduction is, because of its clarity and comprehensiveness, the best introduction to Hegel's philosophy.

He supports this claim, in some prefatory remarks on Hegel's system, by the reasonable argument that since for Hegel philosophy can be reached by a dialectical and historical progression upward from lower grades of thought, Hegel's history of philosophy is really his philosophical theory of philosophy. In the progressive development that is the history of thought, thought produces its own objects and becomes increasingly aware of the fact, to the point, in Hegel's own philosophy, at which it recognises its identity with infinite spirit and with its object, the consummation of freedom and reason. The infinite object, which religion represents pictorially as external, is grasped directly by philosophical reason as internal to it. Philosophers, one might say, have previously been content to imitate Aristotle; with Hegel they turn to imitating Aristotle's God, the pure thinker whose only object is himself.

Another piece by Hegel which is sometimes chosen to serve as an introduction to his work in general is the preface (a substantial affair, seventy-two pages in Baillie's translation) of *The Phenomenology of Spirit*. A new translation of it forms the last main chapter of, and largest chunk of Hegel proper in, Kaufmann's *Hegel*. Just after it in the *Phenomenology* comes an introduction, seventeen pages in Baillie, a somewhat vertiginous critique of the idea that philosophy is an investigation into the nature of knowledge. How, Hegel asks in effect, can we seriously inquire whether certain beliefs are knowledge unless we have already made a presumption about what knowledge really is? So any examination of knowledge must also be an examination of the standard or criterion by which claims to knowledge are assessed.

Heidegger's *Hegel's Concept of Experience* (New York, 1970) prints this introduction on its left-hand pages, the right-hand pages being given up to some commentary by Heidegger himself. Those hungry for enlightenment are met with such observations as this: 'the absoluteness of the Absolute – an absolution that being absolvent absolves itself – is the labour of unconditional self-certainty grasping itself.' The general impression conveyed is that Hegel, for all his bad ratiocinative habits, inwardly realises that the Absolute is present 'within' us. This is, we may presume, another plug for 'openness toward Being', whatever precisely that may be.

In *The Religious Dimension in Hegel's Thought* (Bloomington, Indiana, 1968).

Emil Fackenheim defends the more or less traditional reading of Hegel against the idea that Hegel is some kind of proto-Marxist existentialist. The central problem in Hegel is, for Fackenheim, the relation of life, in particular religious life, to philosophical thought. He raises various intelligible questions arising out of Hegel's doctrines: does the conception of philosophy as absolute knowledge imply that the philosopher somehow *is* God? Is Nature contingent and self-subsistent or wholly dependent on Spirit? How much of Christianity is left by the Hegelian philosophy which claims to be the truth that Christianity imaginatively represents (Fackenheim argues that Hegel is more a Christian than a speculative pantheist)? Does the 'fragmentation' of the modern, post-Hegelian world show his attempted reconciliation of religion and speculative philosophy to have failed?

The argument is carried on in a bold, forthright manner and in a persuasive form, enriched with plentiful material from the history of religion and philosophy. But I have the feeling that it could have gone on indefinitely in its dialectical way, ever new contradictions emerging and importunately demanding reconciliation. Once an intelligent man like Fackenheim has grasped the Hegelian vocabulary and the liquid procedures of quasi-reasoning appropriated to its use, there is really nothing to stop him. Thinking about the infinite slides readily into infinite thought.

Before we leave Hegel the metaphysician, mention should be made of A.V. Miller's new translation of Hegel's *Science of Logic* (London, 1969). This was first translated into English in 1929 by Johnston and Struthers, and has not, perhaps, been read much. Nevertheless Miller (who has also translated that contentious and hitherto unavailable work the *Philosophy of Nature*) was prepared to undertake this arduous labour. It reads well, as well as it possibly can, no doubt, if faithful to its original. In particular great trouble has been taken to avoid reproducing the objectionable chunks of German word-order which the fatigue of Hegel translation often causes to slip by.

There are good reasons why Hegel's metaphysics, for all the obscurity of its presentation and the elusiveness of the general picture of the world it seeks to convey, should exert a continuing fascination. It claims to provide a rigorously reasoned foundation for a spiritualistic account of the nature of things, in place of such flimsier supports as mystical intuition or magical anecdotes or communications from the dead. Its extraordinary scope, the breadth and variety of its creator's learning, and the integrity of his admittedly baffling intellectual style endow it with a formidable quality that demands attention. It was said of J.H. Stirling's *Secret of Hegel* (1865), the first substantial book on Hegel in English, that its author knew how to keep the secret to himself. The secret is still far from fully revealed. In the concluding part of this article, I shall go on to consider recent studies of the other, the social, political, and historical, sides of Hegel's work, which are much more accessible than his account of the universe.

In the first part of this article I discussed the current state of opinion about Hegel, his relation to previous philosophy, in particular that of Kant, and went on to consider his theory of knowledge or method and its most grandiose application in his general metaphysics. I concluded that recent studies of his account of the universe in general, even Ivan Soll's very good one, had not succeeded in making clear what Hegel took the relations of Nature and Spirit to be, in particular whether Spirit should be conceived as something like the God of theism or rather as human mentality taken as a collective whole. I turn now to the application he makes of his dialectical method of reason to the specifically human subject matter of society, politics, and history. Here its implications are very much clearer and, if there has been vigorous controversy over what precisely they are, the issues in dispute, I shall suggest, are within reasonable distance of being settled.

Raymond Plant's *Hegel* does for Hegel's social philosophy very much what Soll's book does for Hegel's metaphysics. I mentioned earlier that for Plant Hegel's social philosophy cannot be understood abstracted from his metaphysics, but the relevant part of the metaphysics is the theory of knowledge or method rather than the theory of God, man, and nature. Plant has something to say about the latter but it has a secondary role since he sees all Hegel's thought as rooted in his social and political experience. In general he sees Hegel's mature philosophy as the culmination of a process of reflection set in motion by a pained awareness of the incoherence and division within men's personalities and between men in society, taking the form of nostalgia for the ancient Greek ideal in which men were not divided into public and private beings, and where state, society, and religion were fully integrated.

Plant stresses the influence on the direction of Hegel's thinking of Steuart's *An Inquiry into the Principles of Political Economy*, which convinced him of the social and psychological importance of economic change. The emergence of commercial, industrial, urban society had deepened the divisions between and within men, and intensified the problem of re-establishing coherence. Yet the process, with its division of labour and of classes, is irreversible. It is a social parallel to the cosmic alienation of men from nature. Where the latter is to be overcome by a metaphysically transfigured religion, the former is to be cured by the state as Hegel conceives it – and to effect the cure he required a strong state.

An issue that emerges here, which Plant does not seem to me to deal with, is that while cosmic alienation seems eliminable by thought, by the transfigured conception of man's place in the total scheme of things supplied by Hegel, actual political change seems required for the reintegration of society. Marx's *Theses on Feuerbach* appear to imply that Hegel's theories (i.e., 'previous philosophy') are a sort of analgesic pill which makes everything look all right. How far is this correct? How far is right thinking about actual social circumstances enough to show that they are all right, or are shortly, and inevitably, going to be? Hegel's conception of the state included a hereditary monarch, a universal bureaucratic class, functional representation by estates, largely free but supervised activity of 'corporations'. In so far as this conception deviates from the actual, is it something men ought to seek to realize or is it going to be realised anyway?

In his final chapter Plant does indeed raise this and a number of other fundamental questions under the highly appropriate heading,

'Transfiguration or Mystification?' and concludes that Hegel's claim that the modern state is truly 'universal' is not really borne out. But the crude question of what is Hegel actually up to – is he prescribing, predicting, or describing – is never forthrightly posed.

Most recent discussion of Hegel's political philosophy in the English-speaking world has taken the form of concrete polemical argument for and against the view that Hegel is to some extent responsible for Wilhelm II and the First World War and for Hitler and the second. The apparent message of Hegel's political theory is that law and the interest of the state transcend and override morality and the interests of the individual. Hegel's 'realism' about war and about the domination of historical epochs by particular states seemed to some a theory fitting such manifestations of German *Kultur* as the invasion of Belgium, the atrocities inflicted on Belgian civilians, and the punitive burning down of the University of Louvain. That line of argument began with L.T. Hobhouse's *Metaphysical Theory of the State*, an attack on the English Hegelian Bosanquet, motivated by the death of Hobhouse's son in battle in the Kaiser's war. The issue was revived by a debate between T.M. Knox and E.F. Carritt in 1940 on Hegel and Prussianism.

This and a further debate of the mid-1960s between Shlomo Avineri and Sidney Hook are the main pieces in Walter Kaufmann's collection, *Hegel's Political Philosophy* (New York, 1970). This is a lively collection of essays, more in the nature of hand-to-hand fighting with bayonets than the more usual long-range artillery exchanges of scholarly controversy. A faintly irritating feature is the partisan intrusiveness of the editor, who embellishes the contributions of Carritt and Hook (for whom Hegel is, broadly speaking, a beastly Hun) with nagging footnotes. Knox is perhaps more successful in arguing, against Carritt, that Hegel was not servile than in arguing that he was not a might-is-right worshipper of the state. Similarly Avineri makes a persuasive case that Hegel was a supporter of rational government rather than a nationalist of the ethnic-cultural variety. But Pelczynski makes less headway against Hook's other charge that he was a bureaucratic authoritarian rather than any sort of liberal.

Both sides to the disputes which Kaufmann referees are equally firm in their rejection of the full fury of Karl Popper's case (in *The Open Society and Its Enemies*). Popper makes Hegel out to be a nationalist, a racialist, a militarist, and an adherent of the *Führerprinzip* by hyperbolic extrapolation of the much milder positions he actually holds. Hegel did think that states should not be bits of dynastic property but should be associated with coherent communities; that in each epoch there is a nation that dominates the scene (but culturally rather than politically); that war is both inevitable and an engine of progress (agreeing on this second point with Popper's paradigm of political enlightenment, Kant); and he assigned a historic role to Great Men. But he was certainly no fascist. He favoured constitutional monarchy with representative institutions, not inspired heroic leaders; he supported autonomous corporations; he lauded reason not intuition; he held art, religion, and philosophy to be 'higher' than the state.

One virtue of Kaufmann's collection becomes clearer when it is compared with Z.A. Pelczynski's similarly named anthology, *Hegel's Political Philosophy: Problems and Perspectives* (London, 1971). Its thirteen essays were specially written for the occasion, a fact that reveals itself in a certain stodgy resolution, an air of heavy breathing, that attends a good many of them. Pelczynski does something to undermine the view that Hegel was in the ordinary sense a state-worshipper by pointing out that by 'state' he means not the government but the whole organised community; K.-H. Ilting uses Hegel's idea that a satisfactory system of law must rest on a shared moral consensus, that civil liberty can prosper only in conjunction with public-spiritedness, to make a suggestive criticism of liberal-individualist accounts of law; W.H. Walsh is agreeably informative about Hegel's philosophy of history, pointing out its extremely Eurocentric character and arguing that Socrates and Luther are the heroes of the Hegelian historical pageant (for inventing morality and bringing the Middle Ages to an end, respectively); R.N. Berki has a good essay on Marx's criticisms of Hegel.

What is very noticeable about many of the essays in the Pelczynski collection is an excessive tolerance toward Hegel's intellectual extravagances that is a widespread feature of writings about him. Everybody knows rather demure and censorious people who number among their friends some drunken and lecherous rascal whose outrages of conduct are genially indulged. He can get away with throwing up at the dinner table, while others are ruthlessly condemned for minor infractions of propriety. Historians of philosophy tend to treat Hegel with an uncritical benevolence that they would never extend to Locke or Mill. I am thinking here not of the moral defects alleged by such critics as Popper, Carritt, and Hook, but of the extreme unintelligibility of much of what Hegel wrote. Of course shrewd *aperçus* do float by on the surface of the murky torrent of Hegelian verbiage. But few dare to take this particular bull by the horns and suggest that the whole quasi-logical apparatus of 'deduction' and 'necessity' and 'contradiction' is no more than a dense incrustation of baroque ornament or, to vary the image, a kind of pastoral idiom in which often interesting opinions are presented.

Burleigh Taylor Wilkins's *Hegel's Philosophy of History* (Ithaca, N.Y., 1974) is a conspicuous example of this kind of treatment. It is not that he is uncritical: he is not inclined, he says, 'to campaign for the resurrection of Hegel's immanent teleology'. But his doubts do not have their proper consequences. 'Failure to accept a position or perspective does not prevent us from appreciating the significance of the position or perspective in question or from making various uses of it.' It is not so much that Hegel's larger principles 'fail to secure acceptance': they are very often absurd or unintelligible. The only thing to do is to ignore them and concentrate on the intelligible and discussable bits.

This is, in effect, the strategy of Avineri's *Hegel's Theory of the Modern State*. A highly, but never oppressively, learned book, it is a brilliant feat of demythologising. Throughout, the more abstruse and ethereal aspects of Hegel are either simply ignored or else translated into concrete, socially realistic terms, a procedure whose conspicuous success amounts to a quiet criticism of the grand panoply of the system. As a result, Hegel the political theorist is presented, despite his own efforts to conceal the fact, as a man with a coherent system of definite and perceptive things to say about the political life of mankind, past and, above all, present. The magnitude of this labour is nowhere revealed by any detailed recapitulation of the interpretative process or any brow-mopping asides of the what-Hegel-seems-to-be-getting-at-here variety. It emerges only in the startling contrast between Avineri's main text and the corresponding footnote citations of bits of Hegel's own prose. Avineri is the Jeeves of the Absolute Idea. To Hegelian equivalents of such Woosterisms as 'dash it all, a conk on the noggin is a bit of a facer' he responds with something like 'I agree, Sir, that a sharp blow on the head is a cause for concern.'

Of course something does get lost in this laundering out of everything but practical good sense. I should be tempted to describe it as the philosophy. What Avineri offers amounts to the comments on the political experience and present political needs of mankind, couched in pretty general terms, of a learned general historian. There is nothing much in the way of rigorous argumentative structure, only an early-nineteenth-century equivalent of the pregnant asides of A.J. Toynbee or W.H. McNeill. Avineri parenthetically justifies this by saying that Hegel's modernity is shown in his shift of concern from the problem of legitimacy to that of historical change. But that is not just a change of interest; it is a change of subject. Furthermore, even when demythologised, Hegel's theory still has implications for the central issue of legitimacy. Even when Hegel's view that the individual finds his true reality as a citizen is translated into the view that in modern industrial society the state must take on an altogether new kind of supremacy it still adds up to the thesis that the individual has only the rights that the state confers on him.

Avineri draws on the whole range of Hegel's political writings, not just the *Philosophy of Right* and the early political essays that have been recently translated, but, most crucially, on his first systematic political writings of the period 1802-1806, culminating in the Jena *Realphilosophie*. Here, more fully than in the *Philosophy of Right*, Hegel develops his ideas about the social and, in particular, economic changes of his own era, which require a new kind of state. In his emphasis on Hegel's concern with the inevitable class differentiation and consequent social problems of industrial societies, Avineri brings Hegel closer to Marx, tunnelling from the other end toward all those recent commentators on Marx who have sought to bring him closer to Hegel. There is a quietly persistent polemical intention behind the level surface of Avineri's exposition, that of undermining the conventional Western liberal account of Hegel's politics, the Hegel you love to hate described by Russell and Popper. According to Avineri, Hegel was not any sort of ethnic or cultural nationalist (indeed he entirely failed to recognise the force of nationalism in the age that followed his own); he was not a statist since he insisted that the economic life of civil society, religion, and private morality should be independent of the state, although he thought that the state should counteract self-interest both institutionally by the mitigation of poverty and by developing public-spiritedness in ideas; he was not a militarist, although he saw that war is the great testing device for the unity and integration of states.

Hegel emerges at the end as a more worldly version of Bosanquet, endorsing educated and incorruptible bureaucracy and the great social reforms of the British governments of the mid-nineteenth century. Avineri does, it seems to me, establish beyond doubt that Hegel was not a totalitarian, racist, or fascist. But he still remains, despite Avineri's denials, pretty much of an authoritarian. The representation of public opinion that he provides for is more a safety-valve for the information of the real bureaucratic rulers than an ultimate control over law and policy.

What is also put beyond question is the fact that Hegel was no toady to the Prussian state that employed him (although, as Avineri points out, for anyone of a toadying bent there were few states more worth toadying to than the progressive, fairly liberal Prussia of Stein and Hardenberg in which Hegel lived and which was very different from the military autocracy of Frederick William IV). His much criticised attack on Fries is put in the perspective of Fries's irrational, and wildly anti-Semitic, protofascism. In favouring representation and a merely symbolic constitutional monarch, he was far from endorsing the Prussian status quo which had neither. His last piece of political writing, an essay on the inadequacy of the British Reform Bill in face of the social problems of British industrialism, was censored by the Prussian authorities. Even if there are some more fiery substances in Hegel than the milk and water of which Avineri represents him as being composed, the monstrous Hun of liberal myth cannot decently survive this cogent and persuasive book.

The blurb on Kojève's *Introduction to the Reading of Hegel* describes it as the best book ever written on Hegel and as one of the few important philosophical works of the twentieth century. It is the content of lectures on the *Phenomenology* given between 1935 and 1939 and reconstituted by Raymond Queneau. Desultoriness and the glitter of philosophical chic are the dominating features of this humanistic, noncosmic reading of Hegel in the light of Marx and Heidegger. One can see that they could have been exciting to the audience to which they were addressed. But they have a tendency to evaporate on the printed page.

A much more accessible book is Hyppolite's *Studies on Marx and Hegel*, a somewhat boneless affair, whose smooth and elegant reasonableness comes over well in translation. Hyppolite holds that the early Hegel had a view of existence not far from that of Kierkegaard, that the French Revolution was the crucial event for him, posing all his problems. He saw it as the first real attempt to reunite the fragments into which man or Spirit had been broken by the collapse of the Greek city-state. He said of it: 'a spiritual enthusiasm thrilled through the world, as if the reconciliation of the Divine and the Secular was now first accomplished.' He believes that Lukács is broadly correct in considering the view that Hegel is basically a theologian to be a 'reactionary legend'. He argues that, in the *Phenomenology*, history and transcendental psychology distort each other, as Haym put it, and that

Hegel's logic corresponds, in a loose and cryptic way, to the history of philosophy. There is a polished fluency about Hyppolite. Raw Hegelian matter is divested of its starkness and effrontery and put forward as the most reasonable thing in the world.

Two recent books consider aspects of Hegel's influence. Brazill's *The Young Hegelians* (New Haven, Conn., 1970) is of more general interest since the interpretation of Hegel it examines, leading as it did through one of its lines of influence to Marx, is essentially the interpretation that lies behind the work of Lukács, Kojève, and Hyppolite. Brazill begins by considering the Hegelian ambiguities from which the young Hegelians took off. Is his philosophy a justification or a replacement of Christianity? In some sense Hegel saw his own age as that in which philosophy somehow takes over from religion and for the young Hegelians that meant that Christ is not God, history is a secular process, not a sacred one, and that Spirit has reached a point in its development of self-consciousness at which it goes beyond Christianity. Most of them, although not Bauer and Stirner, saw nature as independent and objective. As Croce put it, they developed the implicitly immanentist or humanist drift of Hegel's fundamental thinking, even if Hegel himself was too bound to the Platonic tradition in philosophy and to Lutheran religion to detach himself wholly from the belief in something transcending the concrete world of nature and history.

Strauss, Feuerbach, the more visionary and speculative Bauer and Stirner, and the more political Ruge are discussed in detail. Generally, the young Hegelians were humanist exponents of action, remote from the resigned philosophico-religious contemplativeness of the later Hegel. The Prussian government saw what was going on. It suppressed the young Hegelians' papers, replaced Hegel's disciple in his chair by the more religious Schelling, sacked Bauer (and thus extinguished Marx's hopes of a university career). By 1843, twelve years after Hegel's death, with the collision of their philosophy with state-supported religious orthodoxy, the young Hegelians ceased to be an effective party or public force.

William H. Goetzmann's *The American Hegelians* (New York, 1973) is much more of a connoisseur's book. If the young Hegelians achieved little as an organised group they still gave rise to Strauss's Biblical criticism and Marx's social theory, things of large and continuing importance. Hegelianism in America requires a very powerful lens to be seen at all. Its loyal adherents among American philosophers were, for the most part, rather dim figures and its chief significance is as something against which the pragmatists reacted: William James against its late-nineteenth-century British form, Dewey against the variety of American Hegelianism in which he had been brought up and which left a lasting impression both on his prose and on his appetite for unification and system. A Hegelian book had come out in America in 1840, but Hegel's philosophy was condemned as pantheistic in 1845 by the president of Oberlin College. Thirteen years later W.T. Harris, who was to become the first US commissioner of education, was converted to Hegelianism by an engaging figure called Brockmeyer who, arriving penniless, went on to make, and lose, a fortune, and who is pleasantly described by Goetzmann as 'an intellectual Daniel Boone'.

Based in St. Louis, Harris's *Journal of Speculative Philosophy* lasted from 1867 to 1893. An idealist tradition in academic philosophy runs from Harris through Palmer, Morris, and Howison to Royce, but the movement is more interesting as an element, a distinctly German element, in extra-academic culture, at odds with rugged individualism in its concern for the community. One adherent enthusiastically identified the Eads Bridge at St. Louis with the concrete universal. A beneficiary of the Hegelian character of the St Louis school system was, Goetzmann observes, T.S. Eliot, a possible explanation of the Bradleyan leanings of Eliot's youth.

Where Hegel is most alive today is as an ingredient in the rethinking of Marxism, associated most closely with Lukács and the 'critical theorists' of the Frankfurt school. One of the most active and enthusiastic exponents of this current of thought to the English-speaking world was the late George Lichtheim. The essays collected in *From Marx to Hegel* (New York, 1971) are largely concerned with the most up-to-date efforts to reincorporate Marx, freed from the positivistic and necessitarian dialectical materialism of Engels, in the great tradition of German speculative philosophy. These essays are informed and lively, communicating a marked sense of intellectual excitement, but somehow from a distance. There is a great flux of names, an equally copious array of assertions as to what Marxism is not, but in a curious way the central substance is missing.

What this really comes to is that for the Hegelianised Marxists of the present day there is a way of studying society that is not confined to the dispassionate registration of what is to be found on its observable surface, but which can penetrate to its inner essence and, in so doing, discern what ought to be done from the very fabric of history itself, in other words, can arrive at a social theory which embodies the principles of a valid *praxis*. But Lichtheim, unlike the critical theorists he applauds, from Horkheimer to Habermas, seems never quite able to engage with this central issue as something in need of argumentative support. Insinuation, appeals to authority, heavy irony about the superficial character of the Anglo-Saxon mind are mobilised to bear a weight they cannot sustain. This guidebook is no substitute for the hard labour of an actual visit. But it is calculated to whet fairly persevering appetites.

There is a form of scholarly skill displayed by historians of ancient philosophy in their production of substantial treatises on philosophers of whose thoughts only a few broken, vatic sentences are left to us. It corresponds to the archaeologist's ability to infer a draped and breasted goddess from a sculptural fragment of an ear or a big toe. The inverse of this craft is needed with Hegel: the capacity to winnow through the great chaos of Hegelian and near-Hegelian words (for most of what we call his works consists of editorial additions from lecture notes) to bring out an intelligible and coherent residue. Avineri has brought this off, in the area where it would be most likely to succeed and where it is of greatest current interest.

Marxisant students have addressed themselves with the most sanguine enthusiasm to Hegel in recent years, repelled by what they see as the intellectual narrowness and ideological bad faith of orthodox analytic philosophy. It has been a case of out of the deep freeze into the cinder box. I keep hearing of young colleagues who have developed an interest in Hegel, but nothing audible or visible seems to come out of it. Some strong spirit should address itself to the cryptogram of Hegel's metaphysics, with Ivan Soll's clarity and concision, but at a greater critical distance. If it turns out, as I am inclined to expect, that Hegel's metaphysics is composed of all the dross in Kant, carefully purged of all his insights, that will at least ease the consciences of those who confine themselves to Hegel as a theorist of society and culture.

17

Victorian Philosophy

In a broadcast talk recently one of the ablest of young British philosophers gave the following compact history of Victorian philosophy: 'German idealism is said to have effected a revolution in English thought in the first half of the nineteenth century, a revolution which did not entirely eliminate its rivals, but established its ascendancy until the end of the century, when empiricism staged a rather more successful counter-revolution.' In fact the brand of German idealism from which the school of Green and Bradley derived was not really introduced to the attention of British philosophers until 1865, the year in which Stirling's *The Secret of Hegel* appeared, and British idealism itself was not established until the seventies with Green's introduction to the works of Hume and Bradley's *Ethical Studies*. The remark I have quoted is simply a howler and its author's utmost disdain would have been called forth by a comparable lapse about any philosophy not so patently unfashionable. That such a mistake could be widely disseminated without correction is a sign of the neglect into which British philosophy between Hume and Russell has fallen.

The general picture of the development of philosophy with which many contemporary philosophers seem to work is simple, tidy, and remarkably exclusive. First there are the Greeks, then the long stupor of the Middle Ages, fitfully illuminated here and there with interesting bits of formal logic. Dawn, of a sort, breaks with the appearance of the great composite rationalist Descartes-Spinoza-Leibniz and the sun really gets up with Locke, Berkeley, and Hume. After Hume British philosophy seems to close down entirely, with the exception of Mill, until Bradley and does not properly start up again until those two youthful Bradleians, Moore and Russell, break out of the wrappings of their philosophical education. At last God said 'let Wittgenstein be' and all was light. The nineteenth century is seen as an exclusively foreign affair, given over to the fantastication of the more dubious patches of Kant, himself a serious philosopher fallen among metaphysicians. One does not need to rate the claims of the Victorian philosophers very high to feel that the later phases of this chronicle are in need of modification and that British philosophers should have some general idea of the immediate forerunners of the movement in which they proudly claim membership. Apart from anything else, as Hegel observed, if you do not study history you may have to relive it.

It is, no doubt, the analytic tendency of British philosophy during the last fifty years that is responsible for such a blithe indifference to the history of the subject. Analytic philosophers are, if anything, not so much indifferent as positively opposed to the history of philosophy for they see it as a time-consuming and intellectually low-grade substitute for serious work in the field. They have authoritative precedents for their point of view. Russell's brilliantly entertaining survey is thoroughly unhistorical, a mass of lively personal impressions of floating philosophical ideas. And where Russell is cheerfully subjective, Wittgenstein is entirely disengaged. There are hardly any names, let alone definite references, in his writings and he is reported to have found the works of Hume unreadable because there were just too many mistakes in them. It is not surprising that with these examples before them many philosophers should treat their predecessors as simply containers for interesting and timeless ideas. From this point of view when a philosopher lived or by whom he was influenced is irrelevant and if such questions seem at all seductive they are dangerous since liable to lead people away from the serious business of philosophy. This attitude of neglect is fortified by the organisation of teaching which bounds lightly from Hume and Kant to Russell and Moore with no more attention to the intervening period than is required for a ritual flaying of the mistakes of poor old Mill. There really has been a revolution in philosophical method and it is natural that in their lively awareness of all the new work there is to be done, of the fresh applications that are possible for the technique of analysis, contemporary philosophers should be impatient of anything that might side-track them. But the early ardour is now cooling a little and sophisticated voices are being raised to proclaim, quite falsely, that there has been no revolution at all. The epoch of consolidation that perhaps lies ahead will be an appropriate time for making up deficiencies of equipment.

More pressing interests are not the only reason for disregarding the history of philosophy. It is also suspect as a favourite preserve of the idealists. Idealism first appeared in England in a historical disguise, the doctrines of Hegel being mixed in to Jowett's introductions to the dialogues of Plato. Hegel has always been presented as a kind of latter-day Greek, a more public-spirited Aristotle. From Hegel on downwards idealism has been understood by its adherents as the consummation of all previous philosophy and the history of philosophy has acquired shape and significance from being seen as a process of continuous approximation to the final truth. The most recent, Crocean, version of this way of thinking identifies philosophy outright with its own history. Collingwood, for example, defines metaphysics as the historical study of the absolute presuppositions of scientific thought. But the excessive claims that have been made for the history of philosophy in identifying it with philosophy itself are not a good or sufficient reason for ignoring it altogether. Disentangled from the embraces of Hegelian metaphysics it can lead a useful and respectable life on its own.

However, as things stand, most large-scale histories of any originality or merit are idealist in inspiration. When analytic philosophers want to consult the history of their subject they must go, if they are wise, to someone like Windelband whose general history of philosophy is still, after sixty-six years, the best thing of its kind that there is. Now Windelband was a neo-Kantian and as far as he was concerned the history of philosophy came to an end with Kant and his romantic successors. His chapter on the philosophy of the nineteenth century begins: '*The history of philosophical principles* is *closed* with the development of the German systems at the boundary between the preceding [eighteenth] and present [nineteenth] centuries ... For nothing essentially and valuably new has since appeared.' The suggestion is that the truth has been found and that there is nothing left, apart from the exhumation of ancient errors, but to cherish and maintain the inheritance. A slightly odd state of affairs ensues. Empiricists who lived before Kant are accorded full respect. Did they not, after all, contribute to the formation of the true and final philosophical system? Hume's work as an intellectual alarm-clock is a little too familiar to be recalled in its conventional terms. But post-Kantian empiricists are taboo. With the 'German systems' ready and to hand they should have known better. There is a parallel here with the critical assessments in the history of thought made by communists. Pre-Marxian liberals are perfectly honourable and acceptable. Thomas More, Winstanley and Voltaire deserve praise for doing the best they could in the circumstances. But post-Marxian liberals, in their unregenerate refusal to see the light, are plain class enemies, the worst, because most insidious, of reactionary hyenas.

Most contemporary philosophers are, then, suspicious in principle of the history of their subject. When they do turn to it they have to rely on highly partisan sources of information and so are helplessly led into taking up the depreciatory attitude of their opponents to their immediate predecessors. In philosophy, as in literature, it is a good thing that from time to time there should be reassessments of the status of the leading figures. Something has been done in recent years for the Stoic logicians and a great deal for Leibniz. Russell and Popper, while not disputing his importance, have cast timely doubts on the moral perfection of Plato. But much remains to be done. There has been nothing like the contemporary reconstruction of the history of poetry. The great materialist tradition from Democritus and Lucretius to Hobbes has been universally denied the esteem it deserves. Both left and right, from Ayer to Collingwood, are at one in their Cartesian dismissal of this way of thinking. On the other hand the importance of Berkeley is generally inflated, perhaps because of the perfect lucidity and elegance of his style. Heroic efforts have not really succeeded in securing for Peirce the attention he is owed. But no oblivion is so profound as that which envelops the British philosophers of the nineteenth century.

There is, of course, the exceptional case that I have mentioned, that of Mill. But his status is equivocal. In the first place he is regarded in complete abstraction from his environment as a muddled continuation of Hume. The Hamiltonian 'philosophy of intuition' which was the occasion of his chief philosophical work is completely unknown. Furthermore he is used with the utmost disrespect as a sort of punch-drunk sparring-partner. His work is treated as an assemblage of dreadful mistakes: wrong about mathematics, wrong about induction, wrong about the mind, and wrong, oh utterly wrong, about morals. Despite his handy formulation of phenomenalism he is not a great philosopher but simply a great reservoir of elementary errors and so a most opportune pedagogical instrument. Mill was a main target for the late Victorian idealists and came in for as large a share of Bradley's abusive polemics as anyone. As a defender and articulator of the methods of natural science, as a believer in their applicability to man and society, as a declared adherent of the empiricist tradition, as an opponent of moral and political authoritarianism, as one who based his ethics on human nature and defined the ends of conduct by reference to human desires, he was naturally exposed to such an assault. What is surprising is that his stock has not gone up with the change of regime. If anything it has gone even further down.

The main explanation lies in the first half of the chapter on hedonism in Moore's *Principia Ethica*, particularly in eight or nine lethal pages in the middle of the passage in question. Here some rather calamitous attempts by Mill to demonstrate what he had declared not to admit of proof are memorably demolished. However fleeting his acquaintance with philosophy there can hardly be an undergraduate student of the subject who does not at least know his way round this cluster of arguments and as a result there are few philosophical doctrines so universally and unreflectively condemned as utilitarianism. But that doctrine does not sink or swim with the unfortunate 'considerations capable of determining the intellect either to give or to withhold its assent' that Moore fastened on in Mill's treatise. Moore's attempt to demolish Sidgwick's view that nothing can have value out of relation to human consciousness or feeling is much less successful. It rests on a rather absurd *Gedankenexperiment* about whose outcome Moore is at once dogmatic and obtuse. Apart from that, a less rigidly disputatious approach to Mill's own arguments would have revealed more than is commonly found in them. Mill's equivocation about the word 'desirable' was a careless way of making Sidgwick's point that value must be relative to human feelings. The fallacy of composition by which Mill passes from 'each man desires his own happiness' to 'every man desires every man's happiness' was his very rough and ready substitute for the widely accepted doctrine that moral convictions are essentially universal in character, that this is part of what is meant by calling a conviction 'moral'. Finally Mill's view that pleasure is the only object of desire is, in the sense in which he intends the term 'pleasure', a definitional truism. Moore's rejection of ethical 'naturalism' is the most significant residue of Kantian thinking in present-day analytic philosophy. The abyss which Kant interposed between duty and inclination has simply been reconstructed along linguistic lines. Nowadays it divides evaluative from descriptive expressions. It is a signal impurity in the revolutionary creed whose elimination is obstructed by hostile *idées reçues* about utilitarianism.

Mill's logic has not done much better than his ethics, though it has not had to undergo such a classical disintegration. Still Frege's handling of Mill is as ferocious as Moore's even if not quite as well known. The first of Frege's three principles of philosophical method was 'always to separate sharply the psychological from the logical, the subjective from the objective,' a point which Bradley constantly insisted on with his distinction of two senses of 'idea'. The implicit Platonism of this admittedly fruitful canon has repelled twentieth-century empiricists less than the empiricist theory of logic against which it was mainly directed. Just lately there have been some signs of a desire to do more justice to Mill. Professor Ryle has said of him: 'Mill's theory of meaning set the questions, and, in large measure, determined their answers for thinkers as different as Brentano, in Austria; Meinong and Husserl, who were pupils of Brentano; Bradley, Jevons, Venn, Frege, James, Peirce, Moore and Russell. This extraordinary achievement was due chiefly to the fact that Mill was original in producing a doctrine of meaning at all ... Nearly all of the thinkers I have listed were in vehement opposition to certain parts of Mill's doctrine, and it was the other parts of it from which they often drew their most effective weapons.' ('The Theory of Meaning' in *British Philosophy in the Mid-Century*, ed. C.A. Mace (London, 1957), p.241.) On the ethical side Professor Urmson has exploded some of the more insistent misinterpretations. But Mill's rehabilitation has only begun. He remains the Dreyfus of British philosophy, the whole established order of things seems to have conspired inadvertently against him.

Mill is at least scorned; the other Victorian philosophers appear to be totally forgotten. I have explained this as a result of the idealists' corner in the history of philosophy, combined with their belief in the work of Kant and Hegel as its apogee. The question now arises: are any of them really worth resuscitating, and if so who? The first thing that needs to be set in order is the bare composition of this segment of philosophical history. I should imagine that most professional philosophers of the present time know no more of Hamilton than that he was mixed up with some dreary muddle about the quantification of the predicate, that unless they have looked into Dean Burgon's *Twelve Good Men* they know no more of Mansel than his name, that they think of Clifford and Pearson as simply progressive-minded popularisers of natural science, of G.H. Lewes as simply George Eliot's lover, and that they have never heard of Ferrier or John Grote at all. Under pressure they would describe the course of philosophy between Hume and Russell in roughly the following terms: first of all there is Mill carrying on in a more or less eighteenth-century fashion, beside him spring up a whole lot of amateur philosophers like Spencer, of materialistic tendency and intoxicated by the doctrine of evolution, at which point the defenders of religion and public order pull themselves together and import a quantity of surplus metaphysical material from Germany, whose rich obscurity soon puts an end to the complacency of secular rationalism.

It is not difficult to get hold of a more complete and faithful account of the course of events. Consistent stories of the period are to be found in Sorley's contributions to the *Cambridge History of English Literature* (1916), in Dawes Hicks' long chapter on 'die Englische Philosophie' in the fifth volume of Ueberweg (1906), in the first part of Metz's large book (1938), and in the last two chapters of Carré's *Phases of Thought in England* (1949). After Hume there were two possible lines of action. Either you could accept Hume and, shutting up shop as a philosopher, turn into a psychologist, the response of Hartley, Tucker and Priestley, or you could attempt an answer to Hume in roughly his own terms. The second course was followed by the Scottish philosophers. What is not sufficiently realised is that they have as good a right to regard themselves as the continuators of the empiricist tradition as has the school of associationists and utilitarians whose chief ornament is Mill. The two groups are the right and left wing factions into which the main empiricist body was divided by the scandalous character of Hume's ideas. Reid's method is very much that which was laid down by Locke, at least as a programme: the careful introspective examination of what goes on in one's head in various forms of thinking. (De Ruggiero describes the works of the Scottish philosophers, not unfairly, as 'psychological museums'.) Dugald Stewart's generally rather hollow and orotund pages come more to life when he is expounding his version of Hobbesian nominalism. Brown fully accepts Hume's analysis of the notion of cause and denies that there is any kind of real connection between cause and effect. But he gets round the starting-point by claiming to intuit the necessary truth of the causal principle. The Lockean procedure of the Scottish philosophers, with its identification of philosophy with the introspective psychology of thinking, the examination of the 'facts of consciousness', led in practice to pretty Lockean results. But they were not hampered by Locke's overt and practically ineffective repudiation of 'innate principles'. They believed, as Locke did, that there could be no quality without a substance and no event without a cause. Unlike Locke, they were prepared to admit the theoretical consequences of their convictions. Their 'principles of common sense', or, as Stewart preferred to call them, 'the fundamental laws of human belief', together with the large number of basic notions on whose indefinability Reid always insisted, make their doctrines interestingly similar to those of the Oxford realists of the first decades of the present century – Cook Wilson and Prichard. The kind of empirical intuitionism that both groups exemplify is an important and continuing strand in British philosophy.

But the most influential echo of Scottish philosophy at the present day is the principle that Moore took over from Reid: 'To what purpose is it for philosophy to decide against common sense in this or any other matter? The belief of a material world is older, and of more authority, than any principles of philosophy.' The only essential change introduced by Hamilton and Mansel is a greater degree of agnosticism; their method and chief interests are the same as their predecessors' were. Hamilton's vaunted Kantianism is thoroughly superficial. All the Scottish philosophers were Kantian to the extent that they were anxious to preserve the fabric of human knowledge from Humean dissolution. But the means by which they tried to carry out this rescue work have nothing but their final outcome in common with Kant's. Where he derives the organising principles of thought from an examination of the necessary structure and workings of the mind, they are content with the more humdrum and economical assertion of these principles as indubitable truths. The following remark on Kant's theory of space is characteristic of the ponderous bluff with which Hamilton hoped to pass himself off as a Kantian: 'The analysis of Kant ... has placed this truth (that the notion of space is not derived from the senses) beyond the possibility of doubt, to all those who understand the meaning and conditions of the problem.' Mill's attack on Hamilton was not, then, a manoeuvre in the conflict of empiricism with speculative metaphysics, as Mill himself was inclined to suggest; it was part of an internal struggle within the empiricist camp.

The other important fact about the Scottish philosophers that is generally ignored is that they were the dominant philosophical school in Great Britain for just about a hundred years. Reid's most important book, the *Inquiry into the Human Mind*, came out in 1764, his two volumes of essays in the eighties. On the pamphleteering level Beattie's stupid but richly rewarded assault on Hume appeared in 1770. At the other end of the period Mill's *Examination of Hamilton* came out in 1865. In demolishing the chief figure of the prevailing school it succeeded in opening the way for something even less sympathetic to philosophers of Mill's persuasion, the Hegelianism that was heralded in the same year with Stirling's *Secret of Hegel*. In the United States the influence of the Scots was more prolonged, though the rise of Hegelianism could well be dated from 1867, the year in which Harris's *Journal of Speculative Philosophy* first appeared.

Left-wing empiricism in the nineteenth century mainly flourished outside the universities. Its orthodox form, as worked out by Bentham and the Mills, was soon elbowed out of the way by a much less philosophically sophisticated evolutionist point of view. Mainly the work of complete philosophical amateurs like T.H. Huxley, evolutionism reached some sort of culmination in the grandiose encyclopedia of Herbert Spencer. It is significant that the metaphysical top-dressing with which Spencer decorated his system is in all essentials lifted from Hamilton. Later Millians, at any rate, such as Bain, Croom Robertson and Sully, were eclipsed by the bold but philosophically shallow eloquence of men like Huxley and Tyndall.

Professor Aiken of Harvard has recently prophesied that Spencer is due for a revival. 'If his own age overrated him,' he writes, 'ours has underrated his merits.' (*The Age of Ideology*, p.170.) I should be more inclined to back two philosophers whose work is in marked accord with a good deal of recent thought and who have been excessively ignored in recent times – W.K. Clifford and Karl Pearson. This neglect has been encouraged by the practice of most historians of nineteenth-century philosophy of lumping them together with the evolutionary amateurs as just one more phase in the general outburst of pro-scientific and anti-religious enthusiasm that followed the publication of the *Origin of Species*. One of the many merits of Professor Passmore's excellent *A Hundred Years of Philosophy* is that he detaches Clifford and Pearson from the company of the pamphleteers with whom they are usually associated and puts them in their proper place beside the great European philosophers of science, Mach, Hertz and Poincaré, whose influence on modern analytic philosophy is more generally recognised. Russell has recalled the excitement with which at the age of fifteen he read Clifford's *Common Sense of the Exact Sciences* and has said of his philosophy of mathematics: 'In this respect, as in many others, Clifford was ahead of almost all the best thinking of his time.' The importance of Mach is not disputed. He was the chief philosophical stimulus for Einstein's great enterprises. In providing the logical positivists with a theory of experience he was as indispensable a forerunner of that movement as were Frege and Russell with their doctrines about logic and mathematics. His role in this matter has been properly emphasised by von Mises. Russell's own theory of knowledge underwent an increasingly Machian development from *Our Knowledge of the External World*, where Mach is singled out for praise even if his views are not wholly accepted, to the *Analysis of Mind*, in which a full-blooded neutral monism of Mach's variety is expounded. But, as Professor Passmore remarks, 'to try to establish "priorities" as between Clifford, Pearson and Mach would be pointless'. Their ideas are more honoured than their names.

With the idealists we return to more familiar country, though even here it is remarkable how little really serious examination their doctrines have been given. McTaggart has been devotedly investigated by Broad, but he is untypical. Dr Ewing's large treatise on idealism is to a quite unrepresentative extent preoccupied with the problem of perception. There is very little of value on any part of Bradley's vast output. The arrival of idealism in Britain is also still something of a mystery, for all the historians' vague gestures in the direction of Coleridge's addiction to Schelling and Carlyle's passion for things German. British idealism is especially interesting as a social phenomenon, as a conscience-stricken reaction against the heartless and vulgar complacency about material progress to be found in thinkers like Spencer. The social doctrine that Spencer extracted from the theory of evolution was grasping and cruel and seemed to underwrite the coarsest excesses of 'materialism' as a style of life. On the other hand thoughtful defenders of religion were on the look-out for some more reputable support for their faith than blind adherence to dogma or the tinkling superficialities of deistic argument. If Bradley's conservatism was of that repellent, sneering kind to which academics are sometimes unfortunately attracted, Green's defence of state intervention is now generally recognised as an important intellectual preparation for the British Labour Party. And the career of Archbishop Temple is as much a part of the history of idealism in its bearing on religion as the truck-loads of Gifford lectures quietly mouldering in university libraries.

In rather different ways, then, the Scottish philosophers and the English Machians would seem to deserve more attention than they usually get. By ignoring the former a hundred recent if not pre-eminently distinguished years of British philosophy are passed over. In the works of the latter are to be found themes of central interest to philosophers of the present time worked out with freshness, authority and extreme literary skill, for both Clifford and Pearson are in the highest class as expository writers. The early chapters of Professor Passmore's book go some way towards correcting the mistaken emphases of his predecessors and providing us at last with a really reliable survey of the immediate philosophical past.

18

Absolute Idealism

Philosophical movements lead two different lives. On the one hand a body of ideas is formulated, published, accepted, and finally superseded; on the other, at the institutional level, leading positions in the academic system are occupied by the exponents of the movement's ideas. Naturally these two careers are not coincident in time. New ideas are normally produced by unimportant people; the holders of important posts disseminate the ideas they acquired in their comparatively unimportant youth. As a result the dating of a philosophical movement is a slightly complicated business.

Considered as a purely intellectual phenomenon the interesting episode of absolute idealism in British philosophy can be dated with a fair degree of precision. The first seriously professional publications in which this point of view is to be found came out in 1874. That was the year of T.H. Green's long and arduously destructive critical introduction to his and Grose's edition of Hume's *Treatise of Human Nature*, of F.H. Bradley's first essay *The Presuppositions of Critical History*, of William Wallace's translation of Hegel's smaller logic (viz. Book I of the *Enzyklopädie*), and also of the beginning of the translation of Lotze's *System of Philosophy* by a group of distinguished British idealists. Two years later the first classic of the school came out: Bradley's *Ethical Studies*, the most explicitly Hegelian of his works.

Green was the acknowledged leader of the school and in many ways its most compelling personality. Beside his career of active responsibility in education and in public life that of Bradley looks pretentious and self-indulgent. Outside the field of technical philosophy narrowly conceived, Green was certainly the most influential of the idealists. He died in 1882 soon after the school was established. The year after, a group of his admirers brought out *Essays in Philosophical Criticism*, in which his more or less Hegelian methods were applied over a broad range of subjects, and his own chief work *Prolegomena to Ethics* was published, as were also the first edition of Bradley's *Principles of Logic* and Caird's short but substantial book on Hegel.

Green's death deprived the school of a prime unifying factor, but its intellectual dominance continued for the next twenty years. Seth, five years after editing the memorial volume to Green, sounded the first note of protest against the dissolution of the theist's God and of the free and immortal human soul in the all-engulfing Hegelian Absolute in his *Hegelianism and Personality*. This introduced a style of opposition to idealist orthodoxy that was to culminate in the system of McTaggart. On the way it made a detour through pragmatism, which never amounted to anything very much in this country, for all the polemical energies and copious productiveness of F.C.S. Schiller. At Oxford Cook Wilson carried on a somewhat furtive resistance to the reigning opinions from the end of the century (his lectures, *Statement and Inference*, were not published until 1926, eleven years after his death). At Cambridge Sidgwick represented an older way of thinking, but Sorley was an adherent and so, more brilliantly and heretically, was McTaggart.

The first really fundamental assault on idealism did not come until 1903, the year of Russell's *Principles of Mathematics* and Moore's *Refutation of Idealism*. Russell and Moore initiated a wholly opposed style of thought. Its uninterrupted development and augmentation of strength make it reasonable to date the end of idealism's full intellectual dominance from that year, just a decade after the idealist movement's most imposing expression in Bradley's *Appearance and Reality*.

But idealist professors continued to head university philosophy departments for a considerable time after 1903. In Oxford J.A. Smith and Collingwood occupied the chair of metaphysics in succession from 1910 to 1941. In Cambridge, although Moore was appointed to a chair in 1925, the year of McTaggart's death, Sorley remained professor of moral philosophy until 1933. In other universities the idealist hegemony was more enduring and persisted in Scotland until very recent years. Until well into the 1920s idealists held nearly all the leading positions in the philosophy departments of British universities and continued to be the largest group in the philosophical professoriate until 1945. Nothing shows the intellectually anachronistic character of this state of affairs more poignantly than the very high level of technological unemployment of idealists within the philosophical profession. A remarkable number of them nimbly overcame this misfortune by becoming vice-chancellors. The Hegelian mode of thought, with its combination of practical realism and theoretical nebulosity, is a remarkably serviceable instrument for the holders of high administrative positions.

Absolute idealism, then, exercised its full intellectual authority in Britain in the three decades between 1874 and 1903. I shall try to explain the rapidity with which it secured its hold to the absence of any very compelling alternative, to the fact that it arose in something very like a philosophical vacuum. For the two decades after 1903 it remained the best entrenched movement institutionally and it still constituted a considerable intellectual force. But after the deaths of Bradley and McTaggart, in 1924 and 1925, and Moore's appointment to a chair in Cambridge in the latter year, no new idealist works of any significance appeared in Britain except those of Collingwood. Twenty years later still its institutional hold was finally lost.

This episode in the history of British philosophy raises a number of interesting questions. The first I shall attempt to answer is that of why it began when it did and, arising out of that, how idealism managed to establish itself so rapidly. That leads on to the problem posed by the very late according of serious attention to Hegel and to the connected problem of the extent of absolute idealism's dependence on him. I shall defend the conventional view that British idealism is, more than anything else, Hegelian in inspiration. I shall end with a brief presentation of the main theses of absolute idealism as systematically dependent on the principle of internal relations, which is itself an ontological expression of the nature of the distinction between reason and understanding as it was conceived by Hegel.

I

First, then, why did absolute idealism emerge in Britain when it did, two-thirds of the way through the nineteenth century, around the time of Stirling's *Secret of Hegel* (1865) and the beginning of Green's career as a philosophical teacher? Perhaps the most substantial reason is that it met two ideological needs that were being felt with a particular intensity. The first of these was for a defence of the Christian religion sufficiently respectable to confront the ever more formidable scientific influences that were working to undermine religious belief. The second was the need for a politics of social responsibility to set against triumphant *laisser-faire*, of political altruism to counter the idea that uninhibited competition between self-interested individuals was the indispensable engine of human progress.

The religious scepticism of the Enlightenment had been directed more against the particular details of Christianity than the fundamentals of religious belief of any kind. Deism was a more common position than atheism; Voltaire, with his belief in a Newtonian regulator of the order of nature, a more typical figure than Hume, with his altogether more radical assault, both philosophical and historical, on all forms of religion. The Incarnation, the literal inspiration of the Bible, the mysteries of the Sacraments and the Apostolic Succession were the targets – not the existence of God. Furthermore, general arguments against religion like Hume's did not depend on any special knowledge for their force, only on a combination of acuteness and courage.

In the nineteenth century, however, autonomous developments in science, undertaken with no thought of their bearing on religion, exerted a dissolving influence upon it in a way that Newtonian physics had not. Geology, for example, by discarding the orthodox conception of the age of the world, supplied a counter-religious account of the nature of the universe in time parallel to that supplied by Copernicus about its nature in space. That, however, was more a difficulty for Christianity, as currently conceived, than for religion in general. The same is true of historical scholarship about the Bible, as exhibited in such works as Strauss's *Leben Jesu*. There is, indeed, no real irony in the fact that the British defenders of religion in the late nineteenth century should have gone for help to the Hegel who, earlier in the century, had inspired the biblical criticism which had contributed to the need for a defence. Hegel may have been, in a broad sense, a religious philosopher in view of his insistence on the essentially spiritual nature of the world. But the Christianity he was prepared to endorse, however laudatory the terms in which he spoke of it, as for instance the 'absolute religion', was remote from the literalism of prevailing religious orthodoxy. His ideas about religion involved a massive disencumbrance of faith from rationally indigestible elements, which were demoted by him to the status of figurative representations of metaphysical truth.

The scientific development that collided with religion in general, rather than orthodox Christianity in particular, was, of course, the evolutionary biology of Darwin. His theory of the emergence of man on the earth, as the result of competitive selection from random variations thrown up among more primitive animal species, struck at the foundations of religion as a whole in two ways. In the first place it disqualified the largest and most emotionally important range of evidence that existed for the argument from design. The gratifying adaptedness of man to the natural world in which he finds himself was now revealed as the outcome, explicable on mechanical principles, of a vast sequence of minute accidents. It no longer demanded to be understood as fulfilling the purpose of an infinite and benevolent intelligence. The argument from design was thus enfeebled, not, as at the hands of Hume, in its more or less elusive logic, but, with much more devastating effect, in its factual premises.

Secondly, Darwinism seemed to refute the dualistic conception of man as a compound of immortal soul and perishable body, of divine reason and animal passion. Dualism of this kind is a central feature of all the higher religions. It had also been a cardinal principle of the great tradition of European philosophers from Plato and St. Augustine to Kant. The idea that man is a material constituent of the natural order, whose distinguishing peculiarities are susceptible of the same kind of mechanical explanation as those of ordinary natural objects, had been confined hitherto to more or less scandalous speculators like Hobbes. The members of the associationist tradition that derived from him had often been enthusiastically religious, for example, Hartley. If the utilitarians proper, in whom this tradition culminated, had hardly been devout, the last and greatest of them, John Stuart Mill, had allowed in his late essay on theism that the hypothesis of a limited God had a fair measure of probability and he had insisted both on the radical distinctness of mind and body and on the irreducibility of the mind to its component experiences. But with Darwin the conception of man as wholly a part of nature acquired a kind of solid factual support that it had never had before, and which had been only faintly anticipated by Harvey's discovery of the circulation of the blood. Darwin did not, of course, strictly prove that man is a natural object, like, if more complex than, any other. The implication could be circumvented by regarding the evolutionary development that Darwin described as the instrument by which God created an earthly vehicle for the immortal soul. But the immediate impact of Darwin's views, supposing them to be true, seemed fatal to the religious view of man and the world.

Darwin's most brilliant expositor, T.H. Huxley, began his career of elaborating the wider implications of Darwinism with *Man's Place in Nature* in 1863, the year of Lyell's geological demonstration of the errors of orthodoxy about the antiquity of mankind. In 1871 Darwin's own *Descent of Man* was published, explicitly extending his principles to the human species. Thus, Stirling's *Secret of Hegel* in 1865 and the group of more professional Hegelian writings in 1874 were very timely, if help for religion was to be looked for in that direction.

Indeed, as a means for the defence of religion, the philosophy of Hegel had two great merits. First, Hegel succeeded in steering religion clear of a head-on collision with science by jettisoning the more factually concrete details of Christianity and by reinterpreting those elements of the faith of which the new scientific developments were most destructive as poetic images of the abstract metaphysical principle of the spirituality of the world. Darwin was fatal to a literal reading of the story of Adam and Eve, but not to the Hegelian reinterpretation of that story as a metaphor for the emergence of man on earth as a crucial point in the self-externalisation of the Absolute Mind.

Secondly, Hegel was himself, in a very large sense of the word, an evolutionist. The dialectical process could be and was understood as setting out the stages of the development of forms of existence in time, though as a matter of rational necessity not cumulative accident. Admittedly, in the little read and regarded part of his work that contains his philosophy of nature, Hegel rejected biological evolution. 'It has been an inept conception of earlier and later "*Naturphilosophie*" ', he wrote (*Encyclopedia*, sec. 249), 'to regard the progression and transition of one natural form and sphere into a higher as an outwardly actual production ... Thinking consideration must deny itself such nebulous, at bottom, sensuous, conceptions as ... the origin of the more highly developed animal organisations from the lower.' Nevertheless, the dialectical process is a matter of the emergence of higher entities out of a conflict between their less-developed anticipations. If Hegel denies its application in a temporal sense to non-human nature as much as to the pure concepts of logic, he does take it to be temporal in its application to the individual mind, in its ascent from sense-certainty to absolute knowledge, and again to human society, in its passage from the primitive tribal family to the fully rational state. It would be no great modification of Hegel's system to regard the dialectic as temporal in nature as well as in mind and society.

The absolute idealists themselves testify to the serviceability of their doctrines for the purposes of religious apologetic and reveal the attractions that this fact held for them. As Muirhead says, 'British idealism has been from the first a philosophy of religion' (*The Platonic Tradition*, p.197). Stirling, the first in the field, is disarmingly explicit about it. Hegel, he wrote, 'is the greatest abstract thinker of Christianity', and again, 'the Hegelian system supports and gives effect to every claim of this religion'; Hegel's views 'conciliate themselves admirably with the revelation of the New Testament'. T.H. Green was a seriously religious man in his plain, earnest, non-sacerdotal way, an evangelical who sought rational foundations for his faith and laboriously worked them out in his conception of the 'eternal consciousness', the 'spiritual principle in man and nature' expounded in the first part of his *Prolegomena to Ethics*. In a Kantian fashion he argues that nature, as we know it, is a related and orderly system, which presupposes the ordering work of the knower's mind in its construction. But for this knowledge to be more than subjective improvisation, unintelligibly set off by a Kantian thing-in-itself, for it to be genuinely objective knowledge, an all-inclusive mind must be presupposed of which our finite minds are in some sense parts. Green affirms that 'there is one spiritual and self-conscious being of which all that is real is the activity and expression; that we are all related to this spiritual being, not merely as parts of the world which is its expression, but as partakers in some inchoate measure of the self-consciousness through which it at once constitutes itself and distinguishes itself from the world ... and that this participation is the source of morality and religion' (*Works*, vol. iii, p.145). If this seems pantheistic, on a natural interpretation, so does Hegel. What is unquestionable is its positively religious intention.

The religious interest is even more prominent in the other, and more unreservedly Hegelian, initiator of British idealism: Edward Caird. His main constructive work, as distinct from the elaborate interpretations of the philosophy of Kant which make up the bulk of his output, are his Gifford lectures of 1893: *The Evolution of Religion*. In them God is defined as the infinite, but not Kantianly transcendent, being that is the unity that includes and fulfils all things. In his little book on Hegel Caird describes him as, and praises him for, securing 'the moral and religious basis of human existence'.

The two great later idealists, Bradley and McTaggart, were not defenders of religion in any ordinary sense and were far from being Christians. Bradley's Absolute is not a mind but a harmonious tissue of experience and in his system metaphysics transcends and surpasses religion much more radically and dismissively than it does in his more Hegelian predecessors. McTaggart, defining religion as 'an emotion resting on a conviction of a harmony between ourselves and the universe at large' (*Some Dogmas of Religion*, p.3), accepts this conviction in a form which excludes God altogether, in however dilute a conception. For McTaggart the Absolute is a community of immortal and disembodied finite souls who are related by love. But the lesser lights of idealism, in particular Caird's pupils Jones, Muirhead, and Mackenzie, followed him in treating metaphysics as a rational fulfilment of the religious impulse.

II

The second large intellectual need that absolute idealism catered for was that for a political theory which, by taking a more exalted conception of the state than that traditional in Britain since Locke and the establishment of a parliamentary monarchy, could provide a more rational solution to the social problems of the age than unhindered economic competition was able to offer. By the mid-nineteenth century the transfer of ultimate political power from the landowning class to the proprietors of industry, symbolised by the repeal of the Corn Laws, was well under way, even if it was not to be finally completed until the time of Bonar Law and Baldwin. Liberalism, at this time, was the party of the manufacturing interest. The freedom from state interference required by industrialists for their economic activities allied with them the parallel interest of dissenters in removing the disabilities imposed for the protection of the established church, an interest whose chief political effect in the later part of the century was to obstruct, complicate, and enfeeble the national system of education. The traditional instruments of government had failed to respond adequately to the major social changes of the period: the great increase in population, the rapid growth of large industrial cities, and the special problems of destitution to which the new forms of social living gave rise.

The progressive, reforming impulse has expressed itself in a fitful and irregular way in the history of British political thought. In the civil war there was an outburst of democratic radicalism of varying degrees of extremity. It seems to have gone underground, even to have disappeared altogether or to have emigrated to the American colonies, until well on towards the end of the eighteenth century. But, since it was at least latently active in the developing social attitudes of the American colonists, when it came to the surface in the American Revolution it evoked a response in Britain from Paine, Priestley, and Price. This type of radicalism, sympathetic to both the American and French Revolutions, achieved its extreme theoretical expression in Godwin's *Political Justice*, but its doubly scandalous character, as unpatriotic in its fondness for the allied national enemies, France and the United States, and as destructive in its attitude to religion, ensured that its influence would be marginal. (Price and Priestley were both devout ministers of religion, but Paine was at best a deist while Godwin, for all his Sandemanian beginnings, was an atheist.)

Thus in the early nineteenth century the only effective reforming tendency in British political thought was the philosophical, rather than democratic, radicalism of Bentham and his followers. In its early phases the utilitarian movement was concerned with the mainly negative task of legal and political reform. That task was negative because seen as one of clearing away the complex and irrational encumbrance of ancient laws and institutions behind which 'sinister interests' lurked and profited. Freed from these obstructions, men, it was expected, would improve themselves and their conditions of life by their own initiative and efforts. The aim of the utilitarians was to clear the path for individual self-realisation. Paine's idea that the community should take positive responsibility for the welfare of its citizens in the largest sense, for their bodily needs by social services, for their spiritual needs by an effective educational system, was altogether opposite in tendency to utilitarian optimism about the self-redemptive potentialities of the free individual.

By the middle of the century much of the work of the movement had been done. The reform of parliament, accepted more in principle than in practice by the Reform Bill of 1832, was more substantially realised in 1867. The chief representatives of secular individualism were Mill and Spencer. In the end Mill came to acknowledge that his paramount aim, the greatest possible liberation of the human individual, needed to be qualified because of the more or less accidental differences of strength between individuals, as is shown by his mildly socialistic revisions in the later editions of his *Principles of Political Economy*. Spencer affirmed individualism with uncompromising ferocity. Where Bentham had, broadly speaking, ignored problems of education and social welfare, Spencer explicitly asserted, on the basis of the evolutionary account of the progress of mankind, that any state interference with the natural elimination of weak and uncompetitive individuals would disastrously impede, if not reverse, the ascent of man up the evolutionary scale. 'The survival of the fittest' is, after all, Spencer's phrase. 'The ultimate result of shielding men from folly', he wrote in his *Autobiography*, 'is to fill the world with fools.' The only proper tasks of the state are the repression of violence and the enforcement of contracts. Spencer expressed these views as early as 1843 in his essay on *The Proper Sphere of Government* and held firmly to them until his best-known exposition of them in *Man versus the State* in 1884. With him individualism (and the celebration of industrial society) reaches its greatest intensity. His dissenting origins disposed him against authority; his unimaginative rationalism was enchanted by the brute productiveness of industrial capitalism, while obscuring from him its destructive side-effects; his evolutionary interests enabled him to see unrestricted competitiveness in, human society as an application of the law of all progress.

One of Green's most quoted observations is his injunction to his juniors to close up their Mill and Spencer and to turn to Kant and Hegel. In saying this he must have had in mind not merely the empiricism of the British philosophers but also the political individualism of which Hegel's *Philosophy of Right* is a sustained criticism. For Hegel Britain was the paradigm *bürgerliche Gesellschaft* and Mill and Spencer were its prophets at the height of its career. Green exemplified in his own life the ideal of socially responsible politics he propounded in theory. He was a town councillor, the founder of a free secondary school, and an active temperance reformer. When he died he was buried in a municipal cemetery. Collingwood, in his *Autobiography*, says that the Greats school in Oxford under Green's influence, 'was not meant as a training for professional scholars and philosophers; it was meant as a training for public life', that it sent out 'a stream of ex-pupils who carried with them the conviction that philosophy, and in particular the philosophy they had learnt at Oxford, was an important thing and that their vocation was to put it into practice. This conviction was common to politicians so diverse in their creeds as Asquith and Milner, churchmen like Gore and Scott Holland, social reformers like Arnold Toynbee' (p.17). It was under Asquith's government that the foundations of the modern welfare state were laid. Gore and Scott Holland were leaders of the Christian socialist movement in the Church of England which sought to detach the church from its association with the propertied classes and those bound to them by habitual deference and to involve it constructively in the life of the neglected urban masses.

Green's theoretical and practical commitment to a new view of the state's responsibilities was also to be found in Bosanquet, who was both author of *The Philosophical Theory of the State* (1899) and secretary of the Charity Organisation Society. Many followed them in both aspects of this concern for an actively benevolent state. Among lesser idealists Henry Jones wrote *The Working Faith of a Social Reformer* (1916) and *The Principles of Citizenship* (1919), J.H. Muirhead *The Service of the State* (1909), works whose titles clearly declare the social and political attitude expressed in them. Here again, as in the matter of religion, Bradley and McTaggart are exceptions. Bradley's chapter on 'My Station and its Duties' in *Ethical Studies* gives a conservative, hierarchical interpretation to the main themes of the Hegelian theory of politics. McTaggart's chapter on 'the conception of society as an organism' in his *Studies in Hegelian Cosmology* understands that conception in a purely ideal sense: the organic society is realised in the ultimate community of mutually loving immortal souls, not in any historically actual state.

Green's responsible collectivism still exhibited some of the native distrust of state power (see R. Metz, *A Hundred Years of British Philosophy*, p.283). The state cannot make men good, it can only create conditions favourable to their moral perfection of themselves. Yet despite this, and despite his insistence that rights are created not by the politically sovereign power but by the indwelling moral consensus of society, his underlying commitment to the Hegelian idea that the state is an essentially moral institution, absorbing and even superseding the individual morality of its members, comes out in his surprising contention that Czarist Russia is not a state. His famous lecture of 1880, 'Liberal Legislation and Freedom of Contract', opposed the defence of privilege and unequal strength by appeals to liberty. He thought little of the liberty that would be infringed by forbidding tenants to contract away their game-rights to landlords, by limiting the sale of alcoholic drinks, and by compelling employers to assume liability for injuries sustained by their employees. Green argued for these infringements, perhaps questionably, as contributing to a larger general freedom. That way of presenting his ideas made them more acceptable to progressive theorists of liberalism like L.T. Hobhouse, despite his hostility to the Hegelian foundations of Green's concrete political doctrines. It is not fanciful of A.B. Ulam (*Philosophical Foundations of English Socialism*) to see in Green an ancestor of the modern Labour Party.

III

A question is raised by the rapidity with which idealism became the dominant philosophical school in British universities. For its success was undoubtedly rapid. In 1865 Stirling communicated his turgid version of the Hegelian message in *The Secret of Hegel*, the first work in English on Hegel that was both detailed and enthusiastic, even if, as I shall show later, Stirling was not by any means the first to bring news of Hegel to Britain. In less than ten years a series of works came out, bearing a strong Hegelian imprint, from those who were to be the leaders and inspirers of a whole generation of British philosophers. For the next thirty years absolute idealism maintained an unchallenged primacy, both in volume of publications and in its hold over the loyalties of university students.

The reasons for this swift conquest are two: first, the debility of the native philosophical tradition, both in the predominant form in which it was radically opposed to idealism and in the form in which it had some broad affinity with it, and secondly the revival of the universities from the torpor of the preceding age. In the 1860s, on the eve of the emergence of idealism, the party-lines in philosophy were much the same as they had been more than twenty years earlier, as described by Mill in his essays on Bentham and Coleridge. The school of experience, of which Mill himself was now the senior luminary, confronted the school of intuition. In the early part of the century the empiricist tradition deriving from Locke and Hume had been most alive in the ethics and psychology of Bentham and James Mill. Although the latter had applied Hume's associationism with mechanical thoroughness to the whole range of mental phenomena, no member of the utilitarian school had addressed himself seriously to epistemological issues before John Stuart Mill and none introduced significant modifications, as Mill did, into the body of inherited empiricist assumptions in this area.

On the other side, the school of intuition to which Mill referred was the Scottish philosophy of common sense. It had been initiated by Thomas Reid in the late eighteenth century as the most respectable of the numerous 'answers to Hume' put out by his contemporaries. It had been laboriously, if elegantly, expounded in the writings of Dugald Stewart between 1792 and his death in 1828. The leadership of the school had then passed from him to Sir William Hamilton, who replaced Stewart's polite facility with a vast accumulation of insecure and heavily-borne learning. Hamilton's ideas were presented in a series of *Edinburgh Review* articles between 1829 and 1833. The first was a metaphysical agnosticism that rested on the thesis that all our knowledge is inescapably relative and conditioned. Secondly, Hamilton upheld a 'natural realism' about perception, which he took to be an immediate awareness of external reality, at least through the sense of touch. Finally, Hamilton added some fairly footling amendments and complications to the syllogistic logic traditionally taught in universities.

Hamilton died in 1856 and from then on the chief exponent of intuitionism was, until his death in 1871, H.L. Mansel of Oxford (in his last few years Dean of St. Paul's), the first leading figure of his school to come from outside its country of origin. He seems to have left no immediate disciples. Spencer and G.H. Lewes drew on his conception of the Unknowable to round out their eclectic and encyclopedic systems. But they did not use it, as he had, to impose a Kantian limit on the possible scope of human knowledge so as to leave room for faith. For them it was at most a respectful gesture towards the idea that natural science, for all its splendid gifts of enlightenment, cannot answer all the questions that men feel impelled to raise about the ultimate nature of things. It could also be seen as an emblem of the open-ended and incompletable nature of scientific inquiry.

After Mansel's death the Scottish philosophy remained alive only in the United States, through the influence of James McCosh, president of Princeton. Calderwood and Veitch were unable to stem the tide of idealism in Scotland and from Oxford it appears to have disappeared without trace. Such resistance as there was in late Victorian Oxford to the school of Green came from the physical realism of the Aristotelian scholar Thomas Case and, later, from the pragmatism of F.C.S. Schiller and his quaint group of associates and from the sporadic critical activity of Cook Wilson, which was

only to take the form of an articulate philosophical standpoint after the turn
of the century in the work of his pupil Prichard.

By the 1860s, then, the established version of rationalism was, in effect,
sustained by one man, Mansel, and after his death soon petered out
altogether. Reid had praised Hume for supplying empiricism with a *reductio
ad absurdum* by the thoroughness and penetration with which he developed
the implications of its assumptions that only ideas, and not real things, are
perceived and that the organising principles of thought are of empirical
origin. Against the second assumption he held that the principles of
substance, cause, and the like are self-evident *a priori* truths. This theory of
first principles resembled Kant's in its results, but it achieved them, not by
the honest if exhausting toil of Kantian deduction, but by postulation
combined with an appeal to candour. A naïve and diluted Kantianism of this
kind could offer no serious resistance to a philosophy such as Hegel's, which
started from a reasoned rejection of Kant's findings, in particular of the
doctrine of unknowable things-in-themselves, and developed by way of a
thorough criticism of the detailed reasoning that Kant had provided for
them.

As a general current of thought empiricism, or perhaps one should say
naturalism, the philosophy which takes the natural sciences to be the
paradigm of human knowledge, received a marked, but somewhat too
intoxicating, stimulus from Darwinism. Huxley embraced the doctrines of
Hume as a philosophical foundation for his general beliefs; G.H. Lewes those
of Auguste Comte. But the richness and variety of the fields which presented
themselves as fit for the application of the evolutionary principle (not just
organic life but inanimate nature, on the one hand, the mind, morality, and
social institutions on the other) caused attention to be drawn away from the
more strictly philosophical bases of triumphant naturalism to the more
congenial business of finding ever-new confirmations in the world of natural
fact for the explanatory power of the new master-principle. The only
significant exception to this tendency away from the central and towards the
peripheral among naturalistic philosophers of the period is to be found in the
work of W.K. Clifford who died in 1879 at the age of thirty-four. Clifford left
behind the raw materials for a British equivalent of the philosophy of Mach.
In the end this was to be set out systematically by the statistician Karl
Pearson in *The Grammar of Science* in 1892.

Now just at the time when the naturalistic philosophy dominant outside
the universities was becoming increasingly unphilosophical under the
influence of Darwinism and when its rationalistic opponent within the
universities was dwindling away, as much, one might feel, from lack of
intrinsic intellectual vigour as from a shortage of gifted exponents, the
universities themselves were beginning to respond to the effects of reform.
The disquiet of the educated public about their ossified condition, in which
intellectual weakness and social exclusiveness reinforced each other, had
been expressed through the reforming commissions. Against dogged
obstruction by the universities themselves the commissions had sought to
create an effective professoriate for the sake of improved scholarly standards

and to remove barriers to admission, both of teachers and undergraduates, so as to ensure an academic population fitted to sustain and profit by them. Those like Mark Pattison who were most concerned about the low scholarly level of the ancient British universities looked to Germany for their models. It is not surprising that the new philosophical movement should be inspired by the last German philosopher about whose classical status there was broad agreement in his own country. There is a certain irony in the fact that Hamilton, whose philosophy was completely swept away from the intellectual scene of Oxford after reform, had been the most vehement propagandist for change. The effective chairs for which he had called so stridently were to be occupied by Hegelians who had no use for him.

In a cursory survey like this it is easy to exaggerate the changes brought about by a reforming movement. Oxford in the early nineteenth century had not been the Oxford of Gibbon's and Bentham's scornful recollections, even less, no doubt, than eighteenth-century Oxford had been. The general level of academic work had been raised by the introduction of competitive, or, at any rate, classified, examinations and the stimulation of serious effort among the taught had not gone without a response from their teachers. The circle of Noëtics at Oriel in the 1830s, led by Whately, had been an indication of intellectual vitality among the younger fellows of colleges. But Whately, although a clever and intellectually vigorous man, had no substantial new doctrine to teach. His logic, somewhat like that of Ramus, had been more a removal of petrified complications than a really new forward movement. Furthermore Whately's initiative had had an altogether too disturbing outcome. The one really major intelligence among his pupils had been that of Newman. The result of the Oxford movement was that its adherents either joined the Roman church and left the university altogether or retreated into a frightened or taciturn conformity about fundamental questions. But twenty years after, in the 1860s, the distrust in the free play of mind engendered by that episode was beginning to dissipate.

IV

British idealism is commonly assumed to be largely Hegelian in inspiration. Although this assumption has been questioned, it is, as I shall argue later, substantially correct. The unsurprising facts that the British idealists were by no means unselective in their attitude to their German master and that they had ideas of their own to develop within the framework with which he provided them do not undermine it. It is, at any rate, clear that they owed more to Hegel than to anyone else.

I have argued that Hegelianism was appropriate to religious and political needs present in the 1860s and 1870s, and that its success here was accelerated by a lack of competition from a moribund intuitionism which had no political implications and underwrote a bleakly authoritarian and fideistic attitude to religion and from a naturalism that, intoxicated with Darwin, was ignoring fundamental issues about scientific knowledge for the more agreeable task of systematising and extrapolating from the findings of science.

These considerations do not wholly answer the question of why it was not until more than thirty years after his death that Hegel should receive serious study and endorsement in Britain. In Germany by the 1840s the Hegelian school had disintegrated. By the mid 1860s it was alive only as a style in the history of philosophy, as practised by Erdmann, Zeller, and Kuno Fischer. In 1865, the year of Stirling's excited welcome to Hegel, Liebmann was issuing the call of 'back to Kant' which was to be the slogan of most academic philosophising in Germany until well after the end of the century.

The explanation needed is, however, implicit in what has been said about the state of British philosophy in the early part of the nineteenth century. Poor communications with the philosophy of the outside world were the result of the parochialism, inertia, and markedly practical bias of the British philosophy of the age. There is a striking contrast between the speed with which knowledge of Kant became available in this country as compared with that of Hegel. Introductory expositions of and selections from Kant's writings were published in Britain in the 1790s, a decade after the first edition of the *Critique of Pure Reason* and a decade before Kant's death in 1804. The only reference in British philosophical writing to Hegel before his death in 1831 is to be found in Hamilton's essay on 'The Philosophy of the Unconditioned' in 1829 and there he is mentioned only in passing, along with Oken, as one of the distinguished followers of Schelling (*Discussions*, p.21).

Eight years earlier, in a supplementary dissertation to the *Encyclopaedia Britannica*, recounting the history of philosophy in Europe since the revival of letters, Dugald Stewart makes no mention of Hegel, although, after some vapid remarks about Kant, he stigmatises the doctrines of Fichte and Schelling as 'sad aberrations of human reason', despite admitting that he cannot make anything of Fichte and cannot read German anyway. The translation in 1832 of the abridgement of Tennemann's history of philosophy gave some account of Hegel's views. But it was not until 1846 that a fairly reasonable account of the main outlines of Hegel's system came from a British writer, in J.D. Morell's book on recent European philosophy. Morell is lumped together with his quite hopeless near-contemporary Robert Blakey (who made some vague remarks about Hegel in the fourth volume of his *History of the Philosophy of Mind* in 1850) by Muirhead as exemplifying the theological prejudice which blinded the eyes of British readers to the illumination available to them in the works of the German idealists. The entirely reasonable comments on Hegel by Morell which provoke this condemnation are that in his system 'theism ... is compromised ... the hope of immortality likewise perishes ... religion, if not destroyed by the Hegelian philosophy, is absorbed in it'. The objection that Hegel is altogether too costly a defender of religion in divesting man of immortality and God of both personality and real transcendence is precisely that voiced by Pringle-Pattison and a host of other personal idealists after him against both Hegel and Bradley.

Morell, who had studied philosophy at Bonn in the early 1840s and whose subsequent career as an inspector of schools is approximately contemporary with that of Matthew Arnold, gives a reasonably detailed, accurate, and intelligible account of the main ingredients of Hegel's system and of the dialectic which is its generating principle. Anyone interested by what he had to say about Hegel must have been led to share his theological disquiet by another publication in the same year which was of ultimately Hegelian ancestry: Strauss's *Leben Jesu*, translated into English by George Eliot.

In 1844, two years before Morell's book, Jowett had made a visit to Germany with A.P. Stanley, largely for purposes of philosophical study. By 1845 he was writing about the study of Hegel, 'one must go on or perish in the attempt, that is to say, give up Metaphysics altogether. It is impossible to be satisfied with any other system after you have begun with this.' Jowett's biographers, Abott and Campbell, report that he and Temple began a translation of Hegel's 'logic' (they do not say whether it was the greater or the smaller one) but that in 1849 it was 'broken off by Temple's being summoned away to public life' (Abbott and Campbell, vol. i, p.129). 'Hegel is a great book', they report Jowett as saying, 'if you can only get it out of its dialectical form.' He had a high regard for Hegel as a critic of Greek philosophy and said 'the study of Hegel has given me a method'. Metz and Faber are surely right in ascribing to Jowett a large part of the responsibility for the effective introduction of Hegel's thought into this country. Even if he did it through teaching and conversation rather than writing books, the people he taught, above all Green and Caird, were those who were to establish the school of absolute idealism.

Jowett's attitude to Hegel itself underwent a dialectical change. By the 1870s, suspicious of the effect of Green's earnest obscurities on the undergraduates of Balliol, he was complaining that 'metaphysics exercise a fatal influence over the mind'. But by 1884, accepting the gift of a bust of Hegel for the Balliol library from Lord Arthur Russell, he adopted a more favourable posture. 'Though not a Hegelian,' he wrote, 'I think I have gained more from Hegel than from any other philosopher.' Of the bust itself he added, 'Hegel looks quite a gentleman.' We may perhaps see this as a symbol of the satisfactory absorption of Hegelianism into British intellectual life.

Hamilton returned to Hegel in 1852, when preparing his early essays for publication as a book. In a massive footnote to his essay of 1829 he objected to the dialectic as founded 'on a mistake in logic and a violation of logic' (*Discussions*, p.24). In an appendix on 'Oxford as it might be', he says: 'I have never, in fact, met with a Hegelian (and I have known several of distinguished talents, both German and British) who could answer three questions, without being driven to the confession that he did not, as yet, fully *comprehend* the doctrine of his master, though *believing* it to be all true.' It would be interesting to know who the distinguished British Hegelians of the early 1850s were, but Hamilton was never much obsessed with mere fact. Like his further remark, 'I am told that Hegelianism is making way at Oxford', it may be an echo of Jowett's teaching.

At this time two independent British philosophers of an idealist tendency, critical both of Mill's empiricism and the Hamiltonian philosophy which opposed it, were active: J.F. Ferrier in Scotland, whose main work *The Institutes of Metaphysic* came out in 1854, and John Grote of Cambridge, whose scattered and somewhat desultory writings on the theory of knowledge appeared in the two volumes of *Exploratio Philosophica*, the first in 1865 a year before his death, the second not until 1900.

Ferrier, according to G.E. Davie's well-documented account in *The Democratic Intellect*, was a dissident Hamiltonian, provoked into speculative extravagance more by his hostility to evangelical pressures against freedom than by any positive affinity to German idealism (he described his own, rather Berkeleyan, philosophy as 'Scottish to the core') or, for that matter, by much knowledge of it. He wrote a short note about Hegel for a biographical dictionary in the late 1850s. Perhaps his relation to Hegel is best brought out by a story of Stirling's who 'found him diligently engaged on a work of Hegel which turned out to be upside down. Ferrier's explanation was that being utterly baffled in the attempt to understand his author the right side up, he tried the other way in desperation' (Davie, op.cit., p.335). There is only a single reference to Hegel in Grote, in which he is mentioned, along with Schelling, as an object of such distaste to Mill as to bring him into agreement with Hamilton on a certain point.

Before Stirling's book, then, although it was possible to find a short but not too cursory account of Hegel's philosophy in Morell, and from 1855 a translation of the *Subjective Logic*, brought into English by way of a French version of the original, the only really effective presentation of Hegel's ideas must have been in the personal teaching of Jowett. By 1860, the year Green became a fellow of Balliol, another Oxford philosopher, Hamilton's follower Mansel, gave a competent survey of Hegel's ideas in half a dozen pages of his *Metaphysics*, whose footnotes make clear his direct acquaintance with Hegel's text. It was in Oxford at any rate that the chief exponent of absolute idealism in Scotland, Edward Caird, acquired the views which, from his appointment in 1866 to the moral philosophy chair in Glasgow, he was to present to his fellow Scotsmen and which soon came to dominate the philosophy teaching of the Scottish universities. Jowett, it would seem, had prepared the ground in such a way that Stirling's book, instead of sinking into the oblivion to which its bizarre and tumultuous style might have destined it, was able to exert a serious influence.

V

The view that British idealism is a late flowering of the philosophy of Hegel is sometimes challenged in an authoritative-seeming way. The point can be made with examples involving the three chief leaders of the school. Green is quoted as saying 'I looked into Hegel the other day and found it a strange *Wirrwarr*'. Taken by itself this suggests unfamiliarity with, as well as incomprehension of, Hegel. It is pointed out that Caird wrote a massive two-volume work on Kant, and republished it in a substantially revised form twelve years later, but produced only a small, and to a considerable extent biographical, book on Hegel. As for Bradley, there is Collingwood's description of his books as 'criticisms of Mill's logic, Bain's psychology and Mansel's metaphysics by a man whose mind was the most deeply critical that European philosophy has produced since Hume, and whose intention, like that of Locke, was to make a bonfire of rubbish' (*Autobiography*, p.16).

In fact Green's remark about 'looking into Hegel' comes from some recollections of him by Henry Sidgwick (in *Mind* for 1901). In the paragraph in which it occurs Sidgwick writes, ' "Hegelian" is a term that I should never have applied to the author of the *Prolegomena to Ethics*'. He goes on, 'I think, indeed, that the term might be defended in relation to some of his earlier utterances; and that his thought during his life moved away from Hegel ... I remember writing to him after a visit to Berlin in 1870 and expressing a desire to "get away from Hegel"; he replied that it seemed to him one might as well try to "get away from thought itself".' So all that is shown is that Green came to think of himself in later years as free from his early dependence on Hegel. As for Caird's concentration on Kant, it must be made clear that he subjects Kant throughout to criticism from a Hegelian point of view and singles out for acceptance from the former just what is absorbed into the philosophy of the latter.

Collingwood's thesis about Bradley is a little more complicated. It comes as part of a general endorsement of the idealists' repudiation of the description of them as Hegelians. If 'they had some knowledge of Hegel', he says, they had 'a good deal more of Kant. The fact of their having this knowledge was used by their opponents, more through ignorance than deliberate dishonesty, to discredit them in the eyes of a public always contemptuous of foreigners.' Green, Collingwood goes on, 'had read Hegel in youth but rejected him in middle age; the philosophy he was working out when his early death interrupted him is best described, if a brief description is needed, as a reply to Herbert Spencer by a profound student of Hume'. Collingwood's reference to the national suspicion of foreigners is significant. Writing as almost the last member of the Idealistic rearguard and during the inter-war period when Hegel was widely regarded as somehow responsible for the German aggression of 1914, as in Hobhouse's indictment *The Metaphysical Theory of the State*, he was anxious to clear his predecessors of war-guilt by association. In general Collingwood's sporadically brilliant works abound with shrill assertions of false or dubious statements about matters of fact which he found annoying.

A much more sensible view is to be found in the remarks by Edward Caird on the subject in his introduction to the *Essays in Philosophical Criticism*, which Green's admirers brought out as a memorial to him in 1883, the year after his death. 'To Hegel,' Caird said of Green, 'he latterly stood in a somewhat doubtful relation; for while, in the main, he accepted Hegel's criticism of Kant, and held also that something *like* Hegel's idealism must be the result of the development of Kantian principles rightly understood, he yet regarded the actual Hegelian system with a certain suspicion as something too ambitious, or, at least, premature. "It must all be done again," he once said' (*Essays in Philosophical Criticism*, p.5).

It is undoubtedly true that no British idealist stood in the kind of discipular relation to Hegel which the more authoritative type of philosopher regards as a criterion of really understanding his message. Such subservience usually presupposes personal contact, which was chronologically ruled out in this case. Nobody, in other words, swallowed Hegel whole. But there is, after all, a great deal of Hegel to swallow. In particular the dialectic, conceived in Hegel's way, as a rigorous and systematically deductive ordering of all the categories from being and not-being, through the abstractions of logic and the increasingly concrete notions of nature and spirit, to terminate in the absolute idea, is nowhere embraced in the work of a British idealist. McTaggart took it seriously enough to devote his first book to a scrupulously rational criticism of its detailed workings. Bradley's distantly respectful attitude is more typical of the movement. In *The Principles of Logic* he writes: 'I need hardly say that it is not my intention comprehensively to dispose in a single paragraph of a system which, with all its shortcomings, has been worked over as wide an area of experience as any system offered in its place' (p.147). Again, he says: 'In this speculative movement, if we take it in the character it claims for itself, I neither myself profess belief nor ask it from the reader' (p.189). The most he will do is to 'profess that the individual is the identity of universal and particular' (ibid.). Even the devoted Stirling is assailed by doubt when he contemplates the ceremonial elaboration of the dialectic: 'the fact is, it is all maundering, but with the most audacious usurpation of authoritative speech on the mysteries that must remain mysteries' (*The Secret of Hegel*, vol. i, p.73).

The British idealists were not, then, slavish adherents of Hegel in all the detailed effrontery of his system. They were thoroughly selective in their approach to him and they had original ideas of their own as well as original applications of his principles to contribute. But it is implausible to suggest, as Collingwood comes near to doing, that their philosophy is an original native growth. In Caird's words they 'agree in believing that the line of investigation which philosophy must follow ... is that which was opened up by Kant, and for the successful prosecution of which no one has done so much as Hegel'. If Coleridge was chiefly influenced by Schelling and Carlyle by Fichte, the professional philosophers owed little or nothing to either and made negligible reference to them. The only serious alternative to Hegel as the chief influence on their thought is Kant.

Although a certain community of basic vocabulary between Kant and Hegel may at first glance suggest that it is an open question which of the two the idealists most closely adhere to, brief reflection is sufficient to show beyond doubt that they are essentially Hegelian in their views about both reality and knowledge. In Kant's view ultimate reality, the realm of noumena, is unknowable by the human mind, except, inconsistently, in the three respects that it exists, that it contains a mental as well as a non-mental aspect and, by implication, that the latter exercises some kind of determining influence on the sensory raw material which it is the business of the understanding to articulate into knowledge. For all his condemnation of transcendent metaphysics, Kant is himself, marginally but essentially, a practitioner of the forbidden art. Hegel, on the other hand, recognises Kant's inconsistency about the transcendent nature of reality and overcomes the difficulty by taking reality, in the form of his Absolute, to be, not something altogether beyond experience and of a wholly different nature from it, but as a logically ideal completion or totality of experience. In this respect the British idealists follow Hegel exactly.

The point is clearly made in a remark of Green's I have quoted before: 'there is one spiritual self-conscious being of which all that is real is the activity and expression ... we are related to this spiritual being, not merely as parts of the world which is its expression, but as partakers in some inchoate measure of the self-consciousness through which it at once constitutes itself and distinguishes itself from the world' (*Works*, vol. iii, p.143). In less ethereal terms, our minds and their experiences are not cut off from reality itself, but are, somehow, parts of it. Bradley, again, does not take reality, the harmonious absolute experience that lies above the level of relations, to be something quite distinct from the appearances which are the objects of discursive thought. For him appearances are all constitutive parts of reality; indeed he suggests that reality is nothing more than the totality of appearances, harmonised into a fully rational system. For the British idealists, as for Hegel, there is only one world, which we apprehend with varying degrees of adequacy, from the crude intimations of sense at one extreme to the absolute knowledge of philosophy at the other. For Kant, on the other hand, there are two worlds, quite distinct from each other; the unknowable or barely knowable order of noumena and the order of phenomena, jointly produced by sensation and the understanding.

The epistemological affinities of British idealism are equally Hegelian rather than Kantian. For Kant there are three distinct faculties involved in our acquisition of knowledge, or our claims to it, at any rate: sense, understanding, and reason. Sense is a passive receptivity and, by itself, is disorderly and inarticulate. Only if its deliverances are synthesised by the understanding can we achieve objective knowledge of phenomena, material or mental. In reason the intellect is exercised independently of the sensations which are the indispensable content for its formative activity. The result is transcendent metaphysics, not knowledge at all, but only a delusive chimera, a 'natural and unavoidable illusion' (*Critique of Pure Reason*, A 298, B 354). Reason is dialectical, then, where this means that 'we conclude from something which we know to something else of which have no concept, and to which, owing to an inevitable illusion, we yet ascribe objective reality' (ibid., A 339, B 397). Its arguments are 'sophisms, not of men, but of pure reason itself'.

Hegel, of course, reverses Kant's comparative estimate of understanding and reason. Understanding, operating in accordance with the fixed principles of formal logic, yields us knowledge of an inferior sort in common life and the sciences, knowledge that is abstract, partial, and deficient. True knowledge is only to be obtained by the employment of philosophic reason, in accordance with the principles of the dialectic. Reason is not the source of errors which, just because so natural and interesting to us, have to be rooted out; it is the only discoverer of ultimate truth. If ultimate reality were, as Kant supposes, noumenal, then reason, with its dialectical procedure, would be delusive. But, in Hegel's view reality is not noumenal; it is, rather, total, infinite, and all-inclusive, and only the dialectical reason of philosophy, apprehending it as a harmonious and unitary system, can give us genuine knowledge of it as it really is and that surpasses the abstraction and limitedness of the understanding.

In this conception of the nature, object, and cognitive potentialities of reason as compared with understanding the British idealists are at one with Hegel. They agree that since reality is not noumenal, not transcendent of experience, reason can give knowledge of it. Where they differ from Hegel is in regard to the supposition that the philosopher, armed with all the powers of reason, can apply it to provide a detailed, systematic, and demonstratively rigorous account of reality as a whole in which are finally ordered all the partial apprehensions of reality through which we progressively approximate to a true and absolute knowledge of it. That is what is meant by Green's remark that it must all be done again. It is the point of Bradley's repeated insistence that we can be sure that all the disharmonies of appearance are *somehow* reconciled in the absolute. The British idealists suspect the presumption with which Hegel applies his leading principles to the detail of the world and thought. But they unreservedly endorse the principles themselves.

VI

There is a comical immodesty about the titles G.E. Moore gave to the two influential works he published in 1903. It is more obvious in the case of *Principia Ethica* with its implied comparison with Newton's masterpiece. But there is a measure of presumption also in the title of his essay of that year: *The Refutation of Idealism*. It lies not so much in the claim, which Moore himself soon abandoned, to have succeeded in the work of refutation but rather in the supposition that the doctrine to which he was objecting, Berkeley's principle that to be is to be perceived, is the essence of idealism. For it was Hegel's, not Berkeley's, idealism that was a live issue at the time he was writing. If the Hegelian philosophy had a slogan it was rather that all reality is spiritual in nature or, even more fundamentally, that there is no truth or being short of truth and reality as a whole.

Russell's essay on *The Nature of Truth* which came out three years later supplies a more perceptive account of the main theme of idealism. He begins by objecting to the coherence theory of truth, in Joachim's version, that it is self-refuting. The thesis that nothing short of the whole truth is more than partially true is itself less than the whole truth. But he does not confine himself to this kind of direct criticism of the coherence theory. He goes on to say: 'the doctrines we have been considering may all be deduced from one central logical doctrine, which may be expressed thus: "every relation is grounded in the natures of the related terms". Let us call this the *axiom of internal relations*' (*Philosophical Essays*, rev. edn. p.139).

One way of showing that Russell's account of the theoretical core of absolute idealism is preferable to Moore's is by considering the main issues with which the idealists actually concerned themselves. Green's lengthy critique of Hume is preoccupied with Hume's atomism, with his conception of reality as an aggregate of items of feeling or sensation, externally related to one another. The same theme is pursued positively in the early, metaphysical, part of his *Prolegomena to Ethics*. Bradley's main object in the first, critical, part of *Appearance and Reality* is to show the incoherent, contradictory character of the categories of the understanding, of discursive or relational thought. The central argument here is that the understanding falls into contradiction by seeking to conceive reality as a complex of things that are at once distinct from each other and from the relations between them.

Another consideration that supports the view that the principle of internal relations is fundamental to idealism is that all the more specific doctrines of the school can be seen as applications of it to comparatively specific problems. Five of these applications are fairly comprehensive.

(1) The first is monism, in Spinoza's sense, the theory that there is only one true substance, the absolute or reality as a whole. It follows from the basic principle, together with the reasonable assumption that everything is related, directly or indirectly, to everything else. It is perhaps most plausible in the causal form given to it by Blanshard (*Nature of Thought*, chaps. 31 and 32). If causality is more than regular succession, it seems it can only be some kind of logical relation of entailment. So, if all events are causally related, they are also all internally related.

(2) The second is the coherence theory of truth. A proposition cannot be considered as true on its own, abstracted from its involvement with other propositions. Furthermore, a proposition cannot be conceived as externally related to the equally abstract fact that the correspondence theory supposes to verify it. The terms of the truth-relation must be systematic and possess a community of character. Proposition and fact are both abstractions from the judgement, understood as a kind of assertive experience, and the ultimate bearer of truth is the total system of coherent judgements which is also the system of experiences that constitutes the world.

(3) The third is the theory of the concrete universal which is put forward to replace the Aristotelian conception of an object as the instantiation by a bare particular of a cluster of abstract universals.

(4) The fourth is the thesis that reality is essentially mental or spiritual in nature. There are two ways in which the doctrine of internal relations supports this conclusion. On the one hand minds are more real, and so more adequate paradigms of reality itself, than material things, because they are more rational and unitary systems. On the other, there is the consideration that thought and being are not distinct and externally related, an idea intimated by the coherence theory of truth.

(5) The fifth application of the doctrine of internal relations is the theory that mind and its objects are internally and thus necessarily related, a particular version of which is the object of Moore's polemic.

There are further, more particular applications of the principle in the fields of art, politics, and religion. In each case the understanding is seen as operating with incoherent abstractions which it is the task of reason to supersede: form and content, state and citizen, the divine and the human.

This system of ideas certainly satisfies two of its own criteria of adequacy. On the one hand it is extremely comprehensive: all sides of human experience, all objects of human interest, except, perhaps, mathematics and natural science, are catered for within it. On the other it is highly systematic and internally coherent. In each of its applications the basic principle of idealism is used to reject an opposition of diverse abstractions developed by the understanding and to establish in its place a concrete and internally related system, which, in its freedom from inner contradiction, is acceptable to reason.

The enchantment of the doctrine is plain enough. But is that a sufficient reason for accepting it? It is clearly not a correct account of the conceptions of things with which we actually think. What is necessarily true of, and thus internal to, an object is, as is often pointed out, relative to the sense of the description we choose to identify it with. As things are none of our descriptions of things involves a conception of their total nature, of everything that is true of them. Our conceptions of individual things are not Leibnizian individual concepts. Critics of the doctrine usually go on at this point to add that the choice between alternative identifying descriptions of a thing is in the end arbitrary. Things have no essences for nothing is internal to the thing itself.

Yet, on the other hand, it is easy to see the attraction of the idea that the fullest possible description of a thing, the one that implies everything that is true of it, is the best or most adequate description of it there could be. To some extent, indeed, the advance of our knowledge of the world seems to confirm this idea. The concepts of science, for example, imply more about the things they identify than the concepts of common observation, which contribute to their development. But the supposition that this process could, in principle, ever be completed is highly questionable. To know everything about anything, as the idealists themselves would admit, must be to know everything about everything. But even if this goal were in principle one that could be achieved, there can be no short cut to it as the doctrine of the cognitive superiority of the reason assumes. It is only by the patient accumulations of the understanding that our conceptions can be enriched.

19
Ethics and the Theory of Evolution

Soon after the publication of *The Origin of Species* it was seen that the theory of evolution might have an important bearing on ethics. Large-scale ethical systems were constructed on an evolutionary basis by Herbert Spencer and Leslie Stephen and interesting suggestions were put forward in essays by T.H. Huxley and W.K. Clifford. More recently, however, evolutionary ethics has fallen into something very like oblivion. The attempts of Julian Huxley and C.H. Waddington to reopen the question have evoked little attention from moral philosophers. The reason for this is the extraordinary authority and influence of G.E. Moore's refutation of ethical naturalism. First presented to the world in his *Principia Ethica* in 1903, it has dominated philosophical inquiry into morals in Great Britain ever since. Moore's way of showing that the concepts and propositions of morality are radically distinct in logical character from those of natural science has been amended and improved but the thesis itself remains an almost unquestioned point of departure for philosophical ethics. One reason why I believe that evolutionary ethics should be considered afresh is that I do not find the doctrine of anti-naturalism, in any of its forms, to be even plausible, let alone convincing. But even if it were correct the issue of the relevance of evolution to ethics would not be closed. As well as his anti-naturalism, Moore has imposed on subsequent ethical inquiry an extraordinarily contracted view of the scope of the subject. As he has practised it, it is little more than a general logical characterisation of the nature of moral discourse. He has had little to say about the internal relations of moral concepts, about the relations of moral to other forms of practical thinking, about the place of moral agency in human nature or about the character of morality as a social institution. He has encouraged in this way an abstract and profoundly unrealistic approach by philosophers to the problems of morality.

I. A PRELIMINARY OBSTACLE: ANTI-NATURALISM

There are a number of different but approximately coincident ways of formulating the anti-naturalist principle. One is to say that moral and natural properties are utterly distinct. Another is to say that there can be no valid inference from scientific or factual premises to moral conclusions. A third is to assert the radical difference of function, and so of kind of meaning, of descriptive and evaluative discourse. In any of its forms the principle regards evolutionary ethics as naturalistic, and so mistaken, since it attempts to make a scientifically establishable matter of fact, the general trend of the evolutionary process, into the rational criterion for the validity of moral propositions.

Moore's own technique for proving the anti-naturalist principle was crude and unsatisfactory. His successors have discreetly drawn a veil over it and replaced it with something much more persuasive. Moore held that the distinction of moral and natural properties could be discerned, first of all, by simple inspection. Take a moral and a natural term, 'good' and 'pleasant' let us say, attend closely to them so that their meanings, the properties they express, are present to your mind and just see if they are not quite different. The belief that any such procedure could possibly prove the point at issue rests on the exploded psychologistic view that concepts, the meanings of words, are mental entities, susceptible of direct inspection. In fact the meaning of a term is an abstract and more or less complicated social practice, the established way of using the word in question. It cannot be fully and finally articulated by any method as simple as Moore's. If it could, the making of dictionaries would be a great deal easier than it is.

A second, slightly more sophisticated, argument says that if any moral term M and any natural term N were identical in meaning the question 'Is this N thing M?' would be insignificant since it would mean no more than 'Is this N thing N?'. The relevant consideration is that if M and N were identical in meaning the statement that this N thing is M would be analytic and the statement that this N thing is not M would be self-contradictory. But this again is not a matter that can generally be decided by inspection, though it can be sometimes. It is possible and indeed common for people to understand the statements that there is not and that there is a largest prime number without knowing that either, let alone which, is analytic or contradictory.

Two further objections to both of Moore's arguments are that his general conclusion rests on an induction from particular cases and that he gives no clear account of the distinction between moral and natural terms. In philosophy inductions are out of place. At best they can suggest hypotheses which must then be proved. Furthermore it is a condition of the acceptability of an inductive conclusion that the general terms which occur in it should be clearly understood so that the relevance of the supposed particular instances on which it rests is beyond question. Without a better interpretation than Moore provides for 'moral' and 'natural' we cannot tell what ethical theories his principle rules out or even attach any definite sense to it.

All these objections are circumvented by the method of arriving at Moore's general conclusion about the logical uniqueness of moral concepts which his successors have devised. This method distinguishes two broad classes of concepts in the light of their respective functions in discourse. There are the theoretical concepts which describe and the practical concepts which prescribe or evaluate. Since the functions of the two are quite different there can be no logical connection between them. In this mode of argument particular cases are used to illustrate, not to support, the thesis. The two sorts of term are clearly distinguished from the start and in such a way that their logical distinctness necessarily follows.

The simplest version of this argument says that the propositions of science are indicative while those of morals are imperative. As Poincaré puts it: 'There can be no such thing as a scientific morality. It is for a reason, how shall I put it, of a purely grammatical kind.' Popper says: 'It is impossible to derive norms or decisions or proposals from facts.' Ayer concludes: 'Ethical statements are not really statements at all ... they are not descriptive of anything ... they cannot be either true or false.'

The first objection to this theory is that not only are moral utterances not literally imperative but that they do not even behave like imperatives. Moral judgments can be expressed in the past tense; imperatives cannot be. We can say 'you ought not to have done that' but not 'don't have done that'. Furthermore we can speak of knowledge, belief and doubt, of truth, probability and falsehood, just as properly in connection with the moral as with the merely descriptive features of actions and their agents. These objections will be resisted. It will be argued that a moral judgment in the past tense somehow embodies a general imperative in the timeless present ('you ought not to have done that' implies 'don't anyone ever do what you did') and that the epistemic terms have a different sense when they occur in moral judgments, that of signifying the nature and degree of the speaker's subjective commitment to the policy he is prescribing. The point of this resistance is the belief that judgments of value have an intimate relation to conduct which is not possessed by ordinary, straightforward descriptions of matters of fact. 'This is green', as theoretical, is used to get one's hearers to think in a certain way about the thing described: 'this is bad' is used to get them to avoid it.

There is an initial difficulty here in the indefiniteness of the distinction between the influencing of beliefs and the influencing of actions. Even if we are unwilling to define belief, with Bain, as a propensity to act in certain ways, it does seem that the connection between holding a belief and acting appropriately is more than contingent. More fundamental, perhaps, is the difficulty of stating just what the special relations to belief and to action in the two cases actually are. We cannot define an utterance as practical, with Stevenson, as one that can or does cause action since any utterance can and utterances of all possible sorts do. Nor does it help to say that utterances are practical if they are *intended* to cause action. Plain statements of fact like 'the building is on fire' can and do cause action and can be intended to do so. Moral judgments like 'Genghis Khan was a bad man' can fail to cause action and can be used without the intention of affecting it, when, for example, I do not suppose my hearer to have either the desire or the opportunity to imitate him.

A more promising account of practicality, provided by Hare, attaches it to any utterance whose sincere acceptance commits the acceptor to acting in a certain way. On this criterion both 'shut the door' and 'you ought to shut the door' are practical but 'the door is open' is not. In general it brings together as practical all those utterances which are direct responses, making no presumptions about the wishes of the inquirer, to requests for advice, to the question 'what shall I do?' But to establish this much logical affinity between judgments of value and imperatives does not establish, though it may suggest, a more comprehensive identity of logical character. Since imperatives are practical some practical utterances are not statements. But that does not prove that moral utterances, being practical, are not statements either. If there were some practical utterances which plainly were statements the suggestion that moral utterances were not statements, which already has all the grammatical and logical appearances against it, would have hardly anything left to recommend it.

But in fact there is such a class of unquestionably descriptive practical statements, namely what I shall call 'appetitive utterances' which indicate the objects or states of affairs that the person addressed will most enjoy or like or will get most satisfaction from. 'You will most like or enjoy the Red Lion' is as good, sufficient and direct an answer to the question 'which hotel shall I stay at?' as 'stay at the Red Lion' or 'the Red Lion is the best hotel'. It is like them and different from 'the Red Lion is the smartest or largest or quietest hotel' in that no contingent presumption needs to be made about the special tastes or requirements of the questioner in order to predict the action that will follow on his sincere acceptance of the advice or, at any rate, to be assured of its relevance to his inquiry. Of course he can accept the statement as correct and still not act on it. The Red Lion may be too expensive for him. But just the same situation can arise compatibly with his sincere acceptance of the judgment that the Red Lion is the best hotel. This is an important point since it distinguishes value-judgments and appetitive utterances, which are defeasible in this way, from straight imperatives, which are not. There can be no serious question that appetitive utterances are both practical, in the way that judgments of value and imperatives are, and factual, capable of being established as true or false. If a man accepts an appetitive utterance addressed to him and fails to act accordingly it must either be that his acceptance is insincere or that he is somehow prevented from following it up or that there is some stronger practical claim on him. The capacity of a thing to give satisfaction, like its excellence or its moral obligatoriness, cannot, without some kind of absurdity, be taken as a reason against choosing it, but its smartness or its largeness or its quietness perfectly well can.

The acceptable residue of anti-naturalism is the important point that there is an intimate relation between judgments of value and conduct; such judgments are logically, and not just contingently, good reasons for conduct of the recommended kind. It follows that there is a logical distinction between judgments of value and neutral, strictly theoretical, statements of fact. But there is no conflict between the practical character of an utterance and its being a statement of fact. Ironically the most persistent and familiar type of naturalist ethical theory, Moore's principal target, the type of theory which interprets moral concepts in appetitive terms, is what derives most support from a reconstructed version of his arguments, while his own brand of intuitionism, which takes judgments of value to report the incidence of non-natural properties, is clearly refuted by it.

A satisfactory ethical theory, then, must interpret judgments of value in practical terms. But to say that is not to rule out all attempts to derive judgments of value from factual premises. Provided that the premises are practical as well as factual there is no logical objection to the procedure.

II. ARE STATEMENTS ABOUT EVOLUTION PRACTICAL?

If my partial demolition of anti-naturalism is to be of any help to the project of finding in evolutionary theory the fundamental ethical criterion, we must see if the relevant assertions of evolutionary theory can be understood as practical in nature. They are not, prima facie, appetitive. To describe some state of affairs or course of conduct as adaptive or biologically efficient is not the same as to say that it will give enjoyment or satisfaction to the person addressed. But I do not pretend to have shown that appetitive statements are the only practical utterances apart from imperatives and judgments of value. To show that these three kinds of utterance are all species of the practical genus is not to show that there are not other species as well.

I believe, in fact, that there is a class of practical concepts, distinct from those of general evaluation such as 'good' and those of the appetitive domain such as 'satisfying', which constitute a further species of the genus and amongst which the relevant evolutionary concepts can be found. These concepts are those of what I shall call, in a broad sense, 'technical evaluation'. A body of scientific knowledge consists of general statements, systematically articulated into theories, which enable us to predict and explain natural occurrences. In most but not all cases a system of technological prescriptions can be derived from scientific theories which tell us what to do if we want to achieve certain results. Consider the case of medicine. Anatomy provides us with a theoretical account of the structure, and physiology of the working, of the human body. Pathology provides us with an account of the nature and causes of diseased or abnormal conditions of the body. From these departments of medical science we can derive the two great branches of medical technology, in other words, of applied medical science or clinical medicine; namely therapeutics, concerned with the cure of disease, and hygiene, concerned with its prevention. The concepts of technical evaluation in use here are, of course, the concepts of health and disease. To characterise a condition of the human organism as diseased is to make a practical statement. It is to recommend that the condition be removed or avoided. One cannot sincerely accept that a condition or course of conduct is healthier than another and fail to pursue it unless prevented from doing so or unless there is some stronger countervailing practical consideration. Furthermore it is absurd to choose a course of conduct just because it is unhealthy and for no other reason, such as a desire to avoid military service.

Health is one of the most obvious concepts of technical evaluation but there are many others. Technology, in a fairly narrow sense, employs the concept of efficiency, perhaps the most general and inclusive concept of this kind. From economics we derive the concept of the economical. Sociology, of a rough and ready descriptive kind, allows the derivation of that technology of conventional social behaviour we call etiquette, with its governing notion of the polite, that is to say the done or expected thing.

Statements in which these technical values are ascribed to objects or policies seem flatly to contravene the conventional dichotomy of the evaluative and the descriptive. On the one hand they are unquestionably practical, in that they are good, sufficient and direct reasons for action and in that there is an absurdity involved in taking them to be reasons against acting in the naturally indicated way; on the other hand they are unquestionably statements of fact, capable of being empirically established as true or false and, furthermore, in the most favoured way, namely by means of scientific investigation. It is really very peculiar that the defenders of the dichotomy should have failed to notice their existence.

In works of evolutionary biology there is a collection of terms which appear to stand for technical values of this kind. Examples are 'adaptive', 'progressive', 'genetically or biologically efficient' and 'anagenetic'. It is not clear to me that these are all different ways of saying the same thing. It would seem natural to call a particular favourable variation adaptive but to describe the present condition of a species or the structure of an organ as biologically efficient. However these biological valuations appear to be logically inter-connected – a variation is adaptive, for example, if it contributes to the biological efficiency of the organ or species involved – and the same ultimate evidence is appealed to for the ascription of any of them. Species, organs and variations are not the only things that can be intelligibly evaluated in these terms. The ends which they serve can equally be served by the modes of behaviour, policies and social institutions which are the subject-matter, in a broad sense, of ethics. Waddington's notion of 'biological wisdom' is simply their application in this field as a criterion for the adequacy of received ethical ideas and practices.

There are two general remarks to be made about this whole class of technical values. In the first place these values are plural, in the sense that they can come into competition with one another, and in consequence they are subordinate and not final. They may, when they come into conflict, require us to adjudicate between them by reference to some overriding principles of value. The most efficient cook or electric fire or garage or electoral system or raincoat is not always the most economical one. Again, the suggestions of economy may be countered by the requirements of health and efficiency; economy and health may all come into conflict with morality. But the fact that technical values of this kind are not final or absolute values does not mean that they are not values at all.

Secondly, these technical values all have some implicit appetitive element. They are ascribed to things in virtue of the contribution of those things to some end and these ends will be ones that are generally desired by men and are generally satisfying to them. Thus the healthy is that which contributes to long and painless life; the efficient is that which produces a given result with the least outlay of time, attention and scarce materials; the economical is that which produces a given result with the minimum cost. That there should be such concepts of technical evaluation requires that there should be certain things which men generally agree in wanting to achieve or avoid. This dependence of technical value on the appetitive is brought out most clearly perhaps by the utilitarian foundations of classical economics. Here certain assumptions are made about human preferences and behaviour which are sufficiently obvious to be regarded as giving a definition of economic rationality. An allocation of resources or of factors of production generally is regarded as economical to the extent that it yields more total utility than any alternative allocation.

In the evolutionary case the relevant, generally desired, end is the effective survival of the human species, its continuation despite the dangers of the physical environment, the hostility of other species and the increasingly perilous character of its internal dissensions. Now if the survival of the human species is a technical end the biological efficiency of some policy or institution is certainly a good and sufficient reason for choice *other things being equal*, just as its efficiency or economy or healthiness are, but it is not a final or overriding reason for choice in all circumstances. Furthermore that biological efficiency is a technical value at all requires that the survival of the species is something that men generally desire. No one would seriously question that in some sense they do but the notion of survival is a highly flexible one and can take many different forms which will evoke rather varying degrees of appetite.

There is a further consideration about the technical values of evolutionary biology which marks them off from some of the others though it applies to some small extent to the value of health. They have a certain ambiguity which is also shown by those puzzlingly sinuous concepts the natural and the normal. To speak of some sequence of changes as an evolution or a progress may be simply to describe it as a change. In the same way the natural or the normal may be simply that which ordinarily or on the average or on the whole does occur. But more usually an evolution or a progress is a sequence of changes in an upward direction, an improvement. Similarly to describe something as natural or normal is usually to imply that it is what ought to happen rather than that it is just what generally does. The point is that it is conceivable that the most biologically efficient condition of the human species at a certain stage of its development might be an entirely non-progressive one. This would be the case if all possible variations were unfavourable. In other words the mere fact of change is of no more value than mere averageness. If we are to derive from the general course of the evolutionary process so far a criterion for the comparison of alternative futures it can only be to the extent that we can regard its present phase as an improvement on its starting-point and not simply as different from it. Text-books of pathology are extremely cautious about definitions and prefer to start off right away with the examination in detail of particular forms of disease. When they do define disease it is often in terms of the barely statistical concept of normality. That is all right in practice since by and large people feel better and manage their lives more effectively if their kidneys are in the same condition as most other people's are for most of the time. But if I feel better, think more clearly and work more efficiently when my temperature is 100 degrees F. than when it is at any other figure it would be thoroughly odd to say that I was permanently ill, and positively undesirable to keep my temperature down to the conventional 98.4. Just as the statistical definition of disease rests on the extra-statistical reinforcement of absence of pain and discomfort and of efficient functioning, so the use of the actual evolutionary process as a criterion of progress requires reinforcement from outside.

III. THE EARLIER FORMS OF EVOLUTIONARY ETHICS

So far we have been concerned with the rather abstract question of the possibility in principle that a contribution should be made to the central problem of ethics by evolutionary biology. I have argued that since the anti-naturalist argument is invalid this possibility cannot be ruled out in advance. Secondly I have suggested that there are some valuations which evolutionary considerations can directly establish. These, however, are not final but subordinate valuations, and are themselves dependent on the appetitive value, the general satisfyingness, of the end of survival to which they relate. It is now time to turn to the positive theories of evolutionary ethics in order to see whether any stronger claim for the ethical relevance of evolution can be justified. Admittedly the survival of the human species is a generally accepted end along with health, economy and efficiency. The question remains – can it be shown to have some more fundamental significance than these other ends?

The first clearly evolutionary system of ethics was Herbert Spencer's. His final criterion of value was 'quantity of life in breadth and depth'. The qualification about breadth and depth shows that he was not taking increase in the sheer bulk of living matter as the ultimate good. But just what else he did mean is not very clear. The words 'breadth' and 'depth' in this connection have an obvious evaluative implication though what it is is not very definite. It would seem to involve multiplicity of species and complexity in the organisation of those species. In fact it is not necessary to go into the matter of his precise intentions here since Spencer clearly recognised the insufficiency of his formula however it was to be interpreted. For he reinforced it with the palpably appetitive notion of 'surplus of agreeable feeling'. He would appear to have realised that quantity of life could increase 'in breadth and depth' with undesirable results.

The most notorious consequence that Spencer drew from his rather diaphanous axiom was that society should not interfere with the workings of natural selection. In practice this involved strenuous opposition to the welfare activities of the state, to the public relief and support of the destitute, the insane, the chronically sick. Spencer even objected to public support of education. In his view society, by attempting to remedy these misfortunes, was interfering with the beneficent workings of natural selection in its weeding out of unsatisfactory human stocks. The trouble with this argument is not so much its conflict with conventional moral responses but its weakness from an evolutionary point of view. A society run on Spencer's lines, with its members pursuing their own interests in a ruthlessly competitive way, would not indeed be a very pleasant one to belong to. It would be full of aggression, cold-heartedness and anxiety. But more to the point, it would be poorly situated vis-à-vis other, less unamiable societies since it would lack internal harmony and thus be weakened in its competition with them. A further consideration, of course, is that Spencer's aim, the elimination of undesirable stocks, of the stupid, the lazy, the feckless, the diseased and so on, is one that can be much more economically attained than by the very blunt instrument of natural selection. Always supposing that broad agreement can be obtained as to which traits are both undesirable and inheritable, it would be much more efficient, as well as much more contributory to Spencer's 'surplus of agreeable feeling', to eliminate them by the methods of artificial selection proposed by the supporters of eugenics.

A social morality directly opposed to Spencer's was derived from the theory of evolution by W.K. Clifford. In his view the essential condition for the evolutionary success of a society was social harmony, a state of affairs in which the individual subjects his own interests to the demands of the 'tribal self'. Much the same point was made by T.H. Huxley when he said that 'social disorganisation follows on immorality'. Man cannot survive on his own but only as a member of a society, and the effective persistence of a society requires that its members should rate the claims of its welfare above their own advantage. Huxley went on to say that it might well be that the self-assertiveness which had been of evolutionary value in the primitive, more or less pre-social, conditions of human life had become a great danger to man as a fully social being.

In its earliest phase, then, evolutionary ethics took the form of 'the gladiatorial theory of existence', in which it was used to recommend the unwavering pursuit of individual interest, and also of the doctrine of the tribal self, in which it was brought to the aid of an, at any rate local, variety of altruism. With apparent inconsistency Huxley went on in another lecture to argue that the main task of morality was not to foster but positively to counteract the cosmic process of evolution with all its injustices. At this stage of his thought Huxley took the view that evolutionary ethics made an illicit play on the word 'fittest'. Those best equipped to survive were not necessarily those who really ought to survive. Spencer's gladiatorial theory was, then, subjected to two, apparently inconsistent lines of attack. On the one hand uncontrolled competition was held to be inefficient from an evolutionary point of view; on the other, the evolutionary process itself was morally condemned. In fact the inconsistency can be removed without difficulty. Huxley's two doctrines can be reconciled by taking him to say that the socially uncontrolled process of evolution has produced a good result by means on which we are now in a position to improve.

IV. THE CENTRAL PROBLEM: C.H. WADDINGTON AND J.S. HUXLEY

Two main points emerge from this discussion of the earlier forms of evolutionary ethics. First, an evolutionary criterion of ethical value seems insufficient by itself and must be reinforced by some further principle for selecting between different possible directions of evolution. Even the most resolute supporter of evolutionary ethics, Herbert Spencer, had to appeal to the extra-biological concept of 'surplus of agreeable feeling'. Secondly, even if the basic evolutionary principle is accepted there is considerable doubt as to just what sort of moral system it endorses. Both of these weaknesses are present in the most recent presentations of evolutionary ethics. Waddington is more resolute than Huxley in excluding extra-biological considerations from the formulation of his fundamental criterion of value but neither of them gives an at all clear or convincing account of the connection between the evolutionary principle of value and concrete moral convictions. Waddington discourses in a confident but uninformative way about 'the discoverable general trend of evolution' while Huxley, though he is copious enough in stating his pacific, liberal, internationalist ideals, does nothing very much to establish their support by the evolutionary principle.

In his book *The Ethical Animal* Waddington puts forward as the fundamental criterion of value what evolutionary biology shows to be most efficient. This is a strong theory since it makes no appeal to extra-biological considerations. He identifies the biologically efficient with what is favoured by the discoverable general trend of the evolutionary process. There is a difficulty here which he does not face. Biological efficiency is a local or relative notion, conformity with the general trend of evolution is not. Thus a particular adaptive variation may in fact contribute to the ultimate extinction of a species. For example, the more perfectly adapted a species is to its existing physical environment the more vulnerable it is to large changes in that environment. The trouble is that the general trend takes place against a background of many more variables than a particular increase in biological efficiency. So a change that increases adaptation to a certain stable context may be a reduction of efficiency when viewed in relation to changes in that environment. A commonsensical social analogue of this situation is provided by the process of industrialisation. A community of highly specialised industrial workers is, in a sense, better adapted to its environment than a community of pioneers but a major disaster of flood and earthquake is more likely to be effectively surmounted by the more primitive community. Waddington's criterion, then, although purely biological, is nevertheless somewhat ambiguous. And the ambiguity is important since the general trend provides the criterion he really wants but only the more local facts about biological efficiency are likely to be at all precisely available. However the problem of specifying the criterion can be deferred for the moment. What matters here is that Waddington's criterion is an exclusively biological one.

Huxley starts from the point that ethics, as a part of the evolutionary process, itself evolves. Evolution has a direction – towards a higher degree of organisation – and this is a movement that the deliberate control of human society should seek to foster. At first it seems that the objective standard which Huxley claims to have found is the simple imperative: keep evolution going. But this soon becomes encrusted with various extra-biological impurities. Human action, he says, should be directed towards the realisation of new *evolutionary possibilities*, it should assist individual *development*, it should further *social evolution*, it should promote *higher values*, the *welfare* and *dignity* of the individual. The italicised expressions are all intended in a non-biologically evaluative sense as becomes clear when he goes on to describe his criterion as that of the *desirable* direction of evolution. Huxley realises that there are many possible lines of future evolutionary development. Unless there were, indeed, it is hard to see how evolution could be relevant to choice. But which of these are we to select as the criterion of value? The one that will occur if we leave things to go on as they are? The one that is most directly continuous with the course of evolution hitherto? Huxley makes his selection by reference to 'higher values' of a wholly extra-biological kind. An ethical theory that requires this sort of reinforcement, however much evolutionary material it makes use of, is not really an evolutionary ethics at all. It is just another teleological system, defining the rightness of actions in terms of their contribution to ends of assumed value, which emphasises that if this contribution is to be correctly worked out attention must be paid to the facts revealed by evolutionary biology about the effects of policies and institutions.

We must return, then, to the type of strong theory, as I have called it, proposed by Waddington. This holds that the general trend of evolution is discoverable and that the ultimate justification of moral beliefs is to be found in the extent to which they further this trend. Waddington does not say what the trend of evolution is in any but the most formal way. His confidence that it can be discovered seems to be based on the general agreement amongst biologists about the ordering of the evolutionary hierarchy. He does offer three indications of biological progress which might be taken as a general account of the trend: increase in independence of the environment, in complexity of relations with environmental variables and in power to control the environment. But he makes no very serious attempt to show how these general criteria of evolutionary progress are to be applied to the actual situations of human choice. One feature of the general agreement about the ordering of the evolutionary hierarchy which might be used is the unanimous opinion that man is the most evolved species, the one that shows the highest degree of biological progress. He has certainly won the contest between animal species in that it is only on his sufferance that any other species exist at all, amongst species large enough to be seen at any rate. In the light of this fact the survival of the human species can be made into a minimal criterion.

There are two possibilities to be considered here. First, we may be confronted by alternative roads to survival, one of which is less efficient or guaranteed of success than the other. Is it really inconceivable that a higher degree of biological security or efficiency might cost more than it is rational to pay? In other words would it be reasonable always to sacrifice Huxley's 'higher values' for an increased chance for the survival of the human species? The danger of being run over can be avoided by spending the whole of one's life indoors but the consequent impoverishment of life is too high a price to pay.

The second and more poignant possibility is one of a choice between survival and elimination. It is, in fact, a somewhat implausible situation since neither outcome is anything like guaranteed for any of the actual choices with which the human species is confronted. But, ignoring this, is it self-evident that we should prefer a continued and miserable life for the species to a short and gay one? The problem of nuclear disarmament is often presented in these terms as a plain choice between the destruction of the human species and communist domination. Now, whatever communist domination might actually turn out to be like, is it not perfectly conceivable that for the human species, as for Victorian young ladies, there can be fates worse than death?

Of course the evolutionary argument is a strong one here. As long as the species keeps going, on whatever terms, there is hope of an improvement in the long run. But some of its apparent force may be derived from the same insecure foundation as Hobbes's view that the right to life was so overridingly important that all other rights should be sacrificed for its sake if necessary. Merely being alive is of no value in itself: If one's right to live is infringed, of course, one has no rights at all but this does not make it of any value by itself. Salt is essential in our diet but it cannot be a staple nourishment on its own.

The same line of argument is applicable to Waddington's criterion of 'anagenesis'. It is no doubt broadly desirable that we should increase our independence of, the complexity of our relations with and our control over our environment. But if such an increase can only be secured by means which involve a considerable deterioration in the experienced quality of life it is not irrational to do without it.

Waddington has an argument to show that an evolutionary criterion is fundamental to ethics which should be briefly considered. The function of systems of moral beliefs, he says, is the mediation of the progress of human evolution. No doubt moral convictions have been an important causal factor in the social development of mankind. But to say this is not to say that the promotion of evolution was the intended purpose of these moral beliefs, nor, more importantly, is it to say that the promotion of evolution is what morality is really and fundamentally for, in the sense that this is the purpose that it ought to serve and by reference to which it should be judged. It is not indeed even true to say that it is *the* function of morality to promote evolution, any more than it would be to say that the function of cars is to eliminate accident-prone strains in the population, of secondary modern schools to keep adolescents off the streets or of the monarchy to provide a focus of social aspiration.

I conclude that the case for the primacy of biological efficiency amongst the set of technical values has not been made out. That it is *a* good cannot seriously be questioned. What has not been shown is that it is *the* good.

V. PROBLEMS OF PREDICTION AND APPLICATION

At various points in the discussion so far the difficulty has emerged of formulating a general evolutionary principle that is sufficiently definite to be effectively applied to the task of judging between conflicting moral beliefs. First of all there are three issues to be considered about the general trend of evolution if its character is to be taken as a criterion of value. (i) Suppose that it is both discoverable and inevitable as, in the eyes of Marxists, the smaller-scale evolutionary movement towards the classless society is. It does not follow that its continuation should be accelerated or assisted. It is perfectly possible to be a Marxist theoretically but an anti-Marxist practically, to believe that the course of history is inevitably towards the formation of proletarianised mass societies and also to believe that one should struggle against this process. One can strive to delay or complicate the birth-pangs of the new order in much the same way as one might strive to resist the onset of senility with tennis, brightly coloured clothing, and vigorous participation in youthful amusements. There will naturally be a certain pathos about this but it may be preferred to gloomy resignation. (ii) Even if we allow that the general trend is good and should be fostered there is the problem of determining precisely what social policies and practices are calculated to encourage it on its way. The disagreement mentioned earlier between Spencer and Clifford shows how firm commitment to the beneficence of the general trend can issue in directly opposed views about the right course of action to adopt. We hardly need evolutionary theory to tell us that nuclear warfare should be avoided or the geometrical progression of population increase be controlled. No doubt there is a good evolutionary justification for our instinctive condemnation of incest but what has evolutionary theory to say about divorce, variations of income, urban styles of living, the allocation of decisions as between society and the individual or the desirable limits of conformity? In short, there are certain rather general ends which have the support of the general trend of evolution, but do not need it since they are broadly agreed upon already, while as far as more particular and intermediate purposes are concerned, and it is these that are the matters of serious controversy, the general trend of evolution does not come down clearly on the side of either party to the dispute. (iii) An explanation of this indeterminacy of guidance is afforded by the consideration, advanced by Professor Popper in his *Poverty of Historicism*, that trends are not extrapolable and do not provide a rationally well-founded basis for prediction. As he rightly insists there is no 'law of evolution' but only a broadly characterised trend towards greater complexity and flexibility vis-à-vis the environment. What evolutionary theory fundamentally consists of are the genetic theories of inheritable characteristics and chance variation and the theory of natural selection. This entails the important but nonetheless tautological conclusion that if adaptive variations occur within a given population these will come to characterise the whole population in a space of time inversely proportionate to the degree of the variations' adaptiveness. The trouble is that there is no sure way of telling in advance which variations are adaptive; that is a judgment we can only make *ex post facto* in order to explain the actual changes in the characteristics of a given population. Popper does not deny that a trend may suggest a *law*, namely a universal statement which, applied to the conditions of a population at any given stage of the trend, may permit the derivation of the later stages. What makes this a somewhat Utopian hope as far as the process of biological evolution is concerned is that the occurrence of variations still appears to be a matter of chance and that the set of environmental variables in their relation to which the adaptiveness of variations consists is exceedingly large, very heterogeneous and contains elements which are themselves of a very low degree of predictability, such as major climatic changes, and also beyond the competence of biology to pronounce upon.

These final considerations bear as well on the possibility of making well-founded judgments in advance about biological efficiency of a less comprehensive kind than those which define it in terms of contribution to the general trend. Even if we wish to judge some variation to be biologically efficient locally rather than comprehensively, to be efficient in relation to an environment which in its broad outlines is presumed to be stable, the outcomes of encouraging or stifling it by deliberate social action will be so complicatedly different that they will be hard to predict and, when predicted, hard to adjudicate between. And although this type of prediction of efficiency does seem possible in principle the artificial assumption of stability on which it rests makes it that much more hypothetical and so unreliable as a guide to action.

VI. FROM BIOLOGICAL TO SOCIAL EVOLUTION

A further limitation on the relevance of biology to even the broadest kind of ethical problem is imposed by the fact that the sort of evolution that is of ethical interest is social rather than biological. There are two independent ways of making this point. It is suggested by some biologists that in fact biological evolution, or, at any rate, the biological evolution of the human species, is at an end. This is a curious and, in its more general form, unplausible assertion. More to the point is the fact that the time-scale of biological change is incommensurable with that of social policy. Where biologists think in terms of millions of years the framer of social policies thinks in decades. However it might be argued that the rough and ready processes of natural selection can be very greatly speeded up by deliberate human interference. The stock-breeder's activities have none of the laborious prevarication of nature's. It remains true, all the same, that it is the socially acquired rather than the genetically inherited characteristics of men which have been responsible for the conspicuous changes in the nature of human life in the historical period, and indeed for much longer than that. Furthermore it is to these socially acquired characteristics that the moral innovator or framer of social policy must primarily address himself. He is concerned with the dispositions, habits and modes of behaviour of men which have been imposed by society in the course of the post-natal process of learning and not with those received through ante-natal genetic inheritance. These social characteristics can be altered from one generation to the next by simply varying the environment in which the learning process takes place.

It is, of course, perfectly all right to talk of the evolution and of the natural selection of these social characteristics. But the limits of their analogy with genetically inherited characteristics should not be forgotten. In the first place our social or cultural inheritance is not biparental: in this respect we are the direct heirs of all the ages. We can acquire knowledge, techniques, values and institutions from anyone, anywhere, at any time by the simple act of verbal communication. The result of an effective system of verbal communication in which it is possible to get words from one place to another and to present them in an intelligible form is an immensely rapid diffusion of social characteristics. The most striking instance of this is naturally the diffusion of industrial skill, nationalist ideology and the technique of urban living from Europe to the non-European world in this century. In the second place social characteristics can be acquired at any age but our genetic outfit is determined by the condition of our parents at the moment of our conception and we shall only pass on anything new to our offspring if the variations occur before we beget or conceive them. Social evolution, then, is certainly a field in which natural selection occurs; unfavourable variations are eliminated by a large variety of failures to communicate them, if their possessors have no offspring to teach them to or no desire to teach them or no success in getting them accepted. But the social law of inheritance is a very much more complicated and amorphous affair than its biological counterpart.

There remains, nevertheless, one sphere in which our genetic inheritance is strictly relevant to ethics and social policy, that of eugenics. There is a number of generally desired or favoured characteristics – intelligence, immunity to some forms of disease, sanity – which there is reason to believe are to a preponderant extent matters of genetic inheritance and whose diffusion through the human population is therefore capable of being brought about by the control of reproduction. T.H. Huxley argued against eugenics that we do not really know what characteristics we ought to breed for. Even if this were true it would not undermine the eugenist's programme. Though we may not be very clear about the properties of the superman we can at least identify various types of subman without much difficulty or dispute. The real obstacle here, as Sir C.G. Darwin has pointed out, is that man is a wild species and so not amenable to any large-scale experiments in controlled breeding. The dilemma is a practical one. Devices for bringing about differential fertility seem to be either ineffective (e.g. family allowances proportionate to income) or socially dangerous and disruptive (e.g. surgical sterilisation).

VII. SOME CONCLUDING CONSIDERATIONS

Despite my rejection of anti-naturalism, then, I conclude that evolutionary biology does not have much to contribute to the solution of the central problem of ethics: the discovery of a criterion for the justification of judgments of value. Although evolutionary knowledge can give rise to value-judgments these are of a subordinate and defeasible nature. Secondly, these judgments of biological value are inevitably of an *ex post facto* character, since the evolutionary process is a trend not a law and one that depends on a unpredictably numerous and variegated set of variables. Finally the evolving and naturally selected human characteristics which are principally relevant to ethics and social policy are socially acquired and not genetically inherited. I agree with the anti-naturalists, then, that there can be no well-founded evolutionary ethics as traditionally understood. It remains to be considered whether our knowledge about evolution can be of use to ethics in any other way. I believe that there are, in fact, two spheres in which it can make a contribution.

(i) *The evolution of moral agency.* Both Waddington and J.S. Huxley lay a good deal of emphasis on the fact that just as morality as a social institution is an evolutionary phenomenon so the moral capacity of the individual, his possession of moral beliefs and their tendency to influence his actions, is something that has evolved. They connect this, furthermore, with the Freudian theory of the formation of the conscience or super-ego. The strictly ethical conclusion they then draw is that since moral agency or the moral sense is not innate the theory of moral intuitionism, which holds that the fundamental propositions, at any rate, of a system of moral beliefs must be directly apprehended, is false. In fact these three considerations – that morality has evolved, that conscience is not innate, and that intuitionism is false – are not logically connected in the way that they suppose. To start with it is perfectly consistent, and for a biologist, one would have thought, rather natural, to assert both that morality has evolved and that conscience is innate. Suppose an initial population whose members' behaviour is dominated by impulses of Hobbesian and amoral egoism. Suppose further that a variation occurs in one or several members of the population, one that equips them with altruistic or public-spirited or self-sacrificing impulses. If Clifford and T.H. Huxley are right the offspring of these emotional mutants will have an evolutionary advantage since they will be able to form a mutual protection society. In due course the egoistic stocks will be eliminated and innate, inheritable altruism will come to characterise the whole population. I am not suggesting that this supposition is in fact correct, though it strikes me as being not utterly implausible if taken in a very broad sense. My only purpose is to point out that to say that morality has evolved is not to say that it has evolved socially rather than genetically. A further point to notice is that the evolution of morality can be understood in two different ways, an external and an internal, so to speak. By the external evolution of morality I mean the movement from premoral egoism to some sort of altruism or social-mindedness. By its internal evolution I mean the movement from concern for the tribe to concern for humanity or the whole sentient creation, from parochial to cosmopolitan morality in other words, or, again, from a crude morality of overt acts to a morality which concerns itself with motivation, or yet again, from a morality which demands rigorously conceived forms of conduct to one that prescribes the pursuit, by any of a range of critically selected means, of certain broad general ends. It would seem reasonable to suppose that the external evolution of morality is genetic even if its internal evolution is social. However, there may be something wrong with the initial assumption of the theory of external evolution, for it supposes, with Hobbes, that the natural condition of men is exclusively self-regarding. But it might well be argued that the initial human population is not like that since it is equipped with an inheritance of social-mindedness from its ancestors among the higher animals. On the whole, then, it seems reasonable enough to suppose that the internal details of individual moral capacity are acquired by a process of social evolution, and so are amenable to the type of explanation offered by Freud's super-ego theory, but that if the broad instinctive substructure of men has evolved at all within the life-span of the species and is not part of the initial genetic equipment of *homo sapiens* it may well have done so genetically.

We may now turn to the supposed incompatibility between the idea that our fundamental moral convictions are acquired and not innate and the intuitionist theory of morals. The source of this belief seems to be the traditional identification of necessary with innate knowledge. Ethical intuitionism, in one of its prevalent forms, has compared moral beliefs to the propositions of logic and mathematics as being unconditionally necessary and, in some crucial cases, self-evident. Plato's doctrine of *anamnesis* sought to explain necessary knowledge in this way and it was against this inference from necessary to innate knowledge that the first book of Locke's *Essay* was directed. The Platonic theory was revived by Herbert Spencer who held that the important discoveries of ancestors were inherited as self-evident certainties by descendants. The point to notice is that even if their innateness is an adequate *explanation* of our possession of beliefs in self-evident and necessary propositions it does not *follow logically* from their self-evidence and necessity. The Plato-Spencer theory, in holding some of our beliefs to be necessary because they are innate, implies that if a belief is not necessary it cannot be innate. This is not to say that if a belief is not innate it cannot be necessary. To show this it would have to be proved that a belief cannot be necessary unless it is innate.

The other main form of ethical intuitionism compares fundamental moral judgments to judgments of sense-perception, arguing that these moral judgments, like the deliverances of the senses, are objective and yet directly apprehended, by a special faculty of some sort, and not inferred. But evolutionary considerations do not rule out a moral sense theory which conceives the moral sense in rather close analogy to the physical senses. The objective and uninferred character of judgments of colour is not undermined by the fact that the eye has evolved or even by the fact that an element of socially enforced convention enters into our actual colour-discriminations.

There is a sense, however, in which evolution does tend to undermine intuitionist ethics. For by treating morality and moral agency as natural phenomena, by considering morality as a functioning social institution, and so firmly connecting it to our desires and satisfactions it repudiates the essentially other-worldly conception of morality which is characteristic of intuitionism. Intuitionist ethics is a kind of secularised version of the ethics of divine command in which the supernatural law-giver is internalised and placed, rather incongruously, alongside our natural inclinations. On this view man is understood to be moved by two radically different and entirely discontinuous sorts of motivation. The evolutionary way of thinking asserts the continuity between the traditionally separated sides of human nature, the

ape and the angel, just as it asserts the continuity between man and the rest
of the animal world.

(ii) *Evolutionary knowledge of means to moral ends.* It would be widely agreed
that evolutionary biology, by contributing to our knowledge about the
consequences of action, can have an important subsidiary place in the
rational formation of moral convictions. This would not be accepted by those
deontologists, like Kant and, even more conspicuously, Prichard, who
contend that the rightness and wrongness of actions is an intrinsic property
of them and in no way dependent on the consequences that accrue to them.
But this rather foolish opinion is more an intellectual curiosity than a serious
challenge. Allowing, as even most professed deontologists do in practice, for
example Ross, that the consequences of an action are relevant to its moral
quality, we may admit that evolutionary knowledge, by giving us a new idea
of the results to which conventionally approved lines of conduct will lead,
may require the critical revision or development of these conventional
approvals. The difficulty here, as we have seen in the fifth section of this
essay, is to determine just what consequences evolutionary theory does or
can predict.

Despite this sceptical reservation there are two reasons for thinking that
evolutionary theory is particularly relevant to the ethical problems of our
age. The first of these is the very much increased rate of change of the human
environment due to the accelerating increase of population and of the
technological complexity of our mode of life. In changing circumstances what
may be called the derivative moral principles, those which ascribe rightness
and wrongness to particular lines of conduct, tend to become rapidly out of
date. For with the change of circumstances lines of conduct come to have
quite different consequences from those in the light of which rightness or
wrongness was originally ascribed to them. Secondly, the nature of the
change reinforces the effect of change itself. In a densely populated and
technologically complex society forms of action have many more humanly
relevant consequences and so acts which were once harmless and neutral
come to be maleficent in their effects. To take a very simple example: the first
European inhabitants of Australia could afford to be careless about the
conservation of natural resources, the disposal of refuse and even the making
of noise in a way that the inhabitants of a modern industrial city can not.

This leads on to a further point. By a series of accidents the morality which
ethical philosophers study has come to be understood in an absurdly
contracted way at a time when it crucially needs to be enlarged. What
Aristotle meant by ethics was a rational inquiry into the whole management
of human life. A contemporary moral philosopher and partly in consequence,
most people who think at all generally about problems of conduct,
understands by ethics the study of immediate, inter-personal obligation. The
currently conventional, narrow conception of ethics is limited in two ways.
On the one side it leaves out in its obsessive Protestant concentration on the
compulsory, the whole business of rational choice between different styles of
life, the topic of the great tradition of *moralistes*. This is an impoverishment of
ethical thinking, but not, perhaps, a very disastrous one. What is left out on

the other side is more vital and indispensable, namely ideology, conceived not as a collection of more or less fanatically held dogmas but as a rational concern with the fundamental principles of social policy. Morality as conventionally understood deals with the rather short-run effects of individual action; what I have called ideology deals with the longer-run effects of collective action. As the world becomes more technologically complex it is the latter type of effects that have an increasing importance for the life of the individual. This is not due simply to the fact that social action is more effective and known to be so but also because large areas of what were once personal responsibility have been handed over to society at large from the family, for example education and the care of the old and ill. The great virtue of the evolutionary moralists is that they are adept in a style of practical thinking which is of a scope appropriate to the problems of our time and set an example which should be more widely followed. Critics often complain about the triviality of 'contemporary moral philosophy. Their protest is just enough in outline but misplaced in detail. It is not so much that we should turn from the rights and wrongs of returning borrowed books by post to those of suicide but rather that we should enlarge our perspective to take in the problems of society as a whole and not those of such an artificial, transitory and fundamentally unimportant group as that of the two parties to an obligation.

20

Croom Robertson

George Croom Robertson, although the first, was far from being the most distinguished editor of *Mind*. Moore and Ryle may fairly be described as the most important strictly professional philosophers of their times in Britain. For each of them there was a more inventive and far-reachingly influential philosopher in whose shadow, so to speak, they worked; namely Russell and Wittgenstein. But these more wayward and prophetic thinkers were anchored only rather loosely in academic life. For the greater part of their careers they had no university post. Croom Robertson, like Moore and Ryle, was a university teacher throughout his working life. Indeed, while they remained in the same university until retirement, he stayed in the same job, that of professor of mental philosophy in University College, London, from his appointment to it at the age of twenty-four in 1866 until the year of his death, 1892, when he was fifty.

Nevertheless, and despite the fact of his close dependence on Bain, who, in effect, chose him as editor and personally subsidised *Mind* during the period of his editorship, he had a profound and persisting influence on the character of the periodical. In the first place, he chose its name. 'It was his happy inspiration', Bain wrote, 'that gave the title, which commended itself to every one' (*Philosophical Remains of G.C. Robertson*, p.xvi). That title embodied not merely the conception of philosophy suggested by the title of Croom Robertson's chair but his own view of the subject. For him psychology was a proper and desirable preliminary to philosophy. 'The real and natural beginning', he said in his inaugural lecture in 1866, 'is a rigorous investigation of the *phenomena* of mind. If all Philosophy must be essentially Philosophy of the Mind, because it views nothing except in express relation to Thought, the question as to the innermost nature of mental action must surely be taken first ... Psychology then is, and must still be for a long time to come, the only true point of departure in philosophy ...' (*Philosophical Remains*, p.3). From the outset *Mind* was described on its cover as 'a quarterly review of psychology and philosophy'. It certainly remained a wholly applicable description until the end of Stout's period as editor in 1920. Thus in no.115 of July 1920, the last but one edited by Stout, the four articles proper are all essentially psychological: on the sensory attribute of order, motives, consciousness, and sleep and dreams. The description persisted on the cover of *Mind* for another fifty-odd years until the general transformation of its physical appearance under the present editor in January 1974, long after it had ceased to apply to the contents. But Robertson's notion of the relation between psychology and philosophy remained fundamental to the editing of *Mind* after his death for a period at least twice as long as his initial editorial stint.

Secondly, although the precise detail of the physical form of *Mind* may have been determined by the publishers or, more probably, its printers (from the beginning until now), the Aberdeen University Press, the general layout has always corresponded to the proposals of Croom Robertson's first editorial remarks in 1876. First, some substantial articles, then a handful of long critical notices of important recent books, then shorter notices of other publications. One early feature of *Mind* that Stout felt the need to revive was the abstracting of important articles from foreign periodicals, a practice that continued to the end of Moore's editorship in 1948. Another that he introduced was much in Croom Robertson's spirit, that of including 'specialist reports' on the scientific detail of psychological research. Finally, there is the matter of 'notes'. In a fitful sort of way these have always been a feature of *Mind*. But in the second half of its existence they have been occasional and brief. In the early days they had something of the gossipy copiousness of the notes in the present-day *Journal of Philosophy*, with news of appointments and retirements and not just obituaries of the great or of people particularly connected with the periodical.

Croom Robertson's view of the proper relations of philosophy and psychology is given full expression in the editorial introduction to *Mind*'s first number that I have mentioned. Here he argues for the inclusion of psychological material in a somewhat defensive way. It will ensure, he writes, that *Mind* is not wholly composed of 'the speculative differences of individual thinkers'. Readers, it is implied, need to have the traditional strife and inconclusiveness of philosophy proper mitigated for them by samples of work on the nature of the mind that is cumulative, co-operative and, in general, encouragingly Baconian. He goes on that the aim of including a good deal of psychological matter is 'to procure a decision on the scientific standing of psychology'. The suggestion is that psychology is very crucially on trial, that now, the mid-1870s, is the time at which it must prove itself to be a true science or nothing at all.

An interesting proposal is that reviewers should suggest themselves. Croom Robertson's attitude to commissioned book reviewing is censorious, parallel to that of conventional morality to commercially-purchased love. 'Criticism of important books that is not founded on leisurely study of them by men who read them naturally in the course of their own work is worth little or nothing when it is not worth much less than nothing'. He is not worried by the fact that more than one self-appointed reviewer might send in a notice of some significant work. If more than one is adequate, more than one will be printed. I have not been able to discover how well this policy worked or if, indeed, it really was seriously put into effect. Double reviewing has occurred in more recent times. *Mind* contained reviews of J.J.C. Smart's *Philosophy and Scientific Realism* by different hands in 1966 and 1967, but that, it was admitted, was the result of editorial oversight.

A third effect of Croom Robertson on *Mind* is more important than either its baptism, even if the name given imports a theory about the nature of philosophy, or its structure and arrangement, which are, after all, fairly natural and obvious. From the beginning *Mind* under Croom Robertson sought to allow expression to the widest possible diversity of philosophical positions. The actual detail of the way in which this hospitable liberality worked out can be deferred for later consideration. The main point to notice here is that this was achieved in what might well have seemed rather unpropitious circumstances.

In the first place Croom Robertson was heavily dependent on Bain. *Mind* was essentially Bain's idea. He selected his pupil Croom Robertson as editor and the subsidy which made the continuation of the periodical possible was conditional on Croom Robertson's remaining editor. It is said to have cost Bain over £3,000 in its first fifteen years to keep it going. After Croom Robertson's resignation and the appointment of G.F. Stout in his place, Bain's role as financial patron was taken over by Henry Sidgwick, who himself helped, shortly before his death, to inaugurate the Mind Association to support the periodical with a regular income from subscriptions. Bain was himself a fairly tough and combative figure. He had achieved an education, after very modest beginnings in life, by strenuous and persistent efforts. In middle life his attempts to secure various Scottish chairs had been obstructed by widespread and, no doubt, entirely well-founded doubts about his religious orthodoxy. Like many others he was enabled to circumvent academic timidity and conformism by political patronage when Sir George Cornewall Lewis, as home secretary, appointed him to a chair at the new united university of Aberdeen. As editor of James Mill and biographer of John Stuart Mill, he was firmly identified with a particular philosophical party. Yet *Mind*, under his protégé, was open to all. He does not appear to have tried to influence Croom Robertson's editorial policy in any partisan way and from what one can gather of Croom Robertson's character it seems highly unlikely that he would have had any effect on it if he had tried.

Croom Robertson himself, although broadly an empiricist of the school of the Mills, was too widely read in the history of philosophy to be a zealot for one particular point of view. Although loyal to what he took to be the essential, empirically-oriented character of the English mind, on which there is an attractively spacious essay in his *Philosophical Remains*, he believed that the tradition of Locke and Hume needed some measure of Kantian correction, even if in a more or less Spencerian form. If he had a bias it was towards professionalism. He was perhaps the first to draw explicit attention to the unprofessional character of English philosophy. (A Scotsman himself, he said that 'by English is here meant in the broadest sense British, inclusive of Irish and Scotch'). In his editorial remarks in the first number of *Mind* he expressed the hope that the periodical would help to remedy the ill-effects of English philosophical unprofessionality. Five years earlier, in the essay on the English Mind, he had not suggested that all the effects were bad but he did wonder whether the epoch of the amateur philosopher was not coming to an end. 'The representative philosophers of England ... have been, with hardly an exception, non-academic in position or even, many of them, anti-academic in feeling ... There was a time, long past indeed, when in England also the highest thought of the country found its utterance in the teaching of the universities, and such a time may come again. Nay, are there not signs that the day of professors is once more at hand, if not already upon us?' (*Philosophical Remains*, p.31). *Mind*, despite the appearance in its pages of H.G. Wells and Lord Balfour in its early years, has shown that his prophecy was correct and has contributed to its realisation.

Croom Robertson was born in Aberdeen in 1842. His father was an ironmonger and he had to make his way educationally by his own efforts. His intellectual abilities made themselves evident while he was still young, as also did the weakness of health that led in' the end to his early death at the age of fifty. He won a bursary at Marischal College at what must by then have been the very early age of fifteen and began his university studies in the same year. At the end of the third year of his course the colleges of Aberdeen were united into a·single university. The consequential problem of there being two professors for each recognised subject seems to have been solved by the austere expedient of pensioning off the older of each pair. Another effect was that Croom Robertson spent a year in Bain's logic class, the beginning of their lifelong friendship.

Croom Robertson graduated with distinction in classics and philosophy in 1861 when he was nineteen and was awarded a scholarship for two years' study at other places. He spent the winter of 1861-2 at University College, London, where he was soon to settle for the remainder of his life. While there he attended the English literature class of David Masson, the copious biographer of Milton, who should have been sympathetic as a fellow-Aberdonian, an enthusiast for higher education for women and an amateur of philosophy. His *Recent British Philosophy* came out in 1865 and went through several later editions. It is a fair and comprehensive survey of the state of the subject at the time of its publication, in which Carlyle is accorded rather more philosophical significance than would now be ascribed to him, either because he was Masson's friend or because Masson came to the subject with the point of view of a student of literature.

From London Croom Robertson went to Germany, first to Berlin where he heard Trendelenburg, then to Göttingen to hear Lotze. This early exposure to the heartland of philosophical professionalism is in contrast to the robust intellectual xenophobia of his philosophical forerunners, such as James Mill, who from a brief glimpse at the *Critique of Pure Reason* saw 'well enough what poor Kant would be at'. After a final stop at Paris he returned to Aberdeen to a lectureship in Greek at £100 a year and to helping Bain with various projects.

In December 1866 Croom Robertson was appointed Grote professor of the philosophy of mind and logic at University College, London. George Grote, the creator of his chair, had already been painfully involved with it. When the new college had opened in 1828 the chair had not been filled. The preferred candidate from a poor field had been a dissenting minister called Hoppus. Grote, supported by Mill and Brougham, had blocked the appointment on the ground that a deliberately unsectarian college should not appoint a clergyman to a chair of philosophy. A year later Mill and Brougham let Hoppus in, to Grote's considerable annoyance, shown in his immediate resignation from the council. After three and a half undistinguished decades of Hoppus the proposal to replace him by the vastly abler, but still ordained, James Martineau brought Grote into the field of battle once again. Amid a good deal of clamour in the press and the council room Grote's wishes prevailed: Martineau was excluded and Croom Robertson appointed. There is a dryly humorous note to the latter's scrupulous account of the whole undertaking in his article on Grote in the *Dictionary of National Biography* which suggests that charm as well as moral probity was a feature of Croom Robertson's character.

From that time on the general pattern of Croom Robertson's life, that of a progressive, public-spirited academic, established itself in a regular way. As well as his teaching, which appears to have been thoroughly conscientious, he was involved in much administration and examining. He gave popular lectures and was active in the movement for women's suffrage, an almost mandatory commitment for a disciple of Mill. For some years he was on the National Committee and in regular contact with Mill towards the end of the latter's life, but resigned over the insistence of his fellow-suffragists on linking the issue of the vote with that of repealing the Contagious Diseases Act, from motives, not of squeamishness, but of policy. He assisted Thomas Spencer Baynes with the preparation of a new edition of the *Encyclopaedia Britannica*, edited with the utmost care the materials on Aristotle left behind by his patron Grote and addressed the Metaphysical Society, that crucial meeting-ground of late Victorian mental luminaries, in 1873.

In 1876 he was appointed, at Bain's instance, the first editor of *Mind*. This work, so carefully and fruitfully carried out, was, together with his excellent little book on Hobbes, the main achievement of the remaining sixteen years of his life. The kidney disease which was to kill him first appeared in 1880 and from this time onward he was frequently too ill to carry out his work unaided.

Croom Robertson's principal scholarly achievement is undoubtedly his little book on Hobbes. As a volume of 236 small pages in the unassuming format of the Blackwood Library of Philosophical Classics, along with Provost Mahaffy on Descartes, Professor John Veitch on Hamilton and even more substantial items such as Edward Caird's volume on Hegel, it could easily be written off as something much less than it is. In the first place it is not only a biography that surpasses everything that went before it (which is not very much, apart from Aubrey's marvellously entertaining and intimate 'brief life'), it remains to this day the standard and most detailed account of Hobbes's life. Secondly, it contains as its sixth and longest chapter, making up about a third of the whole, a most perspicuous and well-organised exposition of whole Hobbesian system: his accounts of logic and knowledge, of the natural world, of human nature and of human society.

Not that Croom Robertson believed that Hobbes's philosophy really was a system. 'The whole of his political doctrine' he writes, 'has little appearance of having been thought out from the fundamental principles of his philosophy ... It doubtless had its main lines fixed when he was still a mere observer of men and manners, and not yet a mechanical philosopher' (*Hobbes*, p.57). This view is the leading theme of Leo Strauss's *Political Philosophy of Hobbes*, in which Croom Robertson is cited as a forerunner, and it is the main object of attack in J.W.N. Watkins's recent *Hobbes's System of Ideas*. As Watkins observes, Croom Robertson was aware of the *Short Tract on First Principles* in which Euclidean deduction is presented as the only source of definite knowledge ('science') and which Hobbes probably wrote some time around 1630, long before any of his works on political theory. Tönnies brought the *Tract* to light only a couple of years before Croom Robertson's *Hobbes* was published in 1886, so Watkins is justified in suggesting that Croom Robertson's footnote, in which he says of the *Tract* that it somewhat alters 'the complexion of the case', was added in proof.

On the other main topic of controversy in recent Hobbes-interpretation, that of whether his 'laws of nature' are principles of morality, Croom Robertson is on the opposite side to Taylor and Warrender. The fundamental law of nature, he says, is 'a precept of reason with a view to self-preservation' (Hobbes, p.141). There is no suggestion that while self-preservation supplies a *motive* for obeying natural law, that law derives its *authority* from its divine commander.

Croom Robertson's teaching seems to have been roughly divided between philosophy proper and psychology, in accordance with the principle of philosophical method mentioned in connection with the naming of *Mind*. The main topic of his *Elements of Psychology* (posthumously worked-up from lecture notes) is perception. The senses occupy the centre of attention from pages 47 to 176 of a book of around 250 pages. To feeling and the will only 30 pages each are accorded. Given his concern with psychology as providing material for the theory of knowledge this bias is perhaps intelligible. He admits that besides 'objective consciousness' directed on to the world of physical things there is introspective or reflexive 'subjective consciousness', the indispensable instrument of the psychologist; but as a theorist of knowledge he is not much concerned with knowledge of the mental as problematic.

In his *Elements of General Philosophy*, amid a good deal of exclusively historical material, there is a historical account of three main philosophical problems: those of universals, of the *a priori* and empirical elements in knowledge and of our knowledge of an external, material world. Considered as argument the treatment of the problem of universals is distinctly sketchy. A judicious mixture of conceptualism and nominalism is recommended but it cannot be said that the various forms of realistic alternative are refuted.

On the topic of knowledge in general the influence of Kant is shown in Croom Robertson's preference for seeing it as a question about the constitution, rather than the origin, of knowledge. In holding psychology to be a necessary preliminary to philosophy he is still insistent that the two inquiries are distinct. He rejects the view that space is as empirical as colour or sound for the reason that association cannot explain the necessary connection between colour and extension. He does not go all the way with Kant in taking space to be an *a priori* form of intuition, but connects it with what he calls our 'organic constitution': we obtain the idea of spatial extension from the 'muscular' aspect of some of our sense-organs, in particular sight and' touch. 'Kant, then, was right in maintaining that our reference of colours to space was part of our original constitution, though what he called pure intuition I call bodily organs' (*Elements of General Philosophy*, p.133). He concludes that what distinguishes the demonstrative sciences which issue in necessary truths is that they are concerned with 'matter as apprehended by activity, by construction; and herein lies their "necessity"' (ibid. p.134). The idea of causation also has a psychological basis: 'our consciousness of being able to put forth activity; our consciousness of volition' (ibid. p.144).

Muscular activity, or 'active sense', is called on again as a cure-all for the problem of perception of an objective, external world. The distinction of subject and object has to be drawn within 'the circle of consciousness' to which we are inevitably confined. Those experiences which either involve or vary with 'consciousness of activity put forth' (primary and secondary qualities respectively) are assigned to the object. The notion of substance, finally, is a projection of something like personality or subjecthood to these objectified complexes of qualities. In a final metaphysical flourish Croom Robertson briefly signals his allegiance to a form of Leibnizian monadism. The ultimate physical constituents of extended matter must be atoms that are themselves unextended. Such insensible things can not be conceived to have qualities, but we must consider them to be endowed 'with a certain activity, with force or energy' (ibid. p.179). So far they are like us: what I am is essentially will. 'Force ... constitutes real existence, and is the fullest expression of mind. Mind exists everywhere ...'. It is these monadological speculations that Croom Robertson was, according to Bain, about to develop at the time of his death and that Rudolf Metz refers to, with perhaps excessive courtesy, as 'an interesting attempt ... to reach a cosmology related to Leibniz's monadism' (*A Hundred Years of British Philosophy*, p.79).

What remains for consideration is *Mind* during Croom Robertson's editorship, the first sixteen years of its life. The active philosophers of the time in Britain can be ranged under half a dozen heads. First, there were more or less traditional empiricists, philosophers of a naturalistic tendency, but not preoccupied or enchanted by the theory of evolution: Bain, Croom Robertson's mentor and guardian angel, in Scotland, Fowler, the Oxford Baconian and, more important than either, Henry Sidgwick. Evolution was the central, generative idea in the philosophical work of Spencer, Huxley, George Henry Lewes, Leslie Stephen, W.K. Clifford and Karl Pearson, as it was at that stage in that of the first and only notable British pragmatist, F.C.S. Schiller. Thirdly, there were the idealists: Green, Bradley, Bosanquet, the Cairds and, in a less orthodox style, Seth (Pringle-Pattison) and James Ward. A fourth, broadly realistic, group comprises the Oxford Aristotelians, Thomas Case and Cook Wilson, and the learned Robert Adamson. The two remaining groups are defined more by subject-matter than by doctrine: philosophers of religion, such as Martineau, Flint and Lord Balfour, and the logicians and methodologists, such as de Morgan, Venn and Jevons.

With this general picture in mind it soon becomes clear on looking at the contents of *Mind* in its first sixteen years how widely Croom Robertson cast his net. In the first number in 1876 there are articles by Spencer, Sully (Croom Robertson's successor at University College), Venn, Sidgwick, Shadworth Hodgson and Bain. The most interesting item is perhaps Mark Pattison's report (the first of a series) on philosophy at Oxford. Flint has a long critical notice of Brentano's *Psychologie vom empirischen Standpunkt*; Bain reviews Spencer's *Sociology* and there is a note by G.H. Lewes on the nervous system. Later in the year there is Venn again on Boole and a thoroughly slashing review of Bradley's *Ethical Studies* by Sidgwick in which he observes that 'uncritical dogmatism is the largest and most interesting element of Bradley's work', refers to Bradley's 'debating-club rhetoric' and sums the book up as 'crude and immature'. Bradley replied in a tight-lipped fashion in the following year. This first, negative attention to the new idealist movement did not prevent its defenders in due course from making substantial contributions to *Mind* in its support. In 1882, the year of his death, T.H. Green published a long three-part article on the possibility of a natural science of man. A year later Edward Caird has a long article on Green's *Prolegomena to Ethics* and Bradley contributes a series of notes, the beginning of a massive flow of contributions in later years. In 1884 Balfour writes on Green's metaphysics of knowledge and Sidgwick on his ethics.

Perhaps the first real scoop for Croom Robertson was the rather dull 'biographical sketch of an infant' by Charles Darwin in 1877. More interesting in that year is Jevons's defence of examinations. William James makes the first of many appearances in 1879. Clifford's central essay on the nature of things-in-themselves came out in 1878. In the early '80s there are articles from Francis Galton (on imagery, naturally), F.W. Maitland (on Balfour and on Spencer), Josiah Royce, Karl Pearson (on Maimonides and Spinoza), F.Y. Edgeworth (on the hedonistic calculus and on chance), Adamson on Bradley's *Principles of Logic* and, a voice from the past, James Hutchinson Stirling (on Kant's answer to Hume).

In 1885 Rashdall discusses Sidgwick's utilitarianism and Pater's *Marius the Epicurean* is reviewed by Croom Robertson's colleague in the English department at University College. Alexander (writing on Hegel's philosophy of nature) and Dewey make their first appearances in 1886. Ward appears in 1887, Bosanquet in 1888 and Seth and Stout in 1889. Santayana supplies a brief version of his doctoral thesis on Lotze in 1890.

There are few individual absentees from my original list of philosophers active in the period and each group of philosophers is very fairly represented. The 'exemplary fairness' of which the contributors to Croom Robertson's retiring-present wrote was no testimonial fiction. What seems also true is that Croom Robertson succeeded in getting material of the highest available quality as well as of the most inclusive scope. If the anthology business of the present age had been developed in the '90s a substantial volume could have been assembled under the title *Croom Robertson's Mind*. Again, when Stout wrote in his first editorial that it was important to fill the pages with 'serious work to the exclusion of merely dilettante productions' this was no aspersion of his predecessor but rather a resolve to carry on as he had done.

Serious and successful editorship is very often damaging in its effects on the editor's own writing. There seems no doubt that this was true of Robertson, who was by all accounts an exceptionally conscientious reviser of manuscripts. Comparing the *Mind* he edited with the writing of his own he did manage to achieve there is no reason to suppose that he made a bad choice.

21

Lou Andreas-Salomé

Lou Andreas-Salomé was the greatest intellectuals' woman of her age, the two decades on either side of 1900; the most distinguished performer since Madame de Staël in her particular field, but unique as a tease, as an exponent of not kiss and tell. Her three principal conquests (Nietzsche, Rilke, and Freud) clearly exceed in distinction the three husbands of Alma Mahler, her only possible contemporary competitor (Mahler, Gropius, and Werfel), and although Rilke was the only one Lou went to bed with she played quite a significant part in the lives of the other two.

She was born in St. Petersburg in 1861, the daughter of a Baltic German general who was in charge of the accounts of the Russian army. In her late teens she fell under the influence of a good-looking Dutch clergyman, Hendrik Gillot, who awoke her voracious intellect with theological discussion and a course of reading. To get over the unhealthy excitement this engendered she was taken to Zurich by her mother in 1880 and embarked on a regime of theological and philosophical study so intense as to be injurious to her health. In 1882 she met Paul Rée, a pathetic character who attempted to shore up his damp soul and forget his unappetising appearance by developing a toughly reductive theory about the origins of conscience.

Rée's close friend Nietzsche was greatly taken with Lou, seeing in her a potentially ideal disciple. They established an odd and unstable triangle, whose abiding memorial is a photograph of Nietzsche and Rée pulling a small cart in which Lou kneels, holding an ineffective-looking whip, its meagre thong dangling impotently. Their plans for studious retirement together came to nothing very much. Rée jealously slandered Nietzsche to Lou, while she, in a dire confrontation with his sister Elisabeth, poured out her revulsion from Nietzsche as a dirty old man. Nietzsche and Lou broke off their relations. Lou says she made the break despite Nietzsche's persistent entreaties: Professor Binion makes a vast and persuasive case for the view that this was a lie.

For the next few years she lived, non-sexually, with Rée, getting a proposal of marriage from the psychologist Ebbinghaus and exciting a considerable emotional disturbance in the breast of the sociologist Tönnies, familiar to all students of his subject for distinguishing *Gemeinschaft* from *Gesellschaft*. In 1886 she married an Oriental philologist, Friedrich Carl Andreas. The marriage was never consummated. This fact must have played some part in the general fruitlessness of Andreas's career, assisted, no doubt, by his nocturnal habits, his intuitive and disorganised methods of thinking, and his inability to adjust himself to the orderly expectations of the German academic world.

Lou soon became associated with the *Freie Bühne* group – in particular with Gerhart Hauptmann – and began to write for their periodical. She assembled a collection of pieces on Ibsen's heroines in one book and in 1894, with Nietzsche safely tucked away inside his madness, another on him in which she exploited their brief but turbulent relationship to the full. A left-wing journalist fell in love with her and attempted, on discovering the nature of her relations with Andreas, to detach her from him. After exciting the amorous propensities of Wedekind and going on outings with Schnitzler she herself fell in love with the poet and dramatist Richard Beer-Hofmann, but he rejected her for the opposite reason from Nietzsche's: he wanted something more simple and earthy, not something higher and more spiritual, than she had to offer.

This seems to have done the trick. In 1895 or '6 the most noticeably obstinate virginity in Central Europe collapsed in face of the vigorous approaches of Dr Friedrich Pineles, known as Zemek. The susceptibility of this change of name to Freudian interpretation is left uniquely unexploited by Binion. Lou's affair with Zemek endured on and off for a number of years and probably led to an abortion. She tried to remove all trace of him from her memoirs, quite possibly because he was not famous.

Lou now made up for lost time. She took on Rilke, the first and greatest of what Binion calls her boy-lovers, in 1897. She lived with him, in her usual intermittent, Andreas-based way, for three years, made two trips to Russia with him, probably had a second abortion on his account, changed his name from René to Rainer, and exercised an analogous stiffening-up influence on his verse, which had hitherto been excessively diaphanous and ethereal. In the end she sent him rather brutally about his business. She heard that Rée, whom she had not seen for years, had died from a fall and chose to interpret this as suicide caused by his loss of her. Zemek was waiting and continued to serve until 1908. Between 1895 and 1905 the bulk of Lou's imaginative writing was produced: novels and stories of an emotionally melodramatic sort.

In 1903 Andreas at last secured a proper job, at the University of Göttingen, and celebrated the fact in the following year by getting the maid pregnant, not unreasonably after seventeen years of *mariage blanche* to Lou. For her a fallow period of illness and thoughts of suicide followed, until in 1911 a new boy-lover, Paul Bjerre, introduced her to Freud. While working her amorous way through various members of Freud's circle – Bjerre, Tausk, Gebsattel – she was talking and writing to Freud and studying psycho-analysis. Soon she was practising as a lay analyst, sufficiently entranced to see patients for as much as nine hours a day and then to undercharge or forget to charge them altogether.

For a while, as might be expected of a Nietzschean, she toyed with the heresies of Adler. Freud was indulgent and eventually welcomed her decision in favour of orthodoxy. He was the main guiding light of her last twenty years, unwearyingly generous to her with time, correspondence, and money, even if he could offer no more than gratitude for her ecstatic and voluminous endeavours to develop his doctrines, great loose effusions which he did not pretend to understand nor, it may well be thought, make any great effort to understand. This would not seem to detract from Freud's reputation for good sense.

Andreas died in 1930. For her remaining seven years Lou consoled herself with a succession of poodles, some dependent daughter-figures, as well as an elaborate exercise in consolatory fantasy, posthumously communicated to the world in 1951 in the disguise of memoirs, and the recruitment into this project of falsifying her past of Ernst Pfeiffer, the inheritor and guardian of her literary estate, a man, it would seem from the frustrations endured by her biographers, brilliantly cast for the role of dog in the manger.

What sort of biography does such a person as Lou Salomé deserve? Something fairly brief and chatty, one might have thought, making the most of her as a particularly colourful example of the emancipated woman of the *fin de siècle* in the central European culture area. Such a work does indeed exist: *My Sister, My Spouse* by H.F. Peters, a German-born professor at Portland State College, who has also written a book about Rilke. Peters leans fairly heavily on Lou's reminiscences and thus, as Binion pretty convincingly establishes, his book contains a good deal of fiction. It is pleasantly written, although a little infected with that rather cloying hotel manager's geniality sometimes imparted by the editors of publishing houses to the manuscripts of academic authors. Another possibility would have been to use Lou as a pretext for a collective study of the vast array of cultural lions that she so indefatigably sought to tame, since by main force she managed to cross the path of a whole generation of middle European writers and thinkers.

Rudolph Binion, a professor at Brandeis whose previous book was a more or less conventional biographical study of three French politicians of the Third Republic, has undertaken something utterly different from either of these in *Frau Lou* (Princeton, N.J., 1968): a psychoanalytic, if here and there trans-Freudian, investigation of Lou's personality from infantile fantasy to post-mortem defense of her system of illusions through the instrument of Pfeiffer. Moreover, he has based it all on a most brilliant, persevering, and microscopic retrieval and use of every possible scrap of evidence.

It is impossible not to admire the astounding pertinacity with which Binion subjects every preliminary polite excuse for a late reply in her letters, every conceivable suggestion on her part of more intimacy with the great than she actually possessed, to a thorough, detective scrutiny. Her minor social dishonesties in correspondence are exposed with the kind of extravagance of detail and conjecture that is usually applied only to the writings of Shakespeare or the more theologically crucial bits of the Bible. Other readers may suspect, with me, that their own correspondence would not stand up much better under this ruthlessly intense illumination. Binion sets about the correlation between what she actually did and what she said she did, however trivial the deed, with the bulldog resolution of a divorce detective on a fat retainer who happens also to be a classical scholar manqué. Nothing escapes his notice. In 1898 she wrote to a woman friend: 'I spent nearly every hour with my mother and family.' Binion is watching: 'This,' he says, 'was an excuse for not having written sooner – phrased to suggest that she had been in Petersburg her whole time away from Berlin.'

Such Pinkerton material is, however, by no means the largest constituent of Binion's quarter of a million words of text, even if it is the occasion for the majority of his 2,425 bibliographical references. What bulks largest is his speculative analysis of Lou's personality. This starts with due boldness on the second page of the main text. 'Her trouble was psychic growing pains which fortunately can, and unfortunately must, be traced to their crude source. This was a craving for her father excited by excretion and attended by darkling visions of re-entering his bowel-womb to repossess his penis.'

Here, one might feel, Binion presumes too much on a very short acquaintance with his reader. He appears to take it for granted that the latter will nod his head, murmuring 'of course, of course,' at the implied causal connection between Lou's excretings and her desire for her father, that he will take cheerfully in his stride the ascription to General Salomé of that odd piece of Freudian anatomy, a bowel-womb, and that he will not merely be ready, as a good mid-twentieth-century educated person, to recognize penis-envy in infant girls but will endorse the view that the baby Lou was animated at the outset of her emotional pilgrimage by a desire to get her penis *back* from her father. On reflection, furthermore, the itinerary she is alleged to have chosen to get to her destination seems a bit quaint.

In general Binion's psychoanalytical interpretation of Lou is conveyed by this kind of presumptuous intimation, as if he were addressing a close and familiar group of fellow-workers who are fully seized of and wholly committed to the theoretical framework of his interpretation. Quite often some utterance of Lou's will be contradicted or otherwise redirected in a footnote with an 'of course' calculated to make the potential critic feel embarrassingly rustic and imperceptive: for example, 'Lou of course loved – through Beer-Hofmann – Nietzsche.' One barely intelligible quasi-explanation follows another; there is never a pause for clear summary and consolidation.

The directly biographical inquiries make it clear that Lou was a liar or, more specifically, a self-inflating fantast. Binion's most glittering demonstration of this is his contrast between the actualities of an uninvited visit by Lou and Rilke to Tolstoy and the richly elaborate fairy tale she subsequently managed to weave out of her recollections of the farcical encounter where Tolstoy was at his gruffest, refusing to recognise his callers whom he had met before, letting Lou in but slamming the door in Rilke's face, all in a setting of general domestic turmoil with the sound of shouts, sobbings, and large thuds coming from behind closed doors. Binion locates Lou's systematic deception of herself and others as well as the doctrine of mystical self-identification with the universe at large, which was the basis of her early theological and her later psychoanalytical musings, in the framework of an all-engulfing narcissism. In such very indeterminate terms he makes a good case, but the precise articulation of his account of her and the way in which the evidence he cites supports it are intolerably difficult to grasp.

It is in his use of her writings, particularly her explicitly fictional writings, to establish this theory about her that the heaviest going in a generally exhausting volume is to be found. Consider this specimen passage: 'Gillot's engagement, which had broken upon her in Kiev, backed up Rainer's behind Dimitrii's – which in effect topped off Witalii's courtship of Margot in Kiev, signifying Gillot's of herself. Predominantly, however, Witalii was Lou as Kolya ...' Lou, Gillot, Rainer, and Kolya (= Nikolai Tolstoi) are real people; Dimitrii, Margot, and Witalii are characters in a story called 'Rodinka'. Even if there is anything to be found out by this sort of procedure, Binion makes its cost in complexity and involution prohibitively high.

Frau Lou reinforces a moral already well enough supported: that really enthusiastic total immersion in psychoanalysis can lead the most learned and intelligent people into a dreadful, sticky, featureless swamp where every familiar object turns out to lose its identity, to be a symbol or substitute or analogue for something else, which in turn yields to the same interpretative corrosion, and so on ad infinitum. Cases in point are Norman O. Brown's *Life Against Death*, a hymn to polymorphous perversity, and Brigid Brophy's *Black Ship to Hell*.

Those unwilling to step off the duckboards of rationality into this kind of morass should not let themselves be discountenanced by accusations of anal anxiety or something of that sort. Psychoanalysers of the more cosmic variety frequently attempt to invalidate rational criticism by attributing it to the personality disorders of their critics. No polemical strategy more openly invites the retort: *tu quoque*. Why on earth should Binion devote such prodigies of skill, learning, and energy to the microscopic study of an eccentric Russian woman whose only work translated into English is the diary of her relationship with Freud? The attention he gives to her smallest utterances is comparable only to that given by a lover to the flat communications of a conventional or indifferent loved one.

It is only fair to say that Binion does in the end step back from his rapt inquiry, but only to announce with the gratification of Jack Horner that his biography is no more than an incomplete sketch, that possible further lines of inquiry stretch off indefinitely in all directions. He does not ask: why pursue the subject at all? Certainly what he has to say about the execution of his project endows it with some of the fascination of A.J.A. Symons's *Quest for Corvo*. Peters, in his more digestible book on Lou, had written at some length of his frustrations at the hands of Pfeiffer: 'At first everything went well ... Pfeiffer seemed genuinely interested ... yet I could not help feeling that he looked upon me as a rather dangerous intruder in his private domain.' Binion records a similar experience with more acerbity. Old Pfeiffer seems to be doing a fine job as censor of his mysteriously appetising accumulation of repressed material.

22

Freud and Philosophy

Freud was not a philosopher and certainly did not think of himself as one. In his own eyes he was a scientist. He committed himself, at an early stage of his career, to the ascetic ideal of true scientific inquiry that Helmholtz had established for the scientific, and in particular medical, profession of the German-speaking world. Helmholtz, who was something of a universal genius, with interests covering the whole field of natural science from mathematics to the physiology of sensation, was a most resolute mechanist. He was hostile to metaphysical speculation in general and, more specifically, to vitalism, the idea that some principle beyond the reach of physics and chemistry must be called upon to explain the nature of living organisms. But he was not averse to *scientific* theorisation. He did not agree with Mach that the concepts of unobservable entities that occur in scientific theories are simply linguistic devices for the representation of regularities in the sensations that we immediately perceive. Helmholtz took them to be genuinely descriptive of the real nature of things hidden from our direct perception. The theoretical part of physical science, he said, 'endeavours to ascertain the unknown causes of processes from their physical effects; it seeks to comprehend them according to the law of causality'. Freud's doctrine of the unconscious conforms with this realistic conception of the nature of unobservable theoretical entities. The influence of Helmholtz's ideas can also be seen in Freud's persistent hope that an independent physiological confirmation would in the end be forthcoming for his theories about the real nature of the human mind.

Freud's commitment to this austerely mechanistic ideal is shown in the rigidly objective style and the emphatically scientistic vocabulary of his writings. At the outset this was, perhaps, a self-imposed discipline, which Freud embarked on to control a leaning towards speculative extravagance that he discerned in himself. It was a disposition that eventually broke out in his late, more adventurous writings on primitive society, war, religion and civilisation. In the period of his major innovations in psychology, when he was tracing a host of things – neurotic symptoms, dreams, everyday errors and slips of the tongue, even works of art – to hidden causes in the domain of infantile sexuality, this uncompromisingly scientistic stance had two noteworthy effects. On the one hand it provoked opposition by the ambitiousness of its claims; on the other, it somewhat mitigated the scandalous character of the detailed content of his views by the impersonal seriousness with which they were put forward. By choosing to present his revolutionary innovations as standard pieces of scientific theory, on a par with the molecular theory of gases or the germ theory of disease, he made the largest possible claim for their objective truth. Although this aspect of his doctrines excited less opposition to start with than their seemingly outrageous content, it has been that which has been most exposed to the criticism of philosophers, especially in the last few decades.

According to Ernest Jones, Freud attended the philosophical seminars of Franz Brentano during his period of medical study in Vienna in the late 1870s. At the time Freud joined the course it had been for two years no longer compulsory for medical students. The fact suggests that he had a distinct interest in philosophy. But there are no appreciable signs in his work of the influence either of Brentano himself or, for that matter, of Aristotle, with whom, in these seminars, Brentano was mainly concerned. In 1879, during his military service, Freud tried to earn a little money by translating some of John Stuart Mill's essays into German. Jones suggests that it was from one of these essays that Freud obtained his knowledge of Plato's doctrine of reminiscence. All that seems to have caught Freud's explicit attention in Mill himself is the variability of his prose style.

As has often been noticed, there are many correspondences between Freud's doctrines and the philosophy of Schopenhauer. Freud's conception of the unconscious as a reservoir of primitive and irrational energies parallels Schopenhauer's theory that the true self is unconscious will. For both of them, consciousness is no more than a device which the unconscious will makes use of to secure the preservation of the individual and the species. Schopenhauer's ideas were certainly available to Freud. When he was thirteen, in 1869, a popularised version of them was published: von Hartmann's *Philosophy of the Unconscious*. Von Hartmann laid a special, *fin de siècle*, emphasis on the pessimistic side of Schopenhauer. The idea that death is the only solution to the problem of human existence has an echo in Freud's notion of the death-wish.

II

But, for all his formal detachment from philosophy, Freud produced ideas whose generality made them of irresistible philosophical interest. In the broader, and more speculative, extensions of his strictly psychological findings, furthermore, he advanced opinions that are indubitably philosophical in a reasonably inclusive sense of the word.

In the psychological theories prompted by his clinical work Freud began by offering explanations only of neurotic symptoms. But the style of explanation contained in these theories was soon seen by him to be applicable to a wide range of other mental phenomena. Dreams, errors and verbal slips appear at first glance to be pointless and irrational waste-products of ordinary, rational, purposive mental activity, as much as neurotic symptoms do. Freud's recognition of unconscious purposiveness in the latter prepared the way for a similar interpretation of the former. The result was a complete inversion of older ideas about the relative importance of rational and non-rational elements in mental life.

The prevailing secular view of the nature of the mind was the variety of psychological determinism derived from Hobbes by the thinkers of the Enlightenment, the Utilitarians and the classical economists. In this view man comes into the world with an initial apparatus of instinctive desires and elemental likes and dislikes. Under the influence of the environment and of ever-increasing knowledge of the causes of pleasure and pain, this primordial repertoire gets transformed into a complicated system of preferences and aversions. It is not doubted that man always has a clear idea of what he wants and of what motivates him to act as he does. To the extent that his actions are irrational it is because his beliefs about what will give him pleasure or pain are ill-founded. The apparently purposeless or counter-productive thoughts and actions, which were the essential evidence on which Freud based his account of the nature of the mind, were brushed aside as of only marginal interest. Either they are purely random phenomena that could be attributed to some more or less mechanical feature of the human organism, as dreams might be seen as the idling of the cerebral engine between bouts of genuinely engaged activity, or they were the result of some breakdown within it.

Freud turned this picture of the mind and of the voluntary behaviour which manifests it upside down. What had formerly been seen as an unimportant miscellany of disconnected exceptions to the generally conscious purposiveness of mental life became, in Freud's hands, the point of entry into a massive domain of unconscious mentality. Its hidden, primordial energies were soon taken to account, not merely for the apparently irrational odds and ends which first revealed their existence, but also for all or most of conscious mental life as well. This amounted to a new form of epiphenomenalism: the idea that consciousness is a by-product of other aspects of the total person, influenced by, but exerting no influence upon, those other aspects: in T.H. Huxley's phrase 'the smoke above the factory'. In earlier versions that theory had taken consciousness to be an epiphenomenon of the body, in particular of the brain and nervous system. Freud made it primarily dependent on the unconscious and its elemental drives. But he connected this, in a speculative way, to the body by expressing the hope, which was mentioned earlier, that a physiological interpretation could be found for the ingredients of the unconscious.

III

Philosophy has always shown a proprietary interest in the study of the human mind. This attitude is embalmed in the old-fashioned designations of university philosophy departments, current until quite recent times, as departments of mental or moral, as contrasted with natural, science. It is not surprising that idealists should define philosophy as mind's knowledge of itself, since they believe that, in the end, everything real is mental. But a concern with the nature of mind has not been peculiar to idealists. The solid triumphs of the sciences of nature have long secured their emancipation from philosophy. Since the eighteenth century, at any rate, philosophers have for the most part followed Locke and Kant, two thinkers particularly enthralled by the magnitude of Newton's achievement, in conceiving the relation of philosophy to knowledge of the natural world in comparatively humble terms, as a matter of systematising and critically assessing its principles and not as providing the truest kind of natural knowledge. Full-blooded philosophies of nature, claiming to deduce its character from metaphysical axioms, have been a minority, in more or less defiant retreat.

The absence from philosophy of a similar modesty about the study of mind can be reasonably attributed to the later and much less complete emergence of a science of psychology, with a body of precise and generally agreed-upon findings to its credit and a generally accepted method of investigation to make possible the decisive resolution of disputed issues. It was not until the late nineteenth century that psychological inquiry became recognisably scientific in its methods. The securest achievements of scientific psychology began with the adoption of the principle that its proper subject-matter is inter-subjectively observable behaviour. Its chief successes have been in the field of those rather elemental aspects of mentality that men share with animals: perception and learning from experience, for example.

There are still many philosophers who would deny the pretensions of psychology, even in its more academic form as the experimental study of behaviour, to be a science at all. Support for this denial is provided by the thinness of its agreed findings, at least as compared with those of physics and chemistry, and by their confinement to the least characteristically human, and thus least humanly interesting, aspects of the mind. In the writings of Collingwood, for example, psychology is allowed to be the science of feeling but is stigmatised as a pseudo-science when it claims to understand the nature of thought. Between body and mind, Collingwood maintains, there is what he calls the *psyche*, to whose contents the distinction of truth and falsehood does not apply. The sub-rational events and processes that it contains are a proper field for the exercise of the experimental methods of natural science. But mind as reason, mind engaged in thinking, truly or falsely, is not a topic for empirical science at all. It can be understood only by the traditional, 'criteriological', sciences of logic and ethics (see *Essay on Metaphysics*, chapters ix-xii). I think that Collingwood is making an important point here, although in a confused and confusing way. This is that knowledge of the causes of our beliefs does not, by itself, entail anything whatever about their validity. But it does not follow from the fact that inquiry into the cause of beliefs is logically independent of inquiry into their truth or justification that inquiry into their causes is improper or impossible. What is relevant at this point, however, is the confusion: the denial to psychology of a crucial range of mental subject-matter.

At least Collingwood allows *a* field to psychology, conceived as a science emancipated from philosophy, that of the 'psyche' with its sub-rational feelings. Wittgenstein seems to go further. There is to be found in his later writings the outline sketch of a theory of human action which has been extremely influential. Its main theme is that actions are not mere natural happenings for which causal explanations can be sought. An action, such as raising one's arm, will typically involve or contain a bodily movement, such as one's arm going up, which is a causally explainable natural event. But thought about action proper moves on a completely different level. To conceive something as an action is to conceive it as realising an intention, as something that is intelligible only in the light of the agent's reasons for performing it, which are of quite a different nature from the causes of the bodily movement involved in it.

It is significant that Wittgenstein disparagingly rejects the common idea I expressed earlier according to which the limited emancipation of psychology from philosophy is the result of its undeveloped state as compared with the physical sciences. 'The confusion and barrenness of psychology,' he wrote, 'is (sic) not to be explained by calling it a "young science" ... In psychology there are experimental methods and *conceptual confusion* ... The existence of experimental methods makes us think that we have the means of solving the problems which trouble us; though problem and methods pass one another by' (*Philosophical Investigations*, p.232). This quotation is, indeed, consistent with the idea that once the conceptual confusion has been cleared up the experimental methods can, so to speak, be given their head. But he really means more than that. Once the conceptual confusion which is involved in taking behaviour to be, not action from reasons, but natural events with causes is cleared up, the greater part of what psychologists have taken it to be their business to investigate will be revealed as altogether beyond the competence of the essentially causal methods of inquiry to which they are committed.

In a more or less Freudian spirit it might seem inviting to explain this refusal by philosophers to relinquish the study of the mind to psychologists as the expression of a retentive hostility excited by the threat of superannuation. But it is just the relevance of this kind of explanation of beliefs to their validity which is the most substantial part of the point at issue. Whatever the emotional origin of the convictions of anti-psychological philosophers that their methods are more calculated to produce an understanding of the mind than those of the psychologists they criticise, it may still be the case that their conviction is well-founded. To take an extreme case: even if the ultimate source of the determination with which a physicist seeks to discover the fine structure of matter is his frustrated infantile curiosity about the sexual activities of his parents, it does not follow that his physical findings will be illusory. The unusual and even laughable character of the fuel has nothing to do with the capacity of the vehicle to reach its destination.

IV

The type of objection I have been considering applies to any form of psychological inquiry that is or claims to be scientific, in that it attempts to discover the *causes* of mental phenomena and of the actions that manifest or express them. A cause-seeking psychology does not have to assume that strict, absolute determinism is true: to try to explain something is not to be convinced that you can explain everything. But it must assume that some mental phenomena and actions have causes if it is to be embarked upon sensibly at all. This assumption touches a sensitive area and comes into collision with two sorts of resistance which are widespread not only among philosophers but among reflective people generally. The first is the common conviction, already discussed, that if our beliefs are causally determined they are invalid. If that were true there would, in a way, be nothing to fear from scientific psychology. For, in any comprehensive form, such a psychology would include itself in the scope of its theories about the causation of beliefs. The beliefs of psychologists, even their professional ones, must have causes as much as any others and so suffer with them the common fate of invalidation. A consistent causal psychologist, then, cannot assert that the causal determination of beliefs entails their invalidity. The second sensitive point is the equally widespread conviction that if actions are causally determined their agents cannot be held morally responsible for them, but I shall not pursue it here.

The philosophical criticisms of psychology that arise from hostility to determinism are directed against psychology in general and not at Freud and psychoanalysis specifically. If he is often mentioned by the proposers of criticisms of this kind it is simply because of his eminence or notoriety as a cause-seeking psychologist. The main burden of recent philosophical criticism of Freud, however, is directed specifically at him and psychoanalysis as contrasted with academic, predominantly behavioural, psychology. It maintains that while behavioural psychology is a genuine science the doctrines of Freud and his followers, although emphatically claimed to be scientific, are in fact nothing of the sort. In its standard version it simply condemns Freud's theories as a kind of arbitrary metaphysical speculation, masquerading as science.

Freud's ideas have fallen foul of the latest developments in the working-out of a leading theme of philosophy of science for more than a century. This is the attempt to supply an account of the logical relations between theory and experience without which, all parties agree, no theory can claim to be scientific. One doctrine in this field, that of instrumentalism, holds that if theoretical concepts of unobservable entities cannot be empirically defined, the theories in which they figure cannot be taken as descriptions of reality, but are no more than calculating devices – rules of inference with whose aid one observable state of affairs can be predicted from another. On this view Freudian theory is a pragmatically convenient myth which connects getting neurotics to talk about infantile sexual experiences with making them better. That would certainly be entirely unacceptable to Freud who was uncompromisingly realistic about his theoretical constructions.

Another doctrine is inductivism, which requires theories, if they are to count as scientific, to be capable of being confirmed by observable states of affairs. An inverted form of this requirement, proposed by Popper, has come to be widely accepted as a criterion for the scientific status of a theory. This is that for a theory to be scientific it must be empirically *falsifiable*; there must be some possible and empirically observable state of affairs which, if it occurred, would refute the theory in question. Since theories are unrestrictedly general they can never be conclusively established by particular observations, however numerous. But they can be overthrown by a single contrary instance. Popper argues persuasively that the more a theory rules out, the more possible falsifiers it has, the greater is its empirical content, the more, in other words, it actually says. Conformably with this, if a theory is unfalsifiable, it is simply vacuous and devoid of empirical content and certainly is no part of science. The manoeuvres which Freud makes to meet this demand demonstrate that it is one he himself implicitly accepts.

V

In what respects are Freud's theories held to fail by this standard and thus to forfeit their scientific status? Popper himself illustrates his criterion of falsifiability by applying it first to such acknowledged pseudo-sciences as astrology and alchemy. He then goes on, more audaciously, to apply it, with condemnatory results, to the doctrines of Marx and Freud. In Freud's case he does not go into much detail. His argument turns principally on the familiar Freudian tactic of disparaging hostile criticism of psychoanalysis as being nothing more than the expression of emotional resistance to it. There is, indeed, a certain intellectual vulgarity about this type of polemical stratagem, which is more at home in domestic quarrels and knockabout debates on social occasions than in controversy about serious and carefully formulated opinions. It is also an invalid argument, for reasons that have already been touched on. The emotional hostility of a critic is no guarantee of the invalidity of his criticism. It is also not much of a ground for even suspecting it. If passionate involvement may blind the critic to the good arguments in support of the view he opposes, it may also inspire him to seek out good arguments against it. To admit this is perfectly compatible with recognising that a calm desire to discover the truth is more likely than partisan passion to lead to valid reasoning.

The real point here is that the doctrine of resistance is not a central and crucial part of psychoanalytic theory. If it were, Popper would be wholly justified in dismissing psychoanalysis as what he calls a 'reinforced dogmatism', a body of theory which insulates itself against any possibility of refutation by including within itself a thesis about the necessary misguidedness of its critics. That Freud should so often have chosen to resort to this rather low-grade intellectual trick is unfortunate. But his offence is to some extent mitigated by the level of intense critical hostility to which his theories were subjected when they were first expounded and before they became, first, a fashion, and then a more or less habitual persuasion of everyone with more than the humblest educational attainments.

In fact Freud did modify his theories as he went along and, if he did excommunicate a good many of his followers when they dared to dissent from him, some of the modifications he made were at the prompting of critics of his theories other than himself. Perhaps the most important revision of basic doctrine, rather than addition to it, that Freud made was the abandonment of his original view that the traumatic events in infancy that gave rise to his patients' neuroses were actual seductions. Here, it seems, his own common sense was enough to convince him that the statistical mass of parental misbehaviour the theory would imply cannot have actually taken place.

What is interesting about this example is that, in replacing actual seduction by sexual fantasy about a parent as the infantile causal factor lying behind adult neurosis, Freud replaced a conjecture that was hard to falsify with one that is practically unfalsifiable. If the hypothesis is that an adult's neurosis is the result of parental seduction in infancy, there are two good reasons for thinking it will be very hard to refute. The alleged event is remote in time from the neurotic condition it is invoked to explain and its private and shameful nature makes it difficult to verify that it actually occurred. But a seduction is at least a fairly definite historical occurrence, in principle accessible to observation. If, in its place, an infantile *state of mind* is held responsible for the neurosis it becomes practically impossible for there to be any independent check on its having happened. If, as is further suggested, the traumatic desire in the infant is unconscious from the outset, is prevented by repression from ever breaking through into consciousness and is not simply repressed into the unconscious at an early stage, a truly independent check is rendered impossible.

Freud has two answers to this line of criticism, neither of which is, on inspection, very convincing. The first is that the neurotic patient can be got to 'recall' the long-repressed desire in question. But, in the first place, there are good reasons for distrusting memory-claims that reach back to such a very early stage of life. Furthermore, the supposed recollection is always prompted by the analyst, trying out his interpretation on the patient's symptoms. The second is that the Freudian hypothesis about the character of the feelings young children have about their parents can be established by the direct observation of children's behaviour. To the extent that this observation reveals such desires, as it is held to, in nearly all children, the unfortunate consequence ensues that either the desires are not necessary conditions of neurosis in adult life or that most adults are neurotic, a proposition that has the near self-contradictory character of the thesis that nearly everyone is much taller than the average. Freud sidesteps this difficulty by invoking further untestable factors: the quantitative strength of the desires involved, for which no technique of measurement is suggested, and the inherited constitution of the patient, which is simply a promissory note that no steps are taken to honour and has the effect of turning the originally challenging theory into the vacuity that certain repressed desires, which occur in the majority of human beings, cause neurosis in those who happen to be constitutionally disposed to become neurotic. Here again the contentious issue of interpretation emerges. Freud admits that the desires mentioned by his theory are not to be discovered by straightforward observation of children's behaviour. They are revealed only to the true believers who know how to interpret the seemingly innocuous conduct of the very young.

So even if Popper rests too much weight on the pseudo-scientific character of the doctrine of resistance the point he is making remains untouched. The item on which he fastens is representative of a vast array of refutation-avoiding devices which permeate Freud's writings. Besides the examples I have given there should be mentioned the extension of terms, conspicuously 'sexuality', well beyond the limits of their conventional application, a linguistic reform misrepresented as a discovery. Then there is the practice of taking the contrary of what the theory predicts as being as much a confirmation of the theory as its originally predicted opposite. A man's strict upbringing should have made him aggressive towards his father. If he turns out to be notably polite to him that is just as good for Freud: politeness is simply the brilliant disguise the unconscious puts on to conceal its actual aggressiveness. There is no room here to follow the tactics Freud uses to preserve his theories from any possibility of empirical falsification in any greater detail. There is an admirable account of them in Cioffi's essay 'Freud and the Idea of a Pseudo-Science' in *Explanation in the Behavioural Sciences* (ed. Borger and Cioffii, Cambridge, 1970).

Before leaving the subject of the unfalsifiable and thus pseudo-scientific nature of psychoanalytic theory a word should be said about a practical test of its efficacy, if not of its descriptive truth, on which its exponents rely – that of therapeutic success. Because of the difficulty of defining the notions of neurosis and of cure with sufficient precision for definite statistics to be assembled this is an issue that is hard to resolve decisively. But it does appear that the condition of neurotic patients is not changed for the better in a significantly higher proportion of cases when the patient has been psychoanalysed than when he has been treated by an ordinary medical practitioner or even than when he has been left to cope with his problem on his own. But even if psychoanalytically treated patients did get better significantly more often than others, it is as likely that the mere fact that someone took a protracted and sympathetic interest in their condition is responsible for the improvement as that the psychoanalytic beliefs of the therapist had anything to do with it.

VI

Finally I want to comment briefly on two points at which the philosophy of Wittgenstein comes into direct contact with the doctrines of Freud. Wittgenstein agreed that psychoanalytic theory is not a science, though more because of his view that human thought and action cannot be causally explained than because of its unfalsifiability. But he was not content to leave the matter negatively there and to remit psychoanalysis, by implication, to the same intellectual Alasatia as homoeopathic medicine, numerology and measurements of the Great Pyramid. He freely acknowledged what he called its 'charm' and thought that it was possible to explain why generally sophisticated and unsuperstitious people should endorse it. He makes two suggestive points in this connection. The first is that, far from outraging and shocking people, the emphasis of Freudian theory on the ultimately sexual source of mental energies and the actions in which they are expressed is for many agreeable and exciting. (Freud himself was prepared to admit this at times.) Secondly, the idea of the unconscious going with one everywhere, with all its hidden power and wisdom, was a comforting thought in a generally hostile and obdurate world, paralleling the common childhood fantasy of an invisible companion or guardian angel.

He went on to say that Freud was not a scientist but something quite different, the proposer of a 'new notation', a new and poetically exciting way of describing familiar things. This does seem applicable to the Freudian technique of extending the range of application of terms like sexuality. There is, after all, a certain analogy between a child's affection for his mother and the literally sexual devotions of adult life. But this account of the 'real nature' of Freud's work is remote from any intention it would be reasonable to ascribe to Freud. At best it is an explanation of the charm that Wittgenstein finds in his ideas. In either case it is somewhat faint praise and was surely meant as such.

That suggests that the enthusiastic development of a more or less parenthetical comparison Wittgenstein made of his method in philosophy with psychoanalytic therapy, a development found in its most opulent form in the work of Lazerowitz, is something that he would not have endorsed. The basis of the comparison is that Wittgenstein does not take traditional philosophical problems at their face value, any more than Freud took neurotic symptoms. Rightly interpreted, the ancient problems of philosophy are simply puzzles, states of conceptual bewilderment brought about by unconsciously perceived, but nevertheless mistaken, linguistic analogies. The relief of these puzzled states has something in common with Freudian therapy. It consists in lengthily talking out the problem until the patient recognises the hidden spurious analogy that misled him. Lazerowitz takes this modest, and perhaps even playful, comparison and blows it up into a full-fledged theory about the nature of philosophy. The theory is that traditional philosophical doctrines are really disguised linguistic proposals, and not the assertions about the nature of the world that they outwardly seem, and are taken by their exponents, to be. He then goes on to maintain, not that the proper way of handling such expressions of conceptual puzzlement is *like* psychoanalytic therapy, but that these doctrines or unconscious proposals are literal neurotic symptoms in Freud's sense and should be treated accordingly.

This position has a noticeable power to infuriate philosophers. Those who keep their heads soon perceive that few arguments have ever more compellingly invited a *tu quoque* retort than Lazerowitz's disguised linguistic proposal to redescribe philosophical theories as disguised linguistic proposals. A measure of wholesome fun can be had by trying to work out precisely what neurosis of its propounder it symptomatically expresses.

23

The Von Richthofen Sisters

On the mauve dust-jacket of *The Von Richthofen Sisters* by Martin Green (London, 1974), a large and sumptuous volume, American in its wide margins and deckle-edged pages (in everything, indeed, but the publisher's name and the price) there are photographs of the two sisters with whom it is ostensibly and initially concerned. On the left is the well-known Frieda, wife of Professor Weekley and then D.H. Lawrence; on the right the much less familiar Else, wife of one Edgar Jaffé and mistress, if Mr Green has got it right, first of Max Weber and, after his death and for a much longer period, of his somewhat resentful rival and younger brother, Alfred.

Else here looks very much like an ardent and high-minded au pair girl. 'How very interesting,' she seems to be saying to herself, 'that the Herr Doktor should take time to show me his etchings when his wife is away.' Frieda looks more like her mother, fresh and indignant off the Lufthansa plane from Stuttgart, shoulders squared and bosom thrust forward, after some such remark as 'This is not, I think, a household-situation which is, for my daughter, fundamentally acceptable'. The implications of this pair of photographs are doubly misleading: temporally, in that Else (born 1874) was five years older than Frieda, and temperamentally, in that Else certainly appeared to be, and, on the whole was, an altogether more bourgeois and respectable person than her sister.

There are, of course, two kinds of people in the world: those who are convinced that there are two kinds of people in the world and those who are not. Martin Green is very much a member of the former party. *The Von Richthofen Sisters* is only vestigially a biography of its two explicit subjects. In it they are used, rather, as jumping-off points for an elaborate exercise in pattern-making and the exploration of parallels. The sisters were both drawn into the fringes of the erotic movement in Germany at the turn of the century by Otto Gross, one of its more excessive leaders. Both resisted total immersion in it by marrying mousy men of an academic type, with stiff collars and rather dismal moustaches: the economist Edgar Jaffé and the philologist Ernest Weekley. In both cases this recoil to the conventional proved too much. Else had a fairly spiritual, on-and-off, affair with Max Weber; Frieda ran away with D.H. Lawrence. Deprived of these great men by death, the sisters settled down with appropriately divergent long-term partners: Else with Max's irritable, industrious brother Alfred, Frieda, after a whirl with John Middleton Murry, with the uncomplicatedly physical Angelo Ravagli.

But these personal details are very much less than the half of it. The accident of their amorous involvement with the two sisters is a pretext for a comparison of the ideas and influence of Weber and Lawrence, who are taken to represent the prime sources of the two great intellectual forces of the age: the criticism-cum-*Weltanschauung* of F.R. Leavis and the functionalist sociology of Talcott Parsons, a new modulation of the 'two cultures' controversy which Mr Green has already discussed, in an idiosyncratically autobiographical way, in his *Science and the Shabby Curate of Poetry*. Objectivity and the analytic intellect are now represented, in a more potent and less provincial form, by Weber rather than Lord Snow.

Else and Frieda grew up in a military and minor aristocratic household. Their father, a fairly conventional Prussian officer, invalided by wounds into the position of an engineer, took second place in the family to the vigorous, impulsive, 'life-affirming' mother. Else, a serious, intellectual girl, became a factory inspector. In 1899 Frieda, aged seventeen, married Weekley. Else married Jaffé in 1902. The year after, Frieda Schloffer, a school-friend of Else's, married the bizarre Otto Gross. He was the son of Hans Gross, author of *Criminal Investigation* (a work much relied on, Mr Green points out, by Inspectors Maigret and Ghote), a kind of intellectualised equivalent of De Maistre's *bourreau*, the consummate symbol of repressive patriarchal authority. The same at home as in print, in Otto he got the son he clinically deserved.

Otto was an extreme sexual libertarian in theory and practice, a cocaine addict and a social revolutionary. His father managed to get him locked up in an asylum on one of the two occasions when he had provided unhappy mistresses with the means of killing themselves. After the collapse of the short-lived communist regime in Munich he fled to Berlin where he died from the effects of starvation, having hidden in a warehouse, enraged by the refusal of his friends to procure drugs for him by violence. During the first decade of the century he seems to have been at his best. He had an affair with Else around 1906 and with Frieda, Mr Green believes, some time between 1907 and 1910. Else had dropped him for an old flame who personified 'the democratic principle' and he tried unsuccessfully to induce Frieda to leave Weekley and fill the vacant position. But she stayed with Weekley until 1912 when she ran away with Lawrence.

Otto Gross was in the forefront of all the more extreme movements of his age. He started out as a pretty wild Freudian, moved from that to the *kosmische Runde*, a group of intellectuals in the Munich suburb of Schwabing, impressed by the matriarchalism of Bachofen and whose leading spirit was the *Lebensphilosoph* Klages (Stefan George was loosely associated with the group). In 1907 Gross became the father of two sons called Peter, one by his wife, the other by Else, thus exciting Mr Green's appetite for parallels. But he was not a simple womaniser. He was sympathetically indulgent to his wife's affair with one Frick (with whom, indeed, he provided her) and he took Regina Ullman as his mistress despite the fact that 'she squinted and stuttered and her nose was misshapen' (although he abandoned her when she became pregnant by him).

The sisters, then, were profoundly affected by Gross, although neither became his disciple. Each of them is seen by Mr Green as working out a less hectic and frenzied version than Gross's of the general theme of transforming the patriarchal world of men, obsessed with discipline and authority, into a world in which the characteristically feminine values of love and pleasure would be dominant. In Frieda's case this was a straightforward matter. Like other *magnae matres* of the time (Mr Green discusses Alma Mahler, Isadora Duncan, Lou Andreas-Salome and Mabel Dodge Luhan) she sought to enhance life by erotic love through attachment to men of a fairly feminine and unbrutal kind, who could be effectively unfrozen. Lawrence, Mr Green says, 'was more of a flirt than anything else'. (In the same way Alma Mahler got on much better with Mahler and Werfel than she did with the uncompromisingly masculine Kokoschka and Gropius.) Else's procedure was more self-effacing and elusive, although she was no conventional bundle of warrior's mindless home comfort. She served as a sensitive helpmeet to the two Weber brothers. Neither sister, it should be emphasised, had any leaning toward the Lesbian aggressiveness of current Women's Liberation. They aimed, respectively, to transform men by enveloping love and to complement them. Neither sought to supplant or suppress them, nor, *a fortiori*, to do without them.

As long as the two sisters are at the centre of attention all is well. Their early lives are illuminatingly representative of the German version of the general movement for personal emancipation among the post-Ibsen European intelligentsia and they came into contact with a lot of interesting people. The fact that they were sisters is relevant. The family was socially elevated enough to have the opportunity for this kind of experimentation, and in its inner structure of an ineffective soldier father dominated by a *magna mater*-ish mother it was pointed emotionally in the appropriate direction. Heredity, no doubt, supplied them with the looks and stamina, early environment with the boldness and self-confidence that they needed for their culturally innovative task.

It is with the shifting of the centre of gravity to Lawrence and Max Weber, their two major love-objects, that the nature of Mr Green's enterprise becomes baffling. Even if Lawrence and Weber were the really influential culture-heroes of the century it would still be an accident that they happened to be involved with two women who were sisters. Mr Green's devotion to patterns inevitably implies that the patterns he elicits are somehow significant. But, to start with, the two involvements were of extremely different intensity. Lawrence spent the last eighteen years of his life with Frieda in a continuous relationship of the utmost closeness. Max Weber and Else were seldom alone together for long and Mr Green does not claim to have proof that they were more than 'good friends'. Else was a close friend of Weber's wife Marianne.

Furthermore, the very different kinds of work for which Lawrence and Weber are important offered very different opportunities for the influence of a woman companion. Imaginative fiction is going to be much more responsive to the texture of its creator's intimate personal life than large-scale theoretical sociology. So not only was Else's relationship with Weber too fitful and limited to affect him much, it could affect him only as a personality and not in the scholarly activity for which he is chiefly important. Mr Green, to establish his parallel, has to concentrate on Weber the man. Now Weber the man was something substantial and something quite distinct from Weber the scholar, a point he memorably insisted on himself in his essays on politics and science as vocations. He saw the two callings as alien almost to the point of incompatibility and was torn between them. But it is Weber the sociologist who is a force in the world today. In a close-printed epilogue of forty-five pages Mr Green argues persuasively that Lawrence's involvement with Frieda had a great influence on him, by bringing him into the Richthofen family, by exposing him to the emancipative eroticism of the Schwabing circle, by her own participation in his work as a writer. There could be no comparable epilogue on the Richthofenian traces in Weber's *Wirtschaft und Gesellschaft*.

The concluding quarter of the main text of the book deals with the spiritual inheritors of Lawrence and Weber. In it Mr Green's love of parallels is at full stretch. Both his heroes he sees as having two principal successors: the first a more or less emotional exploiter of the hero as man, the second a more faithful repeater of the hero's message. The exploiters are Middleton Murry and Jaspers. They do have something in common, at least negatively, since neither is recognisably a disciple of the great men by whom they were preoccupied. But their reactions were utterly different. Murry subjected Lawrence first to malice, in his *Son of Woman*, and then to a mixture of edifying distortion and highly critical reverence. Jaspers paid little attention to Weber the theorist but hero-worshipped him as an exemplar of authenticity in personal conduct. Murry, one feels, was fundamentally ill-disposed to Lawrence, while Jaspers was utterly devoted to Weber the man although entirely impervious to his style of thinking and to the things he thought.

A more direct and objective connection obtains between Lawrence and Weber and their chief living celebrators, neither of whom ever met them: Leavis and Talcott Parsons. But at this point the pursuit of parallels seems to have gone finally off the rails. Parsons has never been a Weberian in the sense that Leavis has been a Lawrentian. There would seem to be nothing in Weber the man to interest Parsons in any way whatever. Furthermore, both these ultimate heirs are too local, being strictly British and American phenomena respectively, and too marginal to the main ideological collisions of the age, in which more central combatants would be Marcuse or Chomsky on one side and Skinner on the other, to bear the heavy load of cultural significance that Mr Green imputes to them.

There is a lot of interesting material in *The Von Richthofen Sisters*, particularly the information Mr Green has to impart about Otto Gross and his milieu, there are several entertaining oddments (for example, Frieda's hearty prescription of sexual intercourse with a young Italian stonemason as a cure for her daughter's depressed feverishness), and some interesting conjectures about the private life of the Weber brothers. Mr Green makes a good case for the beneficially enhancing effect of Frieda on Lawrence's writing, which came into operation midway through *Sons and Lovers* and correlates well with the pronounced difference in quality between *The White Peacock* and *The Trespasser* and everything that came after them.

But this solid stuff is not presented as part of a straightforward life and times of the sisters. In subordination to Mr Green's larger design it is put forward in an irregular and fragmentary fashion. The book's remorseless patterning, its pursuit of elusive similarities, analogies and coincidences, overrides historic detail in the attempt to impart some vital, but never explicitly stated, significance in the history of ideas to the pure accident that two important figures, in very different parts of that history, happened, at about the same time, to be emotionally involved, to very different extents, with two sisters, one of whom was indeed remarkable, but the other of whom was surely not.

24

The Frankfurt School

It is a commonplace that the Marxist faith shows a marked similarity of structure to the Christian religion. The dialectic is God, Marx is his, or its, prophet, the revolution is the Last Judgment, and the classless society is the Promised Land. If the history of the two creeds is compared some further suggestive parallels emerge. Both began as the beliefs of small and unimportant-looking millenarian groups: the Disciples and the International Working Men's Association. The evident failure of the millennium to arrive led to accommodations with reality: the Roman Catholic Church and Soviet Communism. The corruption of these accommodating strategies, their exploitations and inquisitions, inspired passionate reforming impulses of a backward-looking kind: the Protestant Reformation and the idealist and humanist revisions of Marxism which have developed since 1917.

It is reasonable to date the Marxist reformation from the publication in 1923 of *History and Class-Consciousness* by Lukács, who may be regarded as the Wycliffe of the movement since, despite all his heresies, he died in the faith. From him has stemmed a body of less compromising Lollards, most notably the critical theorists of the Frankfurt school. Their Institution for Social Research was founded at Frankfurt in the year in which Lukács' book was published. In the Hitler years they moved physically, if not altogether spiritually, to the United States. At the end of the 1950s the leading figures returned, in something like glory, to Frankfurt. Since then a second generation of critical theorists has emerged under Habermas and has come to occupy a commanding place in the social thought of the *Bundesrepublik*. More recently still, as a thoughtful reaction to the anarchic extravagances of the student rebellion of the late 1960s, critical theory has received both attention and adherence in the United States, where Marcuse, one of its leading original exponents, had been the half-gratified, half-reluctant object of a cult in the period of turmoil.

On the whole it has been hard for British readers to gain a balanced and comprehensive view of this most intellectually serious and articulate version of neo-Marxism. For the most part the writings of its exponents have been locked up in comparatively inaccessible publications in German. Those that have been translated, notably works by Adorno and Habermas, have not, one might say, been translated far enough. Many of their works are now available in (mostly) English words, but the structure of their thinking remains too cryptically Teutonic and Hegelian to secure entry into the British mind. To get into a position where it is reasonable to think one has really grasped what they are trying to say, it has been necessary to wait for people brought up to speak and think in English to undertake the stern labour of interpretation.

During the last years of his life George Lichtheim was the most conspicuous supporter of the Critical Theorists in this country. In numerous articles, particularly reviews in the *Times Literary Supplement* of German republications of the classics of critical theory, now collected in his *From Marx to Hegel* (London, 1971), he heaped scorn on the inveterate empiricism and positivism of English-speaking social theory and praise on its German critics. But it was difficult to tell from his knowing but enigmatic allusions just what it was that was being argued by the critical theorists and what was to be put in place of the despised social theory of positivism. More light, at least on the sources of the doctrine, was available from Lichtheim's little book on Lukács and from Alasdair MacIntyre's somewhat one-dimensionally critical book in the same series on Marcuse. But for more systematic discussion of critical theory we have had to wait until the last few months.

Two fairly cursory survey volumes are now available which serve admirably to locate the Frankfurt school in the general development of Marxian thought since Marx. The first of these, Peter Hamilton's *Knowledge and Social Structure* (London, 1974), which is sympathetic without being rigidly partisan, is really an account of the sociology of knowledge, of the idea that sociological explanations can be provided for the social doctrines people hold, from its beginnings with Vico and Montesquieu through to the phenomenological sociology of Alfred Schutz. But it contains in its first half, which deals with Hegel, Marx, Lukács, the Frankfurt school and Lucien Goldmann, a lucid, if somewhat inelegantly written account of what may be called the intellectual resistance to the mechanisation of Marxism in theory and practice. On the level of theory this mechanisation is ordinarily attributed to Engels and consists of the view that consciousness, thought, or theorisation is merely epiphenomenal, a dependent by-product of autonomous processes at work in the material base of society. On this view proletarian class-consciousness is the direct result of the exploitation of workers by a capitalism that brings them explosively together in great masses in its factories. It seems to imply that Marxist theorising itself plays no crucial part in the historical process it describes. Marx himself skirted round this issue by saying that knowledge of Marxist theory could help men to ease the birth-pangs of the new classless order that was inevitably coming anyway.

On the level of practice, mechanisation took the form of the Leninist doctrine which made the Party the sole and unquestionable repository of true knowledge and required absolute obedience to its decisions. Lenin allowed in principle for free critical discussion before the moment of decision. But, as it worked out, the leader of the Party became a transcendent oracle, so that the main intellectual task of his subordinates became that of working out in advance what he was going to decide so as to keep out of trouble.

Lukács' essential claim was that the proletariat would not automatically develop the sort of class-consciousness that would inspire them to the kind of revolution Marx had in mind. Such a consciousness had to be 'imputed' to them, in effect by enlightened Marxist intellectuals, presumably organised in the vanguard party. As the error underlying mechanisation, Lukács identified *reification*, an idea derived by generalisation from the concept of fetishism in Marx's critique of classic political economy. Classical economics, according to Marx, was a form of ideological false consciousness. It erroneously attributed the status of substantial things to capital and to abstract labour conceived as a commodity, when these in fact were human activities. Just the same error, but on a larger scale, is present in mechanistic Marxism, which reifies or fetishises the material base of society. In consequence theory is mistakenly sundered from practice; it is represented as a dependent outcome of practice and not, as it should be, as dialectically interacting with it.

Lukács, who chose to remain in the Soviet orbit after the collapse of Bela Kun's communist republic, was constrained to recant his heresies. But they were kept alive by Max Horkheimer and the critical theorists of the Frankfurt school, whose freedom of thought and expression remained unimpeded, first in the Weimar Republic and then, after Hitler, in the United States. Where Lukács had been inspired by the incompatibility of the authoritarian party (creator of the NEP and pursuer of crudely, unculturedly economic goals) with the freedom of the intellect, the chief impetus to the Frankfurt school was the more general failure of Marx's prediction to be realised. The Leninist party could be seen as an outcome of the fact that there was hardly enough of a proletariat in Russia to make a revolution. Outside Russia, in societies where there really were industrial proletarian masses, the proletariat had evidently failed to develop a revolutionary class-consciousness. A new bearer of revolutionary consciousness had to be found. It turned out to be that old hero of the tradition of German idealism: Reason – a somewhat reified or fetishised name for Marxist intellectuals who took seriously the Hegelian elements in Marx.

The story that Peter Hamilton tells from the standpoint of the sociology of knowledge is also to be found in Neil McInnes's *The Western Marxists* (London, 1972), an account of the 'remystification of Marx', which covers Sorel, Gramsci, Korsch and the more anarchic and romantic elements of the New Left as well as Lukács and the Frankfurt school. Where Hamilton is clearly sympathetic to the movement of thought he discusses, McInnes is not, but he takes it seriously enough to have studied it thoroughly. He is an Australian and, I should judge from certain turns of phrase and thought, a pupil of John Anderson, the remarkable and influential Sydney philosopher, who in the inter-War years incorporated Marx and Freud into more traditional philosophy (the latter being represented in his case by the naturalistic metaphysician Samuel Alexander, rather than Hegel, whom the critical theorists recruited for the same task).

These features of his background give him three advantages. First, like all Andersonians, he writes with force, lucidity and economy. Secondly, unlike the analytic philosophers of Britain and America, he is quite familiar with, and finds nothing odd in, the idea that there is such a thing as social philosophy and that the views of Marx and Freud should be part of it. Thirdly, and more elusively, there is none of that slight bourgeois embarrassment that affects the dealings of Anglo-American philosophers, such as they are, with Marxism, an anxiety occasioned by the brutal character and content of Marxian polemics and that expresses itself either in the form of abstract scholarly civility, as of an old-fashioned social worker in a slum district, or (at the opposite extreme) in the form of rhetorical bluster which shifts attention from the theoretical matters at issue to the enormities of Stalin and the KGB. It is as if, being Australian, he is not made nervous by references to things like social class and hunger.

Covering a wider field of Marxist thinking than Hamilton, he considers the critical theorists' application of Freud, in which they see capitalism as a spiritual repressor in addition to being a material oppressor. He interprets Lukács' view that art and other products of high culture can transcend history and society as revealing that his fundamental hostility is not so much to capitalism as to industry itself. He maintains his clarity and poise as he follows the course of ever more hyperbolical Hegelianisation in Lukács and the Frankfurt school, through which the ideal proletariat becomes the 'subject-object' of history, a new interpretation of Hegel's Absolute Spirit, and is taken to be accessible only to dialectical metaphysics, with the consequence that science and logic are rejected as mere reifications or fetishes.

In general, McInnes sees the neo-Marxists as swallowing Weber's social identification of science and logic with economic rationality. Agreeing that economic rationality, particularly as confined for its ends to the growth of production, is not the only kind of rationality, he sensibly observes that that does not imply that it is not rational at all. Narrowly economic ends must take their place in competition with other ends and science and logic are relevant to the pursuit of any of them; they are not essentially tied to the narrowly economic.

So much for the general picture. We may now turn to more specific consideration of the critical theory of the Frankfurt school. There could be no better introduction to the history of the movement than Martin Jay's *The Dialectical Imagination* (Boston, Mass. and London, 1973) which covers the period from its foundation in 1923 to its reinstallation in Frankfurt around 1950. It is hard to see how this could have been better done. Jay has not merely read the works of the critical theorists and studied the public surface of the movement's life. On the one hand, he shows a masterly apprehension of their sources and contemporaries in central European social thought; on the other, he has gone deeply enough into the minor empirical detail of his subject of study to relieve and illuminate his account with a well-deployed accumulation of more personal and evanescent items, matters of personal tension and friction, the private attitudes of the members of the group to each other, their work and the current state of the world. The result is a brilliantly rounded presentation. It is in no way to qualify my praise of Jay's gifts and the use he has made of them to say that he perhaps chose an ideal moment to carry out his project. At the time he set about it the main figures were alive and available for interviews, and correspondence and their private papers were not lost or dispersed, while they were old enough not to mind use being made of them. This is a magnificently authoritative piece of work, which, and this is not a left-handed compliment, will not need to be done again.

Jay is plainly sympathetic to the doctrines of the Frankfurt school. In the introduction he asks how intellectuals critical of society can avoid having their protest embraced and absorbed by the culture they are protesting against, illustrating the point by the taming of the avant-garde, existentialism, and the counter-culture. The implication is that the theoretical seriousness of Critical Theory has preserved it from a comparable trivialisation. But in the main body of the book he is a self-effacingly neutral recorder, a position somewhat at odds with that of the movement he admires and has so devotedly studied.

The story begins with the endowment by Felix Weil, a rich young businessman with interests in South America, or, more precisely, by his father, of an Institute of Social Research, attached to the University of Frankfurt. From the beginning both administrative and intellectual leadership were centred in Max Horkheimer, although he did not become the official director until 1930, after two more senior and established people had held the post. Of the major figures associated with the group Horkheimer is probably the least well known. He is by far the least copious writer among them. His one book in English, *Eclipse of Reason*, came out in 1944 and made little impact. This was largely due to the Aesopian caution of the Frankfurt school in America. In order not to provoke their American sponsors, such as Columbia University and the American Jewish Committee, their commitment to Marxism, idiosyncratic and wholly free of party taint though it was, was concealed by the wrapping of Marxian thoughts in liberal-democratic verbiage. Thus an Oxford philosopher of broadly Hegelian sympathies could review *Eclipse of Reason* as if it were an unusually brief series of Gifford lectures by a professor in Scotland.

Horkheimer's main writings were articles in the Institute's journal: the *Zeitschrift für Sozialforschung*, since collected in two German volumes as *Kritische Theorie*. When, as announced, they come out in English, Horkheimer's central position should be easier to understand. The chief original members of the group, besides him, were Friedrich Pollock, an economist who attributed the capacity of capitalism to survive the depression to its transformation into a new form of state capitalism; and Theodor Wiesengrund-Adorno, student of Husserl, Kierkegaard, musicology, consultant to Thomas Mann on the composition of Mann's *Dr Faustus*, the most pyrotechnically highbrow and, it must be said, unintelligible of the group.

In due course other recruits joined. Herbert Marcuse, whose *Reason and Revolution* of 1941 was the first, and for a long time the only, book by a member of the group to be widely noticed in the English-speaking world, and who developed the theme of capitalist civilisation as a repressor of men, an obstruction to possible happiness; Leo Löwenthal, student of mass culture and the sociology of literature; Franz Borkenau, who was led by his experiences in Spain into becoming the most learned and passionate exposer of organised international communism; Franz Neumann, whose *Behemoth* was the first theoretically serious major interpretation of the social system of Nazism; Erich Fromm, the Freudian revisionist; Walter Benjamin, the literary theorist; and finally, the only gentile among the school's leading members, Karl Wittfogel, the theorist of Oriental Despotism. All of these but Marcuse and Löwenthal were fairly loosely committed to Horkheimer's principles and in various ways drifted away from association with the school.

During the period covered by Jay's study the members of the Institute were active over an impressively wide range of fields. While Horkheimer concentrated on fundamental issues of theory and method, Adorno worked on music and mass culture; Marcuse on the psychological, utopian dimension of neo-Marxian hopes and on the deformations of Marxism in the theory and practice of the Soviet Union; Löwenthal on Dostoevsky, Ibsen and Knut Hamsun; Borkenau on the transition from feudalism to capitalism; Neumann on Nazism as the last stage of capitalism; Fromm on the repressive patriarchal attitude of Freud; Wittfogel on the 'hydraulic societies' of Asia; Pollock on the forms of late capitalism.

In 1934 the Institute re-established itself in New York, under the protective wing of Columbia University, after a short stay in Geneva, but the bulk of its output, and, in particular, the *Zeitschrift*, continued to be published in German. After 1940 this linguistic isolation came to an end. In its new, English-speaking, form the work of the Institute took on a more cautious, conventionally liberal-democratic tone, appropriate to its somewhat precarious status in exile. A further element of Americanisation was its involvement in collective projects of a broadly empirical nature. First, there were its studies of anti-Semitic prejudice, in which the school's leaning towards theory was shown in the rejection of the simple questionnaire technique, followed by naive American sociology, for a method of interpretative interviewing. Then, after Adorno had followed Horkheimer to California (he went there for reasons of health), there was the massive inquiry which issued in the six volumes of *The Authoritarian Personality*, a study of rigid, aggressive conformism, anticipating the informal concept of current, everyday social thinking of the 'hard hat'.

It was not only language that isolated the school from their environment in exile. There was also their money, which enabled them to keep themselves institutionally to themselves. With commendable prescience they had got their endowment from the Weil family out of Germany at the time the Nazis were coming to power. The calls on it were heavy after 1940 and many members of the school found themselves in service to the US government. But an independent nucleus was always preserved.

There was one group of American, perhaps one should say New York, intellectuals at the height of their powers and cohesion in the 1940s with whom the members of the Frankfurt school in exile had a large affinity of interests and with whom, had they not been so self-enclosed, they might have communicated fruitfully. The circle associated with *Partisan Review*, edited by

Philip Rahv and William Phillips, had a very Horkheimerian constellation of interests: Marx, Freud and avant-garde art and literature. Both groups had been driven from orthodox, Moscow-defined Marxism by the degradation of Stalinist tyranny, its ossification of thought, its enslavement of art and literature to propaganda, its maniacal vilification of everything in contemporary culture, from Freud to surrealism, that was not an obvious instrument for the immediate purposes of Russian state power. But, philosophically, the *Partisan Review* circle were attached to the reigning New York liberal philosophy, Dewey's socially concerned pragmatism, which saw science, not as an obscurantist fetish, but as man's best resource for liberation and progress.

Horkheimer was aware of *Partisan Review*. A reference to it in his *Eclipse of Reason* is one of the small signs that show it not to be a work of more or less traditional Hegelian piety about the capacity of reason to establish ends and not merely to find means for them. But it is a critical reference, a rejection of the view that current hostility to science expressed what Sidney Hook called 'a new failure of nerve'.

After the War was over the Frankfurt school looked back to Europe and in 1949 Horkheimer, Adorno and Pollock returned to Frankfurt itself, where Horkheimer became rector of the university some years later, although Marcuse and Löwenthal remained in the United States. Their main concern in this later period was what they saw as the skill of late capitalism in the manipulation of men, the erosion by various means – in particular by deluging people with commodities which the culture industry worked to convince them they really wanted – of individual, critical, protesting thought. But, when radical students did protest, in the interests of a liberation that went far beyond release from economic exploitation, their response was unenthusiastic. The dominant style of student radicalism, its barbaric irrationality and destructiveness, its pursuit of instant, infantile gratifications, was repulsive to them.

The conflict was symbolised by the notorious occasion when students disrupted a lecture of Adorno's by getting a naked girl to go up and display herself to him at the rostrum. As Jay observes, 'the Institute's members may have been relentless in their hostility towards the capitalist system but they never abandoned the life-style of the *haute bourgeoisie*'. One feature of that life-style was a conception of the university as sacred ground. But it could be said that the Frankfurt school had brought it on themselves, by their attacks on the 'instrumental reason' which it is the prime activity of universities to exercise and develop, and their view that a full realisation of the utopian possibilities available to man involved the fundamental liberation of primary, Freudian instincts.

Since the retirement and death of most of the leading figures in the first generation of the school their work has been vigorously continued by others, most notably Jürgen Habermas and his pupil, Albrecht Wellmer. Habermas is as obscure a writer as Adorno, although his inscrutability is of a different kind. Adorno's writing is wild, rhapsodic and sibylline, the sort of tumultuous free association of ideas that might be encountered at a very highbrow party very late at night (see *Negative Dialectics*, tr. E.B. Ashton, and *The Jargon of Authenticity*, tr. Knut Tarnowski and Frederick Will, London, 1973), Habermas, on the other hand, is a parody of a German professor and writes with a knotted involution beside which the works of Kant seem like the directions on a tin of soup.

Three of his works are available in translation: *Toward a Rational Society, Knowledge and Human Interests* and *Theory and Practice* (Boston, 1970, 1971, 1973). The first of these is a collection of scattered essays, three on universities and the student rebellion, three on the social role of science and technology. The last of them, 'Technology and Science as "Ideology" ', is a more than usually straightforward presentation of the theme that traditional, orthodox Marxism gives an inadequate account of class-conflict and ideology for our scientific and technological age.

He describes *Knowledge and Human Interests* as 'a historically oriented attempt to reconstruct the prehistory of modern positivism'. It starts from Marx and Hegel and takes in Comte, Mach, Peirce, Dilthey, Freud and Nietzsche. The 'positivism' at which it is directed could as well be called scientism, the idea that all true knowledge is scientific in the sense of the natural sciences. The same historical orientation is present in the essays which make up *Theory and Practice*, the bulk of which are reinterpretations of Hegel and Marx.

Habermas brings more to critical theory than an astounding professorial heaviness and density. Where his predecessors had called on Freud for a less crude and nebulous conception of human happiness than Marx's – negatively freedom from economic exploitation, positively a vague notion of doing what one wants to – Habermas sees in the psychoanalytic relation between therapist and patient an illuminating image of the role of the social theorist, who is to render those to whom he speaks autonomous by enabling them to understand their own situation in the social world. Another novelty is the favourable view he takes of the later Wittgenstein: for seeing that aspects of language are rooted in 'forms of life', for seeing philosophy as a procedure for releasing men from bewitchment by language and for arguing that human actions cannot be causally explained in the way that merely natural happenings can be.

A less demanding mode of approach to the most recent developments of Critical Theory is provided by the three connected essays that make up Wellmer's *Critical Theory of Society* (New York, 1971). In the first of them the school's standard objections to positivism are presented, with reference, among others, to Popper and Carnap, who appear, quite recognisably, as theorists and partisans of the 'empirico-analytical' conception of science. The second is an historical excursus which persuasively argues that Marx himself, for all the value of his critique of fetishism and false consciousness, was too much of a positivist, that he treated consciousness too much as an epiphenomenon of material processes and wrongly supposed freedom to be the inevitable outcome of economic necessity. In the course of the essay Wellmer insists, in the anti-Leninist manner of Rosa Luxemburg, that the revolutionary movement must realise social freedom within itself if it is to impart such freedom to society as a whole. In the concluding essay he suggests that Horkheimer's account of Marx as an authentic dialectician is more a critical revision than a straight interpretation of intent. Marx was not, in his view, free from the notion that it is man's purpose to control nature, a notion that leads to the repressive 'denial of nature in men' and to the control of men by more obvious instruments of social domination.

Before I turn to the statement and criticism of the main principles of the critical theory of society there are two other works that I should mention. The first of these is *Aspects of Sociology*, a collective work by the restored Frankfurt Institute for Social Research that first came out in German in 1956 (Boston, 1972). Originally presented as radio broadcasts, it has a fairly high degree of intelligibility, described by Horkheimer and Adorno in their preface as a 'loose, improvisatory character'. The basic principles are first set out: the need for a social theory that is 'critical', not barely descriptive, and that treats society as a totality, drawing on psychology, history and economics, not as an array of reified groups composed of abstract individuals. Depth psychology is called on for investigation of the masses; culture, an ethical and spiritual concept, is contrasted with the atomistic and material notion of civilisation. The second half of the book contains chapters on the fields of the Institute's more empirical research: the sociology of art and music, the family, prejudice and ideology.

Another useful introductory book, although it aims to do more than serve as an introduction, is Trent Schroyer's *The Critique of Domination* (New York, 1973), which has the advantage of up-to-dateness, one of its seven chapters being on Habermas. Schroyer writes with an almost pedestrian lucidity that is a welcome change and he shows a measure of American pragmatism, or perhaps one should say practicality, in firmly relating the elevated generalities of Critical Theory to the actual historical situation of late capitalism in America.

The first two chapters, following a standard, but usefully clear, introduction on 'the need for critical theory', discuss alienation: from culture in Hegel and from work in Marx. Hegel had the better conception of what alienation was, but unlike Marx, no proper understanding of how recognition of it was related to struggle against domination. In the next two chapters the original case of the Frankfurt school against positivist social science is expounded and its further development by Habermas outlined. In the three concluding chapters Schroyer moves off on his own. He maintains that the critical theory of the 'cultural Marxists' must be reunified with original Marxism and that it must stimulate empirical research into 'contemporary domination' if it is to be more than 'an abstract utopian ideal for estranged intellectuals'. In the final chapter the concepts of Critical Theory are brought interpretatively to bear on some of the actual facts, pretty broadly sketched, of present American society.

Schroyer is very much his own man: he has an almost Boy-Scout impatience with what he suggests are the self-indulgences of Marcuse (in pessimism) and of Habermas (in hyper-scholarly refinement). Critical Theory, excited by the inadequacies of orthodox Marxist practice, has, he clearly feels, been used far too much for the evasion or deferment of practice and not enough for the contribution to a more rational and effective practice that he believes it qualified to make. This is critical theory in a generally clean-cut and open-necked form, remote from the respectively lugubrious and rococo involutions of Marcuse and Habermas. The vernal and sanguine activism that leads Schroyer to dissent from them makes him a conveniently incisive recorder of what their views essentially are.

The fundamental doctrine of the Frankfurt school can be summarised in four principles.

(1) *The critique of positivism.* The prevailing positivist or scientistic conception of social science is a form of false consciousness which reifies or fetishises what are really humanly alterable processes, endorses the status quo under a misleading veil of value-neutrality and at once ideologically encourages and supplies the instruments for prevailing varieties of social domination.

(2) *The idea of critical theory.* An adequate social theory must embody a critical exposition of the irrational dominativeness of society as it is, and can do so only by a philosophical apprehension of society as a totality of humanly alterable processes, not as a plurality of reified fetishes, and in a historical, not abstractly timeless way.

(3) *The critique of Marx.* For all the excellence of his synthesis of Hegel and materialism, Marx is defective in supposing, through insufficient emancipation from positivism, that the proletariat will inevitably bring about a revolution that will eliminate alienation and dominance; he treats thought too much as an epiphenomenon; his conception of what men need to be alienated from is too narrowly economic, the causes of human misery and frustration include, but go far beyond, the existing system of property-relations.

(4) *The critique of present society.* Advanced industrial society, in its communist as well as in its late capitalist form, is irrational; in it men are both politically and economically dominated from outside; but, through cultural manipulation, they are lulled into a false acquiescence in their condition at the expense of the real interests of human nature.

How well-founded is the critical theorists' rejection of positivism? It seems to maintain that positivist social science is both false and undesirable. At the outset there is a measure of inconsistency between these two claims. If positivist social science is false how does it manage to supply an effective social technology for the socially dominative purposes it is alleged to endorse? Critical Theorists are far from questioning the instrumental competence of the instrumental reason used by the agencies of domination. It would be more reasonable to say that they exaggerate the extent to which the governments of advanced societies have reduced their citizens to a condition of passive, ideologically narcotised submissiveness.

It is certainly true that most of those who believe that, if there is to be any well-founded social theory, it must be (in the sense objected to) positivistic, are far from dogmatic about its success so far in combining approximation to truth with substantial content. The most intellectually impressive bit of positivist social theory, namely theoretical economics, is abstract, hypothetical and of rather precarious application to the economic facts of life. Where positivist social theory is directly applicable to the facts, as in the more empirical parts of sociology, it seems too often to be a mass of desultory fragments and to be rather trivial and obvious. Theoretical sociology, on the other hand, has all the abstractness of economics without its clarity and definiteness of concepts and without its internal intellectual rigour.

Some light on the claim that positivist social theory is false may be gained from considering the doctrine of Marx that inspired it: namely, that classical political economy is a form of false consciousness. The error of the classical economists, for Marx, is that they, fetishise or reify human processes into substantial things. Against that it may be replied that positivist social theory is generally committed to methodological individualism, the insistence that trans-human social objects (institutions, groups, social systems and movements) are nothing more than individual human beings related to one another and interacting in certain specific ways. The reducibility of social objects was asserted in explicit opposition to the Hegelian doctrine of objective mind, which seems to hold that institutions and so forth transcend the individuals of whom they are apparently composed and that institutions determine men rather than the other way round.

What Marx really seems to have been getting at is a tendency, undoubtedly present in the orthodox economics of his time, not so much to treat abstractions as substantive things, but to treat them as *unalterable* things. The 'iron law of wages' is one pertinent example. Another is Malthus's law of the necessarily greater increase of population than of food supplies. Not only did nineteenth-century positivists assert as categorical necessities what were in fact connections dependent on conditions that were not themselves unalterable; they typically used these in a socially pessimistic way, to prove the impossibility of morally desirable schemes of social reform. But the fact that, in their unconditional form, these laws of immutable necessity have been refuted is something from which positivist students of method have learnt. *If* the population always more than reproduces itself and *if* food supplies always stand in a fixed or decreasing ratio to the amount of labour applied to their production, starvation must follow of necessity. But the *ifs* have to be taken seriously. However reasonable and familiar the suppositions they introduce may be, those suppositions are not themselves necessarily true. It may be added, *ad hominem*, that Marx was very much in the iron laws business himself. In objecting to his notion that socialism is inevitable the Critical Theorists are consistently pointing this out.

Marx may well have been correct in supposing that ideological preferences encouraged nineteenth-century economists to ignore the conditional nature of their predictions of the inevitable outcome of current tendencies. Nevertheless they went wrong, not because they were positivists but because they were bad positivists, led by the emotional attractiveness of not unreasonable assumptions into taking those assumptions to be categorical necessities. Furthermore, the fact that their assumptions were ideologically inspired does not itself show that they were false. Only the empirical facts to which the assumptions refer could do that. What it can do is serve as an explanation of the mistake that they made.

Positivists, then, are, if anything, less given to reification of non-human social objects than Hegelians. The allegedly mistaken consequence of reification – that of treating social laws as categorically and unalterably necessary – is simply a mistake and no part of positivist method. It is a mistake that may well be caused by ideological preference but, as the example of Marx himself shows, it is one that is not confined to defenders of the status quo. In any case the ideological attractiveness of a belief to a particular person may explain why he believes it, but is in no way a proof of the falsity of the belief and only weak and indirect evidence of its falsity.

The undesirability of positivism is argued by Critical Theorists on the ground that it is an implicit, and to that extent deceptive, kind of propaganda for the status quo. This is more a matter of bare assertion than of argument. Such sketches of argument as appear are far from persuasive.

In their *Dialectic of Enlightenment* Horkheimer and Adorno maintain that a love of fact is somehow psychologically equivalent to a fear of social change. Someone hostile to social change may well be inspired by that feeling to factual inquiry in the hope that it will reveal that the change he dislikes is impossible or will have side-effects that everyone would wish to avoid. But, equally, someone in favour of social change may be induced on that account to seek out the alterable conditions of the state of affairs he deplores so as to set about altering it effectively. Are textbooks of pathology really covert propaganda in favour of disease? If I say that you have egg on your tie am I implicitly praising this eccentric type of ornamentation?

It is, no doubt, true that a possible use to which the findings of positivistic, fact-loving social scientists may be put is the manipulation of the discontented masses for the sake of preserving the status quo. If those findings are, in the straightforward, empirical sense, true they may help to preserve it. But they can just as well be used for the opposite purpose, just as a sub-machine-gun can be used for one purpose by a policeman and for an opposite one by a terrorist or freedom-fighter. Sometimes an increase of knowledge leads to an increased sense of impotence (whether cheerful or melancholy); but sometimes it leads to an increase of power, whether to preserve or to change. In general, Critical Theorists supply no reason whatever for supposing that the exclusive connection they believe to hold between positivism and the defence of the status quo actually obtains.

I am not saying that there is no evidence; only that they do not bother to collect it. The fact that sociologists were involved in 'pacification' programmes in Viet Nam no more proves the point than the fact that Stalin smoked a Dunhill pipe (cf. Djilas: *Conversations with Stalin*) proves that he was really a British agent.

A better case than they make out could be made. Classical economics can be used very readily as an apologetic. It seems to imply that under competitive capitalism, utility is maximised. But there are two large and familiar logical jumps in that inference. In the first place actual capitalism only very distantly realises the conditions of utility-maximisation: it has always been riddled with theoretical 'imperfections', of competitiveness and of knowledge. What is more, the utility realised is of a pretty non-Benthamite kind; it is distorted by the way in which effective demand is distributed. Finally, the whole range of human satisfactions is far from covered by the utilities that enter into the workings of the capitalist market. All the same classical economics does incline to represent the system it analyses as the paradigm of rationality in choice.

It would be relevant to inquire to what extent positivist social theorists have in fact been determined partisans of the status quo. It is often said that the great sociological theorists, enchanted by the complex equilibrium of the social system, are largely conservatives, fearful of radical change. It would be more correct to say that they were pessimists. But so might any student of the outcome of revolutions come to be. And pessimism is far from peculiar to positivists. It is poignantly present in the later writings of the old guard of the Frankfurt school, particularly Marcuse and Adorno.

Adorno somewhere compares the positivists' outlawing of speculation to the prohibition of liquor, as leading only to more and worse of what it aimed to prevent. There is a comic element to the comparison, which a sociologist of knowledge might impute to the fact that Adorno's father was a wine-merchant. Drunkenness is, after all, a social problem. The swilling of Hegel is not always a very beneficial undertaking. If he is a critical theorist then Critical Theory can certainly endorse the status quo as much as positivism is alleged to.

There is neither space nor need to consider the other three principles at any length. The weaknesses of Critical Theory are plainly implied by the deficiencies of its exponents' attack on positivism. What it amounts to, in concrete terms, is some exceedingly dubious, abstract and unargued methodology at one extreme; some questionably empirical, even if quite suggestive, research on comparatively detailed issues (such as the decline of the family and anti-Semitic prejudice) at the other, and, in between, a body of vigorous and interesting cultural criticism.

This last element is what really counts. The ideas of the Critical Theorists about mass culture as a manipulative device for the containment of social discontent – or about the need for a broadly psychoanalytical supplement to the Marxist conception of human fulfilment – carry out, in heavy philosophical and sociological disguise, the sort of task performed by Matthew Arnold in the nineteenth century and George Orwell in this one. It might be said that the intensification of the intellectual division of labour has undermined the business of cultural criticism. Academics abstain from it because of a positivistic conviction that they should stick to their professional lasts. Literary intellectuals, intimidated by academics, either avoid it or go in, like Norman Mailer, for extravagant, subjective gesturing. So it could be said that the thick crust of philosophico-sociological word-play in which the members of the Frankfurt school wrap their more penetrating thoughts is simply a protective device. If there is anything in this idea, it must seem that with Habermas the pie is nearly all crust and no filling.

The Frankfurt school's critique of Marx is reasonable enough, but it does not depend logically on their more abstract philosophical doctrines. Many would agree that a liberating revolution is not inevitable, that ideas have a real social influence, and that Marx's conception of human fulfilment is limited, hopelessly indeterminate in its positive aspects, and utopian in a bad, wishful-thinking, sense of the word. But such agreement does not extend to the assumption that concern with factual truth, a commitment to logic and the rules of evidence, necessarily obstructs an interest in the improvement of the social condition of mankind.

The Critical Theorists contend that contemporary society is irrational. That is entirely acceptable if it means that society can be improved, that many of its institutions do not serve the purposes that men want them to, or do so only at an extravagant cost. But to claim, as they go on to do, that it is uniquely and hyperbolically dominative is surely rhetorical guff. In advanced societies resistance to conformism is at an unprecedented level. It is the subjects of General Amin and Chairman Mao who are really dominated and those tyrants, like Henry VIII and Nicholas I of Russia, have managed to achieve their effects with no reliance whatever on the findings of positivist social theory.

25

McLuhan

Any effort to get a clear view of Marshall McLuhan's doctrines is seriously discouraged by his explicit and repeatedly expressed scorn for old-fashioned, print-oriented, 'linear', rationality. By rejecting as obsolete the humdrum business of setting out definite theses, assembling evidence in support of them, and undermining actual and possible objections, he opts out of the usual argumentative game of truth-seeking, rather in the style of a chess-player who kicks over the table. In this situation ordinary criticism is enfeebled by an uncomfortable suspicion that it is missing the point.

Although he writes books plentifully sprinkled with the familiar vocabulary of linear rationality ('thus', 'therefore', 'it follows', 'it is clear that'), there is, I think, no doubt of McLuhan's seriousness about this negative and seemingly self-destructive commitment. For although his books are recognisably books, for the most part full of moderately grammatical prose, they do deviate in various ways from standard forms of exposition. The two main works look ordinary enough at first. But the chapters of *The Gutenberg Galaxy* are mostly short, have no numbers, and have very long titles. What really enforces one's bewilderment are the not infrequent cases where the title-aphorism has only a very remote connection with the chapter beneath it. The thirty-three chapters of *Understanding Media* do have titles of a familiar, Vance-Packardy sort (e.g., 'Clocks: The Scent of Time' and 'Television: The Timid Giant'); seven of them are about media of communication in general, the rest about twenty-six particular media (or near-media, e.g. clothes). But the content, of the later chapters at any rate, is largely jottings, transferred, it would seem, from the notebook with a minimum of working-over. However dense and organised the prose may look, what it says is connected more by associative leaps than logical linkages. With *The Medium Is the Massage* (with Quentin Fiore, New York, 1967) a rather thin diet of prose is eked out with a great deal of typographic space-wastage and photographic interruptions, in an attempt to produce something nearer the specifications of his theory.

In varying degrees, then, his writings avoid conventional, linear logic and he instructs his readers to approach them in a non-linear way. *The Gutenberg Galaxy*, he says, is a 'mosaic image' not 'a series of views of fixed relationships in pictorial space'. You can, in effect, start anywhere and read in any direction you like. The same spirit is revealed in McLuhan's regular tactic for dealing with objectors. He sees such linear automata as bogged down in a desperate 'unawareness', so dominated by the print medium to which they are bound by habit and professional interest that they are simply not equipped to see what he is getting at.

Quite a good way of arriving at a general idea of what he is up to is provided by *McLuhan: Hot and Cool*, a collection of thirty items mostly about, but a few by, McLuhan, finished off by a thirty-six-page dialogue between McLuhan and the editor (ed. G.E. Stearn, New York 1967). The items about him vary from fairly devotional pieces, among which is a quite astounding architectural meditation in the McLuhan manner by an architect called John M. Johansen, through the slightly nervous display of interest by Tom Wolfe, to the somewhat predictable broadsides of reflex liberal ideology from Dwight Macdonald and Christopher Ricks. These are mostly rather short pieces, and even if the commentators had any inclination to give more than the most cursory survey of McLuhan's ideas (as Kenneth Boulding, a shrewd but amicable objector, clearly has), they have not had the space for it. An interesting feature of this collection is the extent to which people writing about McLuhan tend to be infected by his style, with its fusillade of scriptwriter's pleasantries, rather in the way that one's voice falls to a whisper when one is talking to a sufferer from laryngitis. What the collection lacks is any extended effort to elicit a reasonably definite structure of theory from McLuhan's writings. I should not make this complaint if I did not think the thing could be done. If McLuhan is desultory (as a matter of principle), he is also exceedingly repetitious; not only does the same quite large but wholly manageable body of leading themes recur time and time again in his writings, they are even presented in the same jocular words (he has a grandfatherly indulgence toward his own phrases). What I wish to maintain is that if we ignore his anti-linear instructions, we can easily discern beneath the thin camouflage of his expository idiosyncrasies an articulate theory of society and culture, with all the usual apparatus of first principles, explanatory supplements, and logically derived consequences. What is more, this entirely linear theoretical contraption is of a classic and familiar kind, having a very close formal analogy with the main doctrines of Marx. To speak just once in McLuhanese: he is an academic sheep in Tom Wolfe's clothing.

The fundamental principle of McLuhan's system is a theory of the main determinant of historical change in society, culture, and the human individual. Such changes according to this system are all ultimately caused by changes in the prevailing or predominating medium of human communication. McLuhan got this idea from the later works of the Canadian economic historian Harold A. Innis, but what the teacher used vertiginously enough, as an interpretative clue, the pupil asserts, with only the most occasional and perfunctory qualification, as the basic truth about causation in history. The main evidence for this proposition is provided in *The Gutenberg Galaxy* in which a vast array of disparate works is ransacked for quotations (they must make up half the book) describing the social and cultural effects of the invention of printing. Print, he tells us, *created* (that is his usual word in this connection) individualism, privacy, specialisation, detachment, mass-production, nationalism, militarism, the dissociation of sensibility, etc., etc.

The connection between cause and effect affirmed in the fundamental principle is explained by the doctrine of 'sense-ratio', which McLuhan derived, it appears, from the work of Father Walter J. Ong. McLuhan associates different historical periods or cultural situations with different balances of emphasis in the communicative and mental life of human beings as between the various senses. Tribal man, with his oral culture, was a conventional being who heard, smelt, and felt the people he was in communication with. Gutenberg man acquires information through focusing his eyes on clearly printed rows of alphabetic symbols. Tribal man brought all his senses to bear on his world in a healthy balance; Gutenberg man over-concentrates on vision and leaves his other senses numb and deprived.

The third element of McLuhan's system is a patterning or schematisation of history, which is achieved by applying the fundamental principle to raw historical fact. Broadly conceived, the schema divides human history into three parts: the remote or pre-Gutenberg past, the immediate or Gutenberg past, and the immediate or electronic future. The first and longest of these eras further subdivides, on closer inspection, into a tribal epoch of oral, face-to-face communication, an ideographic epoch, and an epoch of alphabetic handwriting (i.e., prehistory, the East, and Western civilisation from the Greeks to the Renaissance).

The final stage of this schema, the electronic future, develops into a large-scale prophecy which also implies a diagnosis of current cultural discontents. With electronic means of communication rendering printed matter more or less obsolete we are on the edge of a new type of society and a new type of man. Indeed the new men are already among us: they are our children with their sense-ratios transformed by TV-watching at an impressionable age, dedicated to 'cool', participative enjoyments like the frug, and altogether alienated from the Gutenberg assumptions of traditional instructional schooling. That is why we get on with them so badly. The coming society will be appropriate to this type of human being. It will be a 'global village', a unitary world of neo-tribesmen, sunk in their social roles and fraternally involved with one another in a way that excludes what their forebears would regard as individuality.

Faced by the inevitable we need some kind of strategy to meet it with. Here McLuhan recurs, with a frequency unusual even for him, to Poe's story about a sailor caught in a maelstrom who saved himself by coming to understand how it worked. As things are, ignorance about the irresistible effects of new electronic media is general and blinding. The first step, at any rate, is to understand them by directing attention away from their content to their form and its effects on sense-ratios. It is not wholly clear that there is a second step, that anything more than understanding is required.

The global village is as welcome to McLuhan as it is inevitable. In *Understanding Media* he says that the faith in which he is writing is one that 'concerns the ultimate harmony of all being'. Generally the social and cultural features of the Gutenberg era that we are about to lose are described in an unfavourable way, their connection with war, inequality, indifference, the mutilation of the self is emphasised. But on the other hand, from the time of *The Mechanical Bride* (New York, 1951) McLuhan has been insisting that he is not concerned with whether the changes he is investigating are 'a good thing', and strongly suggests that this is a crude and unenlightened sort of question to ask. Rudolph E. Morris in *McLuhan: Hot and Cool* is sufficiently impressed by these protestations of detachment to praise the book, quite wrongly, for its freedom from moral indignation (a fairly dense cloud of moral steam rises from McLuhan's collar on page thirteen of *The Mechanical Bride*, for example). Despite his insistence on detachment there is no doubt that he strongly favours the future as he describes it.

Finally McLuhan has a special intellectual technique, both of exposition and defense. His procedure is to heap evidence up in tumultuous and disparate assemblages, with little critical appraisal of his sources – unless they deviate very grossly in some way from one of his main theses – and with only the most tenuous thread of topical relevance to connect them. To justify this shapeless and enthusiastic technique of almost random accumulation he falls back on the idea that he is producing a mosaic, not a linear argument. In fact he is producing a linear argument, but one of a very fluid and unorganised kind. Objectors are discounted for benighted visuality and obsession with print. Yet McLuhan not only writes books, he is immensely bookish, in the manner of some jackdaw of a medieval compiler or of Burton in *The Anatomy of Melancholy*.

The analogy between this system and Marx's is plain enough to be set out briefly. Each system begins with a general interpretation of history, an account of the ultimate cause of historical change. Each applies this to arrive at a schematisation of the actual course of historical events. For exciting, practical purposes each schema divides history into three parts: the remote past (before print or capitalism), the immediate past (print or capitalism), and the immediate future (global village or classless society). But the remote past can be divided further, into prehistory (the oral tribe or primitive communism), the East (ideographic script or slave economy), and the early West (alphabetic script or feudalism). Both McLuhan and Marx devote their main work to the shift from the early West to the immediate past: as *The Gutenberg Galaxy* tells what print did to the scribal culture, so *Capital* describes the emergence of capitalism. Each system concludes its historical schema with a prophecy of imminent major change to a state of affairs that is nebulously described but enthusiastically welcomed. In each case the welcomed future is a reversion, in a major respect, to the initial phase of the whole historical process. McLuhan and Marx both present strategies for dealing with the inevitable. Marx calls for an activist endeavour to ease the birth-pangs of the coming order; McLuhan, less exigently, calls for an effort to understand, best pursued by reading his works. Both are strongly in favour of the future that they predict, for all its obscurity of outline. Finally both have a brisk way of disposing of hostile critics. They have a self-sealing device against any possible attempt at refutation: the theory predicts it and explains it away, what Popper calls 'reinforced dogmatism'. Objectors must be visual or bourgeois.

To point out this analogy is not to criticise McLuhan, except in so far as he maintains that his ideas cannot be set out in a conventionally systematic way. But it does put one on one's guard. A system of this form embodies two crucial elements about whose acceptability very general and very elaborately worked-out doubts have been raised: a schematisation of history which implies the inevitability of a predicted state of affairs and a strongly positive evaluation of this none-too-clearly-described inevitable future.

There is clearly something in McLuhan's fundamental principle, just as there is in Marx's. Major changes in styles of communication do have large effects. What is wrong here is the violent exaggeration with which McLuhan blows up a truth about the causal relevance of media into a full-blooded and unqualified theory of historical change. What he usually does is to argue that some change in media of communication is a necessary condition of a certain major social or cultural change, and then to represent his discovery as an account of what *created* the major change in question. Print, he says, created the large national army of modern times. Now it may be that the large national army does make a good deal of use of printed matter for such things as training manuals and quartermaster's forms. But the railway, as indispensable for rapid mobilisation of large numbers, is obviously more important. Anyway McLuhan's timing is all wrong here. The print age, for him, begins about 1500, but the type of army he has in mind first appears in the mid-nineteenth century with the American Civil War and Bismarck's wars against Austria and France, or, at the earliest, with the armies of the French Revolution and Napoleon. During the three preceding, print-dominated centuries, armies had been small bodies of mercenaries or long-service professionals.

He might, at this point, reply that the mass army of modern times was created by nationalism and that nationalism was created by print: Q.E.D. Even if we allow the questionable assumption that creation is transitive in this way, this still will not do. For how does print create nationalism? By stabilising the vernacular? But were not Elizabethan Englishmen nationalistic even though most of them were illiterate? Or is it enough that the ruling class should be literate? Then why was eighteenth-century Italy not nationalistic?

Here, right at the foundations of McLuhan's system, a persisting vagueness of terms makes it difficult beyond a certain point to see precisely what is being said. Media, he contends, are the ultimate causal factors in history. But what is a medium? Much of the time the term is taken in a fairly ordinary way to mean a technique for the communication of ideas between human beings. It is in this sense that the concept of a medium occurs in his schematisation of history. But in *Understanding Media* roads, clothes, houses, money, cars, and weapons are all included in the repertoire of media discussed, things which either do not communicate information but carry altogether heavier loads, or which communicate information only as a very minor and peripheral function (as a nun's habit says 'don't ask me to have a drink with you'). In this extended sense a medium comes to be any item of technology, and the sense in which the fundamental principle is to be taken becomes very much diluted. Nevertheless, McLuhan's fundamental principle does make a point and he has certainly assembled evidence relevant to it which is impressive in its bulk and often intellectually stimulating.

This is less true of the schematisation of history that he derives from its application, which simply draws old and familiar distinctions between historical periods in a new terminology. What everyone is used to calling modern history is renamed the Gutenberg era, ancient and medieval history is renamed the era of alphabetic script, the epoch of the oriental empires is renamed the ideographic era. This would be all right in a modest way if it served to confirm a well-known distinction and to deepen our understanding of it. But here a pedantic-looking doubt must be voiced. What does he mean when he says of some medium that it is *the* dominant medium of a given historical period? Does it mean that everyone was preoccupied with it, in which case the Gutenberg era began in Europe only a hundred years ago with a fair approximation to universal literacy? Or does it mean that *the* medium of an era is the one through which the ruling class acquires most of its information or most of its important information? In that case the beginning of the Gutenberg era is pushed back to where he wants it all right (1500 roughly), but the basis of his claim that we are on the edge of an electronic age dissolves. This serious indeterminacy is one that he generously exploits. He says that England is much less visual and print-oriented than the United States. Yet England was the first country to exhibit most of the social and cultural symptoms of Gutenbergian domination: mass-production industry, big cities, individualism, nationalism, etc. Allowing himself this degree of freedom he deprives his schematisation of any definite content.

At this point his explanation of his fundamental principle by means of sense-ratios needs to be considered. Once again a very simple point seems to have been exaggerated into confident and unqualified assertions which cry out for justification. It is reasonable and enlightening to say that tribesmen do not have a detached, impersonal point of view of a visually conceived world stretching out uniformly from them in space and time. But to talk of sense-ratios suggests a kind of mathematical precision about this kind of perception which he nowhere begins to achieve. To raise a very simple question: why does he say nothing about the blind? Plenty of blind men display all the marks of extreme visuality in his terms, are individualised, specialised, detached and so forth. But how can this be possible for people who have been blind since birth and have had to get their information either tactually through Braille or auditorily through a reader?

This becomes highly important when he arrives at the final stage of his schematisation, his prophecy about the electronic age just ahead of us, peopled with its global villagers. All the alleged products of print are declared moribund and about to disappear: the individual, privacy, specialisation, detachment, militarism, nationalism, mass-production, and so forth. In their place the world will become a unity of emotionally involved tribesmen, aware of everything that is happening everywhere. The real basis for this prediction is his account, in terms of sense-ratios, of the effect of TV on people accustomed to it from early life. TV, he says, is a cool medium, whereas print is hot. It involves the collaboration of its watcher in what it presents, for he has to fill out its low-definition picture with imaginative efforts of his own, while print, where everything is clear and determinate, imposes a passive receptiveness on the reader.

My limited observation of children's TV habits makes me doubt this. If the show interests them they watch it with passive absorption; if it does not they leave it buzzing on around them and get on with something on the floor. But I would not rest the case on such anecdotal material, particularly since the effect is alleged to take place at a fairly subconscious level, as inaccessible to naive observation as it is to modification or control. It seems reasonable, however, to argue that despite its low pictorial definition TV leaves a lot less to the supplementative imagination of its watchers than print does to its readers. But even if electronic media do decrease detachment, as they might be held to do by the very lifelikeness of their representations, why does he infer that this involvement will inevitably be fraternal and charitable? There is no necessary connection whatever between making people more emotional and excitable and making them more humane and unselfish. Words like 'sensitive' and 'involved' can be used to mean either sympathetically concerned with the welfare of others or, more neutrally, just concerned. No doubt young people at present are more given to global idealism than their elders, but then that is nearly always the case; having few other responsibilities they can afford this emotional expenditure.

Again it is not at all clear why the involving nature of exposure to electronic media should eliminate individuality. If print makes men passive it should, according to McLuhan's own argument, presumably be well equipped to stereotype them. No doubt there are many forces in the world making for Riesman's other-directedness, but TV with its rapid diffusion of advertisers' ideas of fashionable life-styles is only one of them.

McLuhan's predictions often go far beyond the global village toward the imminent formation of a kind of cosmic, preverbal consciousness. Media, like all technologies, extend or externalise our faculties. In particular media extend our senses. Electronic media, he goes on, extend or externalise the central nervous system. Here he has really taken off. Certainly tools can augment the power and precision of our muscular operations. In line with this, media strictly so called can be regarded as ways of improving the performance of our sense-organs, though this more accurately applies to things like microscopes and telescopes. Going a little further still, we can allow that computing machines can assist and improve on the thinking work of the central nervous system. But this is not to say that computers or other media detach our faculties from us altogether, that they literally externalise the human capacities they reinforce.

Perhaps a community could enslave itself to a computer by programming it to make social decisions on the basis of its inflow of information, and by linking it up with machinery designed to put the decisions into effect. Such a community would be well advised to put the main power switch in an accessible position. But since in our entropic universe destruction is easier than construction, the descendants of people clever enough to construct such an appliance ought to be clever enough to blow it up if it gets out of hand. Moreover, whatever sort of computer it is, it will not be preverbal in McLuhan's lavish sense: its tapes may have combinations of 1s and 0s on them instead of ordinary words but it will not operate with blank tape. I have almost certainly misunderstood McLuhan on this topic, probably by taking his word 'externalise' literally. If he does not mean it to be understood in that way, all he can mean is that there will be a collective consciousness – or subconsciousness – of the kind an excited patriotic crowd might have, with everybody thinking or feeling the same thing. We must try to avoid this unappetising prospect by leaving TV-watching in its current voluntary condition and keeping more than one channel going.

McLuhan describes the electronic future in reasonably attractive ways on the whole. Not least in the phrase 'global village' itself with its intimations of rusticity, friendliness, the simple life. But his neo-primitive future does seem to be without most of the things which men have laboriously struggled to achieve and in virtue of which, despite everything, they still think of themselves as superior in more than brute strength to the other animal species: freedom, individuality, foresight, even detachment, the indispensable condition of rationality itself. In so far as the outlines of the electronic future are clear they are by no means enticing, but then in so far as they are clear the arguments on which their inevitability is based are very far from persuasive. And in so far as they are not clear there is nothing to take a position for or against. But anyway taking a position about the future has little point in McLuhan's system, since it is not shown how the understanding he offers is related to any possible action. What he really offers is a kind of general relief from historical anxiety: Amazing things are going to happen but considered in themselves they are not at all bad, and the disturbance of their arrival can be brought within manageable bounds by one's being intellectually prepared for them.

Whatever else he is McLuhan is consistently interesting. His scope is unlimited and there are the added attractions of his remorseless and all-inclusive contemporaneity and his jokes. Contemporaneity is a rapidly wasting asset. *The Mechanical Bride*, which is now sixteen years old, has a largely camp interest. The jokes often seem a little automated, like those in a Bob Hope show. His technique has a Gutenbergian repeatability. 'Money,' he says, 'is the poor man's credit card.' Why not 'Gratitude is the poor man's tip' or 'Changing the furniture around is the poor man's interior decoration'. But there are so many of them that the strong can carry the weak. What he claims to offer is much more than this, a general scheme of individual and social salvation. Compared to all such schemes it perhaps makes the least exacting demands on those who would like to follow it. They do not have to mortify the flesh or hurl themselves against the armed lackeys of the bourgeoisie or undergo 500 hours of analysis. All they have to do is to read a few books, a curiously Gutenbergian device. If, as I have argued, the scheme does not stand up very well if approached with the good old linear questions, 'Just what does he mean?' 'Is there any good reason to think that it is true?' they must remember that they were offered salvation at a bargain price.

26

Russell's Philosophical Development

The story that is told in Russell's *My Philosophical Development* is one that has been told before, by him and by others, but this particular presentation of it stands out by reason of its comprehensiveness and its authority. It is a rather austerely intellectual autobiography, sticking firmly to the topic announced in its title, and the non-philosophical aspects of the author's character and interests take as modest a place in it as Collingwood's do in his not altogether dissimilar *Autobiography*. What makes a comparison of these two intellectual self-portraits so tempting is the almost diametrical opposition of their authors. Russell is an aristocrat, an influential public figure too lively and multifarious to be contained for long in a university, a communicator who writes to be understood and believed, a mathematician still despite many years away from mathematics, a moral and political radical, an atheist and a lifelong defender of science as the most solid and enduring achievement of the human intellect. Collingwood was a scholarship boy, the son of an unsuccessful literary man, a pure example of the obscure and ineffectual don, who made out that he was too busy to answer criticism or to take part in college administration or university politics, an elaborately conscious stylist, almost as much a historian and an archaeologist as he was a philosopher, essentially a reactionary for all his autumnal flirtation with Marxism, a Christian (up to a point) and an embattled critic of the pretensions of science. Yet there are affinities at the deeper levels of personality. Both of them are astonishingly self-confident, fearless and unequivocally forthright about their beliefs, with a self-confidence, indeed, that often turns into arrogance. Both were propelled into philosophy by their dissatisfaction with the received intellectual foundations of a first-order discipline and, in particular, by their disgust with the incapacity of the philosophers they first encountered to say anything useful or relevant to that discipline. It is not altogether surprising, then, that for all their differences they should both, looking back on their work, find in it a good deal more unity and coherence than most of their readers do and, more specifically, that they should both make the delightful discovery that their most famous early work contained far more truth than, in their long neglect of it, they had ever suspected.

It is natural that a philosopher, reflecting on a sequence of ideas that he has lived through more intimately than anyone, should see only gradual shifts of emphasis and interest where outsiders have claimed to discern basic changes of doctrine. Russell admits to only one major philosophical change of mind, dating it in the years 1899 and 1900 and describing it as the adoption of logical atomism and of the technique of Peano. In general, he says, philosophy has always been important to him as an instrument for the rational defence and justification of some extra-philosophical body of beliefs: first religion, then mathematics, finally science. In some engagingly characteristic selections from a diary he kept when he was sixteen he is to be seen jettisoning the immortality of the soul and the freedom of the will (the former for some unstated reason is taken to be inevitably borne down in the destruction of the latter) as incompatible with the existence of an omnipotent God. God was soon to follow the other members of the Kantian trinity into the abyss. Until shortly before the war of 1914 his main business was the articulation and defence of mathematics, in particular through the purifying elimination of unnecessary or metaphysical assumptions and of invalid logical trickery. By the time Wittgenstein appeared at Cambridge the whole gigantic structure had been hesitantly and in what he still considers an unsatisfactorily rough and ready manner steered past the jagged reef of the paradoxes. At this point Russell was convinced by Wittgenstein that the propositions of mathematics are simply tautologies and the whole great achievement of *Principia Mathematica* seems to have been deprived by this of interest and importance for him. So, from the end of the 1914 war, Russell's work in philosophy has been almost exclusively concerned with the justification of science. In 1903 he had said that induction, where it was not disguised deduction, was 'a mere method of making plausible guesses'. In his mature epistemology, two decades later, the body of scientific beliefs is taken, as a presupposition of the whole inquiry, to be broadly true on the whole and, at any rate, to be more likely to be true than any other comparable region of our beliefs, in particular than the results of philosophical speculation. If Wittgenstein's theory of logical truth, in appearing to Russell to prove the merely conceptual and vacuous character of mathematics, led him to change his subject-matter, he took with him to the new undertaking the same philosophical technique that had been so successful in the investigation of mathematics.

> Taking it for granted that, broadly speaking, science and common sense are capable of being interpreted so as to be true in the main, the question arises: what are the minimum hypotheses from which this broad measure of truth will result? This is a technical question and it has no unique answer. A body of propositions, such as those of pure mathematics or theoretical physics, can be deduced from a certain apparatus of initial assumptions concerning initial undefined terms. Any reduction in the number of undefined terms and unproved premises is an improvement since it diminishes the range of possible error and provides a smaller assemblage of hostages for the truth of the whole system. (*My Philosophical Development*, p.219)

The title of this book's last chapter aptly summarises the major shift in question: Russell speaks of his retreat from Pythagoras. Once mathematics seemed to him a timeless, abstract structure which it was the philosopher's task to reveal in all its inhuman and apodeictic splendour. The discovery of its tautological nature showed it, in Russell's view, to be all too human; its claim to rigorous necessity was defeated by the shifts required to elude the paradoxes. In science, however, there was a body of beliefs that at least approximated to knowledge and, in its dependence for truth on the non-human world, to impersonality. With the technique of analysis the philosopher can at least work with the modest aim of reducing its deliverances to order.

Russell acknowledges four main personal debts in philosophy. First to G.E. Moore for his liberation from idealism, for the view that fact was independent of our knowledge of it. Fact is not constructed by mind, as in the Kantian tradition, but present, more or less obscurely and uncertainly, to it. Secondly to Whitehead for Ockham's razor, 'the supreme maxim of scientific philosophising', that is to say for the technique of reductive analysis. Thirdly to William James for neutral monism and thus for liberation from the dualism that divides the world into acts of consciousness on the one hand and their non-mental objects on the other. Finally to Wittgenstein for the depressing revelation that all logical truth is tautological and for showing the crucial importance for philosophy of the relation of language and fact.

The general upshot, stated in his second chapter, 'My Present View of the World', is in essentials the same as that expounded in the 'Excursus into Metaphysics' which closes the *Philosophy of Logical Atomism*. The world is a vast assemblage of more or less homogeneous events, overlapping one another and causally related in various ways. Some, but very few, of these are data of experience and are so linked by memory-chains as to constitute minds. What Russell has called cosmic piety enforces the recognition of the very small place of data amongst the totality of events. Arguments from physics, physiology and the common facts of sensible illusion require the admission that only the most abstract and structural features of unperceived events can be reliably inferred. The general acceptability of science entails that there are unperceived events; to form rational beliefs about them we have to rely on principles of non-demonstrative inference. The object of philosophy is to show how the character of the whole order of events can be derived from the rather meagre sample of its contents that, wrapped up with various subjective accretions, is directly revealed to us.

Russell's first organised philosophical refuge from the disturbance of his early theological doubts and his dissatisfaction with mathematics as taught for the Tripos of his day was the absolute idealism of Bradley. He reproduces some early writings in the Hegelian idiom in this book and unequivocally disowns them. But, as might be expected, they are distinctly ingenious and considerably more lucid than most writing in the same mode. Moore's revolt against idealism was effected through the analysis of perceptual experience as a relationship between a mental act of awareness and a non-mental, indeed often physical, object. Russell's critical divergence from Bradley was on the issue of relations. His initial point of attack was on the coherence theory of truth as presented by Joachim which he saw to be a special case, a particular application, of the doctrine of internal relations. For the coherence theory truth cannot lie in a relation between unintelligibly heterogeneous propositions and facts, it must be found in the unitary, internally related character of a systematic whole. Moore's epistemological realism, like Russell's correspondence theory, is a consequence of the rejection of the necessity of internal relatedness. In Russell's case there was an added support for the externality of relations that derived from mathematics. The notion of a series is essential to mathematics and series are logically generated by asymmetrical relations: 'is the successor of', 'is greater than' and so forth. But asymmetrical relations cannot be reduced to properties or attributes of the terms related, without the regressive assumption of a further asymmetrically relational fact. 'George is older than John' only reduces to 'there are ages x and y, such that George is x and John is y' with the addition of 'x is greater than y'. The admission of the externality of relations, then, and with it the recognition that the world was, as it appeared, a real plurality of things, was required by the interpretation of mathematics as much as by Moore's perceptual realism and his own theory of truth. Russell describes the move as leaving the Hegelian hothouse for a Platonic jungle in which an indiscriminate plurality of disparate entities prowled. Even if subsequent analytic economies have reduced the multitude of species on view in his ontological zoo it has never ceased to contain a vast plurality of individual beasts.

If reflection on mathematics led to a pluralism that was at first excessively fecund it also provided the remedy, a technique of analysis which made possible the elimination of the more outlandish existences. The systematic derivation of mathematics from logic showed that numbers – whether complex, real, rational or natural – were 'linguistic conveniences'. The same treatment was less convincingly applied to the classes in terms of which numbers were defined, classes being none too helpfully identified with the set of things satisfying a propositional function. The most influential assertion of a type of symbol's incompleteness, however, was the theory of descriptions. In the light of that theory the topics of discourse were divided into real and apparent subjects, the former referred to by logically proper names, the latter by descriptive phrases. The analysis of descriptions was originally introduced to cope with the troublesome but intrinsically not very engrossing class of non-existent subjects of discourse, with the fictional and the imaginary. In Russell's first articulate presentation of the theory of knowledge, in *The Problems of Philosophy* and in the second half of *Mysticism and Logic*, it was put to a more ambitious use. The distinction of proper name and description was seen here as the logical correlate of the traditional distinction between immediate and inferred knowledge. By asserting this connection Russell provided a point of entry for the analytic procedure of his mathematical investigations into the field of empirical knowledge.

It is usual to divide Russell's career as an epistemologist into three phases: first the highly qualified, Lockean, empiricism of *The Problems of Philosophy*, in which physical objects were inferred as the transcendental causes of sense-data and *a priori* knowledge was held to record the outcome of inspecting the timeless interrelations of subsistent universals; next the period of logical atomism strictly so called, running from *Our Knowledge of the External World* to the *Analysis of Mind*, in which material things were identified in almost phenomenalist fashion with the class of their appearances; and finally a period of progressive retreat from radical empiricism, beginning with the overtly causal theory of perception of the *Analysis of Matter* and continuing steadily to the mildly Kantian theory of non-demonstrative inference in *Human Knowledge*. Looking back on *The Problems of Philosophy*, Russell now finds less to disagree with than he had expected. 'I no longer think that the laws of logic are laws of things; on the contrary, I now regard them as purely linguistic.' He sees the more refined entities of mathematical physics – points, instants and particles – as accessible to Whiteheadian analysis. He admits, too, by implication, that the matter of physics cannot be left in the transcendental autonomy accorded to it by his first account of the subject and that it must be constructed out of some less inherently elusive stuff. He concedes that on first recognising this he indulged in a brief flirtation with phenomenalism whose fruit was an article (chapter 8 of *Mysticism and Logic*) which sought 'to exhibit the hypothetical entities that a given percipient does not perceive as structures composed entirely of elements that he does perceive'. But in *Our Knowledge of the External World*, he rightly points out, two further classes of elements are admitted: the sense-data of others and sensibilia, that is 'the appearances that things present in places where there are no minds to perceive them'. A consistent phenomenalism, he holds, in agreement with its more penetrating defenders, must start from a solipsistic basis, the unobserved must be defined in terms of possible sense-data of *mine*. He is surely correct in saying that this has never been more than momentarily his own position.

Russell, in fact, has always been opposed to a strictly subjective point of view in the theory of knowledge. A more or less Cartesian critical procedure has always been controlled by the assumption of the general acceptability of science and, underlying that, by the cosmic piety that recognises minds and their knowledge to occupy only a very small place in the universe. There are numerous and recurring testimonies to this fundamental theme. To start with he was faithful to the act-object distinction he had acquired from Moore long after Moore had seemingly lost interest in it as being of no service to the purposes of realism. In the *Problems*, Russell firmly distinguishes the act of sensation from the sense-datum itself, for even if sense-data cannot be identified with material things we do not have to conclude that they are mental. He dropped the act-object distinction only when, following James, he believed it possible to regard the experiential stuff of the world as both physical *and* mental in virtue of its relations to other experiential elements. On Russell's version of neutral monism it was the exceptional case for events to fall within minds, that is to be associated with nervous systems and to stand in mnemic relations to previous events so associated. He accepted neutral monism, in other words, only when he could see a way of depriving it of any mentalistic flavour. The same preference for the physical comes out in the theory of sensibilia, for these, despite the hypothetical look of their verbal expression, are construed by him as being as fully actual as sense-data. It was the phenomenalist look of the word 'sensibilia', no doubt, that led him in due course to drop it in favour of 'events'. A more extreme and provocative form his preference has taken has been the widely disputed view that sense-data, the events that are noticed or directly observed, are in the brain. The argument for this distressing conclusion is simply that the immediate causal antecedents of sense-data are indubitably in the brain and that the terms of a direct causal relation are spatially continuous. The assumption that completes the argument, of course, is that sense-data, as a type of events, are in the real world, in space, and so are physical as well as mental. His preference for the physical is recognised as an emotional bias in his comment on the celebrated passage by F.P. Ramsey: 'My picture of the world is drawn in perspective, and not like a model to scale. The foreground is occupied by human beings and the stars are all as small as threepenny bits. I don't really believe in astronomy, except as a complicated description of part of the course of human and possibly animal sensation.' When Russell says that this passage expresses precisely what he does *not* feel he is not supposing that it is to be taken literally. Ramsey does really believe in astronomy; a sentence or so earlier he has been admitting, while disdaining, the vastness of the heavens. But Russell plainly suspects that the literal sense of Ramsey's remarks is just what a subjective, phenomenalistic philosopher should believe in all consistency. In the light of all this it is surely more correct to think of Russell as a hesitant materialist than as a none too thoroughgoing phenomenalist. It is characteristic that he always prefers to use scientific arguments derived from the physiology of perception and from the physics of the transmission of light and again from the profoundly non-perceptual picture of material things given by physics in order to establish the chief and traditional ground for his hesitation, the thesis that material objects are not directly perceived.

There is an interesting analogy between the course of Russell's thought about the theory of knowledge, about philosophical logic and about ethics. In each case, under the initial influence of Moore, he adopted an only very insecurely empirical brand of realism. In rejecting this first standpoint he has never gone as far in the opposite direction as he has seemed to in the light of the lines of development favoured by his successors. His final position has always been an uneasy compromise between Moore and his and Moore's more radical successors. Thus in the first decade of the century he held a Cartesian view of the distinctness of mind and matter and a Lockean view of perception; he held both individuals and universals to be real and mutually irreducible; and he believed moral propositions to convey information about a transcendent order of values in the manner of *Principia Ethica*. Like others at first, he was more affected by the phenomenalistic implications of Moore's investigations into sense-data than he was by Moore's compensating doctrine of common sense. One side of his early logical realism (the theory of Moore's *Nature of Judgment*) was abandoned in the face of Wittgenstein's theory of logical truth; he no longer regarded *a priori* knowledge as descriptive of the timeless realm of Platonic abstraction. With others again he was more impressed by Moore's refutation of ethical naturalism than by Moore's insistence on the objectivity of moral propositions. The natural termination of these developments was the positivism of the 1930s, which combined a phenomenalist epistemology with a nominalist philosophy of logic and a non-descriptive theory of ethics. Russell never went so far. Against phenomenalists he maintained the reality of unperceived events, against nominalists he maintained the reality of universals, against emotivists he maintained the relevance of human desire to moral propositions and in his theory of the goodness of 'compossible' desires sketched the outlines of a fragile, tentative ethical objectivism. Now in each case, it seems to me, the part of his original opinion that he was led to abandon was really more congenial to him, more in line with the fundamental and dominating tendency of his thoughts, than the part he retained. Thus in the theory of knowledge he has really been much more concerned to save the reality, the independence from mind, of perceived fact than to establish the rigorously empirical credentials of his conception of the external world. In philosophical logic he has been reluctant, emotionally and intellectually, to reconcile himself to the view that necessary truth is formal. There are numerous signs of this dissatisfaction: his attempt to find an empirical foundation for the formal concepts of logic, his retention of universals, his implicit abandonment of the view that logic is the essence of philosophy, his emphasis on the continuity of philosophy and science. In ethics he has come as near to utilitarianism as he can without overt conflict with the anti-naturalist principle, the third dogma of modern empiricism. I am suggesting, in fact, that Russell is fundamentally a materialist, baffled by respect for Moore's neo-Cartesian sense-datum theory, a utilitarian, baffled by respect for Moore's doctrine of the logical autonomy of judgments of value, and, most important of all from the point of view of his influence on and reputation among contemporary philosophers, a logical realist, baffled by respect for Wittgenstein's theory of the analytic or tautological nature of necessary truth.

It is important that Russell's nominalism is only skin-deep, since those who accept the exclusive and exhaustive division of statements into the analytical and the empirical are committed by doing so to a certain view of philosophical method. They commonly and naturally draw the boundary between the two realms of discourse in such a way that philosophy is included with logic and mathematics amongst the *a priori* disciplines. In his early writings, ironically enough, Russell was more explicit about the connection of the three disciplines than anyone: in *Principia Mathematica* the identity of mathematics and logic was exhibited, in *Our Knowledge of the External World* (where he has more definite things to say about philosophical method than anywhere else) not only is it argued that logic and philosophy are identical ('every philosophical problem, when it is subjected to the necessary analysis and purification, is found either to be not really philosophical at all, or else to be, in the sense in which we are using the word, logical') but the view that *Principia Mathematica* is the paradigm of a properly constructed philosophical system is asserted.

We start from a body of common knowledge, which constitutes our data. On examination, the data are found to be complex, rather vague, and largely interdependent logically. By analysis we reduce them to propositions which are as nearly as possible simple and precise, and we arrange them in deductive chains, in which a certain number of initial propositions form a logical guarantee for all the rest ... The discovery of these premisses belongs to philosophy; but the work of deducing the body of common knowledge from them belongs to mathematics, if 'mathematics' is interpreted in a somewhat liberal sense. (*Our Knowledge of the External World*, p.214)

Since that time Russell has never been so forthright and precise about the proper method of philosophy but it is plain that he would dissent in a number of ways from the realisation of his early ideal to be found in, for example, Carnap's *Logische Aufbau der Welt*. He would reject its rigorously phenomenalistic starting-point as insufficient, he would insist that principles of non-demonstrative inference are required to move from propositions embodying concepts of one level to propositions embodying concepts of a higher level, above all he would insist that the presuppositions of the whole undertaking could not be merely tautological but must be scientifically grounded.

What is odd about Russell's methodological position is that it was he, in *Principia Mathematica*, who gave the first and by far the largest and most impressive example of the method of logical analysis, and he who, in the years immediately following its publication, gave the principles of this procedure their first clear articulation. Yet since the apparent theoretical trivialisation of his great achievement he has been silent or vague, at any rate generally unconcerned, about questions of method by comparison with his peers. His philosophical practice has been extraordinarily various, his philosophical enterprises have stood in no clear systematic relationship to one another; such comments about method as he has made have been rather off-hand repetitions of earlier formulations. Beyond the recommendation of a rather unspecified technique of analysis he has done little more than urge philosophers to concern themselves with the critical reinterpretation of science and common knowledge, to tackle problems piecemeal in the approved manner of the sciences and to adopt a standpoint of ethical neutrality. Compared with the place of questions of method in the attention of Moore and Wittgenstein this is very little. Moore's practice was, from the earliest days, strikingly uniform and the nature of this practice, the problem of analysis, was one of his three principal philosophical interests. In Wittgenstein the nature of philosophy itself takes pride of place amongst philosophical problems and, as a far more successful interpreter and rationaliser of his own practice than Moore ever was, he has transmitted to a whole generation of philosophers, for better or worse, an unprecedentedly high degree of methodological self-consciousness.

Russell's unconcern with problems of method may help to explain two rather surprising facts: first the conflict between his own view of his philosophical career as solidly continuous and the more common opinion which got its most extreme expression in Broad's remark about Russell's producing a brand-new philosophy every few years and, secondly, the marked and mutual lack of sympathy between Russell and his natural heirs, the main body of present-day analytic philosophers. As to the matter of change of views: if Russell has not been so unwaveringly fixed in his opinions as Moore (most of whose final doctrines were clearly stated in his recently published lectures of 1910 and 1911), he has not undertaken the kind of radical transformation of his entire philosophical position that marks off the late from the early Wittgenstein either. Yet his views appear more fluid and inconsequent than Wittgenstein's because they are not subject to the integrating pressure of a precise idea of philosophical method. (I am ignoring here the unacceptable claim, made by and on behalf of Wittgenstein, that, in his later phase at any rate, he had no philosophical doctrines.) Changes of detailed opinion effected in order to bring those details into line with a persisting idea of method look like merely internal adjustments. Where there is no such idea of method the detail is all and any major change in it looks like a completely new start. In Russell's case the extent of change has been exaggerated largely for this reason, but also because he has never bothered to emphasise the continuity of ideas underlying such changes in terminology as that from *sensibilia* to *events*, because he tends to express his convictions in a forceful and unqualified way, because he has always believed that philosophical problems should be tackled piecemeal anyway and, in practice, by any suitable procedure that lies to hand and, finally, because with the passage of time the main subjects of his concern have varied. In fact, most of the leading doctrines of the latest period of his thought, whether it is taken to start with the *Analysis of Matter* in 1927 or with *The Limits of Empiricism* in 1936, are fairly explicitly foreshadowed in *Our Knowledge of the External World*. That early masterpiece asserts that the experiences of others and also unperceived events must be acknowledged, that principles of non-demonstrative inference are required to support belief in them and from this it follows that the minimum ontology of science and common knowledge must contain trans-empirical elements. Since verification must be in terms of private, sensible occurrences that in its turn entails that not all our beliefs can be strictly verifiable. His positive theory of the verification of basic propositions in the *Inquiry* (the rather surprising view that to verify them we must observe the causal relation between the belief and the experience that verifies it) and the doctrine of non-demonstrative inference in *Human Knowledge* are additions rather than modifications, the filling of gaps that in the latter case at least were openly acknowledged in early writings.

When one considers the magnitude of Russell's philosophical achievement the prevailing estimate of his philosophical importance, amongst academic philosophers at any rate, seems curiously low. On the whole, while according the highest respect to his work in strictly formal logic, they regard his early epistemology as an interesting appendage to Moore and his later epistemology as without interest or relevance to the pressing concerns of the moment. Now in the first place such a view ignores the fact that not only did Russell take an absolutely central place in the creation of modern formal logic but that he is both the identifier and principal creator of modern philosophical logic. In chapter 2 of the *External World* he gave the name 'philosophical logic' to the study of the forms of propositions and his own doctrine of logical atomism has been unquestionably the most substantial single contribution to it. The whole apparatus of logical classification in terms of which philosophical analysis is now conducted is largely owed to him, and no one has done more to give the problem of reference the place it now occupies. Besides these two varieties of logic he has made contributions of the first importance to the philosophy of mathematics, to the theory of perception, to the philosophy of mind and to the topics of causation and probability. He has been active, in a way that is only minor by his own standards, in ethics, the history of philosophy (and here, surely, his *Leibniz* is the most distinguished modern book *about* a philosopher) and in the philosophy of religion and politics. It so happens that two major blanks are two of the most prominent interests of his successors: the problems of necessity and other minds; but beside what he has produced these gaps bulk fairly small. When contrasted with Moore, with his extraordinarily narrow range of interests (the relation of sense-data to material things, of observable facts to judgments of value and of *analysans* and *analysandum*), his acute inflexibility, which kept him circling continuously round a small, fixed set of theoretical possibilities, and his general intellectual unadventurousness, Russell should surely cut a larger figure than he commonly does. I suggest that the explanation of this disregard is a joint effect of the methodological impurity of Russell's practice and his general lack of interest in questions of method at the level of explicit theory, despite the fact that he more than anyone invented the characteristic method and, even more important perhaps, the characteristic tone of modern analytic philosophy. Curiously it was his own logical inquiries that made possible the development of that theory of the analytic nature of philosophical theories in the light of which his own insistence on the relevance of scientific evidence to philosophical problems and on the hypothetical character of his proposed solutions is so unfavourably viewed by his successors.

Russell, of course, vigorously reciprocates their disregard. In a long concluding chapter in the present book he reprints a number of detailed criticisms which are often petulant and sometimes weak. Of his successors, he writes: 'I have been unable, in spite of serious efforts, to see any validity in their criticisms of me'; of Urmson: 'I am unable to see any cogency whatever in the arguments that Mr Urmson advances'; and of Strawson: 'I may say, to begin with, that I am totally unable to see any validity whatever in any of Mr Strawson's arguments'. Not *any* shred of validity in *any* of them? This blustering unfortunately blinds Russell to the extent to which the ideas he is criticising are continuous with his own? For example, he attacks Warnock for pointing out that '∃' or 'there is' can introduce statements of markedly different logical character. Warnock argues against Quine that the ontological commitments of 'there is a prime number between 5 and 11' and 'there is a pear tree in the garden' cannot be construed in the same way because the truth of the two statements is established in quite different ways. In conflict with that Quine had maintained that the reference to classes was as ineliminable from the one as the reference to material objects was from the other. Now Russell asserts in the course of the discussion that both numbers and classes are 'linguistic conveniences', whereas an indispensable part of Quine's case is that classes, at any rate, are not. Russell, in fact, has boldly rushed to the defence of a questionable interpretation of the symbolism of formal logic, in the course of defending which he reveals that this interpretation is in flat conflict with his own view of the type of statement in question. Does he really want to underwrite any interpretation of his logical symbolism against any criticism of the omnicompetent power of that symbolism to reveal philosophical truth, however much the interpretation in question conflicts with his own? Criticising Strawson, he says that Strawson's theory simply confuses the problems of descriptions and egocentric words and that he has already dealt with egocentric words, although Strawson does not acknowledge the fact. He has certainly recognised that there *are* such words, but this, though important, is a platitude. What matters is the use that Strawson makes of it in *On Referring* to show how a sentence with a given meaning can be used in different circumstances to make different statements and to refer to different individuals. Many of these criticisms (though not all, by any means: there are some shrewd questions put to Ryle) are polemical in the bad, merely disputatious, sense.

Russell's overall charge against his most recent successors is that they have turned away from trying to understand the world to a trivial concern 'with the different ways in which silly people can say silly things'. There is a serious point under this none too sensible observation. Post-Russellian philosophy has passed through two distinct verbalistic phases, the first of formal conventionalism in which it seemed to be the philosopher's task to promote arbitrary intellectual constructions controlled only by the criteria of consistency and systematic elegance, the second of grammatical authoritarianism in which it seemed enough for the philosopher to set out in the most refined detail the prevailing rules of ordinary discourse. That this phase is closing is clearly enough shown by the publication of books like Strawson's *Individuals* and Stuart Hampshire's *Thought and Action*. Beyond the mere description of a conceptual apparatus, actual or projected, lies the world in which it is to be employed and in which are to be sought and found the reasons or justification for the apparatus's taking the form it does. This view of the subject-matter of philosophy as being language at work in the world derives from the abhorred later Wittgenstein, most notable to Russell for his 'suave evasion of paradoxes'. Perhaps no modern philosopher was closer in sympathy to this new, concretely pragmatic, attitude to language, as against free construction or dutiful and unquestioning submission to accepted practice, than F.P. Ramsey. Much admired both by Russell and the present-day philosophers he so much deplores, Ramsey might, if he had lived, have prevented the rather sad and quite unnecessary hostility between them.

27

Popper 1: Objective Knowledge

Sir Karl Popper must surely be acknowledged, now that Russell, Moore and Wittgenstein, the three great influences of the century so far, are dead, as the most important and interesting of living British philosophers. The only matter for controversy here is the adjective 'British', since Popper's *Logik der Forschung*, in which the comprehensive set of original ideas he has ever since been exploring and developing were first formulated, was written and published in the mid-1930s, when he was still an Austrian and living in Vienna. But that powerful work has been much more read in its English dress as *The Logic of Scientific Discovery*, and all his subsequent writings have been published in English: *The Open Society* and *The Poverty of Historicism* while he was teaching in New Zealand; his two rich essay-collections, *Conjectures and Refutations*; and now *Objective Knowledge* (Oxford, 1972) while he was at (or just in retirement from) the London School of Economics.

There are two features of his work and influence which distinguish him from the other leading philosophers of his time. The first is the way in which his ideas have been taken up, applied and endorsed by major figures in other disciplines. The art historian E.H. Gombrich and the biologists Sir Peter Medawar and Sir John Eccles are not merely cultivated men, working in other fields, who have found Popper's philosophy interesting and suggestive; they would not, I think, object to being described as practising Popperians.

Secondly, there is the remarkable width of the areas of subject-matter in which Popper's ideas have found fruitful application. He has himself written about the philosophy of science, natural and social, the philosophy of history, the theory of knowledge in general, political theory, the philosophy of language and logical theory. His pupils and followers have gone further afield: Lakatos into the philosophy of mathematics, Agassi into the history of science, Jarvie into the philosophy of anthropology, Bartley (who should perhaps be described as an ex-follower) into the philosophy of religion. Watkins and the highly independent and idiosyncratic Feyerabend have gone further into Popper's own primary domains of politics and history and of the methods of science respectively.

But despite the wealth and power of his ideas his reputation has been slow in reaching an appropriate height. There are two reasons for this: the first circumstantial, the second more fundamental. He first came to the notice of the English-speaking philosophical world in the mid-1930s with publication of his *Logik der Forschung* in a series of books by members of the Vienna Circle: Schlick, Carnap, Neurath, their Berlin associate Reichenbach, all contributing items to it. It was natural that he should have been taken to be much more one of them than he actually was. That impression could only have been strengthened by the favourable view of many of his ideas taken by Carnap, the best-known and most productive member of the Circle.

The initial doctrine of the *Logik der Forschung* is that the propositions of science are demarcated from those of metaphysics by their empirical falsifiability. Now, a leading preoccupation of the Vienna Circle (and the part of their work that at this early stage was most closely followed in the English-speaking world) was their attempt to formulate a counterpart principle of verifiability to distinguish scientific sense from what they regarded as metaphysical nonsense. But Popper's difference with the Vienna Circle was more fundamental than that of how the solution to a given problem should be formulated. He was offering a solution to a different, even if not unrelated, problem. For him metaphysics was non-science, but it was not non-sense. In view of the rigid insistence by critics and commentators that Popper's doctrine of falsifiability is a new formulation of the positivist criterion of meaning, a measure of exasperation on his part – of somewhat egocentric emphasis on what precisely he has said and meant – becomes understandable. It is as if the only review received by a passionately serious play had been one in the *Tailor and Cutter* which concerned itself exclusively with the style of the actor's suits.

A favourite argument against Popper has turned on the consequence of his falsifiability doctrine, one that he quite explicitly drew from it, that unrestricted existential statements of the form 'there exists at some unspecified place and time a thing of a certain kind' are metaphysical because they cannot be falsified conclusively. But, said Popper's critics, such statements are plainly significant, so his doctrine is false. He, however, had never held them to be meaningless. His view was that they could not be regarded as scientific in the way that restricted existential statements about the existence of things of certain kinds at specified places and times – the vital falsifiers of scientific hypotheses – are.

This misinterpretation might not have been very important in itself if it had not diverted attention from what Popper saw as the really crucial part of his work, to which his falsifiability criterion of demarcation is only a preliminary: his account of the growth of scientific knowledge. There are two sides to it – one factual or genetic, the other logically evaluative or justificatory. Science in fact grows (according to Popper) not by the mechanical induction of general propositions from accumulated reports of particular observations but by the imaginative formulation of hypotheses which are then tested and, unless they elude all efforts to falsify them, revised or replaced. On the side of justification, hypotheses are made rationally acceptable not by the accumulation of positively confirming instances but by their successful survival of the most pertinacious attempts to find falsifying ones. In the first chapter of *Objective Knowledge* this theory is given a careful and finally authoritative expression, under the bold title of 'Conjectural knowledge: my solution of the problem of induction'. Its two sides are clearly distinguished but interestingly connected by a 'principle of transference' which states that what is true in logic is true in psychology (in the case in hand, that theory is prior to observation).

The genetic or psychological side of Popper's view about induction is now widely accepted; the logically evaluative side is less so. Everyone would agree with Popper (and David Hume) that no amount of positive confirmation of a hypothesis *entails* its truth. There is less agreement with them that positive confirmation adds nothing to the *probability* of its truth. Popper's argument for this much stronger conclusion rests on a disputable interpretation of the concept of probability. He says that positive instances confer no probability on the relevant hypotheses 'in the sense of the calculus of probability'. But there is no such sense. The calculus of probability concerns the logical relations of probability-judgments to each other. For example, if the states of affairs described by p and q are independent of each other, the probability of both p and q being true is equal to the probability of p multiplied by the probability of q. It does not determine what the logical relations are between judgments of probability and the categorical statements of fact on which they must depend for their acceptability.

Popper argues that since Hume is right about induction – since positive instances neither entail nor make probable the corresponding hypotheses – the traditional problem of induction is insoluble. What he offers instead are criteria for rational preference between competing hypotheses. One hypothesis is better than another if (*a*) it has not been falsified while the other has been; or (*b*) it has more content, and is thus more falsifiable, than the other. Comparison in respect (*b*) is, he admits, only possible within narrow limits. The question that is not raised is whether any hypothesis is rationally preferable to accepting no hypothesis at all and thus to forming no expectations whatever: the position of the radical sceptic about induction.

The justificatory comfort Popper offers is, then, pretty cool. What lies behind it is a particularly vigorous response to Einstein's refutation of Newton. For over two hundred years the marvellously articulated splendour of Newton's achievement had encouraged the assumption that the findings of developed physical science are unshakably certain. The 1919 expedition to the southern hemisphere verified Einstein's prediction about light from stars in line with the sun but refuted Newton's. Philosophers of science have inclined to see this as involving no more than a marginal revision of classical physics. Newton was nearly – rather than absolutely – right. But Popper is surely correct in emphasising the vast difference at the level of theory between the two systems of celestial mechanics. The conclusion he draws is that science is essentially tentative and always open to revision. As he neatly observes, there is something self-refuting about the belief in induction. The picture of the world provided by science is one in the light of which the fact of successful scientific prediction is highly improbable.

In the years since the *Logik der Forschung*, Popper has derived a large body of further consequences from his falsificationist theory of scientific knowledge. He has applied it memorably in new fields (most notably in his refutation of the historicist doctrine of universal laws of historical development); and he has added new refinements such as his theory of verisimilitude or truth-likeness. In *Objective Knowledge* a much larger forward step is taken with his theory of 'objective mind' or 'world 3'. It is this, implicitly present in his earlier work, that constitutes the more fundamental and less circumstantial reason that I mentioned earlier for the surprisingly small amount of attention that his ideas (apart from a misrepresented account of his criterion of demarcation) have received from philosophers at large.

Russell, Moore, and the long line of analytic philosophers that derives from them, have all, in his view, approached their philosophical investigation of knowledge with a Cartesian or subjectivist presupposition about what kind of thing knowledge is. They took it to be a mental state of particular individuals. He maintains that although knowledge is, in general, the product of the mental activities of individuals (although books of logarithms can be produced by computers), knowledge proper is the thing produced and not the psychological incidents that accompany its production or use. Knowledge and language too are objective structures produced by men in interaction with their environment which have effects of the utmost importance on both the men and the environment: evolutionary devices analogous to birds' nests and spiders' webs.

Negatively, this objectivist conception of knowledge involves a criticism of what Popper calls the common-sense theory that knowledge is based on infallible items of given, empirical information supplied by the senses. This is the topic of his long second essay in which he distinguishes it from common-sense realism, the view that there exists a physical world independent of anyone's mental states; he accepts this although he holds it to be metaphysical and unprovable. Crucial to his rejection of the Cartesian adoption of immediacy (or directness) as the criterion of truth is his claim that the senses are, as evolved organs, 'theory-laden' in the sense that they react to stimuli with in-built propensities of expectation.

A theorist of subjective knowledge might reply that the cognitive defect he ascribes to the senses has always been a first principle of subjectivism. It does not follow from the fact that our senses are imperfect recorders of the external world which sets them in operation that we do not have infallible knowledge of the subjective end-point of those operations.

There is more to question on the positive side of his new theory. In distinguishing world 3 of objective mind from world 1 (the order of physical things and events) and world 2 (the order of minds and their subjective states) he invokes the names of Plato, Bolzano, and Frege as anticipators of his position. Now what they believed to exist, over and above material things and mental states, was a timeless order of logical essences or abstractions, of universals and propositions that were somehow there whether any actual mind ever conceived or asserted them or not. On the other hand, he remits to world 3 the books and papers of which libraries are composed. But these, it would seem, are not timeless abstractions but concrete denizens of physical world 1 as are the supposedly analogous birds' nests and spiders' webs. In other words the qualifications for admission to world 3 are radically unclear. The things he puts in it are in some cases Platonic, that is things that could possibly be thought even if no one ever does think them, and in others Hegelian, things that someone has thought and expresssed. This unclarity is particularly evident in what he says about mathematics. The natural numbers are, he insists, man-made (birds' nests again). But things like the infinitude of the prime numbers (and, no doubt, analogous things not yet discovered) are objectively, factually there as unintended, unexpected, but irresistible results of our construction of the natural numbers.

This ambiguity of abstract thinkables and actual thinkings reappears in the general account Popper gives of objective knowledge as at once man-made and yet largely autonomous. What is man-made is physically realised expressions or registrations of knowledge. What is autonomous is the logically related structure of abstract essences. Again, he says that while the mental states of world 2 stand in causal relations to one another, the 'objective thought-contents' that make up world 3 stand in logical relations (pp. 298-9). But he also maintains that world 3 – now conceived in a non-Platonic, non-abstract way as publicly accessible embodiments of knowledge – exercises a causal influence on the mental states of world 2 and through it, by way of technology, on physical world 1.

I conclude, then, that as so far expounded Popper's world 3 of objective knowledge is a logical hybrid, a kind of philosophical mule, troublesome and infertile. But I am also sure that there is an important idea in it, that of public or common knowledge, provided that this is conceived as knowledge that is man-made, concretely embodied, and of such a character as to undergo evolution. This needs to be separated from the Platonic element of Popper's actual presentation of his doctrine: separated, that is, from the notion of an existing order of timeless, abstract essences, accessible to some kind of intellectual intuition, but prior to and massively transcendent of all actual human thinking.

I should hold that objective knowledge thus conceived is reducible to actual items of human thinking (world 2) and to the physical embodiments thereof (world 1). But that does not imply that it is somehow not real. Objective knowledge in this sense is just one more social institution, and Popper has himself argued for 'methodological individualism', the view that institutions are reducible to the individual people that compose them or to their acts and states. Yet he would agree that men are made what they are to a great extent by the institutions of which they are members.

What is most valuable in Popper's recent doctrine of objective knowledge arises from Darwin's evolutionary theory, just as his original philosophy of science derives from Einstein's revolutionary advance on Newton. Darwin's discoveries had a number of large effects in areas of thought outside biology. They strongly suggested that man is a part of nature. They explained the phenomena of natural adaptation without recourse to the theological hypothesis of an intelligent Designer of the universe. They encouraged a large variety of more or less fierce social theories, hostile to the idea that the community should encumber itself with the support of its weaker members. But perhaps their deepest implication was epistemological: that human knowledge is an evolutionary product, in a state of constant change, by which men adapt themselves to their environment. This idea is intimated in Marx's views about *praxis*. It became explicit in the philosophy of the pragmatists, especially that of Peirce, from whom (by way of Ramsey) it penetrated to a small but discernible extent into the later philosophy of Wittgenstein. This evolutionary view of knowledge – which completes Popper's long insistence on the fallible and tentative character of what we call scientific knowledge – is squarely opposed to the Platonic intellectualism or essentialism with which Popper, rather incongruously, combines it.

Popper's theories are always interesting and original and rich with potentialities of further application. Their originality, it seems, has ironically deprived them of what they themselves assert that every theory must have to be strong and worthy of acceptance: penetrating criticism based on a serious understanding of what they actually are. Popper's contemporaries have too often mangled selected bits of his thought so as to fit them in with their own preoccupations.

A conspicuous virtue of his work is the undeviating clarity and definiteness of the language in which it is expressed. Popper, conformably with his view of language as an instrument, is hostile to concern with the precise meaning of words. Yet he has a moral passion for rational intelligibility. In his view it is to be sought by simplicity of statement, by readiness to re-express a thought in different words, by explicitness and avoidance of the oracular and the allusive. This commitment to limpidity and openness of expression is something he has most effectively communicated to his pupils and followers, and to none of them more than to Bryan Magee, whose *Popper* (London, 1933) is a recent edition to the Fontana series of Modern Masters.

Magee has done an admirable job of work. He supplies a complete and balanced picture of Popper's thought from its first beginnings up to its latest developments, brings out the interconnections between its very various parts, and explains the special excitement readers of Popper get from the sense he communicates that his ideas bear significantly on all sorts of matters outside professional philosophy proper.

If he presents Popper's philosophy as a rather isolated thing, only tangentially related to the main current of the philosophical thinking of the age, this is because (for the reasons I have mentioned) that is too much the way it has been. Since there is no body of informed and serious criticism of Popper's thought to draw upon, the book may seem a bit uncritical. Some of the small amount of serious criticism that there is is too easily dismissed. The only real objection Magee makes to Popper's views is to his negative conception of the functions of government. Popper's liberalism allows government to intervene in the life of its citizens, but only to diminish suffering and remove evils. Magee, as a social democrat, would wish to charge it with the positive augmentation of the quality of life.

In a work of this size, directed to the general reader, it is natural that the more technical aspects of Popper's philosophy should be largely passed over. But rather too little is said about probability. The vital thesis that favourable singular instances not only do not entail but do not confer any probability on hypotheses is dealt with in a single sentence. Nevertheless this is an absolutely faithful account of Popper's ideas, presented in delightfully crystalline prose, and it fully justifies the inclusion of its subject in the ranks of modern masters.

28

Popper 2: Political Theory

The three great exponents of classic liberalism – Locke, Bentham and John Stuart Mill – make up a dialectical sequence. Locke based his advocacy of minimal government, charged with the negative task of protecting the life, liberty and possessions of individuals, on the premise that men have certain axiomatic natural rights. He conceived these principles of natural right as the self-evident objects of a kind of intellectual intuition analogous to that which supplies the foundations of mathematics. The necessity, and also the narrowly drawn limits, of government he took to be deducible from these principles in conjunction with the fact of human moral imperfection. Since men claim these rights for themselves, while self-interestedly failing at times to respect them as they apply to others, one of them has to be given up so that the remainder may be effectively maintained. The exception that has to be foregone is complex and procedural: the executive power of the law of nature, which concerns the ascertainment of natural laws, their application to particular cases and the enforcement of their application through sanctions. For Locke the right to the greatest possible freedom is second in importance only to the right to life. That there is such a right is a basic, intuitive moral truth.

For Bentham and James Mill liberty, and such associated liberal preferences as equality and democracy, are not axiomatically good. Their justification, to the extent that they are justified, is derived from the degree to which their assurance contributes to the general happiness. On this view the principle of utility alone is self-evident. In fact, as far as liberty and democracy are concerned, Bentham and James Mill thought that they were to a very large extent justified by considerations of utility. Bentham believed that happiness would be maximised by allowing men a very large freedom of choice in their actions since men are, by and large, the best judges of what will make them individually happy. James Mill favoured democracy as the form of government most likely to serve the common interest since it is the only one in which the rulers have a reliable motive, the desire to retain their power, for seeking the happiness of all. They were less explicit about equality. But as extreme environmentalists they rejected all notions that some men were innately superior to others. There is at least an egalitarian flavour to Bentham's elusive formula 'each to count for one and none for more than one'. Furthermore, some measure of equality in the distribution of the conditions of happiness is implied by the project of maximising utility. The allocation of an instrumental good to some man who has one already will generally produce less utility than its allocation to someone who has none at all.

John Stuart Mill inherited a commitment to the principle of utility from Bentham and his father, but qualified their concrete development of it in a number of ways. In the first place, he had a somewhat more complicated conception of utility than their narrowly hedonistic idea of it. His view is expressed in his unsatisfactory argument for the superiority of the 'higher pleasures' in his *Utilitarianism* and, more significantly, in the important, if fleeting, reference to 'the permanent interests of man as a progressive being' in his essay *On Liberty*. Secondly, his endorsement of liberty is so unqualified as to go beyond the reach of utilitarian justification and almost to reinstate it as a natural right in the manner of Locke. On the other hand he did not have his father's breezy confidence in democracy. He saw it as likely to install the tyranny of the majority, to enforce the general pursuit of mediocre ends and to inhibit individual freedom. He favoured its administration in comparatively small doses as a way of educating the mass of mankind in political responsibility and public spirit. Finally, while passionately committed to liberty in its intellectual, political and personal aspects, he came to question the desirability of unrestricted economic freedom and, in the later editions of his *Principles of Political Economy*, argued for redistributive taxation.

Since the time of John Stuart Mill there has been no comparably original, sensitive and systematic defence of the whole range of liberal ideals. His complex and imperfectly utilitarian arguments for liberty, equality and democracy, in which the dangers of each for the others are acknowledged, has remained the authoritative presentation of the liberal creed. There has been a direct tradition stemming from him in which the moderately socialistic features of his later thinking have been further developed, as in the welfare-state liberalism of such theorists as Hobhouse, prepared, as Mill was not, for the risk to liberty involved in state education. There has also been a more rigidly libertarian current of thought, whose most distinguished contemporary exponent is Hayek; from its distrust of state power, it supports an extreme individualism even at the cost of massive inequality. But until the publication of Popper's *Open Society* there was no large-scale reformulation of liberal doctrine that has presented it in a significantly novel way.

In the preface to his book Popper describes it as 'a critical introduction to the philosophy of politics and history', and the dedication of its companion volume, *The Poverty of Historicism*, is to 'the countless men and women of all creeds or nations or races who fell victims to the fascist and communist belief in the Inexorable Laws of Historical Destiny'. Popper's immediate enemy, then, is modern totalitarianism in its fascist and communist forms. But he does not primarily attack it by direct advocacy of its opponent, whose endorsement of democracy conflicts with totalitarian insistence on absolutely authoritarian government, and whose liberalism opposes the totalitarian commitment to the total control of the life of the individual in the interests of a total transformation of society. Popper's primary target is a thesis in the philosophy of history, not in the philosophy of politics, the doctrine of historicism. It holds that the proper goal and most fruitful achievement of social and historical inquiry is the substantiation of a general law of the historical development of society. Historicists believe that with such laws the next stage of social development can be prophesied and that the content of this prophecy is the only rational determinant of correct political action, action, that is to say, which is appropriate to the inevitable historical future. His main argument, then, is that totalitarian politics rests for its support – at least to the extent that it claims intellectual respectability, to be more than a collection of ideological prejudices – on historicism.

At the same time, like the classic liberals, Popper defends liberty, democracy and equality directly, on moral grounds. His primary argument against historicism is designed to show that the ideals of liberalism are not impossible, that there is no discoverable historical necessity which rules them out altogether. Having defended the idea that liberal ideals can be realised, he goes on to argue that they should be. The basis of his argument here is utility, not self-evident natural rights. He rejects the general essentialist doctrine of intellectual intuition for a number of reasons. He goes on to argue, more specifically, that absolute principles of liberty and democracy are invalid because logically paradoxical. His utilitarianism differs, however, in two major respects from that of either Bentham or John Stuart Mill. In the first place, largely on the basis of a theory of rational social action of an anti-utopian or gradualist character, he formulates his principle of utility in a negative way, as *eliminate suffering* and not as *maximise happiness*. Secondly, he does not regard his principle as a truth or item of possible knowledge but as a demand or, more mildly, proposal.

There are, then, two principal strands to Popper's overall argument: one methodological, designed to refute the allegedly historicist foundation of the totalitarian rejection of liberal democracy; the other ethical, in which a moral point of view is proposed entailing the desirability of the liberal-democratic programme whose possibility has been established by the critique of historicism. The particular, gradualist or piecemeal version of democratic liberalism that Popper supports is defended on broadly methodological grounds. We do not possess the kind of social knowledge required for the overall reconstruction of society; rational social action is not directed to ultimate, utopian ends. But there is much more to his position that is relevant to political theory than these main themes. First of all there is his argument that absolute principles in politics, of freedom, tolerance, democracy and sovereignty, are logically defective. Furthermore there is a large number of particular discussions of political interest, about nationalism, about the prospects of preventing international conflict, about laissez-faire and interventionism and about the attractions of totalitarianism in a time of disturbing social change. In what follows I shall first examine Popper's critiques of historicism and utopianism, then his moral defence of liberal democracy and his contention that absolute political principles involve logical paradoxes and turn finally to some of the specific issues that are comparatively independent of his main argument.

I. HISTORICISM

Popper's more direct arguments against historicism are to be found in *The Poverty of Historicism*. There is, first, a short 'formal' refutation in the preface. The course of history is affected by the growth of knowledge; we cannot predict the future growth of knowledge; therefore, we cannot predict the future course of history. This carries less than complete conviction since the knowledge that affects history may not be the same as the knowledge that cannot be predicted. The knowledge that directly affects history is applied, technological knowledge. We may be able to predict *that* a certain technological problem will be solved, for example that of finding a military use for atomic forces, a considerable time before we know *how* to solve it. Popper's point, however, in holding future knowledge to be unpredictable, is not the simple, verbal one that future knowledge that is known now is not purely future knowledge.

More convincing, at least in being less elusive, are his more detailed arguments attributing methodological confusions to historicists. The two great models of systematic predictability by analogy with which historicists advance their claims are both bad guides. The solar system, far from being a standard instance of a law-governed system, is a rare and unrepresentative case. A small number of variables is involved and the system as a whole is very little affected by extraneous factors. The supposed 'law' of evolution, on the other hand, is not a law at all. At best it is a trend. More correctly it is a unique historical reconstruction in which the laws proper of genetics, amongst other things, are invoked to order a mass of data about organic species and their environments. It affords no ground for rational extrapolation into the unknown future. Such a 'law of evolution' as Spencer's famous formula about differentiation and integration is too vague and elastic to imply any definite predictions at all.

Popper does not discuss the analogy which seems to have weighed heavily with the such ardent historicists as Spengler and Toynbee. This discerns a parallel between a society or a civilisation and a living organism. Every organism has a characteristic life-span which divides into a regular sequence of developmental stages. Certainly the analogy is very loose. A man is a single, continuously identifiable material object. A society or civilisation is not and, indeed, the identification of one such entity as an individual is highly problematic. Toynbee's apparented and affiliated societies merge into one another in a way for which there is no parallel in the relations of human parents and children. Popper's anti-inductivism prevents him from criticising historicism on the ground of the small number of instances of the development of single societies on which it rests. The developmental pattern of human ageing is highly reliable predictively. It is a paradigm of the inevitable. Knowledge of it could be used rationally in prediction long before there was any knowledge of the laws explaining the passage from one of Shakespeare's ages of man to the next. It follows that the predictive employment of recurrent patterns of development is not irrational as such.

So, it would seem, the historicist project is not doomed from the outset. Historicist theories must stand or fall by their ordinary empirical merits, by their ability to withstand our most resolute efforts to falsify them, as Popper has taught us. Their falsification is a task for historians rather than philosophers.

But, despite their frequent dramatic suggestiveness, such theories do not do very well. Marx's predictions for the comparatively immediate future have been uniformly false. The misery of the industrial proletariat has not increased; the proletariat has not become the immense majority of the population; revolution has come not in industrial but in peasant societies. If we assume, as there is good reason to do, that no such theory is well enough confirmed to base confident rational predictions on, the question arises of the extent to which totalitarian political doctrines depend on them. Popper does not try to substantiate the proposition that totalitarianism rests on historicism directly but connects the two through three great philosophers, Plato, Hegel and Marx, whom he holds to be, first, historicists, and, secondly, the crucial theorists who provide foundations for totalitarianism. Let us examine these two claims.

Popper's characterisation of Plato as a historicist is based on an interpretation of the theory of forms and on the doctrine of a regular pattern of political degeneration set out in book viii of the *Republic*. The forms, according to Popper, are at once the ideal or perfect paradigms of their kinds and the first originals of their particular instances. If this is correct then the first is the best; the most primitive form of state or society is the one which most closely resembles the ideal exemplar. The first and best society, for Plato, is one in which the wisest and most god-like of men is king. It is followed by a heroic or feudal timocracy, then by plutocratic timocracy, which gives way to lawless mob-democracy and, finally, to tyranny.

I think that Popper has shown beyond doubt that there is a historicist strain in Plato. He connects Plato's law of political degeneration in a biographically convincing way with the despair inspired in Plato, as it had been in Heraclitus, by the anarchically democratic disturbances of the age. Does he also show Plato to have been a totalitarian? There can be no question that he irreversibly corrects the idea that the *Republic* is the ideal training-manual for high-minded and public-spirited administrators, Jowett's bible for a higher civil service, selected by examinations. Plato's ideal state is one in which political power is monopolised by a rigidly closed class of rulers and is thus a particularly virulent form of authoritarianism. Numerous typical features of modern totalitarianism are present in Plato's construction. The ruling class has the discipline, *esprit de corps* and selfless dedication of the parties founded by Hitler and Lenin. Lying is laid down as an indispensable technique of government. Popper's argument that Plato is a racialist leaves a gap yawning between Plato's proposals for the deliberate breeding of rulers and the genocidal atrocities of Hitlerism. There is little of the emphasis on terror in Plato that there is the theory and practice of Lenin and Hitler. Finally, the ruled, although wholly without political power, do seem in Plato, if only by default, to be left pretty much to their own fleshly devices. There is no suggestion of the kind central to modern totalitarianism that all the citizens should be wholly made over into cogs in the machinery of state.

But, if Plato is rather an extreme authoritarian than a totalitarian proper, the question still arises of how far his political doctrines, which however they are to be described are radically opposed to democratic liberalism, depend on the strain of historicism in Plato's thought. Now although, as I have agreed, this strain is undoubtedly present, it does not seem to be the main source of Plato's authoritarian politics. The historicist strain is entirely *congruous* with Plato's politics, but what the politics actually follows from are the premises that rationality and knowledge are the proper qualifications for political power and that these intellectual virtues are substantially present in, and dominate the personalities of, only a small minority of mankind. Together with the functional principle that each man should do what he is, under the naturally unequal distribution of capacities, most fitted for, these premises about the nature of reason and human inequality entail that the ideal form of government is the dictatorship of an intellectual elite.

There is no need to argue the claim that Hegel and Marx are historicists, or the claim that their historicism is fundamental to their political doctrines. What is open to question is Popper's view that they are both totalitarians and, what is more, the originating theorists of fascism and communism respectively. Although, as has often been pointed out, Popper's discussion of Hegel is somewhat intemperate, there is plenty of substance in the charges he brings, not least against Hegel's polluting effect on the language and argumentative procedures of German philosophy. As far as his formal recommendations about government are concerned Hegel can most accurately be described as an authoritarian of a constitutionalist kind. Although his legislature has a representative element, the representation is functional rather than democratic. The legislature has limited powers. The real ruler is the bureaucracy, unified in the person of the sovereign. But, as Popper sees, the formal constitutional apparatus is not the substance of Hegel's political doctrine. He lists six Hegelian theses which are all typical features of fascism: (1) nationalism, as expressed in the views that the nation is the collectivity to which the individual must subordinate himself and that the aim of a nation must be to be the dominant one of the epoch; (ii) the view that states are natural enemies which assert themselves in war; (iii) the view that the interest of the state is the highest morality; (iv) glorification of war; (v) the creative role of world-historical great men; and (vi) the elevation of dangerous heroism above bourgeois mediocrity. Even if none of the institutions typical of fascism is proposed by Hegel – the party, the police working through terror, the propaganda ministry working through lies – his belligerent, nationalistic collectivism, in which the individual has value only through his service to the state, anticipates the frame of mind, the prevailing mood, of twentieth-century fascism. Hegel is a much less *respectable* figure than his strictly constitutional recommendations suggest or than his current apologists try to make out.

All the same this is at most a matter of broad temperamental affinity;

fascism is more a lunatic continuation of Hegel's politics than a direct realisation of it. Hegel is more the theorist of Wilhelmine than of Hitlerian Germany. There is a marked lack of connection between Hegel and fascism at the other end. Hitler's personal disdain for precise theoretical commitments has often been pointed out. The little bit of Rosenberg's *Myth of the Twentieth Century* that he actually read he condemned as 'too abstract'. The most solid element in his personal ideology was the maniacal drivel about racial purity which supplied his movement with an identifiable opponent and a solution to the pseudo-problem of the root of the world-wide conspiracy to drag Germany down. Finally, in so far as there is a correspondence between the morally objectionable 'background material' of Hegel's politics and fascism it does not extend to Hegel's historicism. For Hitler Germany's struggle for world domination was a heroic risk, not a foreordained necessity – more a Kierkegaardian leap than an irresistible dialectical transition.

But, despite all these reservations, there is an underlying respect in which Hegel's social theory prepared the way for modern totalitarianism. For it was Hegel who produced the most massively systematic and influential critique of individualism, and fascism is simply the most radical assault on the moral ultimacy of the individual. Popper himself is prepared to accept collectivism in one of its methodological senses, namely as a theory about the proper character of explanations in the social sciences. He sides with Marx against Mill in rejecting the idea that all the laws of the social sciences should be deduced from a universal psychology of human nature. But that, he insists, has no implication of *moral* collectivism, the theory that the ultimate criterion of value is the welfare of the collective.

It may at first seem frivolous to question the connection between Marx and the communist party since the Russian revolution. But anyone who denies, as since the close study of Marx's early writings there is every reason to do, the idea that Marx was a totalitarian implicitly does so. Marx's own writings contain hardly any totalitarian elements. Marx's ideal society is, indeed, anarchistic, the state has withered away. The vast totalitarian apparatus of Soviet Russia and its colonial dependencies was entirely created by Lenin and perfected by Stalin. The idea of an elite party of dedicated revolutionaries is a Leninist invention. The only explicitly totalitarian element in Marx is largely verbal: the word 'dictatorship' in the phrase 'the dictatorship of the proletariat'. Marx himself was a libertarian, an angry and acrimonious one no doubt, and the possessor of a cantankerously authoritarian personality. Accuracy, as much as devotional zeal, would justify the description of the Russian state religion by its priesthood as Marxism-Leninism rather than Marxism. This is not to say that the Marxist element of the compound, and, in particular, Marxian historicism, is not a crucial ingredient of the whole. But as originally formulated by Marx, although utopian and violent, it was not totalitarian. What Marxian historicism actually predicts, wrongly as usual, as the outcome of proletarian revolution is a social condition in which men, wholly liberated from economic necessity and the oppressive institutions that it has hitherto required, pursue their varied forms of self-realisation in equal and total freedom.

It must, then, be concluded that the connection which Popper seeks to establish between historicism and totalitarianism by way of Plato, Hegel and Marx is rather tenuous. Plato and Hegel were both moral collectivists and the political doctrines they derived from their collectivism was both strongly authoritarian and contained various totalitarian features: in Plato rule by a caste and a fairly rudimentary racialism, in Hegel aggressive nationalism. But Plato was not much of a historicist and, although Hegel was, in neither case is their near-totalitarian politics very closely connected with their historicism. Marx, although very much a historicist, was not a totalitarian at all.

A final point before leaving the subject of historicism is that while at most associated with, and nowhere essential to, totalitarianism, it has been, at least until the present century, at least as closely associated with liberalism. Condorcet is only the most systematic of the many liberal thinkers who have supposed that liberal democracy was inevitably destined to triumph by some law of progress. This is implied by a sentence that Popper italicises in his favourite quotation from H.A.L. Fisher: 'the fact of progress is written plain and large on the page of history; but progress is not a law of nature'. The error that Fisher is correcting here is that of *liberal* optimism. It is natural that anyone who wants some large historical change to come about should keep his spirits up by finding reasons for thinking that it must do so. The desire for change is the fundamental thing; the historicism is only a reassuring addition. The need for such reassurance is not confined to totalitarians.

II. UTOPIANISM

'Utopianism' is one of those polemical words which writers hasten to mobilise for meanings of their own. In its most usual sense it refers to the indifference to the practicability of their proposals that is characteristic of the devisers of Utopias or ideal societies. In common speech to call a scheme utopian is to object either that it is absolutely impossible to realise or that it cannot be realised without unacceptable costs. Thus to show that some ideal is not utopian is to show that it can in fact be realised, at an acceptable cost, and that can best be done by specifying the steps leading from the present state of affairs to the projected one, tracing out the side-effects at each stage.

The claim of Marx and Engels that their socialism is free from the utopian character of all previous socialism rests on a curious intensification of the procedure of setting out the steps of the realisation of the ideal. They contend, not merely that capitalism *can*, but that it *must*, give way to socialism. The energies squandered by utopian socialists on the detail of the desired end they put to the demonstration of its inevitability, to such an extent that the end in question was hardly described by them in a positive way at all.

Popper's conception of utopianism is something different again. He uses it to cover any large-scale project of social reconstruction – more specifically, the view that rational political action should always be guided by an ultimate end which takes the form of a fully worked out plan of an ideal social order. Such a 'holistic' conception of social engineering he regards as disastrously misguided, and he puts forward in its place a conception of piecemeal social engineering, in which reform is directed towards the elimination of the most pressing present evils.

His underlying argument for this conclusion is that our knowledge of the workings of society is altogether inadequate to the tasks which utopian social engineering imposes on it. The social sciences aim to discover the unintended consequences of human action. These are always manifold and, inevitably, more or less surprising. He also assumes, in effect, that most or significantly many of them will be undesired as well as unintended, being more fearful of bad effects than hopeful of happy accidents. For Popper rational action must always take account of the imperfections of our knowledge. All programmes of change should advance in small steps so that unexpected ill effects can be corrected as soon as they arise and before they do too much damage.

A second argument for piecemeal reform is that there is likely to be much more agreement about the desirability of removing specific present evils than about a remote, complex ideal. Thus its realisation will have to be achieved in the face of opposition and can be pursued resolutely only by authoritarian means. Generally, as he argues, the exponents of large-scale *social* revolution recognise that violence is indispensable for the securing of their ends.

A further consideration is that a programme of utopian social engineering will take a long time to carry through. Might not the ideal come to seem less attractive with the passage of time? There is injustice in imposing the burdens of change on those who have to live through the process of radical reform and delivering all its alleged benefits to those who experience its fulfilment.

In his essay 'Utopia and Violence' in *Conjectures and Refutations* Popper develops further his point about the minimisation of disagreement. Not only will there be more disagreement about comprehensive ideal schemes than about present evils whose elimination is desirable, but the disagreement will be more intense, even religious, in character, thus increasing the likelihood of violent persecution of dissenters.

Popper's arguments for gradualism in social reform are in close correspondence with his ideas about the nature and growth of scientific knowledge. Science, in his view, is gradualist in two respects. It progresses not by the discovery of large, definitive truths but by approximation to truth, by the development of theories of increasing verisimilitude. Secondly, it advances cumulatively by the steady amendment of its tradition of beliefs and methods. However, Popper is less averse to revolutions in thought than in society. No blood is spilt in intellectual revolutions.

There is plenty of empirical confirmation for his scepticism about utopian social engineering. Revolutions, notoriously, produce results that bear little relation to the intentions of their initiators. It is, all the same, possible to admit the substance of this point and still favour large-scale revolutions founded on utopian myths. Sorel contended that gradual reform never really achieves anything, in the long run. Small concessions by the privileged to the oppressed are in due course counteracted, once they have served their purpose of palliating discontent.

But on closer inspection Sorel's argument seems doubly defective. Although relatively peaceful and gradual processes of social reform have not eliminated differences of power and wealth altogether from social relations, and do not seem likely to do so, they have got rid of some particularly extreme varieties of inequality: those embodied in the relations of master and slave or lord and serf. Furthermore slavery and serfdom have not been removed by violent revolution. To the extent that they have been resuscitated in this century it has been in just those countries where violent revolutionary change has taken place.

III. LIBERTY, DEMOCRACY AND EQUALITY

Popper is insistent that the obsession of philosophers with close examination of the meaning of words is misguided and fruitless. Certainly he regards it as a moral obligation to use language clearly but he holds that no amount of antecedent explicit defining of terms can eliminate confusion and misunderstanding. Definitions can only be as precise as the defining terms that they employ. For effective communication what can be done is to convey what one has to say in such a fashion that it does not depend on any special interpretation of the words one uses. It is consistent with this, therefore, that he should spend little time on the task of precisely articulating the terms which express the liberal values that he endorses.

In the case of liberty, for example, he is prepared to condemn what he sees as Hegel's identification of it with self-obliterating service to the state as a distortion. On the other hand he does not work with a strictly negative conception of freedom in which it is seen as the absence of intentional restraints on action. 'A certain amount of state control,' he writes, 'in education, for instance, is necessary, if the young are to be protected from a neglect which would make them unable to defend their freedom, and the state should see that all educational facilities are available to everybody' (*Open Society*, vol.1, p.111).

Again his conception of equality seems to be much more political and legal than economic. In pointing out that most of the specific proposals for institutional reform listed in the *Communist Manifesto* have in fact been carried out, at least in the advanced Western democracies, he comments in a parenthesis about the proposal for the abolition of all right of inheritance: 'Largely realized by heavy death duties. Whether more would be desirable is at least doubtful' (*Open Society*, vol.2, p.141). He favours intervention by the state to prevent the excesses of unrestrained laissez-faire capitalism but he defends this as required for the protection of the 'economic freedom' of the workers rather than as a means for eliminating economic inequality.

For him the important point about democracy is that it is that method of government in which the public can change its rulers without recourse to violence. More positively he approves it as the institutional scheme which allows conflicts in society to be resolved by rational argument and persuasion rather than by violent coercion. If an anti-democrat were to argue that in practice rational argument does not play a large and decisive role in democratic politics, Popper would no doubt reply that democracy, according to him, only *allows* for it. He has not claimed that democracy ensures it. He might go on to claim that authoritarian government excludes it.

He does not directly confront the problem posed by Mill and de Tocqueville of the possible degeneration of democracy into majority tyranny. In an essay on the subject in *Conjectures and Refutations* he is critical of public opinion, however, if it is regarded as the ultimate seat of political authority. It is never as unanimous as its singular name might suggest; since it is anonymous it is irresponsible; the majority is not always right, it may be neither well-intentioned nor prudent. His endorsement of democracy is consistently minimal: it is the least evil form which that necessary evil the state can take. 'Only democracy provides and institutional framework that permits reform without violence, and so the use of reason in political matters' (*Open Society*, vol.1, p.4).

In particular, Popper expressly abjures the claim that democracy will necessarily choose the best policies. Its virtue, for him, is that it is the style of government which will most probably and most rapidly correct bad ones. He is hostile, generally, to any inference from the indubitable fact of natural human inequalities to the conclusion that some elite should be authoritatively empowered to rule. The reason for this is his conviction that knowledge is at once imperfect and social. The truly intellectually superior man is he who knows how little he knows rather than the sage gifted with esoteric insight, a Socratic fallibilist, not a Platonic shaman. Anyone, however specially gifted may err, and the only way in which sound knowledge may grow is through the social give and take of unrestricted critical discussion. He goes on to draw the rather large conclusion that 'institutions for the selection of the outstanding can hardly be devised'. Virtuoso rulers will naturally select obedient drudges as their successors. This may be appropriate for a society dedicated to the Platonic programme of arresting all change but not for anyone who believes that there are defects in society which can and should be eliminated.

With regard to the prime liberal ideals, then, Popper is a consistent pluralist. Neither liberty nor democracy is an absolute good; indeed he argues that attempts to formulate unlimited principles of freedom, tolerance or popular sovereignty are logically paradoxical. Freedom, if it is to be fairly distributed and even worth having, requires a measure of intervention by the state and thus at least local or partial limitation of freedom.

Before going to consider this thesis of the paradoxical nature of absolute political principles brief mention should be made of what Popper has to say about the nature and functions of the state. His distaste for essentialism, and for the obsession that flows from it with definitions and the meaning of words, rules out his giving an account of the 'essential nature' of the state. But he is prepared to answer the questions: 'what do we demand from a state?

What do we propose to consider as the legitimate aim of state activity? Why do we prefer living in a well-ordered state to living without a state, i.e. in anarchy?' (*Open Society*, vol.1, p.109). The answer he gives is that he wants protection for his freedom and other people's freedom, or again, protection against aggression from other men. He goes on 'I am perfectly ready to see my own freedom of action somewhat curtailed by the state, provided I can obtain protection of that freedom which remains' (*Open Society*, vol.1, p.110).

The prominence of his references to freedom in this passage suggests that its equal distribution and protection is the main service he demands from the state and, also, that he equates the protection of freedom with security against aggression. But only on an irresponsibly inclusive interpretation of freedom can it be taken, as here, to be the prime target of aggression. Locke's other two values, life and property, are just as much the objects of aggressive violence as freedom. Security of life and property are just as much ingredients of the well-ordered rather than anarchic state he demands as freedom in any ordinary sense of the word. Security, for other things beside freedom, seems to be more fundamental than freedom itself. The potential for conflict between the requirements of freedom and security is not really dispelled by Popper's assertion that 'there is no freedom that is not secured by the state; and conversely, only a state that is controlled by free citizens can offer them any reasonable security at all' (*Open Society*, vol.1, p.111). Popper here tends to make use of his anti-essentialism as a license for a degree of imprecision which obscures important problems and conflicts.

IV. THE PARADOXES OF POLITICS

Political beliefs, according to Popper, are not certifiable by any form of intellectual intuition. To the extent that they are evaluative they are not confirmable propositions at all, but demands or proposals. To the extent that they assert or assume causal connections in the social domain, they are conjectural, and are only rational in so far as they have been exposed to the social process of critical discussion. Most political convictions embody both evaluation and beliefs about social causation, the relation of means to ends in social action. In putting forward the thesis that certain types of absolute political principle are paradoxical a further limitation is implied on, as it were, the logical form of such principles. To avoid paradox we must not say 'X ought always to be done' but, much less categorically 'in most circumstances X is probably the best thing to do'.

The topics of the principles that Popper holds to be paradoxical are sovereignty, democracy, freedom and tolerance. In fact they make up two closely related pairs. The principle of democracy is a special case of the principle of sovereignty; tolerance is logically connected with freedom, being abstention from interference with it in its intellectual and personal forms.

In what way are these principles paradoxical? A principle of sovereignty, for example the democratic one: *the people at large should have absolute political power*, allows for the possibility that the people may exercise its power by assigning its sovereignty to a tyrant. This is not a point that is original with

Popper. It lies behind the insistence of many traditional definitions of sovereignty on its inalienability. A practical recognition of this liability to mishap is made by systems of law which distinguish constitutional laws from laws of other kinds. The principle of sovereignty gives the central core of the constitution, and the law-making power which it assigns does not extend to the constitution itself. (Normally, of course, some provision is made for amendment of the constitution but the distinction becomes otiose if the amending authority is not in some way different from the ordinary law-making sovereign.)

This has its merits as a practical device, although it is not indispensable – there is no such distinction in the legal and political arrangements of Britain. It is, however, intellectually unsatisfactory. Whatever reason there may be for assigning authority for making positive laws to a person or group will equally be a reason for giving them authority over the constitution. If the people at large are more qualified than anyone else to make laws in general, how can the founding fathers of a previous age be regarded as specially qualified to draw up just one particular set of laws?

Principles of sovereignty of an unrestricted sort are only paradoxical in a fairly weak sense. The statement A, namely 'the statement A is false', logically entails, and is logically entailed by, its own falsity. An unrestricted principle of sovereignty does not even entail its own falsity. It entails only the potentially inconsistent conditional 'if the sovereign says someone other than he should be sovereign, that someone, and not he, should be sovereign'. It would be better to describe such principles not as simply paradoxical, but as potentially self-refuting.

The logical defects of the principles of unlimited freedom and tolerance are even less formal. Popper's point is that if everyone is left absolutely free of control by the government then the strong will be able to oppress and enslave the weak and there will be less freedom all round. The solution to this puzzle is surely that since freedoms are competitive, since one man's freedom is another man's bondage, there can be no such thing as absolute freedom for all. In particular freedom is not going to be maximised by leaving people free to diminish the freedom of others.

Popper concludes that tolerance should not be extended to the intolerant. But what is tolerance and who are the intolerant? There are very real problems about the application of this forthright-looking principle. Intolerance can take many forms. At its mildest it is a matter of believing that certain things should not be allowed, should, perhaps, be forbidden by law, and giving reasoned expression to these beliefs. Next there is the stage at which people are incited to prevent the disliked activities by non-legal violence or the threat of it. Finally there is the situation in which the intolerant have, constitutionally or otherwise, acquired control of the state and make and enforce intolerant laws. Popper maintains that if the final possibility is realised it is reasonable to use violence so as to put state power back in tolerant hands. As for the second possibility, since it involves violence, or the threat of it, or incitement thereto, it is not only non-legal but illegal. One does not have to adopt an essentialist view of Weber's definition of the state in terms of its monopoly of legitimate violence to suppose that any adequate legal system will prohibit all but the most marginal kinds of violence not positively authorised by the state, for example, for immediate self-defence against physical assault. Non-legal violence is forbidden because it is violence and not because of its object. Violent intolerance is on the same footing as violent theft.

But what of the first possibility, that of merely intellectual intolerance? Would Popper have thought the Weimar Republic justified in banning *Mein Kampf*? There is surely something to be said for letting the enemies of freedom come out into the open. It is even more important, for the sake of freedom, to put the onus of forbidding free expression very firmly on the intending suppressors and not to license it generally against anything about which a charge of intolerance can be contrived.

V. NATIONALISM AND COSMOPOLITANISM

An interesting feature of *The Open Society* is the extent to which it reflects the political experiences of Central Europe in the years between the wars. Popper concludes many of his chapters on Marx with illustrations from the melancholy history of that time and place. In this connection he discusses the problem of international security as it presented itself at that time and states his belief that the aggressive criminality of nations, taken as natural by Hobbes and exulted in by Hegel, could be controlled by an extension of the methods by which nation-states keep crime under a measure of control within their own borders.

To help justify this belief he argues against the idea that the nation is an especially real or natural community. Of Wilson's principle of national self-determination he says: 'How anybody who had the slightest knowledge of European history, of the shifting and mixing of all kinds of tribes ... could ever have put forward such an inapplicable principle is hard to understand' (*Open Society*, vol.1, pp.50-1). He goes on: 'Even if anyone knew what he meant when he spoke of nationality, it would be not at all clear why nationality should be accepted as a fundamental political category, more important, for instance, than religion, or birth within a certain geographical region, or loyalty to a dynasty, or a political creed like democracy' (*ibid.*, p.51). It is natural that the concept of nationality should seem particularly indeterminate to a German-speaking Austrian, born under the Hapsburg Empire and coming to maturity in the truncated Austrian republic created by the treaty of Versailles. But for all the difficulty of supplying a clear and explicit criterion for the concept (a fact which should not be all that much to its discredit to the anti-essentialist Popper), it remains a large and emotionally important feature of most people's notion of themselves. Whatever forms of international organisation men are led by political and economic prudence to develop, it seems certain that the bricks out of which the construction is built will be nation-states.

VI. CONCLUSION

There is a great deal more to *The Open Society* than has been discussed here. The greater part of the book is devoted to the interpretation and criticism of Plato and Marx, carried out with the greatest scholarly thoroughness and, at least as far as Plato is concerned, with epoch-making originality. There are important developments of Popper's general theory about the nature and growth of scientific knowledge as applied to the social sciences and history. There are numerous parenthetical discussions of the greatest interest of philosophy, education, the relations of morality and religion and of the tradition of irrationalism in post-Kantian German thought.

As a contribution to political theory its importance seems to me to be twofold. In the first place it carries further the project of supplying empirical foundations for democratic liberalism beyond the point to which Mill brought it, in much the same way as Mill advanced from the merely abstract or formal empiricism of Bentham and his father. The instrument of this important revision is Popper's correction of Mill's theory of the nature of scientific knowledge. For any utilitarian political justification is necessarily based on knowledge of the social consequences of human actions. Bentham acknowledged this in principle but relied in practice on nothing much more than the psychological common sense of the Enlightenment. Mill saw that the social sciences would have to provide the required knowledge of consequences and recognised that it would take a much more complex and tentative form than the naive proverbial wisdom thought sufficient by his utilitarian forebears. Popper's aim is directly continuous with Mill's and the measure of his superiority to Mill in this respect is that of the superiority of the *Logik der Forschung* to Mill's *System of Logic*. This would be enough to make *The Open Society* a really substantial addition to the literal canon.

Secondly, although in the earlier part of this essay I have questioned the closeness of the connection between the historicism it is Popper's main object to refute and the anti-liberal or totalitarian politics of this century, I should not deny that there is a connection between them. Ideologies typically ground social and political valuations in general theories about the universe, human nature or society and its history. In our age social and historical foundations for ideologies have, through the influence of Hegel and Marx, come to prevail over cosmological or psychological ones. Large historicist theories have not, I think, been as positively productive of totalitarian ideologies as Popper suggests. But those that, in the circumstances of our epoch, have supplanted the law of inevitable progress of nineteenth century liberal optimism have created the presumption that the liberal experiment is doomed to fail. If blind faith in progress has turned out to be an error, Popper has shown that its opposite is no better founded.

29

Philosophy in America

There is a famous unkind remark about American philosophy by C.D. Broad which runs something like this: 'Old philosophies never die; they simply go and start a new life in America.' This was excessively patronising when it was first made, presumably some time in the 1930s. It is now wildly inappropriate, with its suggestion that America is, philosophically, a client culture. All the same there are two retrospective elements of truth in it.

The first is that the organisation of philosophy departments in American universities does tend to embalm styles of philosophising that have once been vigorous but have lost their vitality. It seems to be felt that all the main established brands of philosophy ought to be represented in every serious department. In consequence, as Ernest Gellner puts it, 'a certain eclecticism is perhaps the most conspicuous feature of American philosophy ... there is at least one Texas Hegelian, one Nebraska phenomenologist, one West Virginia Wittgensteinian, one Ohio Kantian, and so forth'. A number of things could be cited as possible causes of this state of affairs. America is the land of consumer sovereignty; the university, as a kind of cultural supermarket in a competitive situation, must try to offer as large as possible a range of intellectual goods. America is also hostile in principle to the idea of monopoly and a kind of spiritual equivalent of the anti-trust laws operates against monolithic domination of university departments by a single point of view.

The second, and more important, element of truth lurking in Broad's remark is that America has, to a very great extent, been a philosophical importer. Along with everything else the successive waves of immigrants have brought philosophical ideas along with them. It is not surprising that Jonathan Edwards, the first important American philosopher, who was born in America in 1703 and died nearly twenty years before independence, should have been closely dependent on Locke. Later in the century, though, America received its first major philosophical immigrant in Joseph Priestley, fleeing from the incensed patriots who broke up his home in Birmingham. The Transcendentalists round Emerson in the early nineteenth century used the German idealism of Kant and his immediate successors against the established local tradition of Lockean empiricism in the manner of Coleridge, and to some extent under his influence. In the mid-nineteenth century the official academic philosophy in America was the respectable Scottish common sense doctrine, originated by Reid's critique of Hume, brought with him by James McCosh from Scotland in 1868, when he came to be president of Princeton for twenty years. At very much the same time

Hegelianism, brought over to the United States by a body of comparatively obscure German immigrants, had secured its first native adherents and found itself a platform in the *Journal of Speculative Philosophy*, founded in 1867.

The period from 1880 to 1914 is commonly referred to as The Golden Age by historians of American philosophy. The most notable philosophical movement of the age, pragmatism, was indeed the first purely home-grown school. Chauncey Wright, its first initiator, was a Darwinian adherent of John Stuart Mill, but Peirce and James were true originals, writing and thinking in different, but both indisputably American, accents: Peirce's polysyllabic, neologistic, tumultuous; James's hearty, colloquial, impatient of pedantry and refinement. Santayana, although only just an immigrant in the flesh (since he lived in America from the age of eight until his early retirement at forty-nine), was very much an unrooted exile in spirit, viewing American culture and society with a self-consciously deliberate European detachment. Royce's ultimate inspiration may have been German but as a Californian he was, despite his studies at Göttingen under Lotze and his long service at Harvard, an almost hyper-American figure.

In the inter-war years to which Broad must mainly have been referring American philosophy was, in fact, as self-subsistent as it had ever been. The most publicly prominent personality was that of Dewey, who occupied a position parallel to that of Russell in this country, if in an altogether less flamboyant and aristocratically perverse style. He combined a commanding influence in technical philosophy with a position of importance in public life as a theorist of education and politics. Whitehead, who arrived at Harvard in 1924 to begin a career as a speculative metaphysician at the age of sixty-three, in effect became an American. The work he did in America was largely discontinuous with the mathematical logic and analytic philosophy of science he had been engaged in with Russell and others in Britain and nearly all his following is American. The American philosopher of the period who has perhaps worn best from the point of view of the present age, C.I. Lewis, was wholly and without reservation American, in his New England origins, his Harvard education under James and, most notably, Royce, who inspired him to his original work in logic, and in his cumbrous, wordy but nevertheless business-like and intelligible style.

As one set of German exiles, in flight after 1848, had brought Hegelianism to America, so another, more distinguished group imported logical positivism after 1933. Herbert Feigl was perhaps the first to come. He was soon followed by Carnap, the school's most fertile and productive leader, by Reichenbach, Frank, von Mises, Hempel, and by the independently critical Gustav Bergmann. Even more influential than Carnap, possibly, was another exile from Hitler, the Polish logician Alfred Tarski, caught in America by the outbreak of war in 1939. Comparably distinguished representatives of other philosophical traditions were much fewer in number. Those that there were too old to have a great influence: Cassirer was sixty-seven when he arrived and died four years later, Maritain nearly sixty when the outbreak of war converted his annual visit to North America into a prolonged stay of over twenty years.

Philosophy in America had, then, fully established its national independence by 1880 to 1890, with Peirce, James and Royce in full production. It is worth noticing that American pragmatism, at any rate, was regarded by Russell and Moore, the leading innovators in British philosophy at the beginning of this century, as worthy of extended critical consideration. (The local brand of pragmatism, in effect the one-man band of F.C.S. Schiller, amounted to little more than an entertaining irritant in the thick hide of the reigning idealism.) They both wrote at length about James (in 1909 and 1908). Russell, writing about 'philosophy in the twentieth century' in 1924, counted it as one of the three main positions of the age, along with the 'classical tradition', as represented by idealism, and the kind of scientific philosophy with which he associated himself. Between 1914 and 1920, indeed, he was himself converted from the view that mental facts all involved a relation between a subject and an object to the 'neutral monism' he had found in James, which holds mind and matter to be no more than different ways of arranging the raw material of experience, which is neither mental nor material.

At the time when Broad's remark was made, then, after the end of American philosophy's Golden Age, with Peirce, James and Royce dead, Santayana retired to Europe and Dewey's main work coming to an end, its suggestion that America was, philosophically speaking, merely the passive recipient of ideas from elsewhere was as little true as it has ever been until the last decade. There were movements of thought in inter-war America which paralleled movements in Britain: New Realism and Critical Realism had affinities with the early theory of knowledge of Russell and Moore. But they were still home-grown. In so far as the leading American philosophers took account of Russell and Moore it was in a negatively critical way. In the chief Critical Realist book, Lovejoy's *Revolt Against Dualism* (1930), Russell's phenomenalistic view of the external world is singled out for special attention in two long chapters. In logic Lewis's critique of the extensional character of Russell's logical theories was the most important development. The line of thought Lewis initiated is still very much alive, both formally in the elaboration of systems of modal logic and philosophically in the application of modal logic to philosophical problems by the possible-world theorists of the present time.

It was not until the late 1930s that American philosophy became anything like the client of Europe that it had inevitably been in its first, small beginnings. The first significant influence was that of the logical positivists, already mentioned. Their interests, at least, largely overlapped with those of C.I. Lewis, although he was passionately hostile to their non-cognitive ethical doctrines. These, however, were to achieve their most thorough exposition from an American, C.L. Stevenson, in his *Ethics and Language* (1944). Nagel, although fundamentally committed to the pragmatic naturalism of Dewey, the reigning orthodoxy above all of New York where both Dewey and Nagel taught, was sympathetic to the positivist philosophy of science. The sympathy is intelligible in view of the closeness of the pragmatic and verificationist theories of meaning, a closeness manifested in positivist endorsement of Bridgman's operationalist account of the concept of science, which descended, as the positivists' own did, from the views of Ernst Mach. Carnap's philosophy of language was colourfully elaborated by Charles W. Morris, with a great embellishment of distinctions. Most important for the future was the adherence to Carnap of W.V. Quine and Nelson Goodman. Quine's major work *Word and Object* (1960), the most discussed American philosophical book of the post-1945 period, is dedicated to Carnap. Goodman's writing has been inspired throughout by the methodological example of Carnap's *Der Logische Aufbau der Welt*, which is for him the unique paradigm of a 'system of logical philosophy', as contrasted with 'amorphous philosophical discourses', a phrase apparently intended to cover most of the rest of man's philosophical output.

British analytic philosophy of the 1930s, in the form it was given by the later work of Moore and Wittgenstein, made a less dramatic impact. A handful of American visitors to Cambridge were the first to bring back the new ideas: Norman Malcolm, later Wittgenstein's first biographer and a tireless exponent of Wittgensteinian ideas in Moorean language, Alice Ambrose and Morris Lazerowitz, who developed Wittgenstein's rather casual comparison of his own methods to psychoanalytic therapy into a fully-fledged theory of philosophical theories as distortions of language unconsciously motivated by neurotic disorders. Of the same general outlook, but more sympathetic to logically-oriented philosophy, was Max Black who arrived from England in 1940 to begin a productive career at Cornell, also Malcolm's university.

By the early 1960s, however, it seemed that this second, linguistic, influence from overseas, for all the modesty of its arrival in the United States, had superseded the earlier, positivistic, source of new ideas. In the volume of the *Princeton Studies on Humanistic Scholarship in America* dedicated to philosophy R.M. Chisholm, an independently eclectic and most accomplished theorist of knowledge, wrote: 'The dominant influence in the 1940s and early 1950s came to be the later philosophy of Ludwig Wittgenstein and the writings of Gilbert Ryle, J.L. Austin and other philosophers teaching at Oxford.'

The period to which Chisholm refers is roughly that of the great days of Oxford ordinary language philosophy which can be dated from Ryle's return to Oxford as professor in 1945 to the death of Austin in 1960. During those years the size and vitality of the Oxford philosophical world made it the place which all enterprising American philosophers wanted to visit. Teachers of the subject flowed in on Fulbright grants, graduate students came in droves to work for the two-year higher degree of B.Phil. that Ryle had invented. Austin's authority and intenseness had the effect of keeping everyone on their toes and of communicating a sense that crucial developments were under way or at least in the making.

His death, Grice's departure to Berkeley and Ryle's retirement do not really explain the exchange of status between Oxford and the leading American departments of philosophy that has taken place over the past fifteen years. That there has been such a move by Oxford and British philosophy generally to the periphery of what it was once the centre cannot be denied. Nothing shows it more clearly than the prevailing philosophical interests of the younger teachers and more animated graduate students of the subject in Oxford. A decade or so ago they were preoccupied with such Wittgensteinian topics as the impossibility of a private language or the non-causal character of explanations of human action. Today they concerned with post-positivist issues of American origin such as the semantics of natural languages, as practised by Donald Davidson, and Saul Kripke's causal theory of reference.

In the heyday of Oxford philosophy in the manner of Ryle and Austin the foundations for this unprecedented reversal of the ancient relationship of colonial dependence were being laid by Quine and Goodman. Quine spent a year in Oxford as Eastman visiting professor in the middle of the Austin epoch and, with a special combination of charm, brilliance and accessibility, made a great many friends. But at that stage he did not much influence people. Oxford philosophers admired the ingenuity and adventurousness of the doctrines he put forward, that there is no clear distinction between analytic and synthetic, that singular terms can be eliminated from discourse and that there is no reason to suppose that the word 'exist' means something different when applied to numbers or sets from what it means when applied to electrons or tables. But they showed no inclination to accept his views. Grice and Strawson attacked him on analyticity, Strawson on singular terms, Warnock on existence. The general view, it would be fair to say, was wholly opposed to the kind of logical regimentation of language which he and Goodman practised, seeing it as a form of the underlying misconception which Wittgenstein in his later work criticised as the central error of his own *Tractatus*.

Quine's rejection of analyticity is a development of an idea in an essay of Tarski's about the concept of logical consequence first published in 1936. 'Perhaps it will be possible,' Tarski wrote, 'to find important objective arguments which will enable us to justify the traditional boundary between logical and extra-logical expressions. But I also consider it to be quite possible that investigations will bring no positive results in this direction.' Quine opted firmly for the second conjecture. In his best-known work on the concept of truth Tarski insisted that the kind of semantics he was pursuing was confined to formalised, artificial languages. He italicised the statement: 'It is only the semantics of formalised languages which can be constructed by exact methods.' The idea of a semantics of *natural* languages, developed by Davidson and others, as represented in the massive essay-collection under that name edited by Davidson and Gilbert Harman in 1972, ignored Tarski's implied discouragement, on account, as they said, of 'the success of linguists in treating natural languages as formal semantic systems'. What they had in mind here, of course, is the work of Chomsky. That work has not served only as a methodological example for those in pursuit of a satisfactory formal technique for the investigation of the prime instrument of thought. Chomsky himself has drawn direct philosophical implications from it, implications destructive of the behaviouristic account of our understanding of language which Quine shared with Skinner and also of the almost universal empiricist conviction that there are no innate ideas. In his *Cartesian Linguistics* (1966) Chomsky was at pains to emphasise the confirmation by his own researches of certain central ideas of seventeenth-century rationalists about thought and meaning.

Chomsky had been a student of philosophy at the university of Pennsylvania while Goodman was the chief philosophical figure there. For all their subsequent differences (Goodman has fiercely criticised Chomsky's theory of innateness) they agree that language must be studied with the formalistic rigour of modern logic. Goodman's hostility to 'amorphous philosophical discourses' is implied by much of the most interesting recent philosophical work in America. Notable here is the work of Kripke, Hintikka, Plantinga and the much less Martian-sounding David Lewis on philosophical applications of modal logic.

Even the revival of political theory in the grand manner in Rawls's *Theory of Justice* and Nozick's *Anarchy, State and Utopia* displays, in what might be felt to be the least likely area, the formalistic tendency of current American philosophy. This revival of political theory was no doubt inspired by upsurge of more or less violent political emotion of the late 1960s. But the way in which Rawls argues for radical redistribution and Nozick for the minimisation of the state and the free flowering of an unconstrained plurality of social life-styles has a high degree of formal and technical sophistication. Where Marcuse draws on the opaque profundities of Hegelianised Marxism, they turn to mathematical refinements of game theory and welfare economics.

At the moment there is no accessible account in English of the recent developments I have cursorily sketched. Quine's ideas, or some of them, are to be found in an admirably simple and agreeable form in his short book *The Web of Belief* (1970, written with J.S. Ullian). Goodman's comprehensive collection of essays, *Problems and Projects* (1970), contains a few non-technical pieces and on their account is less arcane than any of his unitary treatises. But for the rest one has to go to the technical texts: to Davidson's and Harman's *Semantics of Natural Languages* (containing a much-discussed work by Kripke), Hintikka's *Models for Modalities* (which begins with a fairly manageable methodological essay), Plantinga's *The Nature of Necessity* and, at the upper limit of technical obduracy, the late Richard Montague's *Formal Philosophy*.

For those who read German there has recently appeared a somewhat less austere aid to knowledge. This is the latest edition of Wolfgang Stegmüller's *Hauptströmungen der Gegenwartsphilosophie* (Stuttgart, 1975). When this originally appeared it was mainly taken up with German philosophers of the most copious and systematic character, such as Heidegger, Jaspers and Nicolai Hartmann. Two chapters at the end were concerned with the type of philosophy practised by Stegmüller himself: one on Carnap and modern empiricism, the other on further aspects of contemporary analytic philosophy. In an English translation of the fourth edition by Albert E. Blumberg (Boston, Mass., 1969) there were also included a long chapter on the philosophies of Wittgenstein and a brief appendix on Chomsky. The new German edition contains all but the appendix on Chomsky in its first volume and devotes the second to very recent developments. In its first half it deals in one chapter with philosophy of language, represented by Chomsky, by Richard Montague and by the theory of speech-acts in Austin and Searle, and in another with eight new areas of philosophical interest in logic and at some length with various ideas of Kripke's. Stegmüller is a lucid, impersonal expositor who gets arguments across as well as conclusions. This new second volume, which also considers recent scientific cosmology, the biological doctrines of Monod and others and T.S. Kuhn's theory of scientific progress, is amazingly up-to-date.

In what I have said about the most recent developments in American philosophy I have confined myself to those formalistic views which have attracted most interest among philosophers here and on which the claim that America is now the philosophical centre of the English-speaking world must rest. But there is a great deal else going on. Chisholm has at least been mentioned; in any account of what is influential Wilfrid Sellars of Pittsburgh should have been. Max Black's selection of articles *Philosophy in America* (London, 1965) gives a much more representative idea of what is afoot than J.E. Smith's *Contemporary American Philosophy: Second Series* (London, 1970) which is largely composed of work by philosophers who are now retired, four of his fifteen contributors having been born before 1900 and only two of them later than 1921.

The recently secured primacy of American philosophy can be traced back, in virtue of its particular style and methods, to the hospitable intellectual and institutional reception accorded in the late 1930s to the European positivists, whose work is being continued and innovatively developed. The impulse those exiles gave has been taken up by the American philosophical community and made its own. This confirms the view of R.M. Harré that the flight of the intelligentsia of continental Europe to the United States caused by Hitler is the most important event of its kind since the dispersion of Byzantine scholars by the Turkish conquerors in the fifteenth century.

30
C.I. Lewis

What are epistemologists for? One conception of the role of the philosophical theorist of knowledge has a consoling quality. It appeals to the epistemologist by assigning him a reasonably dignified position, and to the general interested public, which it sees as his clients, it has the merit of taking him to be socially useful. This is the conception of him as the professional guardian of the standards of rationality. Beliefs abound, reasons are adduced in support of them, claims to knowledge are advanced. The task of the epistemologist, on this view, is to act as an umpire who closely observes all this cognitive play and blows his whistle when the rules of justified belief are infringed.

The run-of-the-mill epistemologist deals with the beliefs of ordinary men: that there are chairs and tables, people other than oneself who think and feel, past events and future probabilities. There is also the more specialised trade of scrutinising the claims made on behalf of the findings of particular intellectual disciplines: history, the natural and social sciences, theology, the criticism of art and literature, psychology, and what may be called substantive ethics, the reasoned affirmation of principles of conduct.

On this view epistemology is, if a science at all, a normative one, an ethics of belief, in W.K. Clifford's phrase, that aims to lay down principles for discriminating justified beliefs from unjustified ones. C.I. Lewis certainly thought of epistemology in this way and, indeed, in very much these terms. He constantly stressed the analogy between logically right thinking and morally right action.

There is something a little vaunting and Promethean about this notion, since it suggests that the epistemologist is somehow above and detached from the cognitive strivings he surveys. Some philosophers have tried to avoid any such immodesty, influenced, perhaps, by the thought that their own discipline is itself just one among many ways in which beliefs are formed and claims to knowledge made.

Three different versions of a humbler idea of epistemology have some currency. First, there is the view of linguistic philosophers that the epistemologist should do no more than describe the rules to which, in their understanding of words like 'know', 'believe', 'certain', and 'probable', their non-philosophical users are already committed. His task is to remind, not to legislate. Secondly, there is the view recently expressed by Quine that epistemology is a part of psychology, an account of the mental and linguistic mechanisms through which beliefs are formed, compete, and persist. Finally, there is the conventionalist view, held at one time by Carnap, which sees the epistemologist as a kind of conceptual entrepreneur, more specifically as a cognitive management-consultant, who devises possible systems of belief-formation and offers them to anyone interested in replacing unreflective habits with an explicit policy.

I do not believe that epistemology can be neutral to this degree. The linguistic philosopher's description is critically selective and the whole point of the rules he propounds is to exclude some actual reasonings and beliefs from their scope. Of course the epistemologist does not prescribe *ex nihilo*, like Rousseau's legislator, to a constituency of cognitive barbarians; he has to build on their fitful intimations of rationality. But his standpoint is inescapably corrective and critical.

However, it is one thing for epistemologists to claim this role, a very different thing for the claim to be effectively admitted by the public at large. It might seem that, for the most part, epistemologists, like contemporary poets, communicate only with each other. If they are to have an influence it must be through the students who pass through their hands and return to the outside world with improved and explicit standards. The exponents of other intellectual disciplines, to whom the epistemologist's more specific injunctions are addressed, are commonly reluctant to receive correction.

There was a notable example of such resistance some time ago when J.H. Hexter applied the ethics of historical reasoning propounded by Morton White to a test case, Mattingly's *Defeat of the Spanish Armada*. For Hexter, Mattingly's book was an incontrovertible example of genuine historical knowledge. Since it did not remotely comply, in his view, with White's specifications, the latter could be regarded as fit only for ornament, not for use.

There is one feature of the history of philosophical theorising about knowledge that is a little at odds with the notion I have been considering of the epistemologist as a socially useful being in his role as critic of our intellectual processes. This is that the greatest epistemologists, by common acceptation, have all defended more or less wild, indeed radically subversive, conceptions of the genuine and proper pursuit of knowledge. For Plato true knowledge was demonstrative in its method and confined for its objects to abstract essences: the contents of the world in space and time lacked the kind of reality which was required for knowledge of them to be possible. Descartes went a little further by allowing that there is also knowledge of one's own current mental states, but he could support the main body of our ordinary convictions only by relying on the principle that a benevolent God, whose existence he claimed to prove, would not deceive us. Hume seemed to himself, and to all of his readers except a group of resolute reinterpreters who take his skepticism to be essentially rhetorical, to have shown that we can know nothing but our own impressions and merely conceptual truths about the relations between our own ideas. Kant, attempting to answer Hume, concluded that we could know the world, but only if it was conceived as largely our own construction; things in themselves being forever beyond our grasp.

There is, however, a body of epistemologists – of the second class, perhaps, by comparison with the great extremists – who lay down altogether less stringent conditions for cognitive salvation: Aristotle, Locke, Reid, John Stuart Mill. These more earnest and responsible figures comment on the methods and results of our common knowledge in a practically more applicable way. The extremists, because of the extravagance of their ideals, can communicate at most a style to the thinking men who are influenced by them. No one, for example, could believe as little as Hume seems to allow, but there is a Humean standpoint of skeptical detachment which has its appeal. Similarly the reorganisation of our beliefs that Descartes recommends, in which all our convictions about the common world are rescued only by subordinating them to the veracity of God, is not accepted by all those Frenchmen whose brisk, abstract, uncompromising mode of reasoning displays his influence.

The moderates accommodate their demands more realistically to the human propensity to believe. In Locke our ordinary beliefs are broadly endorsed, even if they show the bruises left by his examination of them, and in Reid the commonsensical dogmas which much philosophy has sought to undermine are sanctified as self-evident truths about the nature of things. It almost seems that the two kinds of philosopher are necessary to each other. The Don Quixotes produce their explosive illuminations; the Sancho Panzas put the pieces together again.

In this century and in the English-speaking world, something like this relation obtains between Russell and C.I. Lewis. Russell's first great achievement was the construction of a purely extensional system of logic. This implied, as Russell eventually came to agree, that logic is not a substantive discipline with a subject matter of its own: it is essentially formal and concerned with the arrangement of substantive discourse about the world, not with making a further addition to such discourse. Lewis's first books rejected this idea in favour of an intensional logic in which attention is paid not merely to the mathematically manipulable *form* of our assertions but to the necessary connections of meaning between the terms they contain.

For most of his career Russell was heavily skeptical about memory and induction and confessed in his last major work, *Human Knowledge*, that scientific theorising could be ratified only by arbitrary postulations about the world it is applied to. Lewis, on the other hand, gave arguments for the necessary reliability in general of both memory and induction and held that the abyss of doubt that Russell claimed to have detected about everything but what is immediately present to the senses is an illusion.

Finally, despite his strong moral commitments, Russell became convinced that there could be no knowledge in the domain of values and that judgments expressed personal emotional attitudes and not objective matters of fact. Lewis, in his later writings, fought this widespread opinion with determination, and even ferocity, insisting that our evaluations do express genuine knowledge about the conditions of human satisfaction and suffering.

It is clear to me that Lewis was the most distinguished American professional philosopher of the last half-century. The date and the requirement of professionalism rule out Santayana, who left the United States for good in 1914 and was more a critic of culture than a philosopher in the narrow sense. Dewey is Lewis's most serious competitor. But although he was a much larger figure and has no doubt had more influence than Lewis through his work (most of all in education), as a philosopher pure and simple he is Lewis's inferior. Despite his rejection of the type of Hegelian idealism in which he was brought up, Dewey retained the edifying amorphousness of its literary and, more to the point, logical style. Lewis, by contrast, is a hard and definite reasoner, although not much more of a stylist than Dewey.

He has now been honoured, five years after his death, by the publication of a volume devoted to him in the 'Library of Living Philosophers', the thirteenth person to be so honoured. These volumes consist of an autobiography, with more or less intellectual emphasis, by the subject; a series of essays by other people on aspects of his work; and a concluding essay, ideally rather long, in which the subject of the volume answers the criticism in the preceding essays. Three volumes in the series, which has been edited throughout by Professor P.A. Schilpp, are essential philosophical reading: those on Russell, Moore, and Carnap. These philosophers evoked some admirable critical essays and provided thorough and serious answers to criticism. Indeed Carnap's reply to his critics is the best study of Carnap's philosophy that there is.

The Lewis volume (*The Philosophy of C.I. Lewis*, ed. Paul Arthur Schilpp, La Salle, Ill., 1968) is not so good as these three major successes. The autobiography, though enjoyable for its revelation of Lewis's gruff, dour character, is brief and peters out in the middle of Lewis's career. The essays, although for the most part sound and decent, are generally a little uninspired. The selection of commentators is largely confined to a kind of philosophical Middle America and there are few arresting performers of the kind whose thoughts would be interesting in their own right. Lewis's reply to his critics is, as he admits, fairly perfunctory. Here, as in other volumes in the series, the subject of the volume was too old by the time the opportunity of commenting at length on his own work came to him to take the best advantage of it. Certainly the next volume announced, which is on Popper, looks more exciting.

The autobiography is interesting about Lewis's early life. His father worked in a shoe factory and got into difficulties for his membership in the Knights of Labor. The young Lewis was brought up on Fabianism and Bellamy's *Looking Backward* and heard and revered Gompers and Debs. He got to and through Harvard only by the skin of his teeth (in 1902 40 percent of Harvard students depended on what they could earn for themselves). By dint of waiting on tables Lewis got his A.B. in three years. By 1912, after various vicissitudes, he had obtained his Ph.D. And so on to the study of *Principia Mathematica*, the devising of his own alternative logical system, and work in the great chaotic accumulation of the papers of Charles Sanders Peirce.

The characteristic stoicism of his mode of self-description cannot conceal the enormous amount of work he got through in his early years. He picks out

Josiah Royce as the teacher who most influenced him but from that point on has little to say about influences, apart from Peirce's papers. In philosophy, as in life, he was a model of old-fashioned New England self-reliance.

All sides of his work receive full treatment in the essays. A strikingly dull piece on his contributions to the history of logic reminds us that for fifty years his *Survey of Symbolic Logic* was the best history of logic in English, indeed it was the only serious one until the publication of William and Martha Kneale's more comprehensive *Development of Logic*. There is a very thorough and detailed essay on Lewis's work as a creative logician by W.T. Parry which, by its references to a mass of logical work somewhat at the margin of current interest, draws attention to the considerable influence Lewis has exercised in this area.

Roderick Firth and Roderick Chisholm are good on Lewis's epistemology. Chisholm has done more than anyone else to develop Lewis's conception of the theory of knowledge as a normative discipline, an ethics of belief. He points out here that Lewis is a strict moralist in this region: for him there are no indifferent beliefs, any belief that is not justified ought to be rejected. Firth, with customary exquisiteness, questions Lewis's assumption that the ultimate foundation of empirical knowledge must be indubitably certain. E.M. Adams neatly points out the uncomfortable relationship, verging on incompatibility, that holds between, on the one hand, Lewis's empiricist assumptions that the basis of empirical knowledge is subjective appearances and that the meaning of words is determined by the experiences with which they are connected and, on the other, his insistence that his view of our beliefs about material things is a realistic one. Realism implies that there is more to the material world than the appearances it presents to us; but how, on Lewis's assumptions about meaning and experience, can the belief that this is so be expressed?

Lewis's work in formal logic has suffered a curious fate. It was undertaken in order to provide an alternative to the system of *Principia Mathematica* which would accommodate within itself, as that system does not, the essential connectedness that we ordinarily suppose to obtain between the antecedent and the consequent, the if-clause and the then-clause, of a conditional statement. Everyone agrees that 'if p then q' is false when p is true and q is false. In Russell's extensional system that is all there is to 'if p then q'. Provided that p is false or q is true, or both, it is true in Russell's system that if p then q. On this view the truth or falsity of a conditional statement can be established simply by considering the truth or falsity of its constituents. It is not necessary to consider the specific meaning or content of the constituents.

It turns out that this rather meager account of the type of statement that is essential to all reasoning conforms to all the rules of inference which we accept in our more reflective moments and which we should want a logical system to preserve, even if it also underwrites as laws certain patterns of inference that are not intuitively acceptable. In particular it is a law of Russell's logic that if p is false then it follows that 'if p then q' is true, whatever p and q may be and however unrelated they are to each other as regards their content. It also follows that 'if p then q' is true if q is true, whatever p and q may be. These 'paradoxes of material implication' impelled Lewis to construct a system which excluded them. But most logicians have accepted them as a reasonable price to pay in oddity for the immense manipulative benefits that accrue from the extensional interpretation of 'if – then'. What such an interpretation makes possible is a purely mechanical way of deciding on the logical validity of patterns of inference in which conditional statements occur and on the consistency of sets of statements some of which are conditional.

So, despite Lewis, extensionalism generally prevails in logic. The result may be a bit of a caricature of our ordinary ways of reasoning but it contains what is essential and is vastly fertile from the point of view of formal construction, a liberating simplification. But Lewis's approach (one should not say 'system', since he devised several, overlapping ones) has not been abandoned. It has found a new employment of an interesting and important kind: as modal logic, concerned with the rules governing the relations of statements containing such words as 'must', 'may' and 'can', 'necessarily' and 'possibly', 'ought' and 'oughtn't'. For example, if p is necessary then p is possible; but if p is not impossible it does not follow that p is necessary. Lewis's logic has not been accorded the position its creator designed for it, that of representing the rules of ordinary assertion, about what is or is not the case. But a more specialised task has been found for it, that of specifying the rules governing assertions qualified by the pervasive range of modal terms, assertions about what must or should or can be the case.

As an epistemologist Lewis's position always rested on a fundamental distinction between knowledge that is necessary and a priori, independent of what actually happens in the world, and contingent, empirical knowledge. For Lewis, necessary truth is determined by the relations between the meanings of the terms we use, while all contingent statements must be somehow reducible to the incorrigible deliverances of immediate experience. A full exposition of this logical dualism, which has been fundamental to much of the analytic philosophy of the past forty years, is to be found in *Mind and the World-Order* (1929), Lewis's first great book on the theory of knowledge. It anticipated many of the doctrines of the logical positivism of the 1930s but presented them in a more perceptive, perhaps because less polemically combative, way. There is still no better defense of the view that all necessary propositions are analytic than the one to be found in that book.

His account of empirical knowledge received its full development in his long *Analysis of Knowledge and Valuation* in 1946. It is the culmination of a long tradition of more or less radical empiricism in English-speaking philosophy; prepared for by Locke and Berkeley, salvageable from the skeptical desperation of Hume, set out plainly in outline form by Mill, broken into a number of brilliant, hasty fragments by Russell. Lewis goes at the problem of accounting for our knowledge of, or at any rate justified belief in, a world of material objects, existing independently of us, on the basis of the momentary and discontinuous impressions of our senses with a cool head, in great detail, and with a solid readiness to follow the argument wherever it may lead him.

It leads him a long way, into investigations of induction (since our beliefs about the material world are in his view derived by generalising from the regularities disclosed in our sense experience), probability (since no such belief is ever certain or finally established), and the nature of counter-factual conjectures (since all beliefs about what we are not here and now observing assert, he contends, what we should be observing if certain conditions were to obtain which in fact do not).

The problem of our knowledge of the external world is perhaps more calculated than any other to inspire the non-philosopher with an amused conviction of the essentially dotty and fantastic character of epistemology. This results from incautious formulation of the problem as that of justifying our belief in a world that exists independently of us. As Reid too mildly remarked, that belief 'is older and of more authority than any argument of philosophy'. Serious doubt of it is more a sign of mental derangement than of conspicuous intellectual penetration. In fact, the point of the problem is not whether the belief is justified; it is, rather, what the justification actually is.

Lewis's handling of the complicated network of abstractions involved is an exemplary display of patient and systematic rationality. It amounts to a demonstration that, if the initial presumption that empirical knowledge must have infallibly certain foundations is correct (and, of that large majority of epistemologists who have supposed this, Lewis is almost alone in arguing for it instead of taking it for granted), our belief in a material world must be justified in his way.

In the last twenty years the theory of empirical knowledge has been considerably transformed by the abandonment of the presumption about empirical knowledge I have mentioned. Various things have contributed to the change. One was G.E. Moore's persistent efforts to distinguish certainty, properly so called, from the much narrower concept of incorrigibility with which Lewis and those of his persuasion identified it. Another is the recognition that it does not follow from the fact that a belief is less than certain, in either sense, that it must therefore be the outcome of an inference.

Lewis accepted this deduction on the ground that probability is always relative to evidence. But that does not, as Lewis thought, entail that all less than certain beliefs must be inferred. Any reason there is for thinking that probability is relative to evidence is a reason for thinking that certainty is relative to evidence too. The type of 'direct realism' propounded by many current theorists of perception sees no logical difficulty in the admission that fallible beliefs about material things can be direct and uninferred reports of our perceptions just as well as the infallible beliefs about sense impressions which theorists of knowledge from Descartes to Lewis have held to be the only possible occupants of this epistemologically basic status.

The main preoccupation of the last twenty years of Lewis's philosophical career was ethics, in a wide sense of the term that embraces prudence as well as morality, indeed, the whole range of principles by which conduct can be rationally guided. This width of scope, in which prudence, as the reflective pursuit of private advantage in the long run, as well as morality with its impersonal ends, is contrasted with the solicitations of immediate desire, marks him off from the majority of recent ethical philosophers by whom morality is considered in an unearthly isolation while all other action-guiding factors, whether rational or not, are indiscriminately lumped together. Lewis's approach draws attention to the fact that morality is not the only or most representative way in which conduct may be rationally guided. The conflicts with which it abounds tend to suggest that evaluation in general is an altogether more chaotic and emotional affair than it is.

Lewis's first publication on ethics was Book III of his *Analysis of Knowledge and Valuation*. Eighty thousand words long, it could have been a substantive work on its own. In it he treated valuation in general, without distorting concentration on moral valuation, in a way that should have been exemplary, but unfortunately was not. In 1955 he published his Woodbridge lectures, *The Ground and Nature of the Right*, in which morality proper is approached more closely but still in a fairly gingerly way. Now John Lange has edited a collection of Lewis's pieces on ethics written between 1948 and 1959 under the title *Values and Imperatives* (Stanford, 1969).

It is an attractively produced and altogether useful volume, understandably a bit repetitive, rendered delightful for connoisseurs of the idiosyncrasies of Lewis's style by a fine array of characteristic touches. As the years went by Lewis's manner of utterance became ever more gnarled and stilted. But although it became an increasingly graceless vehicle of thought, it remained entirely serviceable. A consistent peculiarity is abstention from articles: 'a' and 'the' are rigidly excluded from many places where they might have been expected. 'Solution of this problem is hard to find', he will say, or 'this doctrine must be subjected to critique of cogency'. Much of his vocabulary is heavily upholstered: words like 'purview', 'pertinent', 'perchance', 'venture', 'gratifying', 'cognize', to offer a random sample, remains of the language of late nineteenth-century protestant edification. Finally, he had a fondness for the subjunctive: 'if it be that ...' and 'it were well that ...'

That this rather elaborate diction only grew on Lewis with time is made clear by the magnificent and magnificent-looking assemblage of the *Collected Papers of C.I. Lewis* brought together under the editorship of John Goheen and John Mothershead of Stanford University (Stanford, 1970). This noble volume contains thirty-five of Lewis's essays, written between 1912 and 1957, divided up into groups of criticism, ethics, epistemology, and logic. A number have not been published before but also here are some of the most influential and best known philosophical pieces of the last half-century (a fact attested to by the frequency with which they have appeared in anthologies) such as 'Experience and Meaning', 'Logic and the Mental', and 'The Modes of Meaning'.

Some excellent published pieces of earlier date have been rescued from comparative neglect, such as his fine 'Facts, Systems and the Unity of the World', a logician's critique of idealist metaphysics. The style of the earlier pieces is much more straightforward than that of his later works. A splendidly cool and authoritative dismissal, written in 1917, of the popular thesis that German idealism was responsible for the 1914 war makes its point with none of the cumbrousness and grandiloquence of his better known prose.

Lewis's chief concern in ethics was to resist what he saw as the destructively sophistical agreement among up-to-date philosophers that judgments of value are neither true nor false and that they express not knowledge but only emotion. His positive view was that there are objective values and that they are unmysteriously empirical. We have a personal, subjective awareness of value in the satisfyingness or displeasingness that we find to be as much a feature of our immediate experience as shape or colour. He saw the relation of objective value to experienced satisfaction as paralleling that between the real shape or colour of things and the shape or colour they appear to have. For a thing or situation to have objective value is for it to have the capacity to yield satisfaction for people in general in ordinary circumstances. There can be illusions of valuation, just as there can be illusions of perception, but they can be identified, as illusions of perception are, by their incongruity with the general testimony of individual experience.

Rightness and wrongness, for Lewis, are properties of actions that are within our control and they are determined by the value of the consequences to which those actions lead. It is important for the critical side of his argument that the terms 'right' and 'wrong' should be widely applicable, not merely to actions being morally appraised, nor just to actions involving bodily movements, but also to 'internal actions' of believing and inferring. For it confronts those who would deny objective validity to judgments of *moral* rightness with the possibility that the same denial should be extended to the assumptions of *logical* rightness on which their arguments depend.

He distinguishes four main fields in which judgments of rightness and wrongness are made: prudence, where the end is a comprehensively satisfactory life for the agent; morality, where the end is justly distributed satisfaction for all; logic, where it is the consistency without which there can be no rational thought or significant speech; and epistemology, where it is cogency or a reasonable prospect of truth. In each of these domains there is a generally valued end, conduciveness to which sets the standard of right for that domain. If ethics, in the widest sense, is the theory of right action, including thought, then, he argued, it disastrously undermines itself if it holds judgments of rightness to be subjective. This for Lewis is an aberration which philosophers have been led into by concentrating on moral rightness alone to the neglect of other kinds of rightness.

The liveliest aspect of the essays in *Values and Imperatives* is Lewis's vigorous development of this theme against the prevailing 'non-cognitivist' orthodoxy in moral philosophy: the idea that value, or moral value at any rate, is not a possible topic of knowledge. He thought it absurd to suppose that the dictates of prudence are not rationally discoverable matters of empirical fact and, since that is so, why should not the same be true of morality? Against the idea that principles of obligation are matters of arbitrary choice he argued that this makes subjective nonsense of the imperatives of logic and epistemology. He often recurs to the pragmatically self-contradictory character of the Cyrenaic's rejection of prudence. The resolution to take no thought for tomorrow is self-refuting since it is itself a thought for tomorrow as well as for today.

In broad outline Lewis's position is close to that of Bentham's utilitarianism, for which the ultimate standard of value is the greatest possible pleasure for all, but it is wider in scope. Lewis did not deny the affinity but laid stress on some points of disagreement. He rejected 'pleasure' as an adequate description of the positively valuable and expressed doubts about Bentham's notion of a calculus of value with its suggestion that problems about the comparison and balancing-off of the pleasures and pains of different people could be settled in a simple, mechanical way.

In the best essay on Lewis's ethics in the Schilpp volume, Mary Mothershill points out that he makes rather too much of this disagreement with Bentham's idea of a calculus. He certainly allows for the comparison and over-all estimation of the values and disvalues realised for different people in the consequences of a particular action. But, as she goes on to show, there is a substantive difference with Bentham in the special emphasis Lewis lays on the satisfactions that come from activity as constitutive of a good life, in contrast to merely passive enjoyment.

For all its elaboration there are several loose ends in Lewis's theory of value. Robert W. Browning points out in a perceptive essay that Lewis does not really address himself to the fact that the value-experiences that things give rise to vary much more from one person to another than do the sense-experiences they produce. A more homogeneous conception of human nature than the facts warrant seems to be presupposed by the idea that an objective, social, impersonal value can be ascribed to things in the way that perceptible qualities like colour can be ascribed to them. Our tastes are more various than our sensory equipment. In particular, the expert or connoisseur has a place in evaluation that he does not have in ordinary perception. No expert is needed to tell us that *The Golden Bowl* is long and written in English, nor is there any persisting doubt about these judgments. But that is not obviously true of the book's value. It is not hard to think of the sort of modifications Lewis's theory would need to meet this kind of objection, but the modifications are needed.

Another important weakness is the very tentative nature of Lewis's engagement with morality proper. To start with he offers two definitions of the domain of the moral that do not coincide. On the one hand, it is tied up with justice or consideration for others; on the other, it is identified with the resultant or over-all value of an act or state of affairs when all particular value-claims have been taken into account. To regard these as the same is to make altruistic self-suppression the ultimate rule of conduct by implying that, in every situation of choice, consideration for others must override all other claims.

In general there is something of a gap between the well-worked-out view that values are matters of empirical knowledge and the conception of the morally right as that which contributes most to the satisfaction of all. We all may agree that it is right to change out of wet clothes and come to this agreement by the same train of reasoning and in the light of a universally shared hostility to pneumonia. There is no such community of reasoning or of attitude toward the taking of human life to sustain an objective judgment about the moral acceptability of euthanasia.

Lewis shows an awareness of this gap by endorsing a description once given of him as a naturalist with respect to the good but a rationalist with respect to the right. This is a somewhat confusing way of recognising his need to connect the idea that each man's satisfaction is a good to him with the idea that the general satisfaction is a good to all. What he offers as a connecting link is the fact that we are social beings. 'The ground of our obligation to another person,' he writes, 'is that we know him to be as real as we are, and his joys and sorrows to have the same quality as our own.' As it stands this goes no further than, if it goes as far as, Hume's grounding of benevolence in instinctive sympathy, an interest in social peace, and the convenience of having the same rules for all.

It is a measure of Lewis's influence that, despite the somewhat old-fashioned quality of his style and approach, he is very much a back-ground presence in two ambitious and resolutely up-to-date books by young American philosophers. In Arthur Danto's *Analytical Philosophy of Knowledge* (Cambridge, 1968), indeed, he is very much in the foreground, being, along with Austin, the most frequently mentioned twentieth-century philosopher in the book. There is only one explicit mention of him in Thomas Nagel's *The Possibility of Altruism* (Oxford, 1970). But Nagel's project, which is to show that morality, the consideration of the welfare of others, can be shown to be rational in just the same way as prudence, the consideration of the welfare of one's future self, is entirely Lewisian.

Danto's book has been unfavourably criticised for its convoluted and ornamental style. It is written with the kind of showy and nervous volubility that suggests a lack of self-confidence. Danto insistently applies the symptomatic word 'banal' to positions from which he is anxious to dissociate himself, as if in terror of the raised eyebrows of some group of arbiters of philosophical chic. I said earlier that Lewis's style was quaint and clumsy, but its peculiarities do not obstruct understanding or slow up the argument. This cannot be said of Danto's. Where Lewis advances on his readers in dun-coloured verbal garments of complex and antiquated cut, which nevertheless do not impede his movements, Danto keeps falling over the elaborately unfunctional folds and hangings of his stylistic fancy dress. (Nagel, however, appears in a tight-fitting scuba-diving rig, in which he moves so rapidly that it is often hard to keep up with him.)

Danto's main thesis is that epistemology is concerned with 'the space between language and the world', that is to say with a group of semantic concepts the chief of which are knowledge, truth and existence. These concepts do not describe ordinary empirical properties of the thoughts and things to which they are ascribed but, rather, the semantic relations of thoughts, sentences and the names of things to the world. The type of very general and far-reaching skepticism that has always provoked epistemological reflection dramatises the gap between our thoughts and the world they refer to by insisting that we are irrevocably stuck on one side of the gap.

Danto holds that the gap is necessary and so is not a ground for skeptical anxiety. His all-purpose cure for doubt is the principle that in order to understand a sentence one must be able to experience whatever it is in the world that makes it true. The possibility of knowledge necessarily follows from the fact of understanding. Without understanding there is nothing about which the question of knowledge can be raised.

On the way to this conclusion Danto disposes, to more or less effect, of various competing accounts of the nature of knowledge; of the idea that true knowledge must be infallible (making very heavy weather of what is at most a partial diagnosis of this assumption); and, more convincingly, of the idea that to know something is to know that one knows it. He accepts the traditional distinction between direct knowledge based on experience and indirect knowledge that is derived from other knowledge already possessed. By laying down the very strong condition that indirect knowledge must be logically entailed by the evidence for it (the usual view is that the evidence for it should be good or sufficient, not logically conclusive) he avoids consideration of the whole topic of justified, as contrasted with absolutely certified, belief which ordinarily forms a main part of epistemological discussion.

His main point, perhaps, is that experience has been traditionally misrepresented as the *object* of knowledge, when it is in fact the *relation* between the knower and the world he knows. Traditional theories (Lewis's as much as Descartes's) maintain that the only direct objects of knowledge are experiences themselves, namely private ideas or sense-impressions. Danto concludes from the fact that sentences about public, extra-mental objects are intelligible that such things can be experienced directly. The traditional view that public, material things can be known only indirectly is nowhere, as far as I can see, refuted, although I agree with Danto that it is in fact false.

Nagel's *The Possibility of Altruism* is an extremely tough, polished, and altogether stimulating piece of work. Most recent ethical theorists, by their monocular concentration on the issue of the precise logical status of moral judgments (are they really statements, true or false; are they implicitly universal?) have taken it as a simple brute fact that people are disposed to make such judgments and to guide their conduct by them. Nagel, adopting the sensible but recently much blown-upon position that the core of morality is concern for the welfare of others, raises the grand old question: why should I be moral, how can it be shown to be rational to pay any attention to the welfare of others except to the extent that doing so can be seen to conduce to my own well-being?

His basic strategy is much the same as Lewis's. If men are conceived as always choosing simply between what morality dictates and the satisfaction of their own desires, their choice of the former is made to look irrationally self-immolating. But such a view, he holds, misrepresents the nature of our situations of choice. In the many situations where no moral considerations are relevant we still have to choose ordinarily between what our present desires suggest and the requirements of prudence, which takes into account the desires we have good reason to think we shall have in the future.

The heart of his argument is that the desires relating to the future which prudence takes into account are not desires we currently possess. To cater for them by taking out insurance, giving up smoking, stifling rude remarks is only rational in the light of the fact that we are beings that endure or persist through time. For most people most of the time it is true that they have a future in which chickens will come home to roost and the displeasing consequences of present gratifications will materialise. One attitude toward conduct that everyone would admit to be irrational is that it is the kind of impulsive living in the present that is uninfluenced by the fact that we are temporally continuing beings.

The next step Nagel takes is to argue that there is another fact, parallel to that of our having futures, which makes a measure of altruism rational (he is not arguing for major self-sacrifice, only for consideration for others) in the way that our futures rationalise prudence. Just as the desires we actually have, rather than have reason to think we shall have, are insufficient to justify prudent conduct, he says, so our natural benevolence and our personal interest in being members of a peaceful and not vengefully disposed society are too weak to justify the kind of consistent and principled concern for others which constitutes the minimum demand of morality. The elementary fact which, according to Nagel, makes it rational to be concerned with the satisfactions and sufferings of others is that they really exist and do rejoice and suffer in just the same way as we do.

Many ethical theorists have been satisfied with the attempt to base morality on its connection to our private, personal interests. Our natural benevolence, as Hume observed, is fairly confined in its operations, largely to the small circle of people whom we love or are fond of. It is, of course, personally convenient to each of us that morality should be maintained as a general institution, but we can easily argue that a few tempting deviations from its requirements can be indulged without damaging it perceptibly, provided that they are carefully concealed and so do not evoke vengeance or inspire imitation. Something more seems needed to justify a fixed and settled practice of altruism, and Nagel finds it in recognition of the fact of the real existence of others.

If I found the parallel argument that our really current desires are too weak to justify prudence both cryptic and elusive it may be because it is a genuinely new and original idea. He does seem to me to have overstated the case in saying that we have in fact very few desires for anything but the immediate future. I now strongly desire many things which I should like to have now if it were possible but which I know I shall have to plan and work for in a protracted way. He could still say, however, that I do not currently desire to be solvent and healthy in twenty years' time (and much of my prudent behaviour is directed toward that end), but only know that I shall desire it when the time comes.

There is a more fundamental weakness, I think, in the parallel he draws between the fact of my future existence and the real existence of others. He says that the concern for others that expresses, our recognition of their equal reality with ourselves does not need to be understood as any kind of 'mystic identification' with them. The recognition that there *are* other people is, after all, a recognition that they are *other* people. But although in conceding the reality of other people I am certainly not taking myself to be in some way actually identical with them, as contrasted with being more or less like them in certain respects, I surely am the very same person as my future self, I am numerically identical with that future being for all our differences with regard to teeth, hair, posture, and general vivacity. The desires for whose satisfaction I cater in my prudent conduct are still my desires, even if they are not my desires yet. The desires of others that I aim to satisfy with my moral conduct are not, and never will be.

But despite these doubts Nagel's attempt to strengthen a weak link in Lewis's ethics seems to me more successful, at least to the extent of deserving a good deal of further and serious examination, than Danto's attempt to circumvent the main problems of his epistemology altogether.

31
W.V. Quine

Modern analytic philosophy is descended from a fertile if temporary union between the revived formal logic of our age and empiricist philosophy. In the last decades of the nineteenth century logic underwent, at the hands of Frege, its most important developments since Aristotle started it off as a systematic discipline. Frege's work seemed to realise the prophetic dreams of Leibniz. With it formal logic came to cover a vastly wider field than the syllogistic logic of Aristotle had ever done. Where the logic of Aristotle was largely confined to the study of inferences owing their validity to the way the words 'all', 'some' and 'not' occurred in them (as in the old favourite: all men are mortal, all Greeks are men, so all Greeks are mortal), the logic of Frege also covered inferences hinging on 'and', 'or' and 'if'. Aristotle's theory of the syllogism turned out to be a rather small, elementary segment of the second main part of Frege's system. Frege's logic was expressed with unprecedented rigour, and as a crowning achievement, seemed to afford a basis of indubitable certainties from which the whole of mathematics could be derived, effecting a unification of the two disciplines.

At much the same time Mach in Austria, and W.K. Clifford and Karl Pearson in England, were adapting features of the traditional empiricism of Mill to the interpretation of physics, a science that Mill knew only as an intelligent general reader. For this new philosophy of science the basis of all knowledge of fact was the reports of immediate, subjective sense-experience. All the statements of common observation and scientific theory owed their significance and truth to these basic assertions, of which they were held to be convenient abbreviations. Concepts of ordinary material things and of the theoretical entities of science were understood as shorthand for the concepts of direct perception: colour patches in the visual field, felt pressures and so forth. Science in this view was an application of Mach's principle of the economy of thought, a concise and convenient notation for the common patterns and regularities to be found in the streams of individual sense-experience.

The union of logic and empiricism was solemnised in the first really independent philosophical writings of the first man to combine the requisite logical and philosophical expertise, in *Our Knowledge of the External World* (1914) and *Philosophy of Logical Atomism* (1918) of Bertrand Russell. In these works the world is seen as an array of individual events of sense-experience, some related so as to constitute minds, some (including many of the previous group) as material things. For Russell the task of philosophy was to use the new resources of logic to analyse the stock of received knowledge, to reveal its ultimate constitution in basic empirical terms where this was possible, and to discard it as illusion where no such reduction could be effected.

Wittgenstein's *Tractatus Logico-Philosophicus* (1922) was the first brilliant wayward child of the marriage, but the parental lineaments were more obvious in the logical positivism of the Vienna Circle. Wittgenstein's chief service to the tradition at this early stage of his career was to provide a congruous account of logic itself, the instrument of analysis. Formal research in the most elementary and fundamental part of the discipline led him to the view that the laws of logic are tautologies, statements that owe their necessary truth not to some unalterable structural features of the world which they might be thought to describe but to the conventions of language by which they are endowed with meaning. The central idea here is that all necessary truths are at bottom alike in nature. The most sophisticated theorems of mathematics are true for the same reason that 'all bachelors are unmarried' is. That simple truism records no substantial truth about the world. It reflects a fact about language, that the same rules are in force for the distinct expressions 'bachelor' and 'unmarried man'. We do not discover that, as a matter of objective fact, all bachelors are unmarried men. The possibility of an exception is ruled out in advance by the meanings that are conventionally assigned to the words in question.

In its standard form, as expounded in the 1930s by Schlick and Carnap, logical positivism consisted of three main doctrines, multiply related to each other: phenomenalism – a theory of factual knowledge, conventionalism – a theory of logic or formal knowledge, and verificationism – a theory of meaning. Phenomenalism holds that all knowledge of fact is or can be reduced to knowledge of immediate experience, conventionalism that the necessary truth of logic and mathematics is due to conventions of language, verificationism that any utterance that is neither phenomenal nor conventional is beyond the pale, metaphysical, without meaning as a statement, and at best an effusion of feeling. Thus for the positivist 'there is an apple here' is really a compact way of referring to a pattern of visual, tactual, and olfactory experiences that could be obtained here. '4 x 7 = 28' is made true by the meanings conventionally given to the numerals, and 'God loves us all', being neither reducible to immediate sense experience nor true in virtue of its meaning, is not really a statement at all but perhaps the expression of a subconscious wish that everything will turn out all right for us in the end.

The pressures of history brought most leading European positivists to the United States at the end of the 1930s, notably Carnap and Reichenbach. They got an intellectual welcome over and above the political asylum open to them as refugees from fascism. To start with, there is a certain broad affinity between positivism and pragmatism, in Dewey's version at any rate, since both are pro-scientific and anti-theological. Peirce, who was preeminently a logician and a philosopher of science, shared the leading interests of the positivists and his version of pragmatism closely anticipated the verification principle. For Peirce the meaning of a statement lay in the observable difference that would result from its being true rather than false. Such a view is remote from the pragmatism of folk-lore, the idea that the true is what works, which is not all that much of a travesty of the position of William James. Then there is a strongly pragmatic flavour to the idea that all concepts but those of immediate sensory qualities are abbreviative constructions to be chosen on grounds of convenience and economy. The leading American theorist of knowledge of the inter-war period, C.I. Lewis, had come, from a pragmatic starting point, very close to positivism by 1929 when the European movement was only just under way. Always a phenomenalist, he was at that time a conventionalist and he was an anti-metaphysician in practice if not by profession.

But just as transplantation seemed to be giving new life to the most developed form of the union between logic and empiricism, the union itself was coming apart. Logic was withdrawing itself from philosophy and assimilating itself to mathematics. A good theoretical reason for this was Gödel's proof, in his epoch-making paper of 1931, that the Frege-Russell ideal of constructing a complete system of logic and mathematics was incapable of completion. So the interest of logicians turned from the construction of one ideal system to the disciplined study of deductive-systems of all kinds from outside. Another reason was the increasing bulk and sophistication of logic itself which converted its skilled practitioners into an autonomous profession, one that had a direct technical application in the theory of electrical circuits and computer engineering.

On the other side, philosophy of a broadly empiricist, non-edifying kind was undergoing a revolt against formalism, that is against the conviction that discourse achieves its ideal form in the propositions of mathematics and natural science and against the connected principle of method which takes translation into the notation of formal logic to be the proper way to distill the substantial content from any kind of thought or speech. The uncharitable explain this revolt by the fact that philosophers in Britain, where it began, ordinarily know a good deal of classics and rather little mathematics or science. But that was more the fertiliser than the seed of the new development.

At any rate since 1945 analytic or empirical philosophy has become less and less formal, more and more grammatical, at first in Britain, more recently in the United States. It has not tried to solve the traditional problems of philosophy in the manner of positivism by a formalistic regimentation of language but has aimed rather to undermine the problems, to expose them as the outcome of hidden, seductive deviations from the ordinary use of words by close study of the way in which language is actually employed. Mathematics and natural science, the ideal forms of thought for positivism, are viewed by linguistic philosophers, usually pretty much out of the corners of their eyes, as just two out of the many going concerns within the whole field of discourse. Wittgenstein, in the later part of his career, and J.L. Austin, the most influential linguistic philosophers, laid great stress on the many other purposes that language can serve over and above the communication of knowledge. For them statement is not the prime function of language but is on a level with advice, incitement, the expression of feeling, and a host of others. Secondly, they dismissed the claims of formal logic to be a canon of rationality. For them it is not a display of the essential structure of rational discourse, but is rather a diagram or even caricature of properly conducted intellectual processes, a highly selective, not a literal, representation of them. Their philosophical method does not pursue economy and system but seeks to make explicit in all their complex variety the rules which govern established uses of words. This informal logic is a conservative undertaking, for it does not judge the forms of discourse it examines by a formal ideal of the communication of truth. It seeks simply to understand the different kinds of generally prevailing discourse and to codify them only to the extent that is necessary for the relief of philosophical perplexity and is possible in view of the complexity of language. Positivism, by contrast, is radical and critical. It dismisses metaphysics and theology altogether and looks down on common speech and the everyday beliefs it is used to express as first crude approximations to the language and the theories of science.

From a distance the two schools may seem as hard to distinguish as are Stalinists and revisionists to the eye of a stockbroker but there is no love lost between them. To their opponents the positivists look rigid and unenlightened followers of Procrustes, the linguistic philosophers look desultory, amateurish, and constitutionally inconclusive. An example may help to convey the difference between their procedures. Both are interested in the concept of cause. But where the positivist seeks for a single defining formula in logical notation for the sense of the word central to science, the linguistic philosopher compiles an open-ended album of its possible uses, registering every nuance and inflection with taxonomical dedication.

But although the union of logic and empiricism is no longer the height of philosophical fashion it was thirty years ago, it is by no means extinct. In Britain its orthodox form is skillfully defended by Ayer, the Hannibalic figure who first brought the elephants of positivism over the Alpine barrier of British intellectual insularity. Sir Karl Popper, never a member of the Vienna Circle but from early days a critical and highly independent associate, is active and influential. And there is Professor W.V. Quine of Harvard, who is at once the most elegant expounder of systematic logic in the older, pre-Gödelian style of Frege and Russell, the most distinguished American recruit to logical empiricism, probably the contemporary American philosopher most admired in the profession, and an original philosophical thinker of the first rank.

Readers who know him only through his contributions to *The New York Review* may have thought him a geographer, since most of them have been reviews of atlases. (But this taste is not peculiar to him among philosophers. Hobbes, Aubrey reports, 'took great delight to go to the bookbinders' shops and lie gaping on mappes'.) What such readers will not have failed to notice is that he is an extremely witty and felicitous writer. Some great philosophical books are very badly written indeed, those of Kant being unrivalled for their combination of eminence and ugliness. Philosophers who are also logicians at least write lucidly on the whole but they can be fairly dull, as witness the greatest of their number, Aristotle and Frege. But many logicians are entertaining as well as clear. Lewis Carroll and Bertrand Russell have contributed to laughter as well as to understanding.

There are several reasons for the fact that logical writings can be funny with no loss of relevance. A relatively superficial one is that the high abstractions with which they deal can be illustrated with any sort of subject-matter, in a way the odder the better. A deductive argument is valid provided that its conclusion must be true *if* its premises are, but it is not required that its premises actually be true (hence the striking rationality of some cranks and madmen). The distinction is instructively enforced by examples in which they are not. A more substantial reason is that logic deals in surprises. If all rules of inference were obvious it would not be worth codifying them. Furthermore the discovery and prevention of paradoxes has been one of the chief engines of logical progress and a paradox is, among other things, a joke in the full Bergsonian sense, the outcome of mechanical reliance on an ordinarily trustworthy instrument. The title essay of Quine's *The Ways of Paradox* is a beautifully concise survey of the nature and significance of paradoxes and the following delightful proof that 2=1 will give some idea of its attractions. Suppose that $x=1$. Then, multiplying by x, $x^2=x$ and, subtracting 1 from both sides, $x^2-1=x-1$. But $x^2-1=(x+1)(x-1)$. So divide both sides of $x^2-1=x-1$ by $x-1$. The result is $x+1=1$. But since $x=1$, $2=1$. QED.

In general Quine's style combines a certain rotundity of utterance with a verbal wit that exploits the submerged associations and resonances of technical terms. But there are also bonuses of straightforward humour. It is characteristic that Quine should replace those traditional bores X and Y in one of his essays by McX and Wyman. Or consider this passage which needs a small glossary. '$(\exists x)$' may be read here as 'there is something of which it is true that', the x's following this symbol as 'it' and '.' as 'and'.

> The incorrectness of reading 'Ctesias is hunting unicorns' in the fashion: $(\exists x)$ (x is a unicorn. Ctesias is hunting x) is conveniently attested by the non-existence of unicorns, but it is not due simply to that zoological lacuna. It would be equally incorrect to render 'Ernest is hunting lions' as: (1) $(\exists x)$ (x is a lion. Ernest is hunting x), where Ernest is a sportsman in Africa. The force of (1) is rather that there is some individual lion (or several) which Ernest is hunting; stray circus property, for example. The contrast recurs in 'I want a sloop'. The version (2) $(\exists x)$ (x is a sloop. I want x) is suitable insofar only as there may be said to be a certain sloop that I want. If what I seek is mere relief from slooplessness, then (2) gives the wrong idea.

I dare say there are low-spirited people who would regard this passage as merely jocose. But it makes an important point with memorable economy, that statements like 'I want a sloop' are ambiguous: the sloop desired may be a particular sloop or any old sloop. The entertaining elements are not detachable incrustations stuck on to the bare bones of the exposition. Some proper name had to be chosen for the lion-hunting example (1); it was a happy thought to pick Ernest as the subject for such a virile predicate.

This special gift of running the workaday virtues of lucidity and concision in harness with the ability to produce audible laughter makes Quine's more strictly logical books unique of their kind. It is displayed in the more important, comprehensive, and full-dress of them – *Mathematical Logic* and *Set Theory and Its Logic* – as well as in his *Elementary Logic*, an introduction to the rudiments of the subject that goes with particular thoroughness into the business of converting ordinary speech into logical notation and vice versa, and in his *Methods of Logic*, to my mind the best of all comparatively introductory books on the subject, in which the hard formal core is buttressed with philosophical commentary on one side and practical hints for the aspiring ratiocinator on the other.

Scattered logical writings not incorporated in previous books make up the bulk of *Selected Logic Papers* (New York, 1966). Its contents are pretty strictly for the initiated, even the article 'Logic, Symbolic' reprinted from an encyclopaedia. This is an amazing feat of condensation with something solid to say in its brief scope about every major topic of interest in modern formal logic. But it must surely daunt all but the cleverest of technically innocent inquirers. *The Ways of Paradox* is made up of twenty-one more generally accessible pieces showing a much higher ratio of prose to logical symbolism. Quine describes the first five as 'semi-popular pieces on logic and the foundations of mathematics'. The remainder comprises all of Quine's philosophical work that has not been either collected into *From a Logical Point of View* or worked into *Word and Object*, his general treatise on the philosophy of language.

Earlier I boiled the standard, Viennese, form of logical empiricism down to three main theses: phenomenalism, conventionalism, and verificationism. Quine dissents from all three but remains in the tradition because his main problems are those of his positivist predecessors, because he employs the same touchstones of rationality, namely mathematics and physical science, and because he follows the same philosophical method, the interpretation of discourse with the apparatus of modern formal logic. Quine is not exactly a positivist then, but he is a continuator of the positivist mode of analytic philosophy. He is the most productive and distinguished of those who have continued in that mode and resisted the informality and desultoriness of linguistic philosophy *à la* Austin and the later Wittgenstein.

Quine's rejection of phenomenalism rests partly on the irreducibility of ordinary statements of objective fact to immediate sensory terms and partly on the inadequacies of such language as we have for the reporting of private, sensory events. There is, in his view, no unique pattern of immediate experience associated with each empirical statement as its certifier. Language does not mirror experienceable fact but stands in a much more complex relation to it. The relation of a belief to the facts that confirm or undermine it is always mediated through other beliefs. So when the facts are contrary to expectation it is not the belief in the forefront of our attention that has to be dropped. The surprise can be accommodated just as well by dropping one of the other beliefs with which the first belief is connected. In an odd situation I do not have to give up my belief that this is a chicken; I can drop the conviction that no chicken has three legs instead.

Quine's position here is not peculiar to him, though his way of presenting it is. Others, for example Popper, have taken the fallibilist line that all empirical discourse stands to extra-linguistic reality in the loose-fitting kind of relation that for positivism was the feature distinguishing statements of theory from statements of observation. What is special to Quine is the very general conception of the interconnectedness of our beliefs that he derives from it. In his view the entire body of our beliefs is up for judgment each time an observation is made, no element of it has a privileged immunity from revision. Pragmatic considerations of simplicity and convenience must decide which of the defendants is to be the victim sacrificed to accommodate an unexpected experience. According to positivism the system of our beliefs is bounded at either end, so to speak, by two kinds of incorrigibly certain truths: at one end by reports of immediate experience, at the other by the necessary propositions of logic and mathematics. These are indubitable and all other beliefs must be manipulated into consistency with them. Quine denies any difference of principle as far as corrigibility is concerned between these pampered darlings of epistemology and other beliefs.

This adventurous kind of holism had been applied before in a partial way, to theories but not to statements of observation, by the French philosopher of science, Duhem. Quine accepts his doctrine about theories but rejects the theory-observation distinction by which Duhem limited its scope. Taking a step further Quine includes in the total range of revisable belief the principles of inter-connection themselves, the truths of logic and mathematics. This is one facet of his most notorious deviation from orthodoxy, his anti-conventionalist denial of any basic difference of kind or principle between that which is analytically true in virtue of meaning and that which is synthetically true in virtue of experience. The positivist tradition saw a sharp discontinuity between (1) descriptive statements about the world and (2) linguistic statements expressing logical relations between descriptive statements. The relations expressed by statements of type (2) were taken to be identities of meanings and to have been established by conventions of language rather than to reflect the objective nature of things. Quine sees only a difference of degree. For him what is called analytic is only more general and less readily revised than what is called synthetic. He contends that the arguments by which the distinction has been defended all turn on a set of words – 'analytic', 'contradictory', 'necessary', 'synonymous' – each of which requires one of the others for its explanation and none of which is clear in itself. Like the terms of theology these terms fit together logically well enough; the hard question is how any of them is to be related to the actual world. Even those least convinced by his arguments must admit that they are deployed with admirable resource and ingenuity. Any doctrine as far-reaching as the dualism of analytic and empirical discourse draws its strength from a wide variety of considerations. Quine's polemic against it has something worth examination to say about all of them. *The Ways of Paradox* (New York, 1966) contains his first assault on conventionalism, which came out in 1935, as well as two recent variations on the theme.

So far I have mentioned two distinction-eroding doctrines of Quine's, those in which continuities replace hard-and-fast frontiers between observation and theory in the field of empirical discourse and between the empirical and the analytic within the field of methodically establishable statements in general. Quine's third main heresy is his denial of a distinction between science in the most inclusive sense, and metaphysics; or, at any rate, between science and a rather temperately conceived ontology. He shares more than a fondness for maps with Hobbes. Both are logician-philosophers with a special respect for mathematics and physics and with powerfully idiosyncratic prose styles. It is clear that Quine has a strong leaning towards Hobbes's minimal ontology, which says that nothing exists but material bodies. In an essay 'On Mental Entities' in *The Ways of Paradox* he propounds a very general version of Hobbes's materialist denial of an ultimate distinction between the mental and the physical. He identifies the mental state of a subject with the physical condition of the organism in question at the time, leaving it to neurophysiology to discover the precise details of the relevant physical states. He is not worried by the possibility that two organisms could truly report different states of mind, although there was no physical difference but position in space between them. If such a possibility seemed to be realised, he would either deny that both reports are true or put forward the irrefutable hypothesis that there is a physical difference between the two that has not been detected.

There is evidence that Quine would like to be a nominalist with Hobbes too and to deny the independent existence of abstract as well as of mental entities, leaving concrete physical things as the only ultimate constituents of the world. What frustrates him here is his conviction that mathematics is true (or if, like everything else, it is in principle revisable, as true as anything is), that classes are abstract entities, and that mathematics makes irreducible reference to classes. Carnap, the main repository of the positivist tradition, has claimed that whereas 'there are molecules' and 'there are black swans' are assertions of empirical fact, such general statements about whole categories of things as 'there are numbers' or 'there are classes' are either truistic consequences of the adoption of a language in which the names of numbers and classes occur, or else disguised ways of proposing that such a language be adopted. True to form, Quine replies by arguing that such reasons as are given for interpreting 'there are numbers' as a linguistic proposal show 'there are molecules' to be one too.

Quine's three main philosophical innovations add up to a coherent theory of knowledge of great boldness and originality which he has for the most part constructed single-handed. He has arrived, by an entirely new route, at a position which has some general affinities of outline with the absolute idealism of F.H. Bradley, another philosophical stylist given to disconcerting negations. But the spirit of the two philosophies could hardly be more different. Quine's aim is to show the essential continuity of all forms of rational discourse. Taking science as ordinarily conceived to be the central form of rationality, he seeks to connect it with direct observation of the world on the one hand and with logic, mathematics, and ontology on the other.

Bradley of course had no such aim. He saw all discursive thought as inadequate to the apprehension of reality, which could be grasped only by a kind of mystical immersion in its undivided flow. Science, in his view, was not the paradigm of rationality but a crude practical instrument.

The final upshot of Quine's philosophy is an assertion of the essential unity of science and, even more, of the ultimate identity of science with all rational thought. He emphasises its unity in opposition to a long tradition of dualism, distinguishing pure mathematics as the achievement of unaided reason from natural knowledge derived from the senses, that stretches back, through Hume and Leibniz, to Plato's separation of knowledge and opinion. The other point could be expressed in a quasi-Paterian formula: All thought aspires to the condition of science. To Quine the devotion of linguistic philosophers to ordinary language and common sense has a Luddite flavour. Science, with its inextricably mathematical and observational aspects, as the most precise and most firmly established body of human beliefs, is the criterion by which all our convictions must be judged.

Quine's theory of knowledge has had a good deal of piecemeal discussion, but it needs and deserves a fuller and more systematic exposition than its creator has yet been able to give it. In this respect *Word and Object* was something of a disappointment since Quine's views about knowledge took a fairly recessive place in it. In Britain at any rate, some of the steam appears to have gone out of the anti-formalist movement. Wittgenstein and Austin are not so reverently regarded now as they were ten years ago, and the philosophical atmosphere is more hospitable than it has been for a long time to Quine's style of philosophising. In the United States the most effective and penetrating critic of anti-formalist linguistic philosophy is Professor Hilary Putnam, who, if not a disciple, is sympathetic to many of Quine's ideas. Most universities teach formal logic to their philosophy students as they have done since the universities of Paris and Oxford came into being in the twelfth century. Quine's work proves that the subject is still of the most direct relevance to the epistemological core of philosophy.

32

Mortimer Adler

Particular academic disciplines do not institute bodies formally charged with the maintenance of ethical standards, as do such professions as medicine and law whose services have a more immediate practical interest. But they do develop some sort of agreement about the line between respectable and less respectable ways of practicing the discipline in question. (At times there is the unfortunate situation of competing doctrinal schools each trying to draw the line so as to put all who are outside the school on the wrong side of it.) This agreement will not exert itself through an explicit apparatus of courts and condemnations. But it has sanctions at its disposal: exclusion from posts, a unanimously dismissive style of reviewing, the conspiracy of silence.

There are three main offenses against academic respectability and they are found and penalised more often, for obvious reasons, in the humanities. They are the pursuit of money, the propagation of ideology (political or religious), and over-weeningness, in other words, biting off more than any ordinary scholar would regard as possible to chew. Money is best pursued by popularisation, the enlargement of the market. The offence here is to conform, against one's better judgment, to the expectations of the herd, to eliminate the intrinsic difficulty of a subject, to make it congenial and attractive at the possible expense of its proper intellectual values. Sir Arthur Bryant, Gilbert Highet, and C.E.M. Joad have been subjected to attack on these lines. In recent years the possibilities in this area have been much enlarged by the industrialisation of popular enlightenment with large illustrated volumes for the coffee table, encyclopaedic works issued in weekly parts with their munificent 'editorships' for men of proved academic distinction, or, at any rate, reputation. But this, as the case of A.J.P. Taylor shows, can be survived. It is, after all, a mode of enrichment that can be indulged in on a part-time basis. It is permissible to pick up some money on the side but not to make it the predominant object of one's efforts.

The offence of ideological commitment is less disastrous, provided that it is not combined with employment by an ideological institution, a church, or a political party. Philosophy is obviously relevant to religion, history and social science to politics; literary study stands in a slightly more remote relation to both. Philosopher-priests are most respected when they avoid the philosophy of religion, politician-historians when they stick to the study of the reasonably remote past. Over-weeningness, even more than ideology, tends to be associated with the achievement of financial success, even if not with its deliberate pursuit. It must be their status as best-sellers that has exposed

Toynbee and Teilhard de Chardin to such aggressive comment. In a way there is something disarming about the explicit pursuit of money. The dun-coloured and respectable, secure in the armour of their cloistered virtue, can afford to dismiss straight money-makers with moderately indulgent raised eyebrows. Those who achieve worldly success apparently without having aimed at it evoke a stronger reaction.

Mortimer J. Adler would, I imagine, be regarded by most professional philosophers as at best a denizen of the twilight zone. To start with, he has been identified with a definite ideological position: orthodox Catholic Christianity and political conservatism. This was the theme of his association during his time at Chicago between 1930 and 1952 with Robert M. Hutchins. The Great Books programme that they devised served the interests of traditional Christian philosophy, more specifically Catholic scholasticism, and involved a rejection of the social and educational ideals of the American version of secular rationalism, which is roughly to say John Dewey. Adler defended philosophical deduction against inductive science, tradition (as incarnated in the Great Books) against progressive innovation, the wisdom of traditional institutions, such as the church, against individual human reason.

But with the passage of time a discernibly commercial aspect, calculated to modify the style of respectable hostility, has come over his activities. There is a Jack Benny situation in which Benny says to a visitor who has admired some article of furniture 'would you like it then' and opens a cupboard to reveal a large roll of wrapping paper and a cash register. Adler's remark, toward the end of *The Conditions of Philosophy* (New York, 1965), 'I am going to risk what looks like special pleading. I hope I may be pardoned for referring here to the programme of the Institute for Philosophical Research ...' has something of the same gently comical quality. The Great Books themselves and the Syntopicon, a large analytical index that Adler has attached to them, have been the subjects of an energetic marketing campaign. I once sent in a coupon from *TV Guide* in order to get a 64-page free coloured brochure about them. I received instead a visit from a man in a station wagon who reminded me of the hero of John Updike's *Rabbit Run*. He could not be induced to sell me the Syntopicon unless I bought the Hundred Great Books as well.

In 1952 Adler founded the Institute for Philosophical Research and has since been its director. It is a body of anonymous toilers who sift from the corpus of philosophical literature all references to some of the leading ideas among the 102 given canonical status in the Syntopicon. Its first bulky fruit was a two-volume study *The Idea of Freedom* (1958, 1961). More recently briefer studies of the ideas of happiness, justice, love, and progress have appeared. Adler labels the work of his Institute 'dialectical'. It resembles the preparation of memoranda for the higher executives of a bureaucracy. It seeks 'to take stock of the whole accumulation of philosophical opinions on a given subject' with a view to constructing from these materials a rational debate about the issue in question. Adler's assiduous dialecticians are under-labourers whose task is to make things easier for those capable of creative philosophical thought. With 97 of the Syntopicon's great ideas still to be dialectically explored the Institute has plenty of work before it.

At various points in *The Conditions of Philosophy* and *The Difference of Man and the Difference It Makes* (New York 1967) the churning noises of this large industrial undertaking are audible, but Adler does not come before the reader of these books as a philosophical entrepreneur. They are substantial treatises on topics of primary philosophical interest, organised in the ordinary argumentative fashion and not 'dialectically', although some of the bibliographical notes testify to the Institute's resources in the way of information retrieval. In the first book Adler lays down the conditions that philosophy must satisfy if it is to recover the general respect that is now accorded to science and history but no longer to it. Mistaken views about the proper conduct of the discipline are criticised. Elements of virtue are discerned in styles of philosophising that are otherwise deficient. The main controversial issue, the English-speaking philosophical environment being what it is, is Adler's insistence that philosophy cannot be simply a second-order, critical or analytic activity, occupied with the clarification of other, substantive varieties of knowledge. It must be a first-order discipline with a subject matter of its own.

The more recent book surveys a good deal of philosophical and scientific thinking, but its main aim is to bring out the essentials of the dispute between those who see man as a part of nature and those who do not. Adler prefaces his inquiry into the existence of a radical difference of kind between men and other things with a general theory about the nature of difference. He concludes that reasoning alone cannot effectively settle the dispute. It hinges on the truth or falsity of the prediction that men will be able to construct a machine which can converse with them as they converse with one another. Adler stakes his implied preference for the view that men are radically different from other things on the prediction that this technological feat will not be accomplished.

The first thing to say about these books is that they are plainly the work of an intelligent and well-informed man. They are written with great lucidity. As far as the main argument is concerned, all the author's cards are laid unequivocally on the table. It is possible to doubt whether Adler's neutrality in the dispute discussed in the second book about the difference between men and other things is as complete as his manner of handling it there seems to suggest. But stating the problem as he does as one of determining just what is in dispute about the uniqueness of man and just what would be needed to resolve it, he is altogether within his rights in adopting the rather unearthly detached manner that he does. He is particularly conscientious about making the logic of his reasoning explicit. He nowhere relies on allusion, rhetoric, or the probable preconceptions of the reader. Considered simply as expositions of rather elaborate trains of abstract reasoning, these books have much to commend them. The style is plain and effective rather than elegant or memorable. There are occasional lapses into malapropism: 'denumerable' for 'innumerable', 'hypothecate' for 'hypothesize', 'protagonist' for 'supporter'.

Adler has done a good deal of homework, particularly in the second book where it is more needed, in both philosophy and science. As well as arguments and theories in the philosophy of mind, ancient and modern, he has carefully assembled material from evolutionary biology, palaeontology, ethology, experimental psychology, neurology, and cybernetics. I am not qualified to pronounce on the thoroughness and representativeness of his selection of scientific material, but in philosophy he covers the available contributions adequately, with one serious exception. This is that he says nothing about the Wittgensteinian philosophy of mind (as expounded by Wittgenstein himself, Malcolm, Shoemaker, Anscombe, and Melden). Yet in no philosophical school is the attribution of man's uniqueness to the fact that he alone is a language-user more emphatic. It may be that the Wittgensteinians' denial of the relevance of science explains his neglect of their ideas. He does tend to skirt around technical complexities (such as the tangled issue of intentionality) which it would be hard to treat with the degree of lucidity he has imposed on himself. But that does not obviously impair the force of what he has to say. So in whatever relation these two books stand to the vigorous corporate enterprise that markets the Great Books and the Great Ideas, they deserve consideration in their own right as contributions to philosophical debate.

The Conditions of Philosophy begins by laying down the requirements that philosophy must satisfy if it is to regain a status alongside, or even a little above, that of science and history. The more controversial and interesting of these are that philosophy should aim at knowledge in the sense of well-founded belief (*doxa*) and not at demonstrative certainty (*episteme*), that it should be carried on as a public, cooperative enterprise, and that it should be substantive, that is, it should be not merely critical, but should have a first-order subject matter of its own. As Adler sees it, existentialism deals with first order questions but in an idiosyncratic, more or less poetic way, while analytic philosophy, although a rational, public undertaking, refuses to address itself to substantive problems of the first order; analytic philosophy studies not the world but our knowledge of or discourse about it.

The requirement of first-order subject matter for philosophy in effect asserts the possibility of metaphysics, a position which was polemically denied by the positivists of the 1930s. But in fact Adler himself rejects the kind of metaphysics the positivists wished to eliminate: the establishment by purely demonstrative means of a general theory of the world. His position is determined by the requirement that philosophy should be well-founded belief, not demonstrative certainty. He agrees with the analytic philosophers that substantive knowledge of the world must be corrigible and rest on experience. But where they say philosophy can be demonstrative because it is conceptual not empirical, he maintains that its fundamental part, because substantive, must be empirical. His requirements of substantiveness and corrigibility go together.

One is tempted to ask why philosophy must have a first-order subject matter. What is so disreputable about knowledge about knowledge as compared with knowledge about matter or life or the human past? There is a hint in Adler's demand for substantiveness of the kind of inverted proletarian snobbery which denies that anything but manual work is really work, or that anything but manufacture is really productive. Do they not also serve who only sit and analyse? But there are other, less rhetorical objections.

To start with he tells us surprisingly little about the detailed content of philosophy's proprietary subject matter. There is a list of problems on page 43, and thereafter, whenever it becomes appropriate to be at all specific about the requirement of substantiveness, he refers back to this brief and unelucidated catalogue. Substantive questions are of two kinds: speculative questions about what is and happens in the world and practical questions about what men should do and seek. Among the list of speculative questions, which is shorter than it looks because of thinly disguised repetitions, are 'the nature of being and existence', 'change itself and the types of change', 'causation and the types of causes', 'necessity and contingency', 'the material and the immaterial', 'freedom and indeterminacy'. But Adler does not seem aware that every problem in the list can easily be given a second-order, conceptual, interpretation: How should the concepts of existence, change, cause, etc. be analysed? What is more, the most obvious method for dealing with the problems in Adler's list is conceptual. What clear sense can be given to the problem of the 'modes of being' other than by raising the question of what the logically distinct varieties of significant assertion of existence are? In a way, of course, there is an empirical element to this inquiry. We must start from our common empirical awareness of the kinds of claims to knowledge of existence that people are actually disposed to make. But this, though empirical knowledge, is still second-order. It does not relate to the contents of the world in general but to claims that are made for knowledge about the world.

Adler rests his case for substantive philosophical knowledge on a distinction between what he calls special experience, which is acquired by deliberate and systematic, or, as he puts it, investigative, study of the world, the evidential basis of science and history, and common experience, the fruit of non-investigative observation. Now there is, no doubt, a difference between observational knowledge that is acquired by deliberate investigation and knowledge that is just passively and casually picked up. But what non-investigative observation yields is common knowledge or common sense rather than philosophy. What is more, having or lacking an investigative origin distinguishes the way in which knowledge is acquired, but not necessarily the kinds of things known. While elusive things like molecules have to be found by investigation, much of science is concerned to establish methodically things that we know already by common observation of the non-investigative sort.

To the extent that common experience does give rise to a proprietary sort of knowledge, then, it is common sense knowledge, not substantive, metaphysical philosophy. Adler assigns two functions to philosophy in relation to common sense. The first is the second-order business of defending it against science and against mistaken philosophical skepticism, a programme indistinguishable from that of G.E. Moore, a founding father of analytic philosophy. Secondly, philosophy should develop theoretical constructions to explain common phenomena. What these are he does not specify, but God, the soul, and universals would seem reasonable candidates for the task in question. This is to conceive metaphysics as a science based on unscientific evidence. Adler's rather vague account of the relation between substantive philosophy and common experience is in fact compatible with the position of the analytic philosopher, for the latter does not suppose his conceptual investigations to take place in thin air. Their field is not that of bare conceptual possibilities but the comparatively empirical one of the conceptual activities that men actually engage in.

Adler is even less specific about the other, practical branch of substantive philosophy. It is, he says, the most publicly useful part of the subject. Science can discover means to our ends but it cannot determine the ends themselves. For them we must turn to the maid-of-all-work: common experience. But how it underwrites moral convictions is left wholly unexplained. To support his claim of the ethical incapacity of science he invokes the familiar doctrine that naturalism is a fallacy: the opinion, imposed by G.E. Moore on a generation of moral philosophers, that judgments of value are logically unique and cannot be deduced from statements of fact. But if this is so, then common experience is as powerless as the special experience science rests on to justify our valuations. To regard ethical naturalism as fallacious is to reject any kind of observational verification of judgments of value.

In *The Difference of Man and the Difference It Makes* the question at issue, whether or not there is a radical difference of kind between men and other things, is not a pure question, to be resolved by common experience alone presumably, but a mixed question, where philosophy has to adjudicate between the competing claims of other bodies of knowledge, in particular between the common-sense presuppositions of our practice of according a unique moral status to human beings, on one hand, and the various sciences which stress the continuity between man, other animals, and even machines, on the other. Toward the end Adler advances a traditional scholastic argument to show that no explanation of man's power of conceptual thought in wholly material terms is logically possible, but he does not rest his case on it. The materialist thesis of basic continuity between men and other, unquestionably material, things would be established if a machine could be built which could be taught to converse with men in the way that they converse with each other. Until such a machine is constructed the materialist case remains unproved.

The first step of his argument is a theory about the kinds of difference that can obtain between different sorts of things. Things differ in kind rather than degree if there is some defining characteristic of one that the other does not share and if there are no intermediaries between them. But such a difference in kind is only apparent if the discontinuity that shows it is merely contingent, if there could be intermediaries although there are in fact none. Real differences of kind may be superficial rather than radical if they can be explained by reference to differences of degree in the explanatory factor. Thus to show that man is unique in the world in a philosophically significant way it must be shown that he differs in kind radically from all other things. If his difference from them could be explained by the greater proportionate size of his brain then he would differ in kind only superficially. The bulk of the ensuing discussion turns on this point. The logically prior question of whether man's difference of kind is real rather than apparent is hardly considered at all.

But as Adler has defined the notion it is not clear that there is more than an apparent difference of kind between men and other things. As a matter of contingent fact there is a marked discontinuity between men, with their propositional language, construction of tools, and reliance on tradition, and the higher animals who merely signal to one another, improvise tools, and inherit instinctive patterns of behaviour. But intermediate cases are conceivable. Dolphins or a lost tribe of Neanderthal men might prove to have the linguistic, technical, and social capacities of moderately bright four-year-old children and imagination could be mobilised to fill the gaps on either side of them in the scale of achievement.

Adler illustrates his account of the concept of difference with mathematical examples. Whole numbers differ in kind, there are no intermediates between 6 and 7, but there are intermediates between any pair of proper fractions: 1/2 comes between 2/5 and 3/5, 9/20 between 2/5 and 1/2 and so on. Adler betrays a naïve realism about concepts in his reliance on this model. It is a form of the Platonic view that ideas are prior to their exemplifications in the natural order. This is far from obvious to those who follow Hobbes, Locke, and Hume in taking our apparatus of concepts to be a human contrivance. For them our concepts are, as Locke put it, rooted in the similitudes of things, but they do not correspond to an antecedently fixed repertoire of natural kinds. Concepts of entities, like numbers, that are themselves conceptual cannot be taken as a guide to the nature of concepts of actual things. The devices with which we classify the objects of experience are influenced in their formation by our interests as well as by the intrinsic nature of the things themselves. Thus a difference in kind in the natural order reflects only a dissimilarity that is definite and interesting enough to lead us to invent a special word to mark it with.

Adler's presupposition of fixed essences in nature is the consequence of a view of the world as the creation of an intelligent being, working in accordance with a preconceived plan. Now it is just such presuppositions that Adler, in his generally careful neutrality, is anxious to do without. However, the application he makes of this theory can survive its abandonment, in a somewhat chastened form. The idea of a difference of kind can still make perfectly good sense for a non-Platonist; such a difference could be said to rest on the solidity with which the conceptual distinctions we have chosen to introduce are entrenched in our way of thinking about the world. Natural differences in kind can still be important, even if they are all, in Adler's sense, no more than apparent.

The possession of propositional language is the vital point of difference for him between men and other things. It differs from the more or less linguistic capacities of non-human animals in two ways: in the nature of its elements and in the manner of its employment. Human language consists of 'designators', expressions that have denotation and connotation, and not of 'signals' which are only causally related to the immediate stimuli that produce them and to the immediate responses they evoke in their hearers. Secondly, it is not instinctive but employed deliberately and with intention. It testifies to its users' possession of the power of conceptual thought, which is something quite distinct from a mere recognitional capacity. Conceptual thinkers can transcend their environment; they are not tied to the here-and-now in their mental processes in the way that non-human animals seem to be.

The power of conceptual thought is clearly an important differentia of the human species. The vital question for Adler is whether it is a superficial difference that can be explained by the greater proportionate size of the human brain or a radical difference which has to be explained by the presence in men of an immaterial factor, an Aristotelian rational soul. Adler resurrects a traditional scholastic proof for the thesis that matter cannot think. Concepts, the instruments of thought, he argues, are universal in nature, but all matter is individual. One could as well argue that an immaterial factor is needed to explain how a lock can secure a door since a lock is a wholly material thing, but the function of securing the door is universal, having indefinitely numerous instances or occasions of exercise.

Although he seems persuaded that his scholastic argument for immaterialism is valid, he admits that it is unlikely to carry conviction with those who take conceptual thought to be a power of a suitably complex brain. Instead he offers the materialists a challenge. If matter can think, let them produce a piece of unquestionably material machinery which by conversing with men as they do with each other can give the same sort of evidence as they do of the power of thought. He must, in the light of his view that it can be proved that matter cannot think, be convinced that this cannot be done. But he is prepared to rest his case on the empirical foundation of repeated failure to bring it off. To all appearances the crucial issue is left open, with its decisive resolution projected into the future. But, in fact, if a machine is constructed that from behind a screen persuades a group of investigators that it is a person, the immaterialist will not have to surrender. He can always say that men have discovered the material conditions that have to be satisfied for God to endow a natural object with a rational soul. For he must already believe some such endowment to accompany the conception of a child.

The book ends with a survey of the consequences that would follow a resolution of the dispute one way or the other. As things are, fortified by our general belief in a radical difference of kind between men and other things, we accord a unique moral status to human beings. For most people it is morally permissible to enslave animals or to kill them for food, but human slavery and cannibalism are to be condemned. The invention of conversational machines will bring the boundaries of the moral community up for revision. Adler clearly does not subscribe to the view that the basic condition for membership of the moral community is capacity for suffering. If he did he would not give so little attention to the intrinsic claim of animals to moral consideration, which, even on his principles, is as securely based as that on behalf of human idiots or the hopelessly senile. But whatever happened, his assertion that if a conversational machine were constructed 'the moral aspects of human life would be rendered illusory' is extravagant. If a conversational machine were to respond to praise and blame as men do it would be worthwhile reminding it of its duties.

Further consequences would arise for religion. The beliefs that human beings are uniquely personal, are the objects of a special creation, immortal and free, would be undermined. But if materialism turns out to be false and there is an immaterial factor in man, it could be argued that it must have an immaterial cause in God. (Adler thinks this argument is new, but its outlines are in Locke.) At the very end he gives vent to a little partisan ferocity at the expense of the new Christians for whom God is dead. If they think that the divine is not in heaven but in the fact of human personality, they might just as well admit it in heaven. For Adler, God and the soul stand or fall together.

These two books, *The Conditions of Philosophy* and *The Difference of Man and the Difference It Makes*, are presentable contributions to current debate about philosophical method and the philosophy of mind, written with admirable clarity and based on fairly wide study. The first book defends a more-or-less Aristotelian, and thus scholastic, idea of first philosophy or metaphysics; the second does not succeed in concealing a commitment to the Aristotelian idea of the rational soul. Both ideas are apt for the defense of orthodox Catholic theology, since the former underwrites the intellectual propriety of natural theology (conceived as theoretical constructions to explain common phenomena) and the latter is a suitable framework for the Christian doctrine of human nature.

But these broadly ideological potentialities are not emphasised. Indeed only in the final footnote of the second book are they recognised by implication, where, considering the possibility of a 'positive strengthening of the immaterialist hypothesis', Adler observes that it 'would have earth-shaking effects throughout the learned world of the future' and on those laymen who 'reflect the naturalistic materialism and atheism of the learned'. There is something about the wording of these comments which suggests that the 'positive strengthening' in question would be entirely welcome to their author.

Nothing, at first sight, could be more sweetly reasonable than Adler's readiness to accept the arbitration of technical progress in the development of mind-like machines as far as the issue of the soul, or 'immaterial psychic factor', is concerned. But on closer inspection this attitude of perfectly disinterested and open-minded neutrality proves to have certain limitations. First, since there is nothing like a conversational machine in existence at the moment, immaterialism has the immediate advantage. Secondly, Adler's insistence on the final decisiveness of machine construction is misplaced. On the one hand, there can always be dispute about whether a machine has really passed the test. On the other, if this has to be admitted, the immaterialist can fall back on the tactic mentioned earlier of allowing that a new mechanical, rather than biologically reproductive, way has been discovered in which men can get God to endow material bodies with souls. Finally, there is Adler's commitment to the proof that matter cannot think, developed in considerable, not to say loving, detail in a long footnote. He regards it as valid and does not rely on it only because in present intellectual conditions it will not secure general assent. But if it is valid then either no conversational machine can possibly be constructed or there is a non-biological way in which men can get God to put souls into bodies.

Adler, I am sure, faces the future with complete confidence. We are, to start with, quite a long way technically from any machine that looks like passing his test. If something that looks like passing it does eventually get produced, a little backing-down will be called for, since Adler rejects with some scorn the idea that God would ensoul a machine; but the ranks could be soon reformed. In the meantime the work of the Institute for Philosophical Research goes on. 'It is currently engaged,' he writes, 'in the study of the whole discussion of language and thought and especially the problem of meaning,' while he himself is working on a book about the problems of moral philosophy. The extreme suavity of Adler's approach, as compared with the ringing anti-naturalist polemics of twenty or thirty years ago, is a sign of the extent to which 'materialism and atheism' have come to prevail among both the learned and the laity. But even in the catacombs preparations are in hand for the better times that are sure to come.

33

Polish Philosophy

The Polish philosophy of this century, best known for its achievements in formal logic, is a most impressive cultural phenomenon. In his extensive study of its vicissitudes during the Stalinist period Zbigniew Jordan observes that its beginning can be exactly dated. In 1895, when he was 31, Kazimierz Twardowski returned from working with Franz Brentano in Vienna to take up a chair at the university of Lwów. While in Vienna he had written an important monograph on philosophical psychology and he could well have gone on to a successful career in the highly professional surroundings from which Husserl, Meinong and the phenomenological movement in general were emerging. At Lwów he found the philosophy of his own country in a loose, amateurish, edificatory condition. Until his death in 1938 he devoted himself to the task of transforming it into what was perhaps the most rigorously and effectively rational philosophical community in the world.

The high standards of professional competence he imposed on the philosophers of Poland can be expressed in two principles which seem straightforward to the point of obviousness. They demand that absolute priority be given in philosophical work to the greatest possible clarity and definiteness of expression and the greatest possible rigour in argument, with all essential logical steps being explicitly set out. In his view humanly interesting conclusions can be left to look after themselves: bright ideas will emerge without the assistance of an academic philosophical profession. The prime responsibility of the professional philosopher is to set an example of intellectual discipline by dedicating himself to the strict critical justification, rather than the invention, of ideas and beliefs.

In due course two main lines of activity developed under Twardowski's influence. The first and better-known of these is the work of the great school of Polish logicians. During the two decades of the life of the independent Polish republic this was the only genuine community of logicians on any substantial scale in the world. The examples of Frege in Germany and of Russell and Whitehead in Britain had had some general influence on philosophy and had inspired an individual here and there to take up full-time work in the field of logic but they had produced no institutionalised study of logic at an advanced level. A good way to measure the uniqueness of logic in Poland is to compare the main elementary text used there, Lukasiewicz's 'Elements of Mathematical Logic', which is at once rigorous and sophisticated, with its contemporaneous English opposite number, Susan Stebbing's muddled and promiscuously put together 'Modern Introduction to Logic'.

The first two major Polish logicians – Jan Lukasiewicz, who died in exile in Dublin in 1956 in his late seventies, and Stanislaw Lesniewski, who died in 1939 at the age of 53 – both came to the subject from philosophy. Both, it seems, felt that Twardowski's principles could be fully put into effect only by going back to absolute fundamentals, to the strictly formal study of deductive reasoning. Lesniewski abandoned philosophy for logic altogether after the 1914 war, repudiating some early, informal essays on logical topics. Lukasiewicz remained interested in the philosophical implications of his logical work but insisted that philosophy was intellectually valueless if it was not solidly founded on modern formal logic.

Both contributed extensively to the subject. Lukasiewicz invented a new, economical notation, devised unprecedentedly rigorous systematisations of basic propositional logic and, by setting on foot the investigation of many-valued logics, created a kind of logical counterpart to non-Euclidean geometry. He also did some very original research in the history of logic. Lesniewski, like Frege and Russell, sought to provide new logical foundations for mathematics and in pursuing this aim radically revised predicate logic and invented a new logical discipline, mereology, concerned with the relation of whole and part.

Their work established a lively tradition and they had worthy successors. Alfred Tarski, the most brilliant of them, who has been in the United States since 1939, produced, in his monograph on the concept of truth, the school's most distinguished achievement. It is still in effective existence in Poland today.

The logicians of a nation whose language is little known do not find this fact an obstacle to general recognition. Important logical discoveries can be expounded quite briefly and will be largely expressed in the near-Esperanto of formal symbolism. Thus the Polish logicians soon acquired an international reputation. But the equally distinguished philosophers associated with them have had to wait much longer. Of the two leading figures Ajdukiewicz has had only a small proportion of his work published in any of the world languages while the two main works of Kotarbiński have only recently come out in English translation, in one case after nearly forty years, in the other after eleven.

Kazimierz Ajdukiewicz, who died a few years ago, is perhaps the more exact, expert and technically ingenious of the two. But he has been less influential than his colleague Tadeusz Kotarbiński, who is now, at the age of 81, retired, but by no means inactive. One reason for this is that Ajdukiewicz has not woven his numerous and penetrating applications of formal logic to central philosophical problems (about meaning, necessary truth and the existence of abstract entities) into a unitary, systematic form, whereas Kotarbiński's work is everywhere connected to a central, governing idea. Another reason for Kotarbiński's pre-eminence is his very remarkable qualities as a man.

In a series of articles in the 1930s Ajdukiewicz developed the outlines of a general theory of language, a kind of conventionalism which sees our conception of the world as determined by the rules through which language is endowed with meaning, rules freely selected from a set of possible alternatives. It is a more radical version of ideas familiar to English-speaking philosophers from the writings of C.I. Lewis and has an even closer affinity to the ideas of Benjamin Lee Whorf, the linguist, who held that the forms of different languages could differ so fundamentally as to make translation between them impossible and could thus lead to entirely unconnected conceptualisations of the world. But Ajdukiewicz came to doubt the correctness of some of the main assumptions of his argument and proceeded no further with this approximation to a systematic position.

Kotarbiński's development was in the opposite direction. Early in his career he recommended a programme of what he called 'minimalism' in philosophy: the study of precise problems of manageable size, in preference to the pursuit of large syntheses (a proposal much like that of a 'scientific method of philosophy' made by Bertrand Russell in his Lowell lectures of 1914). But as his reflections accumulated he found, rather to his surprise, that they had a common systematic backbone. This was the theory, first called reism and later concretism, that the only true, genuinely referring names in language are the names of material bodies, whether sentient or not. According to this doctrine all the terms of ordinary and scientific discourse that purport to refer to things other than material bodies – to properties, relations, classes, mental states, social institutions and so forth – are only apparent names or 'onomatoids'. Such apparent names are, in effect, handy abbreviations. To understand the meaning of sentences in which they occur is to be able, in principle, to translate them into the usually much more complex sentences, referring only to material bodies, which they abbreviate.

The general formula of reism implies three more specific doctrines: first, a radically realistic theory of perception which takes material things and not private sense-impressions to be the direct objects of the senses; secondly, a nominalist theory of logic, mathematics and discourse about meaning; and, thirdly, a 'somatist' theory of mind which holds that every statement about a conscious, experiencing subject is about a particular, specially organised kind of material thing, viz. an organic body. The general upshot is variety of materialism, but of a new kind, semantic rather than scientific, based on the logical analysis of language and not on the findings of the natural sciences.

Since 1945 many English-speaking philosophers have come to accept conclusions that correspond to those of Kotarbiński, although, oddly enough, only as a result of largely breaking away from the logically-inspired assumptions about philosophical method he accepted. Austin and others have undermined the conviction, common to almost all theorists of knowledge since Plato, that private impressions are the immediate objects of perception. Wittgenstein and Ryle have been widely followed in their interpretation of mental activity in general and of the apprehension of meanings in particular in terms of the behaviour, or dispositions to behaviour, of embodied human beings, an approach which rejects Descartes' dualism of the mental and the physical as well as Plato's dualism of the concrete, changing objects of sensation and abstract, timeless objects of understanding. But in 1929, when Kotarbiński first rejected them in the work now translated by Olgierd Wojtasiewicz under the unappealing title *Gnosiology* (Oxford, 1966), the sense-datum theory of perception and a dualistic account of mind and body were almost universal assumptions of the more up-to-date British and American philosophers. Russell, Moore and C.I. Lewis, for example, never really shook themselves free from them.

The first 385 pages of *Gnosiology* are a translation of the lightly revised second edition of what was originally published under the title 'Elements of the Theory of Knowledge, Formal Logic and Scientific Method'. From the time of its publication it was the leading Polish philosophical textbook. It was well qualified for the role since the original ideas it contains are embedded, as a statistically small part, in a broad, informative and economical treatment of the whole range of topics listed in its original title. Instead of reworking the entire text in the light of criticisms and second thoughts Kotarbiński has added 130 pages of later essays on the controversial issues involved. The book concludes, rather characteristically, with the long, appreciative but nevertheless very thoroughly critical review that Ajdukiewicz wrote when it first came out.

It is not surprising that, after forty years, the book should show some signs of wear and tear. In the preface to the second edition Kotarbiński claims no more for it than the interest of a historical document. But that is over-modest. It remains a uniquely thorough presentation of a substantial and currently lively point of view, one whose chief supporters in the Anglo-Saxon world at present are the 'Australian materialists' such as J.J.C. Smart (cf. his 'Philosophy and Scientific Realism'). It is distinguished from comparable works in English by its tentative, conjectural character. On the whole English-speaking analytic philosophers present their views in a demonstrative, apodeictic way. They speak of proof and necessary consequences and argue by *reductio ad absurdum*. But it is strange that philosophers who regard physical science as the paradigm of human knowledge should adopt the expository stance of traditional abstract speculation, of Aristotle and Aquinas. Those who do deviate from this practice, like Wittgenstein and Austin, express themselves with a colloquial, even chatty, inconclusiveness. Kotarbiński evinces a well-founded scepticism about the mathematical finality of particular demonstrative-looking arguments in philosophy without lapsing into desultoriness and coaxing. He takes his book's sub-title, 'A Scientific Approach to the Theory of Knowledge', with a proper seriousness.

In 1965 the same publisher brought out, under the title *Praxiology*, a book originally published as *A Treatise on Good Work* by Kotarbiński in 1955. Its first appearance had a special political interest since it was the first non-Marxist philosophical book to be published in Poland from the time of the imposition of the full Stalinist freeze in Poland in the late 1940s. It contains a civil reference or two to Marx and its subject-matter is in some sort of accord with the Marxist principle of the unity of theory and practice, but its style and method are entirely in the Polish tradition of formally explicit rationality. Its aim is to lay the foundations of a science of efficient action. In its first half definitions are elaborated of some leading concepts of such a science: simple and compound action, preparation, cooperation, conflict and so forth. In its second half principles of efficient action are extracted from common-sense practical wisdom, supported by a wide range of examples and classified with reference to the possible stages of practical undertakings to which they relate. Kotarbiński anticipates the criticism that he is simply giving a scientific appearance to the content of such proverbs as 'more haste less speed' and 'a stitch in time saves nine'. The generality of the principles at which he arrives is what he offers as an answer. There is certainly no objection in principle to the idea of supplementing piecemeal and empirical rules of thumb in this field by precise, general and systematically arranged rules of efficient conduct. *Praxiology* is not very systematic but Kotarbinski does not claim that it is more than a beginning. And he has at least devised a reasonable vocabulary for the organised and deliberate discussion of the subject.

Kotarbiński has been a prominent figure in Polish public life for a long time, throughout the seismic and mainly terrible period since the death of Pilsudski in 1935. He has not only maintained his integrity in fearful circumstances but has consistently acted with the highest civic courage. The regime of colonels that succeeded Pilsudski had some near-Fascist features. Among them was an institutionalisation of Polish anti-semitism that seems mild only in comparison with the German example. When Jewish university students were compelled to occupy a designated area in lecture-rooms they protested by remaining on their feet during lectures. Kotarbiński, I have been told, abandoned the rostrum and delivered his lectures from their part of the hall. He managed to survive the war, unlike a book he had written on Francis Bacon, all the typescript copies of which, distributed around Warsaw, were destroyed in the rising of 1944. After the war the Russian-imposed regime sought to benefit from the public esteem in which he was held by appointing him rector of a new university in the manufacturing town of Lodz. At the end of the 1940s the demands of the regime led him to resign. With the return of Gomulka to power in 1956 he became president of the Academy of Sciences, in place of some police-state functionary, and made good use of this position for the protection of intellectual freedom. Although he is now retired he is still active in defence of the liberal principles which he, more than anyone in Poland, incarnates.

The movement of thought that Twardowski originally inspired penetrated far beyond formal logic and analytic philosophy. It had a strong methodological influence on a progressive group of Catholic philosophers. Twardowski's example led to the development of a common language for rational communication between thinkers of very different ultimate loyalties. In a way his closest follower is Roman Ingarden, the phenomenologist, widely known for his work in aesthetics, who brings the characteristic rationality of this Polish tradition to bear on material treated with formless enthusiasm by Scheler or heavily pedantic elaboration by Husserl. A full and clear account of the whole movement is now available in English in Henryk Skolimowski's *Polish Analytical Philosophy* (London, 1967), which does not confine itself too narrowly to the area marked out by its title. I can do no more than mention the existence of this book since I was the author's academic supervisor while he was writing the dissertation on which it is based.

There is also a briefer survey of the same field in Part 1 of Z.A. Jordan's *Philosophy and Ideology* (London, 1963). However the main theme of this work is the changes undergone by Marxist philosophy and sociology in the period between their effective emergence in Poland in the wake of Russian occupation and the dissolution of Polish Stalinism in 1956. Until 1948 or 1949 other schools of thought were allowed to continue in public existence; their adherents were allowed to lecture on these ideologically sensitive subjects and to publish books and articles about them. By the end of the 1940s the exigencies of totalitarian rule required an intellectual equivalent of the absorption of all the permitted, 'progressive' political parties in the Polish United Workers' Party. The rational philosophers of Twardowski's tradition were in effect silenced by being confined to lecturing on logic or to translating classical philosophical texts into Polish. But they do not seem to have been unbearably oppressed. Although the leading figures were exposed to anathematising assaults by rather unskilled ideological hacks they were allowed some right of self-defence. They were not imprisoned or killed or even prevented from doing some sort of intellectual work. The only fatal casualty among philosophers was himself a Marxist, Pawel Konrad. In his essay 'Responsibility and History' Leszek Kolakowski wrote of him: 'he has been withdrawn from historical circulation, murdered by the missionaries of great historical justice'. In general Stalinist oppression seems to have been less hyperbolic in Poland than in the other Russian colonies in eastern Europe. Gomulka was not tortured and killed like the leading 'national communists' of the other satellites. He was not even subjected to the ignominy of a 'trial'. But some of the credit for the comparatively humane treatment accorded to the bourgeois philosophers of Poland must be given to Adam Schaff who was until recently the chief ideologist on the central committee of the Party as well as a copiously productive author.

Schaff, who is Jewish, was trained as a lawyer before the war, which he spent in Russia. Before Gomulka's return he seems to have been something very close to the dictator of Polish intellectual life. Between 1946 and 1955 he published five substantial books. Although highly partisan productions they were at an altogether more elevated level than the buffoonery of the then president of the Academy of Sciences, who said in 1952 that scientific societies should not demand academic qualifications from their members but should throw themselves open to 'working people, rationalisers and shock workers', whose perspicacity and good judgment, unburdened by the routine of academic thinking, would discover the weak points which escape the mind of a scientist (cf. Jordan, pp. 165-6). Schaff survived the thaw without a tremor and has only recently fallen into disfavour, partly because of his flirtations with the subjective problems of existentialism about the meaning of life and moral responsibility, for which he says Marxism must find an answer, and partly because of his race, in the atmosphere of the revival in a Marxised form of traditional Polish antisemitism.

Jordan goes with massive detail into the efforts of Polish Marxists to make Marxism intellectually respectable in a society accustomed to rational thinking from its academic philosophers and sociologists. They have occupied themselves with the problem of determining the relation between formal logic, so well established in Poland, and the elusive dialectical logic of Marxist scripture. They have been exercised about a set of epistemological issues arising from Lenin's naive causal theory of perception, from the connected idea that truth is a 'reflection' of objective reality (with its disconcertingly antiquated implications about logical and mathematical truth) and from the notion that all truths, except perhaps the first principles of Marxism, are relative and partial. Kotarbiński's reism had prepared an atmosphere inhospitable to Marxist hypostatisations of social forces and institutions, to the treatment of such things as social classes and methods of production as substantial, independent existences. Finally there was much discussion of the Marxist principle that all thinking is ideological. This doctrine, if strictly generalised, undermines itself, for it implies that it is itself a piece of ideology, a practical weapon in the class struggle but not an objective truth. An ironically liberating factor in this debate was Stalin's sibylline rejection of the theory of the linguist Marr. Marr was wrong, according to Stalin, in supposing all forms of consciousness, in particular the institution of language, to be ideological in nature. This led Jakub Berman, of all people, the Polish Beria, to go so far as to deny the ideological character of science.

Jordan makes a good case for the view that once the Polish Marxists had made the decision actually to think about their articles of faith, instead of relying on dogmatic intonings and 'administrative measures', the dissolution of theoretical orthodoxy was inevitable. 'The outcome might have been very different,' he writes, 'if Polish philosophy had not been steeled for generations against any form of irrationalism by a systematic cultivation of logical and other scientific procedures.' Polish rationality, like Polish patriotism, turned out in the end to be tougher than Marxism. He suggests that the story may have a general significance. Although Polish philosophy was as technical and specialised as the academic philosophy of the English-speaking world, which is so often chided for its social irrelevance, 'the philosophers' consistency, persistence and reasonableness ... left their imprint on the course of social and political events'. The habit of rationality fostered by Twardowski's pupils acted as a Trojan horse inside the citadel of the Marxist faith, to which it had gained admission because of the aim of the Marxists to dominate thought as well as conduct.

Philosophy and Ideology is not easy reading. It is written in perfectly reasonable English and there are only occasional symptoms of that Polish difficulty with the definite and indefinite articles of our language whose emblem is the sentence from a Polish savant's lecture on English grammar: 'In English language definite article always precedes noun.' What is rather wearing is the very high level of abstraction at which the discussion is carried on. The Polish intellectual scene is described as if occupied not by persons but by large bodies of words. It thus comes as a refreshing shock when one reads: 'It was the manuscript of the treatise *On Happiness* for which Tatarkiewicz risked a shot in the back to save it from the gutter where it was thrown during a personal search in 1944.' Elsewhere it might not occur to the reader that the names he was reading referred to things that had backs to be shot in.

In 1965 Schaff published a large book called *Marxism and the Individual*, altogether different in nature from his books in the monolithic period of Polish Marxism. It has not yet appeared in any language but Polish, but some idea of its contents can be from a collection of short articles he brought out in English in 1962, called *A Philosophy of Man* (London). In it he says that Marxism must give some answer to the questions raised by the existentialists – personal, even subjective, questions about morality and the meaning of life which it has hitherto brushed aside as reactionary and idealistic. In this short work he turns out to be much better at raising these neglected questions, and at rejecting existentialist answers to them, than at providing any but the most sketchy Marxist answers. At this stage he rejected also what he saw as the obsession of revisionists like Kolakowski about the young Marx's anthropocentric interest in alienation. It must be Kolakowski he has in mind when he writes: 'If one can only repeat that morality takes precedence over politics, one confesses only one's poverty – it does not help in political practice.' In the more recent work, however, Marx's theory of alienation plays a fundamental part: the dominance of a historically correct regime does not automatically produce that ideal society in which the problems of the individual wither away.

The publication of *Marxism and the Individual* was the occasion for an attack on Schaff by Jozef Chalasinski, a distinguished sociologist whose conversion to Marxism in the late 1940s had added a considerable feather to the intellectual cap of the regime. In it he links up Schaff's view that socialism does not necessarily abolish alienation with various ideas of Martin Buber and Daniel Bell about the 'homelessness' in the world of 'universal man'. Chalasinski's ostensible objection to universal man is that he is an unhistorical entity; his real objection is that he is a Jew. This was at once perceived by Kotarbiński, who came to the defence of his beleagured opponent Schaff. 'We should regard it as an honour,' he said in the polite but unequivocal protest he published early last year, 'if our country, while remaining a Polish home, were to be friendly to universalists and prove to be for them as good as a universal home.' Now that Gomulka's regime is trying to enforce hostility to Israel on its subjects this position will need further support in Poland.

If Schaff was the ablest thinker the newly-imposed communist state in Poland had at its disposal to start with, Leszek Kolakowski is undoubtedly the most talented person to grow up as a Marxist within the new system. Although he began his studies in 1945 under Kotarbiński, his basic convictions were Marxist and his main interests have lain in social philosophy and in the history of ideas (his first large professional publication was a treatise on the idea of freedom in the philosophy of Spinoza). A study visit to Russia in the early 1950s encouraged him in the belief that Marxism was in need of revision. By the time Polish Stalinism collapsed in October 1956 he was established as the chief radical critic of Marxism from within. Between 1955 and 1957 he wrote a series of powerful essays which focussed and gave direction to the attitude of the young dissident Marxist intellectuals to the upheaval that returned Gomulka to power. They have been collected in German in *Der Mensch Ohne Alternative* (Munich, 1960) and a good many of them have appeared in English here and there (one of them, on the concept of the Left, in a recent number of the *Evergreen Review*). It may be hoped that any English version of this collection will contain, as it does not, that splendidly scornful washing-line of dirty linen, 'What Socialism Is Not'.

In this, the most politically direct of his writings, Kolakowski says we must begin by seeing what socialism is not. Seventy-two acid negations follow. Among other things socialism is not 'a state in which there are more spies than nurses ... a state in which one is responsible for one's ancestors ... a state which always knows the will of the people before it asks them ... a state which does not like to see its citizens reading back numbers of newspapers.' 'That was the first point,' Kolakowski concludes. 'But now listen attentively. We will tell you what socialism is. Well then, socialism is a good thing.'

Most of what he has written, however, and all the items in *Der Mensch Ohne Alternative*, are of a more complex and theoretical order than this very plain statement. It could have been written by any democratic socialist but, in 1955-57 at any rate, Kolakowski was a Marxist, however sweeping may have been the revisions he wanted to make of Marxism. Indeed it was just because he was a Marxist that he was in a position to express himself so forcefully in that period of very relative liberalisation. In an essay on current and obsolete aspects of Marxism he rejects institutional Marxism, the official ideology of communist states, as a rather degraded form of revealed religion. But he has difficulty in specifying just what intellectual Marxism, the only tolerable alternative, actually is. Some of what Marx said is just false. About much of contemporary social reality Marx has nothing to say. The truths of Marx's materialist interpretation of history have passed into the common stock of knowledge and as far as they are concerned there is no more need to make a profession of being a Marxist than there is of being a Newtonian or a Darwinian. What Marxism comes to is a rationally critical attitude to social facts, a determinist method for the interpretation of history and reliance on a set of interpretative categories like *class, capitalism* and *ideology* and also, as elsewhere appears, a humanitarian moral commitment to the support of the exploited and oppressed.

Much of Kolakowski's more professionally philosophical work has dealt with the theology and metaphysics of the seventeenth century. He has applied it in his uniquely thorough exploration of the familiar analogy between institutional Marxism and dogmatic religion. In the most brilliant essay in this collection, 'The Priest and the Jester' (which is available in English in *The Modern Polish Mind* ed. Maria Kuncewicz, Boston, 1962) he reveals the theology hidden in modern secular philosophies, including Marxism. They can offer an eschatology (e.g. the idea of communist society as heaven) and a theodicy (solving the problem of evil in history by asserting that suffering and error play an essential part in the realisation of the ideal final end). Modern historiosophers, of whom Marx is the most important, provide all the main satisfactions of traditional theology. Conventional 'rationalist' polemic against the supernaturalism of religion is naively irrelevant; it attacks the husk but not the core. Against the priest, of whatever persuasion, with his conservative determination to hold fast to certain revealed ultimate truths, Kolakowski subscribes to the position of the jester, negatively vigilant with regard to all absolutes.

His adherence to what he sees as authentic Marxism, to a historical vision which insists among other things on the social determination of beliefs, brings about an interesting instability in his point of view. Intellectuals must be freed from institutional constraint if they are to perform the useful function of seeing that the decisions of the communist party are wise rather than the otiose one of slavishly praising them. But the ideology they produce will still be ideology, indispensable for effective social action, but under the determining influence of social conditions. Ideological convictions can have no eternal, objective validity. But it is better that they should be associated with true beliefs about what can be objectively known, something that is ruled out by institutional Marxism which shores up its ideology with plain falsehoods about current social fact.

The most important themes of Kolakowski's revisionism are brought together in his large, exciting, somewhat chaotic essay on responsibility and history. One simple, rational thesis it presents is that our basic moral convictions, however they may vary and however much they are influenced by social and historical circumstances, are far more certain and well-founded than any historiosophical prophecies about the inevitable course of future history. To the extent that the Marxist account of what is historically inevitable is worthy of credence it is vague and leaves open many possible ways of reaching utopia. To the extent that it is definite enough to require the abandonment of universally accepted moral beliefs for the effective pursuit of the ideal goal it is superstitious dogma. Kolakowski insists as firmly as any positivist that no conclusions about the moral desirability of an inevitable state of affairs can be validly derived from the fact of its inevitability. But his main point here is that nothing very definite has really been shown to be inevitable.

His twists and turns in attempting to reconcile the thesis that moral beliefs are socially determined with the claim that they are better founded than the historical predictions on whose account the 'realistic' revolutionary would set them aside, both of which he wishes to affirm are perhaps more honourable and persistent than ultimately satisfactory. This is also true of his efforts to reconcile Marxian social determinism with a view of individual moral responsibility almost as extreme as Sartre's. His final conclusion is that as agents we cannot predict our own choices, that for the individual only the last is inevitable, and that to regard oneself as fated to act in a fixed way is to treat oneself as dead.

'Responsibility and History' begins with a dialogue between a Revolutionary, who is prepared to stake everything on effective cooperation with the inevitable course of history, and an Intellectual (or Clerk, in Benda's sense) who, for the sake of moral purity, is prepared to detach himself altogether from public, political activity. To the Revolutionary the Intellectual is a futile aesthete; to the Intellectual the Revolutionary is an opportunistic scoundrel. In 1955-7 Kolakowski was anxious to find a third position, politically involved like that of the Revolutionary, but morally autonomous like that of the Intellectual. He would seem to have hoped that the communist party, ideologically guided by a free intelligentsia, could produce a society that was at once morally respectable and politically progressive. He did not explicitly put in question the principle of one-party rule, though this may have been simply expedient recognition of what, at most, Russian power would permit. (Another false either-or, in his view, was that between complete submission to institutional Marxism and the totalistic anti-communism adopted by 'renegades' like Koestler. The prevalence of monolithic anti-communism was a triumph for Stalinism, whose most active opponents conformed precisely to the Stalinist picture of them.)

In more recent times Kolakowski's relations with the party have changed, both institutionally and intellectually. In October 1966 he was finally expelled from it for the culminating offence of taking part in a celebration of the tenth anniversary of the liberating upheaval that brought Gomulka back to power. It is a measure of the Gomulka regime's regression to authoritarianism that it should feel impelled to punish the recollection of the hopes with which it was inaugurated. An essay on Jesus Christ as prophet and reformer, written in 1965, and published here in a sort of English, villainously misspelled, in the *Tri-Quarterly Review* for spring 1967, suggests that he has moved closer to the position of the Intellectual in 'Responsibility and History'. Christ, Kolakowski says, 'was a model of that radical authenticity with which alone every human being can give real life to his own values'. There is a moral attitude that, in the European world at any rate, is essentially bound up with Christ, an attitude that sets love above law, rejects violence, proclaims that all men are of one family, asserts the insufficiency of purely material ends and regards human temporal existence as incapable of being made perfect. It is an attitude which must not be carried away in the general decline of institutional, supernaturalistic, Christianity. To endorse it is to affirm a priority of moral to political considerations that must be impossible for a Marxist. At best it would be consistent with *ad hoc* alliance with organised Marxism for specific, morally acceptable purposes.

Whatever his current position may be, Kolakowski remains the most interesting Marxist thinker of the post-Stalin period, very much more sophisticated than the rather crude though personally most admirable Milovan Djilas. It is to be hoped that his writings will soon be available in English in a less fragmentary way than they have been hitherto.

Index